Praxial Music Education

D1214957

PRAXIAL MUSIC EDUCATION

Reflections and Dialogues

Edited by
David J. Elliott

OXFORD
UNIVERSITY PRESS

OXFORD
UNIVERSITY PRESS

Oxford University Press, Inc., publishes works that further
Oxford University's objective of excellence
in research, scholarship, and education.

Oxford   New York
Auckland   Cape Town   Dar es Salaam   Hong Kong   Karachi
Kuala Lumpur   Madrid   Melbourne   Mexico City   Nairobi
New Delhi   Shanghai   Taipei   Toronto

With offices in
Argentina   Austria   Brazil   Chile   Czech Republic   France   Greece
Guatemala   Hungary   Italy   Japan   Poland   Portugal   Singapore
South Korea   Switzerland   Thailand   Turkey   Ukraine   Vietnam

Copyright © 2005 by Oxford University Press, Inc.

Published by Oxford University Press, Inc.
198 Madison Avenue, New York, New York 10016

www.oup.com

First issued as an Oxford University Press paperback, 2009

Oxford is a registered trademark of Oxford University Press

All rights reserved. No part of this publication may be reproduced,
stored in a retrieval system, or transmitted, in any form or by any means,
electronic, mechanical, photocopying, recording, or otherwise,
without the prior permission of Oxford University Press.

Library of Congress Cataloging-in-Publication Data
Praxial music education : reflections and dialogues / edited by David J. Elliott.
p. cm.
Includes bibliographical references and index.
ISBN 978-0-19-538507-6
1. Music—Instruction and study.   I. Elliott, David James.
MT1.P712 2004
780'.71—dc22   2004041467

1 3 5 7 9 8 6 4 2

Printed in the United States of America

To four wonderful music teachers
—praxialists, all:
Jim Elliott
Glen Wood
Bob Cringan
Gordon Delamont

Suppose we were able to share meanings freely without a compulsive urge to impose our view or conform to those of others without distortion and self-deception. Would this not constitute a real revolution in culture?

—*David Bohm*

Acknowledgments

This book belongs to the eighteen authors in this volume who devoted a great deal of time, thought, and energy to this project. To all of you: my sincerest gratitude for your dedication, patience, and encouragement during the production of this book.

A very special "thank you!" goes to my dear friend and colleague, Wayne Bowman. In addition to authoring two essays for this volume, Wayne produced one of his essays in extremely short order, as a special favor to me, to support my initial proposal of this book to Oxford University Press.

To Maribeth Payne, the editor of *Music Matters* and the original editor of this book: my heartfelt appreciation for your continuous support, encouragement, and wisdom.

To Kimberly Robinson: thank you for your patience, attentiveness, expertise, and kind consideration.

To Janet Beatty, my Executive Editor: my sincere gratitude for your wise counsel and your enthusiasm for current projects.

Finally, Dr. Marissa Silverman, Adjunct Assistant Professor of Music Education at New York University, provided enormous assistance toward the first publication of this book and, now, this edition.

Contents

Contributors

Margaret Barrett is Professor and Head of the School of Music at the University of Queensland, Australia. She has published on children as composers in many scholarly journals. She is the editor of *Research Studies in Music Education.*

Wayne D. Bowman is Professor of Music and Music Education at Brandon University, Canada. He has published extensively in the areas of the philosophy of music and music education and is author of *Philosophical Perspectives on Music* (Oxford, 1998).

Pamela Burnard is Senior Lecturer in the Faculty of Education at the University of Cambridge, England. She teaches courses in arts and music education. She has published extensively in the areas of children's compositional development and teacher education and is editor of *British Journal of Music Education.*

Robert A. Cutietta is Dean of the University of Southern California's Thornton School of Music. Prior to his appointment at USC he was Professor of Music Education and Director of the School of Music and Dance at the University of Arizona. His research interests lie in the psychology of music, especially the musical perception of elementary and middle-school-aged children.

Lori-Anne Dolloff is Associate Professor and Coordinator of Music Education at the University of Toronto, Canada. She is an active choral conductor and arranger. Her publications include journal articles on the development of teacher identity and elementary music education.

David J. Elliott is Professor of Music and Music Education at New York University. From 1973 to 2002 he served as Professor and Coordinator of Music Education at the University of Toronto. He is the author of numerous journal articles and book chapters. Also, he is a frequent speaker at conferences and universities worldwide, an active performer, and an award-winning arranger and composer.

J. Scott Goble is Associate Professor of Music Education at the University of British Columbia, Canada. He has published on topics in the history and philosophy of music education, the semiotics of music, and music cognition. In addition, he is an active choral and orchestral conductor.

Wilfried Gruhn is Emeritus Professor of Music Education at the University of Freiburg, Germany. He is the author of numerous journal articles and books on the relations among music pedagogy, music cognition, and brain research. One of his most recent books is *Neurosciences in Music Pedagogy* (2008).

Marja-Leena Juntunen is Assistant Professor of Music Education, University of Oulu, Finland. She also teaches at the Sibelius Academy of Music. One of her special interests is Dalcroze pedagogy.

Constantijn Koopman teaches at the Royal Conservatory of The Hague. His articles have appeared in the *Journal of Aesthetics and Art Criticism*, the *Journal of Aesthetic Education*, the *Oxford Review of Education,* and *Educational Philosophy and Theory.*

Marie McCarthy is Professor and Chair of Music Education at the University of Michigan. She has published numerous articles and book chapters on topics in music education history, philosophy, and sociology. She is the author of *Passing It On: The Transmission of Music in Irish Culture* (1999).

Dr. Jeffrey Martin has taught university music composition, improvisation, and electronic music in Singapore. In addition to his interests in music cognition, he is a practicing secondary school music teacher and music department head in Shanghai, China.

Patricia O'Toole has served as an Assistant Professor of Music and Music Education at the University of Buffalo, Ohio State University, and Ohio Wesleyan University. An active choral conductor, researcher, and music educator, she is the author of numerous articles on gender issues and multicultural music education. Dr. O'Toole founded the Gender Research Group of the Music Educators National Conference and is the music education editor for *American Women in Music since 1900: An Encyclopedia* (2001).

Thomas A. Regelski is Distinguished Professor of Music, Emeritus, at the School of Music, State University of New York, Fredonia. His many articles on philosophy, sociology, and psychology have appeared in journals in Europe, Japan, Canada, and the United States. He is author of *Principles and Problems of Music Education* (1975) and *Teaching General Music* (1981), and *Teaching General Music in Grades 4-8: A Musicianship Approach.*

Sandra L. Stauffer is Professor of Music Education at Arizona State University, where she teaches undergraduate and graduate courses. She has published in various music education journals and authored educational materials for symphony orchestras. Her current research is a longitudinal study of student composers, elementary through high school.

C. K. Szego is Associate Professor in the School of Music and the Department of Folklore at the Memorial University of Newfoundland, Canada. An ethnomusicologist with a strong interest in music transmission and learning, Szego's work focuses on how people construct musical meanings, especially in multicultural environments.

Kari K. Veblen is Associate Professor of Music and Music Education at the University of Western Ontario, Canada. Her publications include *Sound Ways of Knowing: Music in the Interdisciplinary Classroom* (with Janet R. Barrett and Claire W. McCoy, 1997), numerous journal articles, and, most recently, a chapter on "Community Music" (with Bengt Olsson) in the *New Handbook of Research on Music Teaching and Learning* (2002). She is a former Chairperson of the Community Music Activity Commission of the International Society for Music Education (ISME) and is currently a member of the ISME Board of Governors.

Heidi Westerlund is Professor of Music Education at the Sibelius Academy of Music, Finland. She serves on the editorial board of the *Finnish Journal of Music Education* and on the foreign advisory board of the *British Journal of Music Education*. She has published widely in music education philosophy.

Sheila C. Woodward is Assistant Professor of Music Education at the University of Southern California. Her research on the effects of music on the fetus and neonate has been presented and published internationally. She has also served as Chairperson (1994–1998) of the Early Childhood Music Education Commission of ISME.

1

Introduction

DAVID J. ELLIOTT

> There are no ultimate sources of knowledge. . . . Every source, every suggestion, is open to critical examination.
>
> —Karl Popper, *Conjectures and Refutations* (1965)

This book is a collection of critically reflective essays on the praxial concept of music and music education I put forth in *Music Matters: A New Philosophy of Music Education* (1995).

The idea for this project came to me while reading a series of books called *Philosophers and Their Critics* (Blackwell).[1] Each book in this series presents several probing essays by different philosophers on the ideas of one contemporary philosopher. (Among the philosophers whose ideas undergo this kind of inquiry are Peter Singer, Willard Van Orman Quine, Daniel Dennett, John Searle, and Jerry Fodor.) Then, following these critiques, the philosopher whose work is under scrutiny offers replies to and engages in dialogues with his or her critics. The aim of this series is to highlight the reality and importance of scholarship as a collective, collaborative, and community enterprise that depends on *dialogue* to refine ideas "in the crucible of close scrutiny" (Lepore, in Dahlbom 1993, ii).

In my view, music education is in need of such books. Most fields have long traditions and sources of critical discourse. Students involved in (say) philosophy, literary theory, psychology, law, and gender studies encounter a wide range of alternative views during their education. They tend to be familiar with the characteristics and techniques of reasoned debate and the hallmarks of fallacious argument. Thus, as professionals, they expect to read and hear rigorous, ongoing, point-counterpoint dialogues about key concepts in their domains.

Music education is young in all these ways. In fact, many music educators still consider it impolite, inappropriate, unprofessional, or heretical to debate ideas, philosophies, methods, and institutions in our field.

Those who feel otherwise have limited opportunities to publish extended discussions. True, we have many journals offering articles and regular book reviews. And, yes, journal editors occasionally take the unusual (and generous) step of devoting a whole journal issue to one theory, book, or movement. The problem is, however, that most journals have too little space to present substantive essays, criticisms, and dialogues *together*. Accordingly, journals often fail to give their readers a reasonable balance of points and counterpoints.

This book attempts to redress some of these problems. The writers speak for those in our profession who believe, with me, that critical thinking, constructive debate, and dialogues are the lifeblood of music education. By means of their essays, they also speak for those who believe that future music teachers must learn to think for themselves and develop their own philosophies based on their own careful reflections.

With these points in mind, I developed this collection of essays with four aims in mind: (1) to contribute to music education philosophy generally and the literature of praxial music education specifically; (2) to listen to, engage, respond to, and learn from the views of my colleagues toward improving and refining another edition of *Music Matters*; (3) to provide a "critical companion" to *Music Matters* that would act as a catalyst for critical thinking among music education students, teachers, and professors; and (4) in all these ways, to provide the field of music education with good models of constructive criticism and mutually enlightening dialogues on basic issues in music education.

Accordingly, I invited an international and interdisciplinary group of contributors to evaluate the praxial philosophy, pro and con, from the viewpoint of their area(s) of interest and expertise (e.g., philosophical foundations, performance, listening, early childhood education, multicultural music education, and curriculum) and offer criticisms.

Indeed, the task of improving, amending, correcting, and refining a philosophy cannot be done alone. The praxial philosophy of music education is a work in progress.

Improving and advancing this theory (or any theory) depends on receiving constructive reflections from informed colleagues. Thoughtful feedback is the only way writers can see beyond their individual limitations, recognize what they overlooked, and understand what they failed to make clear.

About This Book and Its Web Site

In an ideal world, I would have invited more contributors from other places (philosophically and geographically) to address additional issues, such as technology and evaluation. I would have included my replies to each author, too; indeed, this was my original plan. But I changed my mind toward the end of this project when I realized I could have my cake and eat it too: I could give each author as much room as possible in the pages of this book and, by using the Internet, I could attach my replies *and* create a virtual place where students, professors, and colleagues could ask questions, post challenges, or offer elaborations on anything about *Praxial Music Education* or *Music Matters*.

So, after you read each of these essays, please visit my website (http://www. davidelliottmusic.com) for my replies to several colleagues' criticisms.

With the help of the internet, and between the poles of high hopes and economic reality, I think it's fair to say that this collection of critical commentaries represents a good balance on several scales: topic coverage, author-gender balance, geographical perspective, and breadth and depth of scholarly and practical focus. At least, this is my hope.

Music Matters: Meanings and Interpretations

Clearly, the unifying element in this collection is my version of praxialism as it relates to the many complex concepts and issues that constitute the nature and significance of music education. The variety in this book comes from two main sources: each author's viewpoint on each different topic, and different authors' interpretations of what I say about the same issue (e.g., in chapter 15, Lori-Anne Dolloff interprets my views on music listening in an entirely different way than Robert Cutietta and Sandy Stauffer do in chapter 7).

These dimensions of unity and variety have two main consequences. On one hand, the discussions in this anthology investigate and evaluate *Music Matters* from more directions and in more ways than I could have ever done alone. As a result, I am more aware than ever of what I have failed to say well, what I need to repair, and what I have overlooked. In many cases I am happy to make these corrections and repairs. But not always, because some authors read or take the same words in *Music Matters* in extremely different ways. In the process, one writer will often counterbalance or refute the claims of another, and vice versa, back and forth. So reading these essays back to back not only exposes my weaknesses, it exposes the mistakes of my critics, too.

This raises an interesting question: How can the same words (in *Music Matters*) produce so many different interpretations? The short answer is: "We do not see things as they are, we see things as we are" (Barlex and Carre 1985). Our eyes do not give us a true and faithful record of things and events in the world. Everything a person reads (and sees, hears, tastes, smells, and touches) is filtered by and through his or her personal understandings, beliefs, past experiences, assumptions, expectations, and preferences.

This may be hard to accept at first because seeing, hearing, tasting, and so forth seem completely natural, "thought-free," and automatic. Thus, we usually fail to notice that our minds continuously generate our very own personal notions of everything in relation to our particular assumptions and beliefs. But this is what happens. Not surprisingly, then, readers and experts often disagree about the meaning of the same word, sentence, statistic, book, method, theory, or event.

None of this is news to people familiar with postmodernism. A basic tenet of postmodern thought is that texts (in the broadest sense of the word—meaning scientific reports, poetry, philosophy, music, and so on) cannot and do not have one true and universally understood meaning. Instead, meanings lie at the nexus of readers' minds and the texts that readers mentally construct and interpret.

Then again, postmodern thinkers vary widely in their interpretations of postmodernism. Rosenau (1992) suggests that we think in terms of "affirmative" and "skeptical" postmodern scholars; within these categories she identifies moderate and extreme factions. In short, it is important to note that postmodern scholars differ about whether texts present several possible meanings to a reader or an *infinite* range of meanings. And because there are many ways to interpret a text, scholars say that texts can be "deconstructed" in terms of their hidden meanings, metaphors, subtexts, political agendas, and so forth.

And what about writers (including authors and critics)? Consider that authors always invite or "cause" multiple interpretations, whether they know it or not. Iris Yob (2001) states the point cleverly: "What we write is wrong" (1). What Yob means is that authors can never be totally correct in what they write because it's impossible for human beings to know and write "the truth, the whole truth, and nothing but the truth" about a topic. There will always be gaps in our knowledge, limits on our perspectives, and biases in the words we select and the statements we construct. As Yob says: "We cannot speak truth for all persons, in all situations, at all times. Every element of what we know [and write] is something of an idiosyncratic construction within our own cultural, political, gendered, linguistic, economic, and personal context" (1).

In the end, then, the best we can do is to examine every argument (pro and con, past and present) and every form of evidence (e.g., logical, empirical, narrative, and ethnographic) that someone offers as support for their view (claim, case, or argument). In doing so, we must respect the context in which the viewpoint was developed and expressed. Then, we should decide what counts on behalf of that view and make a case for our position, pro or con, with the understanding that someone else may scrutinize our view—someday, somewhere—for further confirmation or rejection.

So, a case for any sort of claim, statement, or theory—whether philosophical, legal, scientific, historical, moral, or ethical—is always provisional. We do the best we can to justify or warrant our claims contextually, in relation to the past and present procedures of verification that scholars understand and apply in our knowledge-generating community.

This process is imperfect. But we must proceed this way because we must act to survive, live, and improve. Better to act on knowledge warranted in the best ways we know than to act impulsively or by trial and error.

The praxial philosophy in *Music Matters* is intended to help music educators make informed decisions on behalf of themselves and their students. Still, *Music Matters* was put forth with all the above realizations in mind. That is, the praxial philosophy, like all theories, is provisional, incomplete, in progress.

For these reasons, *Praxial Music Education: Reflections and Dialogues* looks outward to our community for assistance in warranting the praxial philosophy, or parts of it—or not. The book asks our knowledge-generating community to scrutinize this set of beliefs for confirmation, amendment, or rejection.

Summaries of *Music Matters*

Before ending this first chapter with brief summaries of each essay in this set, I will now summarize what I consider important themes in the praxial philosophy. I hope these digests will be adequate as a review for readers who have already read *Music Matters* carefully, as an introduction for those who have not read the book, and as a primer for readers who think they know a little about praxialism from a lecture, a book review, a journal article, or rumors.

The Praxial Philosophy: A Brief Overview

The praxial philosophy begins with an explanation of the nature and significance of music. Based on this foundation, I go on to explain the nature and values of music education.

A major theme of this philosophy is summed up by the word "multidimensional." In *Music Matters* I aim to develop a multidimensional concept of music and musical works, a multilayered concept of musical understanding, a multifaceted concept of musical values, and a diverse approach to achieving these values.

Practically speaking, I suggest that achieving the aims of music education depends on developing the musicianship and listenership of all music students, through engaging students in: performing-and-listening, improvising-and-listening, composing-and-listening, arranging-and-listening, conducting-and-listening, and listening to recordings and live performances. I emphasize that music making of all kinds—and, of course, the rich kind of music listening required to make music well—should be at the center of the music curriculum.

Recorded music (e.g., CDs and audio tapes) and talk about music have a very important place in music teaching and learning, but not the central place. Lectures about music and recordings of music should be included in music teaching situations in such a way that they weave continuously in and out of a teacher's ongoing efforts to empower students to make music well—to perform and improvise, and to compose, arrange, and conduct as frequently as possible.

I propose, also, that developing our students' musical creativity (in all forms of music making) overlaps and extends the process of developing our students' musicianship. In other words, we can and should develop our students' musicianship and creativity simultaneously.

All students can learn to be creative music makers, but doing so requires that teachers allow and encourage students to make creative decisions while they are learning to perform and conduct and that they teach students the various kinds of knowledge they need in order to improvise, compose, and arrange music in several (i.e., a reasonable range of) musical styles.

In summary, the praxial philosophy urges a comprehensive and reflective approach to music teaching and learning. It is based on detailed arguments for the views that: musical works involve many layers of meanings; that musical understanding involves many closely related kinds of thinking and knowing; and that the significance of music in human life can be explained in terms of many important life values.

Praxialism recommends, further, that to achieve the values of music, music teachers ought to emphasize the interpretive aspects of music as a performing and improvising art and (again!) that composing, arranging, and conducting, all of which demand keen listening, should be taught frequently and in direct relation to a reasonable diversity of musical styles during the course of our students' musical education.

I said a moment ago that the praxial view begins with an explanation of the nature and significance of music. Let me be more specific now.

On the Nature and Significance of Music

The praxial philosophy of music education rests on two premises. The first is that the nature of music education depends on the nature of music. The second is that the significance of music education depends on the significance of music in human life. In other words, the most reasonable way to explain the nature and values of music education is to begin with an explanation of the nature and significance of music.

THE NATURE OF MUSIC

"Pieces" of music are, of course, central to what "music" is. But is it reasonable to assume that an explanation of the nature of musical works will yield a comprehensive understanding of the nature and values of music? No. Beginning with works of music risks the possibility of producing a narrow and implausible concept of music and, therefore, a narrow and implausible philosophy of music education.

So, let us begin with the observation that the auditory events we call "musical works" usually result from the actions of people (e.g., performers performing; improvisers improvising, and so on) who live in particular times and places and who make musical products or works of all sorts (e.g., notated compositions, improvised songs) in relation to histories and standards of musical practice (whether they know these histories and standards formally or informally).

In short, musical products—performances, improvisations, compositions, and arrangements—are enmeshed in and derive their nature and significance from their contexts of creation and use. Even the structural details of musical patterns (melodies, harmonies, and so on) owe their characteristic features to the reflections of music makers who work at particular times in the history of their musical cultures. Works of music are, therefore, artistic-cultural constructions, and our personal acts of music listening involve complex cognitive-affective construction processes that also operate in relation to our sociocultural beliefs.

Accordingly, listening intelligently to music of any kind involves and yields several interconnected dimensions of meaning: affective, interpretive, structural (i.e., musical elements), expressional (i.e., musical expressions of emotion), representational, social, ideological, and/or personal meanings.

In this view, the auditory events we call music engage and challenge our powers of consciousness (attention, cognition, emotion, intention, and memory) on many levels: pieces of music are multidimensional challenges and, therefore, thought-and-feeling generators.

And MUSIC, considered broadly and socially, is the diverse human practice of making sounds of particular kinds for listeners who understand (informally or formally) how to listen for these particular kinds of Musics (e.g., Japanese koto music, Dixieland jazz, or Donegal fiddling).

I suggest, also, that the performing art of music (which involves acts of performing, improvising, composing, arranging and/or conducting) depends on a multidimensional form of understanding called musicianship that always includes music-listening abilities, or what I call "listenership."

Musicianship and listenership are two sides of the same cognitive coin. Listenership involves the covert (mental) construction of intramusical relationships (within works) and intermusical relationships (between works) through the same kinds of knowing that make up musicianship: procedural, formal, informal, impressionistic, and supervisory musical knowing. The knowings required to listen effectively for the musical works of a given practice involve the same kinds of knowing required to perform, improvise, compose, arrange, and/or conduct the music of that practice.

THE VALUES OF MUSIC AND MUSIC EDUCATION

Music and music education have many values. One of the most important categories of musical values is created (as the psychologist Mihaly Csikszentmihalyi suggests) when there is a balance or a match between our musicianship (however naive or advanced) and the wide range of cognitive-affective challenges involved in listening to or making music (as performers, improvisers, composers, arrangers, or conductors). When our levels of musicianship match the challenge-levels of the pieces we interact with, we achieve the central values of musicing and listening: namely, musical enjoyment (or "flow"), self-growth, self-knowledge (or constructive knowledge), and (through continuous involvements with music over time) self-esteem. In this view, musicianship is not only a rich form of thinking and knowing, it is a unique source of one of the most important kinds of knowledge humans can achieve: self-knowledge.

In addition to these values, musicing (of all kinds) and musical works extend the range of our expressive and impressive powers by providing opportunities for us to create musical expressions of emotions; musical representations of people, places, and things; and musical expressions of cultural-ideological meanings. This range of opportunities for musical expression and creativity offers people numerous ways of giving artistic-cultural form to their powers of feeling, thinking, knowing, valuing, evaluating, and believing, which, in turn, challenges other listeners' conscious powers and musical understandings.

I wish to emphasize, also, that musical style-communities are significant because the musical works they produce play important roles as unifying cultural artifacts: that is, cherished musical works are crucial to establishing, defining, delineating, and preserving a sense of community and self-identity within social groups. Musical pieces and musical style-communities (or practices) constitute and are constituted by their social contexts.

Additionally, teaching and learning a variety of Musics comprehensively, as music cultures, is an important form of multicultural education. Why? Because the process of learning and "entering into" unfamiliar Musics activates our self-examination and the personal reconstruction of our relationships, assumptions, and preferences about other people, other cultures, and other ways of thinking and valuing. Inducting learners into unfamiliar musical practices links the central values of music education to the broader goals of humanistic education.

Last, if music making or listening proves beneficial for the development of students' spatial, mathematical, or scientific (or other cognitive) abilities, then these benefits will most likely develop more deeply and frequently to the degree that music education programs become deeper and more available to all students.

These perspectives on the nature and significance of music provide the basis for my praxial recommendations about what music teachers ought to teach, and how.

Praxial Music Education and Seven Basic Issues

Another way to summarize the praxial philosophy is to address seven basic issues, or "curriculum commonplaces," that are present in most types of teaching-learning situations, whether formally (in a curriculum or a lesson plan), or informally (in a teacher's mind or in the processes of teaching and learning). The issues I mean are aims, knowledge, learners, teaching-learning processes, teachers, the teaching-learning context, and evaluation.

AIMS, OR, WHY TEACH MUSIC?

The praxial philosophy holds that music has many important values. Self-growth and self-knowledge—and the unique emotional experience of musical enjoyment that accompanies these—are among the most important values of music and music education. These values should be at the center of every teaching-learning episode. They are accessible, achievable, and applicable to all learners, providing that we develop their musicianship and listenership progressively and in balanced relation to a variety of significant musical challenges over time. To the extent that we enable our students to achieve these values, music education will also contribute to the development of their self-esteem and self-identity.

In addition to these values, musicing and listening extend the range of people's expressive and impressive powers by providing us with opportunities to formulate musical expressions of emotions, musical representations of people, places and things, and musical expressions of cultural-ideological meanings. When this range of opportunities for musical expression and creativity is combined with the opportunities presented by texts in vocal and choral works, music makers gain numerous ways of giving artistic form to their powers of thinking, knowing, valuing, evaluating, believing, and feeling, which, in turn, challenge listeners' conscious powers and musical understandings.

On the basis of the cognitive, affective, and social richness of musicing and listening, praxialism also argues that musical works play an important role in establishing, defining, delineating, and preserving a sense of community and self-identity within social groups. Also, teaching and learning a variety of Musics comprehensively, as music cultures (through a praxial approach), amounts to an important form of multicultural education. Entering into unfamiliar musical practices activates self-examination and the personal reconstruction of one's relationships, assumptions, and preferences. In the process of inducting learners into unfamiliar musical practices, music teachers link the basic values of music and music education to the broader goals of humanistic education.

KNOWLEDGE

What should music teachers teach? Asked another way: what knowledge is most worth learning by all music students?

My answer is: musicianship. Musicianship is the key to achieving the values and aims of music education. Musicianship, which always includes listenership, is a rich form of procedural knowledge that draws upon four other kinds of musical knowing in surrounding and supporting ways. Musicianship is context-sensitive, or "situated": that is, the precise nature and content of musicianship and listenership differ from one musical practice to another.

Although verbal knowledge contributes importantly to the development of musicianship, verbal knowledge about music is secondary to procedural knowledge in music education.

LEARNERS

Musicianship and listenership are not abilities given naturally at birth to some people and not to others. They are forms of cognition—very rich and complex forms of thinking and knowing. All humans are born with the "hardwiring" (that is, in our brain mechanisms) to learn how to make and listen to music at a competent level. This does not mean that everyone can become a Mozart. It means that most people can learn to make and listen to music well—that music learning is achievable and applicable to all people.

Accordingly, all music students ought to be taught in the same basic way: through performing, improvising, composing, arranging, conducting, and, of course, listening to live and recorded music whenever possible. Listening ought to be taught and learned in direct relation to the music that students are learning to make and also in relation to recorded music presented in relation to and in the context of their active music making.

Howard Gardner (1991) agrees with this view: "in the arts, production ought to lie at the center of any artistic experience. Understanding involves a mastery of the productive practices in a domain or discipline, coupled with the capacity to adopt different stances toward the work, among them the stances of audience member, critic, performer, and maker" (239). So there should be no differences between and among music education programs regarding the fundamental contents of the music curriculum: the achievement of musical values through the development of musicianship and listenership. However, there will (and should be) differences between and among music education programs depending on the levels of students' musicianship and listenership and the kinds and levels of good music that teachers choose for (and, perhaps, with the cooperation of) their students. In addition, music programs will differ in the kinds of music-making media (e.g., wind instruments, voices, string instruments, and electronic instruments) chosen for (or with) one's students.

TEACHING-LEARNING PROCESSES

Music education is not only concerned with developing musicianship-listenership and musical creativity in the present. An essential part of our task is to teach students how to continue developing their musicianship in the future.

The praxial view suggests that the process of developing musicianship is a particular kind of learning process that students can engage in and learn how to employ themselves. The keys to this process are targeting attention, progressive musical problem-solving, problem-finding, musical problem reduction, critical reflection, and the creative generation and selection of musical ideas. Implicit in all these processes is the broader requirement that all music students be engaged in rich and challenging music-making projects in classroom situations that are deliberately organized as close approximations of real musical practices. Again, Gardner (1990) supports these principles from a developmental perspective: "students learn effectively when they are engaged by rich and meaningful projects; when their artistic learning is anchored in artistic production; when there is an easy commerce among the various forms of knowing . . . ; and when students have ample opportunity to reflect on their progress" (49).

TEACHERS

Teachers who are musically competent themselves should carry out music education. Musicianship and teaching ability (or "educatorship") are interdependent. One without the other is insufficient. To teach music effectively, we must know our subject—music. We must embody and exemplify musicianship. This is how children develop musicianship themselves: through actions, transactions, and interactions with musically proficient teachers.

Becoming an excellent music teacher depends heavily on learning to reflect in and on our teaching efforts as we endeavor to develop and match our students' musicianship with appropriate musical challenges.

Novice music teachers require music education professors who can model musicianship and educatorship through their own vivid examples. Teacher education programs ought to be deliberately organized to prepare future artist-teachers through excellent models of teaching and excellent examples of diverse musical materials.

TEACHING-LEARNING CONTEXT

The praxial philosophy focuses on achieving self-growth and musical enjoyment in the thoughtful actions of music making and listening. Teachers and students should work together to meet the musical challenges involved in realistic musical projects through reflective music making.

Each musical work that students are learning to interpret and perform (and improvise, compose, arrange, and so on) should be approached fully—as a full-course meal — as a multidimensional challenge to be made artistically and listened for intelligently in all its relevant dimensions (interpretive, structural, expressional, and so on).

In support of artistic listening in context, carefully selected recordings ought to be introduced parenthetically, in direct relation to the musical practices into which students are being inducted. Similarly, verbal musical knowledge should be filtered into the continuous stream of music making and listening as needed.

The praxial music curriculum is deliberately organized to engage learners in musical actions, transactions, and interactions with close approximations of real music cultures. The praxial curriculum immerses students in music-making projects that require them to draw upon the musical standards, traditions, lore, landmark achievements, symbol systems, gestures, and creative strategies of the musical practices of which their projects are a part.

From this perspective, the music teaching and learning environment is itself a key element in the music education enterprise. The musical actions of learners are enabled and promoted by the interactive, goal-directed swirl of questions, issues, and knowings that develop around our students' efforts as reflective musical practitioners. The praxial curriculum is itself informative.

How does the curriculum-as-practicum look in action? When small and large performing ensembles (e.g., a class choir, guitar ensemble, African drumming ensemble, string ensemble, jazz ensemble, or wind ensemble) are developed and realized in relation to the above principles, and students engage in performing, improvising, composing, arranging, conducting, and music-listening projects, then the school music classroom, or the community music situation, becomes a reflective musical practicum: an approximation of real music-practice situations, or music cultures. The music-practicum context feeds back to students by revealing what counts in their developing musicianship.

EVALUATION

There is an important distinction between evaluation and assessment. The primary function of assessment in music education is to provide feedback to students about the quality of their growing musicianship. Learners need constructive feedback about why, when, and how they are or are not meeting musical challenges in relation to musical standards and traditions. Overall, then, the assessment of student achievement gathers information that benefits students directly in the form of constructive feedback. Assessment also provides useful data to teachers, parents, and the surrounding educational community.

Building on the accumulated results of continuous assessments, evaluation is primarily concerned with grading, ranking, and other summary procedures for purposes of student promotion and curriculum evaluation.

Students need to learn how to assess their own musical thinking by learning what counts as good music making and listening in a given musical style. To become independent judges of musical excellence in the future, students need regular opportunities to reflect on the results of their musicianship and that of their peers. It follows from this that assessment is the joint responsibility of teachers and students.

Because musicianship differs substantially from the kinds of verbal knowledge taught in scholastic settings, there is no justification for using standardized tests in music. There is justification for a moderate number of paper-and-pencil tests and written assignments about the verbal knowledge components of musicianship (music theory and music history). But overall, conventional methods of evaluation are inappropriate in music education because they rely too heavily upon linguistic thinking.

Praxial: The Word

The last point in this summary concerns the word "praxial." What does it mean?

"Praxial" comes from the Greek word *praxis*. Praxis does not simply mean "action" or "doing." As Aristotle used it in his *Poetics*, *praxis* connotes action that is *embedded in and responsive to a specific context of effort*. (My friend and colleague Philip Alperson was the first to use "praxial" in the field of music education philosophy. See Wayne Bowman's discussion of "praxial" in chapter 3 of this book.)

I call *Music Matters* a praxial philosophy because this word captures a key idea of this philosophy: that a full understanding of the nature and significance of music involves more than an understanding of pieces or works of music.

"Music," fully understood and fully taught, involves processes and products (actions and outcomes) intertwined. "Praxial" is meant to convey the idea that music pivots on specific kinds of human doing and making (to me, listening is a doing and a "making" in the sense of a mental construction process; "music making" speaks for itself) that are purposeful, contextual, and socially embedded.

By calling *Music Matters* a praxial philosophy, I want to highlight the importance of teaching and learning "music" as a particular form of action (i.e., listening, or making and listening simultaneously) that is purposeful and situated and, therefore, is revealing of one's selfhood and one's relationship with others in a community. "Praxial" emphasizes that music (as products and processes) ought to be understood in relation to the meanings and values evidenced in actual music making, music listening, and musical outcomes in specific cultural contexts.

The Essays in This Collection

The praxial philosophy has traveled widely during the last decade. Scholars, teachers, and students have become increasingly interested in the origins, history, and conceptual underpinnings of this view. In chapter 2, Marie McCarthy and Scott Goble address these topics in their detailed explanation and interpretation of the last fifty years of music education philosophy. In doing so, they contextualize the topics, reflections, and dialogues in this book and situate the efforts of some of the most venerable scholars in our field. In my response (on this book's Web site), I offer some additional ideas on the development of praxialism in relation to postmodern thinking and what sociologists now call "the practice turn" (e.g., Bernstein 1999; Schatzki, Cetina, and Savigny 2001).[1]

In chapter 3 Wayne Bowman "situates" praxialism philosophically. (Tom Regelski continues in this vein in chapter 12 from a different perspective and with different results.) Bowman analyzes the philosophical foundations, concepts, practical implications, and scholarly influences on *Music Matters*. He organizes his discussion in terms of three key issues: performing, multicultural music education, and musical works. For the most part, Bowman believes that praxial tenets do not support my views on these three issues.

I disagree with Bowman on several points. In my reply I point out errors in his criticisms, reasoning, and readings of my words. This point-counterpoint between us makes for a lively dialogue that grows deeper and wider when readers compare chapter 3 to chapter 8 (Bowman's second contribution to this collection) and to three other perspectives on performing, multicultural music education, and musical works contributed by C. K. Szego (chapter 11), Pam Burnard (chapter 14), and Lori-Anne Dolloff (chapter 15).

Constantijn Koopman takes a decidedly negative view of *Music Matters*. In chapter 4 he questions what he believes to be my "cognitive account of musical value," my "exclusive focus on cognition at the cost of feeling," and my "neglect of listening as an independent way of engaging in music." In making these statements, Koopman echoes critics who advocate the philosophy of "music education as aesthetic education" (or MEAE), as Koopman also does. However, a lively debate emerges if you compare Koopman's thoughts with the ideas of other thinkers in this book, such as Wilfried Gruhn (chapter 5), Jeff Martin (chapter 9), and Pam Burnard (chapter 14). Also, I argue (in my reply) that Koopman's claims depend on a straw-man version (his interpretation?) of the praxial philosophy.

In chapter 5 Wilfried Gruhn examines the processes and substrates of music cognition as this term applies to both music making and music listening. Gruhn contradicts several of Koopman's claims (chapter 4) while adding support to Sheila Woodward's views on early childhood music education (chapter 13). Based on his research and the illustrated reasons he offers, Gruhn goes on to suggest strategies for practical music teaching and adjustments to my views on this topic.

Gruhn's ideas match current research findings in the field of consciousness studies (e.g., LeDoux 2002). On the other hand, the views of Gruhn and Koopman clash on several points.

Action-as-knowledge is a key concept of praxialism. In chapter 6 Heidi Westerlund and Marja-Leena Juntunen investigate several senses of the word "action" with special attention to the human body, which plays "a crucial but (unfortunately) a taken-for-granted and opaque role in the development of agency." They focus particularly on "the musical mind and body within a naturalist framework of holistic duality but without dualism."

Since Émil Jaques-Dalcroze had similar concerns, Westerlund and Juntunen take the opportunity to compare his venerable ideas with key tenets of the praxial philosophy. In the process, they articulate several interesting criticisms of and recommendations for the praxial view. For one thing, they suggest that I err by offering a theory of "embrained knowledge" instead of "embodied mind and knowledge." I believe Westerlund and Juntunen are mistaken on this point and others, for reasons I give in my response. However, they are correct on other points that I accept gratefully.

In chapter 7 Robert Cutietta and Sandra Stauffer critique the praxial view of music listening. Their thinking strategy employs several hypothetical "inside" and "outside" listeners to test the praxial view. Among other things, they question whether performing experiences improve students' music listening abilities.

My reply refutes most of the claims made by Cutietta and Stauffer. In my view, their arguments depend on their inaccurate and incomplete reading of *Music Matters*.

Wayne Bowman's second contribution to this collection (chapter 8) probes the pros and cons of teaching performing and listening. This essay is an exquisite example of a philosopher probing all sides of important issues by means of a point-counterpoint dialogue with himself. Among Bowman's many elegant statements (which he later qualifies and questions) is this: "listening without benefit of performance experience is predominantly an aural (all-ears) experience, it might be argued, whereas performance-informed listening is a profoundly corporeal experience in a highly inclusive and broadly distributed sense."

If you find yourself persuaded by one side of Bowman's point-counterpoint dialogue, I encourage you to continue reading. Weigh all his points in relation to each other and in relation to the essays by Szego (chapter 11), Cutietta and Stauffer (chapter 7), and Woodward (chapter 13). Then, consider reading my reply, which agrees with some of Bowman's concerns and counters some of his criticisms.

Like Pam Burnard (chapter 14) and Lori-Anne Dolloff (chapter 15), Jeff Martin is an experienced composer and teacher of composition. In chapter 9, Martin probes the cognitive and social aspects of composing; examines relationships among composing, improvising, performing, and listening; and questions common concepts of the terms "composer" and "composing." Among other issues, Martin questions my suggestion that teachers should "include composing, alongside performing and improvising, 'as time permits.'" I engage Martin's criticisms and suggestions in my reply.

Margaret Barrett (chapter 10) focuses on musical creativity—specifically, the "systems view" of creativity. By this she means the contextual, sociocultural view I adopt and advocate. Although Barrett supports this view to a large extent, she argues that "our recognition of the sociocultural dimensions of creativity also requires that we acknowledge the complexity of these dimensions and the diversity of ways in which children participate in musical communities of practice within and without the school setting."

One of the key questions I debate with Barrett in my reply is whether it makes sense to separate children's musical creativity from adult creativity, as she wants to do. In other words, is Barrett correct when she conflates age and ability in her theory of creativity? I think not. It is not difficult to give many examples of children who learn how to compose and improvise very original and stylistically significant works that, in the judgment of adult experts, match or surpass the creative products of adult musicians. And, of course, a few exceptional children (e.g., Mozart and Mendelssohn) become adult masters at early ages. In short, my reply offers an alternative to Barrett's age-specific view of creativity.

In chapter 11 the ethnomusicologist C. K. Szego examines several key concepts in multicultural music education and presents "a number of counterexamples and arguments to soften Elliott's position on performance and listening." In doing so, she joins the dialogue on these issues that begins in chapter 3 and continues in chapters

7, 8, and 12 through 15. In addition, Szego offers several original points, pro and con, on the roles of performing and listening in multicultural music education. She also probes the concepts of authenticity and multiculturalism to help music teachers "avert simplistic models in the actual delivery of music education."

Although I agree with most of Szego's excellent points, my reply offers several thoughts on the needs and situations of school music teachers that she (and other ethnomusicologists) often omit to consider, let alone value.

In chapter 12 Tom Regelski discusses the philosophies supporting different curriculum orientations. In the process he offers a penetrating analysis of the assumptions underlying music education as aesthetic education and praxialism. This detailed background prepares the way for several discerning questions about my version of praxialism compared to his version. Regelski follows this with constructive enhancements, refinements, and alternatives to my ideas, many of which I accept.

In reply, I address Regelski's version of praxialism and correct some non-problems he creates. I go on to suggest that our differences are minor; indeed, most of what he wants to see in a praxial philosophy are easily accommodated or already included in *Music Matters.*

Overall, music education philosophers pay too little attention to research in the field of early childhood music education. In chapter 13 Sheila Woodward corrects this neglect by linking her research and that of other early childhood specialists (e.g., Custodero, Sims, and Scott-Kassner), to music education philosophy generally and praxialism particularly. Among Woodward's most important themes is that "music learning takes place from before birth, whether adults play an active role in the process or not."

The setting for Pam Burnard's reflections (chapter 14) is her "Musical Creators Club," where students develop musicianship in the context of a practicum that revolves around composing, improvising, performing, and listening. Burnard examines praxialism in relation to many details that make this general music program (her Creators Club) effective and enjoyable. Many readers will find Burnard's descriptions and analyses engaging, affirming, and inspiring. Readers who take the time to compare her views with others in this book (e.g., Cutietta and Stauffer, and O'Toole) will find dramatically different interpretations of what *Music Matters* means.

In chapter 15 Lori-Anne Dolloff examines praxialism from her multiple standpoints as an elementary music teacher and teacher educator, a composer and arranger, and a children's choral conductor. In doing so, she expands important points I could only outline in *Music Matters*. For example, in the process of explaining why "praxialism is compatible with many traditional approaches to elementary music education," including those of Orff and Kodaly, she also explains why "Orff and Kodaly teachers who take a praxial perspective will differ with their colleagues about two main issues: choosing repertoire and organizing curricula." In the process of addressing many other topics in the area of elementary music education, Dolloff discusses "integrated arts" in relation to multicultural music education, thereby adding her voice to the reflections on this topic by Szego (chapter 11) and Bowman (chapter 3).

The last two essays in this book differ significantly from others in this book. In chapter 16 Patricia O'Toole approaches the praxial view from the standpoint of her "feminist politics." She explains why she is uncomfortable with the praxial view as it relates to matters of gender, class, and race. In her view, music is primarily about identity affirmation; in contrast, O'Toole believes I am mostly concerned with the "technical and performative aspects of musicing, which offer musicers limited identities."

I find O'Toole's teaching narratives especially moving. I value the way she speaks her personal truth about (and in) the contexts they occur—whether teaching fifthgraders, observing Charles Keil's MUSE program in Buffalo, or working with her university choir. I want O'Toole (and others who share her views) to feel included; it troubles me that she does not. So, in my reply I examine our differing views on praxialism in relation to our individual perspectives on gender, race, class, and also the chauvinism that permeates much of our discourse.

In chapter 17 Kari Veblen probes *Music Matters* from two interlocking perspectives: her long-standing commitment to and documentation of Community Music projects worldwide and her research expertise in the areas of narrative inquiry, biography, and ethnography.

In addition to reinforcing some of Regelski's points in chapter 12, Veblen maintains that "the praxial view of musical values falls short in explaining some key benefits of Community Music programs." Point taken, as I explain in my reply.

I know I speak for each and all the writers in this book when I express the hope that you will find the following reflections and dialogues engaging, stimulating, and informative.

Note

1. Ernest Lepore is the general editor of this series of books, which includes, for example, *Dennett and his critics* (Dahlbom 1993).

References

Barlex, D., and C. Carre. 1985. *Visual communication in science*. Cambridge, UK: Cambridge University Press.

Bernstein, R. J. 1999. *Praxis and action: Contemporary philosophies of human activity*. Philadelphia: University of Philadelphia Press.

Dahlbom, B., ed. 1993. *Dennett and his critics: Demystifying mind*. Cambridge, MA: Blackwell.

Gardner, H. 1990. *Art education and human development*. Los Angeles: J. Paul Getty Trust.

———. 1991. Assessment in context: The alternative to standardized testing. In *Report of the commission on testing and public policy*, ed. B. Gifford. Unpaginated.

LeDoux, J. E. 2002. *Synaptic self: How our brains become who we are*. New York: Viking.

Popper, K. 1965. *Conjectures and refutations*. New York: Harper & Row.

Rosenau, P. M. 1992. *Post-modernism and the social sciences: Insights, inroads, and intrusions*. Princeton: Princeton University Press.

Schatzki, T. R., K. K. Cetina, and E. von Savigny, eds. 2001. *The practice turn in contemporary theory*. New York: Routledge.

Yob, I. M. 2001. Editorial. *Philosophy of Music Education Review* 9 (1):1–2.

2

The Praxial Philosophy
in Historical Perspective

MARIE McCARTHY AND J. SCOTT GOBLE

Since the 1950s music educators have witnessed striking developments in the philosophical foundations of their profession. The purpose of our chapter is to explore and interpret these developments and, in the process, to historically situate praxial concepts of music education. Specifically, our chapter accounts for developments within each decade since 1950, though the reader will note that there is much overlap between decades as themes and trends continue from one to the next. Also, we wish to emphasize that because each philosophical perspective emerged and was shaped by the social, political, and cultural values of its time, we approach the professional literature with this in mind.

As a basic orientation to this chapter, we suggest that the primary philosophical perspectives of the last fifty years may be termed "utilitarian" and "aesthetic" and that a new "praxial" approach to music education philosophy has appeared in recent years.[1] In addition to depending on ideas drawn primarily from Western aesthetics, music education philosophy has been increasingly affected by concepts from related disciplines such as psychology, sociology, and ethnomusicology.

The Evolution of Music Education as Aesthetic Education

Societal developments in the 1950s and 1960s (e.g., the cold war and the civil rights movement) affected education, influenced the way music educators viewed their subject, and altered our profession's rationalizations for music in the K–12 school curriculum. Prior to the 1950s music education had been associated with a variety of functional values, reflecting its role in social, physical, moral, and intellectual development. In post–World War II years, discontentment was rising among music edu-

19

cators who were not satisfied with recognizing such values as the basis for their work (Leonhard 1965, 44–45).

Owing at least in part to this discontentment, a number of scholars—such as Allen Britton, Harry Broudy, Charles Leonhard, Bennett Reimer, Abraham Schwadron, and Ralph Smith—began to work toward formulating a new philosophy built on principles drawn from Western aesthetics.[2] These writers were influenced principally by the ideas of John Dewey, Susanne Langer, Leonard Meyer, and James Mursell. According to Broudy (1957) and McMurray (1958), a philosophy of music education must entail not only a statement of beliefs, but also a clear articulation and critical refinement of those beliefs based on experience. The view that a philosophy was a resource for practicing music teachers—"one of the most practical things a teacher can have" (Leonhard and House 1959, 84)—was a pervasive theme in the literature (see also Broudy 1957; McMurray 1958). Expanding this idea, Leonhard advocated strongly that musicians and music educators at every level should participate in the creation of a profession-wide philosophy. Leonhard held that the process could not take place "within the vacuum of the academic ivory tower" (1966, 18). Indeed, connecting philosophy to the grass roots of the profession and demonstrating how it might serve teachers were primary concerns of the emerging advocacy movement in music education.

At the same time, these scholars believed that whatever form the new philosophy might take, it would need to be sufficiently comprehensive to unify the profession (Leonhard 1965, 43). From the middle of the 1950s onward the music education literature began to support a professional philosophy based on principles taken from aesthetics (Mark 1988, 111). Accordingly, the notion of "music education as aesthetic education" met with little or no opposition upon its introduction. Based on the values of the era and the needs of the profession, a philosophy grounded in aesthetic principles held the promise of providing a suitable alternative to formulations used during the progressive education era, when the functional values of music education had been emphasized. An aesthetic philosophy would focus on music as a form of fine art and provide music educators with a more respectable basis for explaining the nature, value, and uniqueness of their subject in the school curriculum.

Leonhard was already writing on musical and aesthetic education in 1953. He asserted, "Systematic and consistent efforts to develop an aesthetically valid philosophy of music education are urgently needed at this time" (26). Notably, the language he used was traditional in its allusion to the "richly abundant beauty" inherent in music. At the same time, his thinking revealed an alignment with new psychological approaches to explaining music and art that were appearing in the writings of Langer and Meyer. Leonhard (1955) also provided leadership in highlighting the need and mapping out an agenda for philosophical research in music education.

As individual scholars adopted the aesthetic philosophy,[3] without considerable debate or discussion, the National Association for Music Education (MENC) also came to support this philosophy. *Basic Concepts in Music Education* (1958)—a publication that emerged from the Commission on Basic Concepts established by MENC in 1954—was a landmark in formally launching the philosophy of music education as aesthetic education. In the first section, "Disciplinary Backgrounds," scholars representing classical realist philosophy, pragmatist philosophy, sociology, and history, among other fields, provided perspectives on music. Many of their contributions reflected the emerging aesthetic philosophy. For example, McMurray began his essay by describing the tenets of pragmatism, but he framed his discussion of music education well within the aesthetic paradigm.[4]

Likewise, *Foundations and Principles of Music Education* (Leonhard and House 1959) added to the considerable momentum of music education as aesthetic education. Leonhard and House asserted the profession's need for having a definitive philosophy of music education, emphasizing that it would be "useful, even essential, for an operation as complex and important as music education" (84). Their call for a definitive philosophy reflected the need for establishing professional security, and it manifested their belief that philosophical unity was the answer.

At the same time, they acknowledged the limitation of the aesthetic paradigm to accommodate youth music and contemporary experimental music that "operate within different aesthetics" (Leonhard and House 1959, 108). While they recommended that such music be integrated into the school music program, they did not provide an account of how the new philosophical approach would accommodate it.

By the early 1960s the aesthetic philosophy had already become significant within music education. Bennett Reimer, Abraham Schwadron, and Ralph Smith elaborated this philosophy and articulated its benefits. The establishment of the *Journal of Aesthetic Education* in 1966 confirmed the strength of the aesthetic education movement by the mid-1960s. This journal served as a forum for publication and debate of philosophical issues in music education and the other arts. Several professional dialogues during the 1960s were also instrumental in popularizing the aesthetic approach, especially the Yale Seminar (1963), the Seminar on Comprehensive Musicianship (1965), and the Tanglewood Symposium (1967).

A qualified commitment to music education as aesthetic education is evident throughout the Tanglewood papers. While some participants (e.g., Broudy) argued for the importance of establishing students' familiarity with the "great classics" of musical art, other participants (e.g., McAllester) believed the approach needed to be expanded to include many different forms of music. The final report of the symposium identified the need for a new aesthetic theory—one based on developments in technology, anthropology, and communication in the previous fifteen years (Choate 1968, 11).

Although the symposium participants recommended expanding the repertoire of school music to include "music of our time in its rich variety" (Choate 1968, 139), it is clear that not everyone agreed that the aesthetic philosophy could accommodate musical cultures and practices beyond the Western musical canon. Still, the majority did agree that all music has aesthetic value. Thus, the aesthetic philosophy was generally affirmed because it was thought to meet the demands of the changing relationship between school and society. Mark observed that in this sense the Tanglewood Declaration provided "a brilliant utilitarian basis for an aesthetic philosophy" (1988, 123).

Among all the scholars wrestling with philosophical issues in music education, Abraham Schwadron faced these tensions with the greatest lucidity as he straddled the line between the need for professional security achieved through a singular philosophy and the realities of a pluralistic society.[5] In his opinion, the classic aesthetic theories of objectivism (or isolationism) and subjectivism (or contextualism) had not resolved the problems of contemporary music education satisfactorily (Schwadron 1965, 131).[6] Thus, Schwadron advocated a more relativistic position—one that emphasized the interrelationship between objectivism and subjectivism. In his most well-elaborated statement on aesthetic education, *Aesthetics: Dimensions For Music Education* (1967), Schwadron attempted to develop a theory based on that position, so that "more inclusive understandings of socio-musical values and related educational means and ends" might be realized (v).

Critical probing of aesthetic theory led Schwadron to confront core disputes and dilemmas, identifying the central problem of reconciling his humanistic vision of musical aesthetics with the purist's view of music as an isolated art, separated from life.[7] He recommended that educators adopt a plurality of theories of art, warning against the dangers of "philosophical and critical dogmatism." Schwadron wrote: "Opposing camps appear to be engaged in the philosophical pursuit of an absolute and universal value system which somehow bypasses the logical recognition that values are relative to and conditioned by cultural groups and periods" (1966, 190). Schwadron displayed the most visionary and comprehensive thinking of his day, but it seems clear that the aesthetic philosophy could not contain the breadth of his thought.

While Schwadron was drawing from anthropology, ethnomusicology, and religion,[8] other scholars were delving into psychology for a combination of reasons: to account for the nature and meaning of music, to validate the premises upon which aesthetic philosophy was based, to organize instruction, and to strengthen their aesthetic rationale for music in education.

This effort drew from a number of sources. The first and most obvious source was the work of Susanne Langer, who articulated a modernist vision of music as "a tonal analogue of emotive life" in her books *Philosophy in a New Key* (1942) and *Feeling and Form* (1953, 27). A second major source was Leonard Meyer, who drew upon Dewey's philosophy and gestalt psychology to address many important issues (e.g., musical meaning, communication, value, and greatness). His most influential book was *Emotion and Meaning in Music* (1956).

A third source was *Basic Concepts in Music Education* (1958), a book intended to "emphasize the emerging trend toward more effective orientation of instructional programs to accepted goals of formal instruction" (viii). This work, coupled with Jerome Bruner's *Process of Education* (1963), foreshadowed the conceptual approach to curriculum that came to dominate music education by the end of the 1960s.[9] The idea of the "common elements of music" served as the basis for developing hierarchies of concepts to organize music instruction.

A fourth source worthy of note was the set of two handbooks authored by Benjamin Bloom and his colleagues. These presented taxonomies of educational objectives. The first (Bloom 1956) focused on the "cognitive domain," while the second addressed the "affective domain" (Krathwohl, Bloom, and Masia 1964). These books provided a theoretical basis for developing course content, planning instruction, and organizing the outcomes of instruction (Abeles, Hoffer, and Klotman 1984/1994, 242). Altogether, these publications laid the foundations for concept learning in music and provided a model for organizing instruction based on identified outcomes and instructional objectives.

Also important to the development of a psychological approach to the arts was the work of the philosopher Nelson Goodman. This eminent scholar applied various cognitive principles to art education under the auspices of "Project Zero," which he founded at Harvard in 1967. His book *Languages of Art* (1968) examined the symbolic nature of the arts in a psychological framework. Indeed, side by side with the rise of interest in educational psychology was the beginning of what Mark has described as a "synergy between philosophy and psychology" (Mark 1996, 67–70). His observation points out the degree to which these disciplines were coming closer together in the minds of music educators at this time.

Alternative Perspectives

Music educators had a rich array of conceptual frameworks available to them in the 1950s and 1960s, but most of the leading scholars in the field aligned their efforts with aesthetic education in order to bring about professional unity, security, and respectability. In light of developments in later decades it is important to acknowledge alternative perspectives that were not then pursued seriously. These perspectives were rooted in educational philosophy, particularly social constructionism, pragmatism, sociology, and the emerging discipline of ethnomusicology. While the criticism is justified that music educators narrowed their conceptual lens, it is important to keep in mind that the disciplines they might have drawn from were not unified philosophically.[10]

For example, Leonhard noted the influence of a number of philosophical schools in educational thinking of the time: idealism, realism, experimentalism, pragmatism, existentialism, and instrumentalism. However, he concluded that it would be impossible to construct a philosophy of music education that could reconcile the conflicting points of view represented by these theories (1965, 43). In his opinion, music educators had appealed principally to educational philosophy to give them direction in the past, and the relative weakness of the profession suggested that it needed to be grounded in a theory more closely associated with music (48).[11]

Pragmatism and social reconstructionism were promoted in certain educational contexts, but they did not seem to offer the type of intrinsic justification for music in education that mid-twentieth-century music educators deemed appropriate and necessary. For example, while Leonhard and House (1959) were aware of the need to integrate socially relevant music into the curriculum, they did not connect that need with the social reconstructionist philosophy being advocated at that time by Theodore Brameld. Brameld's anthropologically centered philosophy had its roots in the 1930s and grew out of the progressive movement. It seems probable that in the move away from progressive ideals, social reconstructionist philosophy had become associated with utilitarian educational outcomes.[12] Pragmatic philosophy might have also contributed greatly to music education philosophy. However, one of the most basic characteristics of pragmatism—openness to different perspectives—was not a hallmark of the music education profession in the 1950s and 1960s.[13]

Sociology also had much to offer music educators. Indeed, our profession may have benefited from this domain of scholarship during the social revolutions of the 1960s. However, the potential for sociological perspectives to strengthen and direct music education philosophy was not realized because sociology was seen to be associated with nonmusical educational outcomes. John Mueller's chapter "Music and

Education: A Sociological Approach" (in *Basic Concepts of Music Education*, 1958) and Max Kaplan's sociologically based view of music (in *Foundations and Frontiers of Music Education*, 1966) represented the most comprehensive statements on the sociology of music and music education in this period.[14]

Still, there is no evidence that the ideas related by these scholars penetrated music education philosophy. Mark has noted music education philosophers' neglect of sociological perspectives in this period: "The new movement toward an aesthetic philosophy was to have the effect of disassociating music education from societal goals, at least in the minds of many music educators. . . The part that conveys to the public its value to society, was missing" (1988, 120). Thus, music education might be said to have existed in a social vacuum.

Ethnomusicologists and cultural anthropologists, such as Alan Merriam and Charles Seeger, also offered progressive philosophical interpretations of music as a socio-cultural phenomenon. Merriam's book *The Anthropology of Music* (1964) provided valuable insights into the functions of music and into music as symbolic behavior, among other topics. Seeger, who addressed music educators on numerous occasions from the 1940s to the 1970s, summarized the plight of music education philosophy:

> American music educators have had to get along with second- and third-hand echoes of European philosophies of music. Besides being considerably distorted, these echoes are somewhat out of date. The foundations of music education in the United States are, then, strictly 20th Century upon their educational side, but garbled 19th Century on the musicological side. And worst of all, the music educators do not know it. (1947, 197)

The primary strength of music education philosophy in the 1950s and 1960s—its efficient adoption of aesthetics as its foundation—could also be considered its primary weakness. By narrowing its conceptual focus, the profession laid the foundations for a philosophy whose parameters and assumptions were unable to accommodate the shifting social and cultural realities on the horizon. Its narrow definition of music focused on the musical work and its intrinsic value; it did not incorporate the emerging cultural view of music in related disciplines.

Since aesthetics was born in the 1700s in the context of a particular European socially elite class, it evolved around a hierarchical view of musical value and greatness that placed Western European art music at the pinnacle of musical repertoires. In an era when increasing knowledge of a wide variety of the world's musical practices was available through research and media, and while it was being introduced into some Western curricula, the aesthetic philosophy for music education was, in essence, ethnocentric.

On the positive side, the development of an aesthetic basis for music education established a cohesive philosophy for the music education community at a time when ideological homogeneity was a societal ideal. Efforts toward philosophical unity were reasonable for a profession in need of security and a society in need of sociopolitical balance. The need for philosophical research and discourse was highlighted, and action was taken to create forums and publications to serve this need. Considerable energy was directed toward developing a philosophical basis for music education's principles, concepts, and values. The foundations were laid for the 1970s, during which the aesthetic movement blossomed at all levels of music education.

The Heyday of Aesthetic Education

Developments in the 1960s began to consolidate the aesthetic education movement, climaxing in the publication of Bennett Reimer's *Philosophy of Music Education* (1970). In this timely book Reimer brought together the various aspects of the aesthetic philosophy in an unprecedented way. His considerable reflection on philosophical issues was evident in his elaborate statement on the need for a music education philosophy; in his clear, logical, and persuasive argument for the adoption of "absolute expressionism" as a basis for music education; and in his design for applying the aesthetic philosophy to music instruction.

Previously, music education advocacy had been associated with philosophy in general terms. Reimer brought this relationship into clear focus and, one could argue, launched a new phase of advocacy in which the values of music education evolved out of a particular philosophical position. Reimer never envisioned that the philosophical position he set forth would come to dominate music education in subsequent years. He wrote that a philosophy "must be conceived as being 'of a time'" and must also give recognition to the fact that it can only provide "a point of departure for practitioners of that time" (1970, 2). His disclaimer was little noted, as the philosophical unity his book helped to effect served to balance the profession in the midst of social and cultural upheavals.

Reimer's book marked the beginning of a phase of "putting aesthetic education to work,"[15] a series of efforts by the profession to implement this philosophy. In 1971 *Toward an Aesthetic Education* was published as a collaborative project of MENC and CEMREL (the Central Midwestern Regional Educational Laboratory). The papers in this collection reflected the thinking of a community of scholars dedicated to the development and implementation of aesthetic education programs, set in the context of a professional organization supporting such development.[16] The development of music education as aesthetic education was supported by the federal government, professional organizations, the music education research community, music textbook companies, and, increasingly, by music educators in K–12 settings (Schwadron 1973a).[17] As Reimer observed at the time, "aesthetic education is now something real" (1972, 29).

The aesthetic philosophy influenced several curriculum projects in the 1970s, such as the CEMREL Aesthetic Education Program (Madeja 1975), the Cleveland area project (Reimer 1978), and Harvard's Project Zero, among others. A feature of many projects, and of aesthetic education in general, was an emphasis on interrelated arts and an interdisciplinary approach to curriculum development (Reimer 1976, 28–29; Tait 1973). Reimer strongly advocated such an approach, stating, "The arts in education hardly know one another. It is time that we begin to recognize our common cause and become more united in pursuing it" (1972, 33).[18] Increased attention was given to interrelated arts programs during the 1970s. Reimer attributed the success of this development to a better and shared philosophical base among the arts (1977, 12). An interrelated arts focus was a primary strength of aesthetic education, especially in the context of the basic education movement of that decade and the ongoing need to advocate for the arts in education.

The aesthetic paradigm and philosophical research developed together. Schwadron (1970b, 1973c) addressed the state of philosophical research, observing that the profession had come far since Broudy asked in 1957, "Does music education need a philosophy?" In spite of shortcomings, Schwadron noted, "the results of a decade of philosophic-aesthetic inquiry are impressive" (1973c, 46). This observation was supported by the increase in doctoral dissertations on philosophical issues reported in the *Journal of Research in Music Education* (Gordon 1964; 1968; 1972).[19] One continuing concern was that music educators were not involved in exploring philosophical questions about music (Schwadron 1970b, 26; Reese 1977). In effect, although the philosophy of aesthetic education was being put into action through curriculum development and textbook production, those who implemented the philosophy in the classroom were not involved in directing its development.

A second concern that surfaced as the aesthetic philosophy was gaining momentum was its hasty adoption and immature application. Reimer observed that even though aesthetic education "is now something real," the reality to which the phrase "aesthetic education" referred remained "disturbingly obscure" (1972, 29). He was not alone in identifying this tension between the nebulous nature of the aesthetic philosophy and its widespread adoption and implementation.

Although Schwadron supported the idea that music education as aesthetic education had "captured the professional conscience" of music educators, he was apprehensive, on the basis of what he perceived as "an eagerness to get down to brass tacks, a desire to build a viable curriculum before a real understanding of aesthetic education is achieved" (1973a, 37). He saw the need for better discourse about aesthetic education, and he warned against premature application of the philosophy to music education (1973a; 1973c).

Similarly, Gonzo argued that although the focus on "the aesthetic experience" represented a "coming of age in music education," it needed a clear definition and a workable form if it was to influence course content, methodology, and curricular objectives (1971, 36). Epperson was willing to ignore "the danger of oversimplifying" that accompanied the adoption of the aesthetic philosophy because musical aesthetics played an important role in integrating and synthesizing "our multifaceted discipline" (1975, 53). Tensions and dilemmas surfaced in some writings, but for the most part advocates continued to articulate the benefits and possibilities of aesthetic education.

Trends Impacting the Development of Aesthetic Education

As music educators adopted the aesthetic philosophy in the 1950s and 1960s, and as it expanded and became institutionalized in the profession in the 1960s and early 1970s, it could have taken several directions. The ways it entered into professional discourse and practice were determined in large part by the educational values and practices of the day, developments in related disciplines, and the economic changes that fueled the basic education movement and intensified the arts advocacy movement (Thompson 1977; Broudy 1978; Sudano and Sharpham 1981).

Research in aesthetic education responded to the widespread value attributed to quantitative research methodology, the measurement of behavioral and instructional outcomes, and the creation of instructional plans around concepts and behavioral objectives. The most popular definition of aesthetic education at the time was "the development of sensitivity to the aesthetic qualities of things" (Reimer 1972, 29), and trends in education and psychology were focused on perception and affective educational outcomes. Thus, it is not surprising that one should find a group of published studies during the same era exploring the effect of developing aesthetic sensitivity on musical attitude, musical expressiveness, and musical perception (Standifer 1970; Lewy 1971; Bullock 1973; Madeja 1975).[20]

Mainstream research in aesthetic education was not without its critics. Goodman (1972) identified the need for "a less simple-minded approach" to explaining the aesthetic experience. Not surprisingly, Schwadron (1970b; 1973a) viewed the research on aesthetic education with reservations and criticisms. He was critical of the "statistical, pencil-to-paper measurements of affective behavior in music," the misleading attempts at classification, and the lack of "penetrating musico-aesthetic inquiry" in music education (1973a, 38). By the end of the decade Reimer was also critical of the "monopoly of experimental research in music education" (Aquino 1979, 43).

Links between psychology, educational psychology, and aesthetic education were developed further in the 1970s, with an emphasis on applying the concept of taxonomies to music instruction and to the goals of aesthetic education (Biggs 1971; Lewy 1971), on expanding objectives to describe aesthetic behaviors and affective outcomes (*Toward an Aesthetic Education* 1971; Lewy 1971; Bullock 1973), and on evaluating aesthetic education programs. An increasing number of scholars used psychological paradigms and techniques to investigate philosophical issues in the teaching and learning of the arts. For example, exploring the arts as symbol systems was a topic that emerged in the realm of philosophy but was subsequently explored from a psychological standpoint (Howard 1972, 8). Ideas from cognitive psychology assisted in meeting increasing pressure to validate music in education. Brain research studies suggested that experiences in the arts stimulate parts of the brain that are not accessed by learning in other subject areas. The arts were thus recognized as contributing to human development in a unique way (Franklin and Franklin 1978). Connections with psychology were further developed during the Ann Arbor symposia held in 1978, 1979, and 1981.

Questioning the Aesthetic Approach

As the 1970s progressed, the aesthetic rationale for music in education began to be questioned. This resulted in large part from the problems created by the national economic conditions of that decade (Mark 1996, 59). Some music educators pointed out the limitations of focusing rationales on the aesthetic qualities of the arts to the exclusion of what they perceived as nonaesthetic and nonmusical dimensions of arts experience. Gary (1975) defined the purpose of music education in a broader context than aesthetic rationales: "to reveal to students what music can do for their lives and to offer as many opportunities for musical learning as they desire and are capable of assimilating" (iii).

The changing views of the MENC were evident in a position paper published in 1977, which stated that although "the important contributions of music to the aesthetic and cultural objectives of education" are more than sufficient to justify its presence in the basic curriculum, "the Conference recognizes that music can make other contributions to the educational and personal growth of the student and that these ancillary contributions may be highly valued in some communities" (59). Threats to music programs in public schools across the nation stimulated the advocacy efforts of this influential professional organization (see Suber and Stearns 1972).

While some music educators explored and drew on utilitarian functions of music education to rationalize its presence in the curriculum, many scholars remained committed to the aesthetic philosophy. Broudy (1978), for instance, refused to acknowledge the utilitarian rationale, arguing that "the aesthetic education program must make its case on its contribution to aesthetic values and the values of aesthetic values and not on its putative non-aesthetic spinoffs" (3). Reimer (1972) also remained strong in his convictions, stating that if music abandons its aesthetic role in favor of a social role, "it becomes a demeaned thing, and the teaching and learning of it are equally demeaned" (30).

Declining confidence in aesthetic education was not attributable only to its inadequacies as a rationale for music education in a time of budget crises. Criticism was also directed at the philosophy of art chosen by Reimer and the state of philosophical unity that the aesthetic approach created within professional discourse (Schwadron 1973b, 1973c, 1975; Lemmon 1977). For Schwadron, the tensions arose principally out of the limitations of the aesthetic approach to accommodate "the nature of the pluralistic society, the many musics, and the variety of accepted modes of thought" (1973c, 49; 1973b, 19–20). He saw a need for incorporating perspectives from ethnomusicology and comparative aesthetics to expand thinking in music education and respond to cultural realities.

Lemmon (1977) was similarly critical of the narrowness of Reimer's philosophy in the context of music as a global phenomenon:

> We may approach what Reimer has done in one of two ways. Either we must
> believe that all musicians . . . work according to the principles of Reimer's theory of art . . . or only those works and activities of musicians that can be shown
> to conform to the conditions laid down by Reimer's theory of art can be justifiably included in deliberations on the nature (structure) and content of a curriculum in music. (8)

In response to Lemmon's observations, Reimer (1977) acknowledged that there are limitations with any philosophy, and he defended his position by expressing surprise at the degree to which his book was embraced in the 1970s. "I would not have quite believed how monolithically the profession would evolve in the 1970s. . . . I envisioned that my own attempts to articulate a philosophy and play out its implications in the curriculum would be matched by alternative efforts" (11).[21]

Alternative views were available to music educators that would have expanded the philosophical foundations of the discipline and provided new perspectives on the nature and value of music. In particular, scholars in ethnomusicology and sociology were publishing research that was highly relevant to music educators. These publications included John Blacking's *How Musical Is Man?* (1973), John Shepherd's *Whose Music? A Sociology of Musical Languages* (1977), and Christopher Small's *Music, Society, Education* (1977).

With the exception of a minority of scholars and practitioners whose thinking was aligned to the radically new insights found in such sources—such as Abraham Schwadron, Barbara Reeder Lundquist, and James Standifer—the music education profession in this decade seemed comfortable maintaining the aesthetic philosophy while adding some new ideas from cognitive psychology. However, when economic changes once again required music educators to explain the importance of music, many responded with arguments that played up the nonmusical outcomes of music education.[22]

As the 1980s began, there was a certain loss of confidence in the aesthetic approach. The era of philosophical unity was drawing to a close. Still, one cannot neglect to acknowledge the legacy of the aesthetic movement. It helped unify thinking within music education and among scholars and practitioners across the arts, and on an international scale,[23] and it elevated the status of music in the curriculum by aligning it with other school subjects. It also assisted in the development of general music programs, and its growth demonstrated how a philosophy could be implemented in practice.

A Period of Philosophical Ferment and New Beginnings

In the United States, philosophical writings on music education in the early 1980s reflected a growing uneasiness within the music education profession as the economic policies of President Ronald Reagan began to channel funding away from the nation's public schools, and as arts education programs were cut back in many school districts. Mark (1982) drew a distinction between "utilitarian" and "aesthetic" rationales for the profession, demonstrating that a factor common to all music education philosophies historically is that each has demonstrated a relationship between music education and the society within which it is practiced. While this was also the case in the United States prior to the mid-twentieth century, he observed, "music is now taught for the sake of music" (15); there is no longer a connection between the philosophy of the profession and societal needs. Mark's distinction came to be recognized widely by the profession as the March 1983 issue of the *Music Educators Journal* included articles by scholars expressing their opinions on the utilitarian-versus-aesthetic question.

Gerard Kneiter reaffirmed the aesthetic philosophy, expressing the conventional view that instructional programs in aesthetic music education should provide for a continuing sequence of significant aesthetic experiences and that the development of musical literacy was among the most critical outcomes of such programs. Patricia

Coates, on the other hand, asserted that the central problem with aesthetic education was that it failed to relate to other kinds of learning. Evidently frustrated with the view of music as "purposeless," espoused by aesthetic education theorists, she wrote: "A facet of the curriculum that believes in its own lack of utility is doomed" (1983, 31). Coates recommended that music educators begin to ground their work in a philosophy of education rather than a philosophy of art.

Simultaneously acknowledging the historical roots of aesthetic education and recognizing the merits of utilitarian views, Kenneth Phillips suggested a pendulum swing "back to a more central philosophy that embraces both the utilitarian and the aesthetic" (1983, 30). He pointed out that aesthetic rationales do not have meaning for administrators, parents, or many others and acknowledged that "in the end, music educators will need a philosophy to which the general public can relate if music is to remain a viable force in public school education" (30). Later that year Charles Elliott observed that a reorientation was going on within the profession, noting that music educators in increasing numbers were beginning to move away from the aesthetic rationale for public school music (1983, 36).

In July 1983 a conference titled "The Future of Musical Education in America" was held at the Eastman School of Music. Of all the presenters, Christopher Lasch brought the broadest perspective (which was rooted in anthropology and history) to the question of why the arts in general "lead such a precarious existence in America" (1984, 11). Discarding stock answers of the past, he pointed out that music had become separated from ordinary life and "surrounded with an aura of sanctity" in Europe during the nineteenth century, and that America had adopted much of this attitude at its inception. Observing that an element of play pervades most human activities, he noted that the American rationalization of work had banished this element from most of the nation's workplaces. In his view, "those who love the arts and deplore their marginal status in American society do not need to develop more enlightened consumers of culture, but to end the segregation of art and to achieve a new integration between art and everyday life" (17).

Regrettably, the profession did not then actively seek ways to implement Lasch's suggestion. Instead, the aesthetic model continued to be reaffirmed in several books published for use within the profession, as well as numerous articles. For example, *Foundations of Music Education* (Abeles, Hoffer, and Klotman 1984/1994), a text for graduate students in the field, rearticulated long-held philosophical, psychological, and sociological perspectives on the work of the profession. Another highly visible work of the decade, *Music, Mind, and Education* (Swanwick 1988), drew its basic themes from the same scholars central to the aesthetic philosophy—Langer and Meyer—although Swanwick attempted to illuminate other psychological and sociological dimensions of musical experience and explain their implications for music education in pluralist societies.[24]

In the mid-1980s other music educators (some of them senior scholars in the profession) challenged the aesthetic education model. Leonhard (1985) took a hard line against many of the overwrought writings on aesthetic philosophy of the time: "current statements are often so vague and esoteric that few people can understand them, especially laypersons" (5). He acknowledged that he had been "at least partially responsible" for the profession's emphasis on aesthetic education during the preceding thirty years. Leonhard went on to say that he had not intended "aesthetic education" to become the primary rationale for the teaching of music in the schools, and he now questioned the credibility of some who were arguing for the importance of music education on aesthetic bases:

> I never anticipated that the concept of aesthetic education would come to be used as the major tenet in the justification for music education. That has, however, happened. As a result, the profession has been sated with vague esoteric statements of justification that no one understands, including, I suspect, most of the people who make those statements. (7)

Leonhard then presented a rationale for music education based on what he termed "realistic" principles, asserting their usefulness in convincing school board members, administrators, parents, and the general public of music's value. He listed eleven benefits he saw as accruing from music education, all stemming from his central belief that music educators are responsible for the preservation, refinement, and transmission of cultural heritage to succeeding generations of Americans. Notably, all of the benefits he enumerated reflected utilitarian values.

Likewise, Colwell (1986) challenged Reimer's aesthetic education philosophy in the twentieth anniversary issue of the *Journal of Aesthetic Education*, remarking that it "lacked sufficient focus to justify the retention of many specialized music programs" (36). Colwell concluded: "On the surface music [education] continues to march forward under the aesthetic education banner, but it is searching for a new gonfalon that is not only more understandable to the general public but closer to what has become accepted educational practice" (37).

While possibilities for a "new banner" were taking rough form in the minds of music education scholars in various quarters, one Canadian scholar, David Elliott, delivered the first in a series of incisive critiques of the aesthetic philosophy. His efforts ultimately opened the door to new ways of thinking about the philosophy of music education.

Elliott completed coursework for his doctoral degree in music education with Bennett Reimer at Case Western Reserve University. Accordingly, Elliott was intimately acquainted with the aesthetic philosophy and in a unique position to evaluate its strengths and weaknesses. In a 1986 publication, Elliott related and applied the perspectives of the psychological theorist Ernest Schachtel to the organization and conduct of jazz education as aesthetic education, expanding the model of the nature of musical perception under the heading of aesthetic education. Elliott argued that Schachtel's theory helped explain how an individual's affective predispositions might contribute to enhancing or diminishing his or her grasp of musical meaning and that they represented an important expansion of Leonard Meyer's work. Specifically, Elliott took issue with aesthetic education's narrow and absolutist concept of musical works, its implausible idea of musical affective experience, and its overemphasis on the use of recorded music in music education. In Elliott's view, "jazz is a way of performing; a way of being in music. Participation, not contemplation, is the hallmark of the jazz aesthetic" (1986, 45). Elliott recommended that jazz educators not allow themselves to be constrained by the aesthetic model and advocated that those invested in aesthetic education expand their model to embrace the uniqueness of jazz (52).

Although Elliott framed his discussion within the scope of aesthetic philosophy, he was apparently finding it sufficiently limited and constraining that he felt it appropriate to take issue publicly with some of its basic tenets soon after the article was published. In 1987 he published an article titled "Structure and Feeling in Jazz: Rethinking Philosophical Foundations." In this discussion he undertook to elaborate a perspective on the musical structure-affect relationship in jazz that was grounded in a broader concept of the musical work, musical parameters, and musical affective experience than the aesthetic philosophy could provide. Elliott offered an alternative to Meyer's model of musical affective experience based on research in the psychology of emotion that Reimer had not considered in the construction of his philosophy. Elliott (1987) concluded his article by summarizing the implications of his work for music education philosophy in general: "It seems appropriate to recommend that the philosophy of music education as aesthetic education—a philosophy built on the premise that music is capable of arousing affect, and that music education is the education of feeling—ought to end its allegiance to a one-dimensional conflict theory of human affective experience" (32). Elliott had identified one of the primary limitations of the philosophy of music education as aesthetic education: its incapacity to account for the range of affective responses beyond those typically associated with Western art music and thus outside the scope of "absolute expressionism"—the aesthetic theory at the core of Reimer's philosophy.[25]

Elliott's critique was validated tacitly by Schwadron, who (as we noted earlier) had long held that aesthetic education would need to be reframed in a way that would allow it to embrace the uniqueness of different musical traditions if it was to continue as the profession's guiding doctrine. In an essay featured in *Music Education in the United States: Contemporary Issues* (1988), Schwadron acknowledged his own involvement in fostering the growth of the aesthetic education philosophy, but he also noted the weakness of the philosophy in accounting adequately for the musical practices of different cultural groups.

> The aesthetic emphasis in contemporary philosophy of music education shows the broad influence of Meyer (1961), Langer (1953, 1967), Broudy (1958), Schwadron (1967), Reimer (1970), and others. One strong theory of musical meaning and value, based on Meyer's aesthetic posture of absolute expressionism and adapted by Reimer, still prevails. It should be understood that, aside from its validity in Western European music (principally as applied to common practice), absolute expressionism is simply not universally applicable. . . . As a theory, however important and even applicable in its own right, absolute expressionism should be viewed as limited; relative, not absolute; Western European, not global. Its educational significance must also be considered with cogent concern for its appropriate application. The large bulk of music, worldwide, calls for musical understanding (of meaning, value, etc.) on other grounds, more contextual and even extramusical. (1988, 100)

Based on this view, Schwadron expressed doubt that a philosophical consensus would ever be possible among music educators within the framework of the democratic pluralist society of the United States. He recommended that the profession make an effort to welcome a number of different theories. Unlike Elliott, however, Schwadron optimistically held out hope that a plurality of opinions could be contained under the rubric of aesthetic education.[26]

In the same volume, Mark (1988) published an essay reframing the aesthetic-versus-utilitarian dilemma. He reconsidered his earlier position on the rationales given historically for music education (Mark 1982) and those given more recently by aesthetic education philosophers. Mark appealed to history to identify common threads in music education practices of the past, discussed factors limiting music education philosophy in a democratic society, accounted for the emergence of aesthetic education in the United States, and concluded by describing what he saw as the role of higher education in teaching music education philosophy.[27] Evidently some members of the profession had difficulty grasping Mark's reconciling synthesis, because the utilitarian-versus-aesthetic polemic did not abate.

Soon after that, Reimer recognized the possibilities for broadening the aesthetic approach that had appeared in Elliott's work. However, he expressed disappointment that Elliott used them to challenge the foundations of aesthetic education. Reimer (1989a, 1989b) outlined what he held to be the past, present, and future of aesthetic education. He defended and, in some respects, redefined the aesthetic position in a way that would subsume some of the criticisms being leveled against it. He addressed the tendency of some music educators to rely on utilitarian justifications for the teaching of music, warning that when music education is conceptualized merely as skill training for performance, then the profession becomes limited by its undue focus on instructional methodologies. He stressed that aesthetic education—with its emphasis on understanding music and musical experience—is not so limited. Then, as an example of how aesthetic education could allow for expansion and transformation, Reimer cited Elliott's article "Structure and Feeling in Jazz," in which Elliott had given an "excellent explanation" of Leonard B. Meyer's recent revisions of his own theories. However, Reimer expressed regret that Elliott had taken the additional step of using these new ideas as a basis for raising questions about the viability of aesthetic education as a philosophical foundation for the profession.[28]

Reimer concluded his discussion by stressing the importance of aesthetic education as a fundamental concept that provided coherence for the profession. He warned that setting it aside would cast music education into a constant state of turmoil over its purpose.[29] He then predicted that two new developments—computer technology and cognitive psychology—would influence music teaching in important ways. Notably, he did not discuss other developments: America's increasing cultural diversity and the attendant societal interest in music from different cultural traditions. In fact, each of these three developments did impact music education in striking ways. But other new developments in cognitive psychology and multiculturalism—and the recognition of their implications—were to have the greatest transformative effect on the philosophy of the profession during the following decade.

Indeed, in 1983 Howard Gardner published an important book stemming from cognitive science research, titled *Frames of Mind: The Theory of Multiple Intelligences*. Gardner's influence was already beginning to penetrate music education and the broader national education forum. He cited physiological and cultural evidence to argue for the existence of a number of relatively discrete human "intelligences" in every human being, including musical intelligence.[30] Gardner's model of mind held major implications for education in all discipline areas at all levels, prompting wide-spread reconsideration of school curricula. His work gave a great boost to music education because it caused educational leaders and administrators to regard music in a new way. As music educators began to see, once one recognizes that the human mind is partly musical (i.e., that the mental manipulation of sound is a natural and unique form of human cognition) and that musical intelligence has relationships to other intelligences, it is a small step to the realization that nurturing its development may be a basic responsibility of public schools.[31]

Gardner's theory of multiple intelligences (MI) gained high visibility during the following years. *The National Society for the Study of Education Yearbook* (1985) took as its theme "Learning and Teaching the Ways of Knowing," reflecting the widespread influence of MI theory in general education. Numerous scholars in arts education incorporated aspects of Gardner's writings directly or indirectly into their own work.[32] Gardner's insights, and cognitive science research in general, gave tremendous support to music education, and a number of scholars undertook their own approaches to studies of musical cognition.[33]

Just as music educators were incorporating concepts from cognitive science into music education research and practice, they were also turning to sociology and anthropology to inform them about multicultural issues. In August 1984 a MENC-sponsored symposium was held on the campus of Wesleyan University in Connecticut. Its purpose was to bring perspectives from social anthropology to the teaching and learning of music in the United States. The symposium, according to the ethnomusicologist David McAllester, was "the first conference to focus principally on a transcultural approach, seeking information from musical practice and thought worldwide" (1984, 2). Indeed, discussions during the five-day conference were based on studies of thirty different cultural groups featuring musical traditions from Polynesia, Africa, Bulgaria, and Native American reservations, among others. McAllester drew a distinction between the understandings of music held by the various cultural groups represented in the conference discussions and those influencing many Americans at the time:

> We are still at least halfway engaged in our myth that art exists for art's sake alone. Few music educators venture so far as to propose that music is a basic tool in teaching morality, ethics, the fundamental values of one's culture, or is necessary to life itself. The study of communities where these powers and functions of music are taken for granted can alert us to their presence everywhere. (4)

Simultaneously, the movement toward including music from cultural traditions ordinarily outside the U.S. public forum was gathering momentum in K–12 music classrooms, as more music educators began to regard their teaching as "multicultural." Some of these educators focused primarily on the performance practices of different cultural groups, illustrating how they could be undertaken in the classroom and placing less emphasis on understanding the social contexts of their origin.[34] Others emphasized that the forms of music undertaken by the members of particular cultural groups must be understood on their own terms as unique expressions of the communities from which they stem.[35] These differences in orientation have persisted within the profession.

A Flourishing Era for Music Education Philosophy

The late 1980s and early 1990s witnessed a number of significant initiatives in music education philosophy. In 1988 the first issue of the *Philosophy of Music Education Newsletter* was published. A Special Research Interest Group (SRIG) for Music Education Philosophy was officially established by MENC in 1990. The first international symposium on music education philosophy was held at Indiana University during July of the same year. The papers from this conference appeared as a special issue of the *Journal of Aesthetic Education* (1991). These essays offered contrasting perspectives from a range of philosophers, music theorists, and musicologists (Jorgensen 1991a, 1-2). Summarizing the content of these papers, Estelle Jorgensen wrote: "The essays in this issue reveal that a variety of views of music education has now emerged. These ideas have yet to be systematically criticized. It remains to be seen how philosophy will develop in music education and what its future directions will be. We have in these essays, however, a glimpse of some of the possibilities" (3-4).

This publication was followed in 1993 by the establishment of the *Philosophy of Music Education Review*, a refereed journal edited by Jorgensen. A cursory glance at the contents of the first volumes reveals a broad range of topics that both revisited philosophical ideas of the past and confronted contemporary issues, with writers drawing from multiple disciplines. The year 1993 also witnessed the birth of the "MayDay Group." Initiated and led by J. Terry Gates and Thomas Regelski, this international community of scholars was founded with two main purposes: "(a) to apply critical theory and critical thinking to the purposes and practices of music education, and (b) to affirm the central importance of musical participation in human life and, thus, the value of music in the general education of all people" (Gates 1999, 15). Aspects of its agenda, titled *Action for Change in Music Education*, were reflected in the philosophical discourse of the decade, a time of intellectual tension due to an evident "paradigm shift" within professional thinking.

Although the aesthetic philosophy was weakened in the philosophical ferment of the 1980s, its strength was evident in the degree to which its language continued to dominate professional discourse. A number of scholars in the field held firmly to aesthetic education philosophy, some of them convinced of its inherent value, others trusting in the professional security that often stems from shared convictions.

Streams of Continuity with the Past

In the 1990s three themes emerged as having strong connections with the past: the use of insights from cognitive psychology as bases for exploring the nature and meaning of musical behavior and music education; the need for increased attention to philosophy in teacher education programs; and continued emphasis on defining the relationship between music education philosophy and advocacy. Aesthetic education scholars continued to draw on cognitive psychology to explore aesthetic experience, since it was clear that exploration based on philosophical reflection alone was not adequate (Reimer and Wright 1992, xi). Efforts to articulate and strengthen the cognitive paradigm in the context of aesthetic education were also evident in *The Arts, Education, and Aesthetic Knowing* (1992), which was the first yearbook of the NSSE (National Society for the Study of Education) devoted to the arts as a field of study. In this book, "aesthetic knowing" was put forth as a "special mode of cognition" (Reimer and Smith 1992, ix). Reimer argued that "aesthetic knowing" provided a convincing rationale for arts education and a powerful set of organizing principles for achieving aesthetic learning (x). Other authors in the publication whose efforts made a significant impact on the field in the late twentieth century were the psychologists David Hargreaves, Howard Gardner, and Mihaly Csikszentmihalyi.

The focus on arts as ways of knowing continued into the 1990s, as evidenced in scholars' writings on music as knowledge, each one bringing a different set of assumptions to their explorations (e.g., Elliott 1991a; Reimer 1992; Swanwick 1994).[36] Additional themes began emerging in the philosophical literature (e.g., "music as communication" and "musical participation as constructing social reality"). Scholars addressed music as discourse, conversation, community, and interaction. The perspectives gained from these explorations advanced a more social view of music (Keil and Feld 1994; Brinner 1995; Jorgensen 1995).

The tension between utilitarian and aesthetic values of music education continued to be highlighted in publications of the 1990s. The growing association of philosophy with the study of the intrinsic values of music, and of advocacy with the extrinsic values of music education,[37] a legacy from previous decades, led to reactions from numerous scholars. In general, two arguments were advanced. First, advocacy statements needed to include both the intrinsic and extrinsic values of a musical education; and, second, the relationship between philosophy and advocacy needed to be clarified (Roehmann 1991; Bowman 1992; Phillips 1993; Jorgensen 1994). For Jorgensen, what was needed was a political philosophy of music education, "one that speaks to ideas of freedom, democracy, community, and the importance of social values of music" (1994, 28). Phillips (1993) and Roehmann (1991) recommended a philosophy that would embrace both utilitarian and aesthetic objectives, one that better served the profession in justifying music education and would unite philosophy and advocacy (Roehmann 1991, 44).

Other scholars disagreed with this thinking, believing that "the issues a philosophy must deal with are usually very different from the arguments one makes to people outside the profession to convince them to support our programs" (Reimer 1993, 10). Similarly, Bowman (1992) stated that "advocacy, although undeniably important, is tangential to philosophical inquiry" (3). In line with many scholars of earlier periods, Bowman approached philosophy as "that process devoted to the systematic examination of the grounds for belief and action" (3). Such a process "works to render the implicit explicit" (4) and "to confront and undo prejudice, to maintain respect for the ambiguity and complexity of reality" (5).

Concerns about clarifying philosophy and advocacy were interwoven with efforts to strengthen the relationship between philosophy and its role in the education and practice of music educators. Writers were critical of the lack of attention to philosophy in music teacher education programs (Jorgensen 1990; Gates 1991; Bowman 1992; Reimer 1993); the inability of music teachers to articulate connections among beliefs, ideas, and actions (Gates 1991; Roehmann 1991); and the lack of a philosophy that adequately explains, unifies, and illuminates practice (Gates 1991). Philosophy for the music teacher needed to go beyond advocacy arguments (Bowman 1992, 1; Reimer 1993, 12). And music teacher education programs needed to help preservice teachers learn to think in ways that are critical and "*habitually philosophical*" (Bowman 1992, 2; italics in the original). Such philosophical thinking would span a broad range of teaching dimensions and not limit itself to issues of musical value. For example, Jorgensen (1990) claimed that music teachers need to be able to make critical judgments and decisions and to justify their choices "on logical, moral, ethical, or aesthetic grounds" (21). Music education philosophy was thus presented as an area that would benefit immeasurably from the insights gained from other disciplines (Jorgensen 1991b, 14). By the mid-1990s an increasing number of music education scholars (including Bowman, Elliott, and Jorgensen) were looking at different aspects of music's meaning and function in life and education.[38]

Tensions of Paradigm Change

In the view of some scholars (e.g., Elliott 1991a, 1991b), it was time to put forth alternatives to "music education's official doctrine" (i.e., music education as aesthetic education). A philosophy was needed that would be broad enough to accommodate the differing worldviews that were gradually being incorporated into music educators' thinking. Shepherd (1991), addressing the politics of music in the academy and the need for change in the study of music in higher education, viewed music education as "an appropriate site from which to reinvigorate the academic study of music" (113). Bowman (1992) welcomed the philosophical ferment and the struggles that were afoot. He believed that the profession needed to be "somewhat more philosophically diverse, somewhat less monolithic from the standpoint of practice, and somewhat less enamored with ideological unanimity than has typically been the case in music education's 'aesthetic era'" (16).

The principal criticisms directed against the aesthetic philosophy of music education included its narrow focus on the "musical work" and its relative neglect of musical context; its embeddedness in the aesthetics of Western art music; its neglect of dimensions of music's significance beyond the aesthetic, such as sociological, political, and cultural meanings (Elliott 1991b; Shepherd 1991; Bowman 1992); its inability to accommodate alternative functions and values of music (Elliott 1991b; Shepherd 1991; Bowman 1992); its neglect of "the epistemological significance of music making" (Elliott 1991a, 23); and its tendencies toward male hegemony (Koza 1994; Lamb 1994). The focus on "music-as-object," a fundamental tenet of the aesthetic philosophy, was now recognized as an inappropriate basis for studying the meanings of music in other cultural settings. The "common elements" and "conceptual" notions of music curriculum development advocated by aesthetic educators were also recognized as inappropriate for teaching such music (Elliott 1989, 1990). Music educators needed a philosophy that would access the meanings of different cultural forms of music and interweave details of musical structure with equal attention to matters of musical context, musical communities (practices), a wide range of musical values, and the humanistic dimensions of music making and music listening (Elliott 1990, 1993).

As the aesthetic philosophy was challenged yet again, its proponents responded, and a lively discourse ensued in the literature.[39]

Emerging Praxial Conceptions

As music educators sought a philosophical view that would accommodate the values and paradigms of contemporary thinking in critical theory, psychology, sociology, ethnomusicology, and cultural theory (to name the major influences), some scholars began to articulate praxial conceptions,[40] the possibilities of which, according to Alperson (1991), were first introduced in two essays by the music philosophers Francis Sparshott and Nicholas Wolterstorff in *What Is Music? An Introduction to the Philosophy of Music* (1987). Alperson (1991) sketched his own praxial approach in which he underscored the importance of understanding art "in terms of the variety of meaning and values evidenced in actual practice in particular cultures" (233). In advocating this approach, he did not intend to abandon the idea of aesthetic experience, since, in his opinion, it answered to "an undeniably important kind of cultural significance" (233). However, he emphasized that the praxial approach was not limited to a consideration of the function of music in aesthetic contexts (234). In Alperson's view, adopting a praxial view for music education would demand a shift away from philosophy to anthropology, and it would require uniting the intrinsic values of music with what had been regarded as so-called nonmusical values—the moral, psychological, sociological, and political meanings involved in musical expression and transmission (237).

Like Alperson, Elliott challenged the appropriateness of the aesthetic philosophy for music education and sought to replace it with a praxial philosophy. Elliott's book *Music Matters: A New Philosophy of Music Education* (1995) represented—and still represents—the most fully developed and publicly visible articulation of a praxial philosophy of music education. This book (intended in part to serve as a new foundational text for graduate courses in the field) spoke to many major issues confronting the profession at the time of its publication. *Music Matters* also addressed and integrated aspects of contemporary cognitive psychology with multicultural and sociological concerns.

Building the foundation for his "new philosophy" upon the research and writings of Sparshott and Csikszentmihalyi, among many other scholars, Elliott set out to present a pan-cultural conception of music and music education based on the premise that each style of music is not just a collection of identifiable products or works of music. In addition, and logically prior, each style of music is a particular group of people—or a "practice," in the sense of a sociocultural community—who make and listen to "their music" in their preferred ways. Following Sparshott, Elliott observed that "[what] music is, at root, is a human activity" that involves doers (makers and listeners), particular kinds of doing (music making and listening), something done (musical works of some kind), and "the complete context in which doers do what they do" (39–40).

Elliott set aside the assumed notion of "aesthetic experience" in favor of Csikszentmihalyi's concept of "flow" (i.e., the experience one has while engaging in a personally valued activity in which one is fully absorbed and which simultaneously tends order and strengthens the self). Elliott drew particular attention to the experience of "flow" in a variety of musical behaviors, including listening, performing, improvising, composing, arranging, and conducting. Overall, he proposed that persons throughout the world who make and listen tó one or more "Musics" (each Music or musical practice having its own traditions of music making and listening) may be viewed as belonging to something even larger: MUSIC, by which Elliott means the huge, infinitely diverse, global human endeavor (43).

From these and other premises, Elliott (1995) argued for an "open concept" of music (see below). Based on this concept, and further explanations of its components (see Elliott 1995, 128–131; 198–201), Elliott asserted emphatically that music has multiple values in life and education.

> *MUSIC is the diverse human practice of overtly* [making] *and covertly constructing* [via listening] *aural-temporal patterns for the primary (but not necessarily the exclusive) purposes of enjoyment, self-growth, and self-knowledge. These values arise when musicianship is sufficient to balance or match the cognitive challenges involved in making and/or listening for aural patterns regarded significantly, but never exclusively, as audible designs.* (128; italics in the original)

Continuing the public dialogue they had begun in earlier articles (e.g., Elliott 1991b; Reimer 1991c), Reimer responded to the publication of *Music Matters* by challenging several aspects of Elliott's praxial conception. Elliott (1997), in turn, identified differences between Reimer's views and his own praxial conceptions. Since that time, the aesthetic-praxial debate has continued unabated as proponents and detractors of both philosophies have contributed their perspectives (see McCarthy 1999; Kneiter 2000).

Regelski (1996) sketched a preliminary description of his own praxial conception of music (and music education), underscoring his contention that all accounts of "good music" must address "what music is 'good for'" (25). Expanding on the work of Dissanayake (1988, 1992), Regelski centered on musical practices as important means by which aspects of a well-lived life are "made special," regarding music making as "a choice by which individuals and groups change or enhance basic human actions in predictable and satisfying ways" (26). Turning his attention to music education, Regelski used the notion of praxis to identify cultural limitations of the aesthetic philosophy, explaining that a praxial conception of music allows the philosophy of music education to extend beyond the Western art music tradition. He asserted that "to teach music properly is to teach—to model and demonstrate through action and practicum—what in *all* the world music is 'good for'" (1996, 35–36). Subsequently, Regelski (1998) explored more deeply the Aristotelian bases of praxis, articulating implications of this inquiry for the philosophy of music and the conduct of music education and demonstrating how a praxial perspective supports conceptions of music as "basic" to general education.[41]

Throughout the 1990s scholars took additional innovative approaches to addressing the profession's philosophical questions—most of them arguably less absolutist than those of the past. In her book *In Search of Music Education*, Jorgensen (1997) set out to "take a dialectical and dialogical view of music education, recognize tensions in need of resolution, and hope that through dialogue these tensions can be worked through and either reconciled or tolerated" (xiii). Instead of entering the aesthetic-praxial debate, Jorgensen focused her attention first on education and the various ways in which it is conceived (e.g., as schooling, training, education, socialization, and enculturation). She then addressed the phenomenon of music, providing a theoretical account of its validity in various cultural contexts or social spheres, also briefly discussing its role in religion, politics, and commerce. Jorgensen concluded her book by identifying a series of dilemmas that the profession faced, helpfully presenting each as a dialectic.

The profession's accounting for the sociological dimensions of music and music education expanded greatly as the twentieth century drew to a close. This expansion was reflected in the publication of *The Social Psychology of Music* (Hargreaves and North 1997) and of the papers of a sociologically oriented group of scholars assembled in the mid-1990s at the University of Oklahoma (Rideout 1997; Rideout and Paul 2000). Shepherd and Wicke (1997) took an innovative, sociologically informed and multidisciplinary approach to longstanding questions of musical affect and meaning in their *Music and Cultural Theory*. Their efforts also hold promise for a reconceptualization of the music teaching-learning enterprise. In his book *Musicking: The Meanings of Performing and Listening*, Small (1998) illuminated the social relativity of musical meaning by analyzing the multidimensional nature of a traditional symphony orchestra concert. The curricular implications of all these efforts and their attendant perspectives have yet to be addressed adequately.

Finally, in this book Bowman addresses what he holds to be the limits and grounds of musical praxialism. He compares and contrasts the praxial orientations of Alperson, Sparshott, and Elliott, elucidating the collective and respective merits of their conceptions and raising issues—most of which transcend the aesthetic-praxial debate—that have not yet been addressed by scholars presently exploring praxial approaches to music and music education. Perhaps most important, Bowman draws attention to matters inherent to music and music education that received relatively scant attention in the second half of the twentieth century. Among these are issues of moral growth, social transformation, and politics, each of which suggests a potentially consequential and vivifying direction for the profession.

Notes

1. Other perspectives of lesser consequence for the practice of music education are not addressed in this chapter.

2. Aesthetics is the branch of philosophy that deals with theories of beauty and the fine arts.

3. We shall use the terms "the aesthetic philosophy" and "aesthetic education" interchangeably with "music education as aesthetic education."

4. McMurray (1958) asserted that music should "become known for its sounds and its felt qualities," thus lending support to the notion of music education as aesthetic education (61). His aesthetic orientation was also obvious in certain of his aims for music education: "to help further awareness of patterns of sound as an aesthetic component in the world of experience" and "increase each person's capacity to control the availability of aesthetic richness through music" (41).

5. Perhaps Schwadron's background in Hebrew music and his interest in anthropology

provided him with a unique, "outsider's" perspective on the concerns of music education. For an analysis of Schwadron's background and intellectual dispositions, see Palmer (1998b).

6. Schwadron (1965) recommended that the profession reconsider its philosophical direction, encouraging a renewed rapport with the social sciences and with a view of the school as an agency for social change (131).

7. Schwadron (1966) wrote: "If we follow the objectivist or isolationist we tend to make art dehumanized and irresponsible; if we follow the subjectivist or contextualist we tend to lose the purity and autonomy of art" (190).

8. Schwadron (1970a) was not alone in his efforts to connect religion and aesthetic experience. Reimer (1962) also acknowledged the complexity of this "relatively unexplored region" and concluded that "music education is, when fulfilling its function, religious education" (99). Reimer continued to explore this relationship in his doctoral dissertation, but he did not carry it forward to his book, *A Philosophy of Music Education* (1970).

9. See Gary (1967).

10. In fact, McMurray (1958) applauded the efforts of music educators in the *Basic Concepts* project for building relationships with "a wider domain of theory and doctrine" (36).

11. Furthermore, Leonhard argued, we cannot ask educational philosophers to create a philosophy since they do not have sufficient understanding of music and music education. Recently, Bowman (1999–2000) has been critical of the profession's lack of rootedness in educational philosophy. It seems probable that the directions taken by music educators in the decades of the 1950s and 1960s are partly responsible for this state of affairs.

12. Not all scholars wanted to abandon educational philosophy of the progressive era. Miller (1966) studied the period in depth and advocated the ideals of liberal progressivism, which acknowledged the contributions of sociology, cultural anthropology, and philosophy "in light of current political, economic, and social conditions in the culture" (16).

13. One scholar who was in a position to influence music educators' thinking—Foster McMurray—adapted pragmatic concepts to fit the aesthetic philosophy. Further evidence of McMurray's bias toward aesthetics appears in the addition to his article ("Variations on a pragmatic theme") in the 1958 edition of *Basic Concepts*. His commitment to aesthetic education is evident from his statement that the purpose of music education ought to be "to teach the values that accrue to human life from experiences with serious music" (59). Music teachers, he argued, must be committed to "teaching about music, and about music that possesses the strongest aesthetic content" (60).

14. Mueller (1958) approached aesthetics as "the discipline, or system of thought, which is concerned with music (or any other art) in its interaction with social life" (92). As a sociologist, he viewed music as a social force; he believed it functioned in multiple ways in the lives of individuals and groups, and not as "a monistic entity" (114).

15. Reimer's phrase (1972).

16. Most papers in this collection were presented at a mini-conference titled "Music Education as Aesthetic Education" at the national MENC convention in Chicago in 1970. Authors in this publication included Bennett Reimer, Gerard Kneiter, Maxine Greene, Ralph Smith, and Charles Gary. It is curious that Abraham Schwadron, one of the most prolific writers on aesthetics in the 1960s, did not contribute to this collection of essays.

17. The aesthetic education philosophy anchors *Silver Burdett Music*, by Reimer, Crook, and Walker (1974): "The Silver Burdett Music program is aesthetic education in action. Its

major goal is to increase the sensitivity of all students to the power of music as an art—to develop their abilities to perceive the art of music keenly and respond to it deeply. Nonartistic values—the social, psychological, physical, and other benefits of involvement in music—are recognized and included, but they are treated as adjuncts to the main purpose."

18. In a similar vein, when interviewed in 1979 about changes he would make in his philosophy, Reimer replied: "If I were to do a philosophy now, it would be applied to all the arts and their potential for education.... [W]e need to be caught up in a much more powerful movement—arts education" (Aquino 1979, 42).

19. Philosophy and philosophical research in the earlier issues were categorized under "Trends, problems, issues, and philosophies in music education." Gordon (1972) included a new section, titled "Aesthetics," which reflected increased attention to research focused on topics in this area.

20. Standifer (1970) investigated the effects on aesthetic sensitivity of developing perception of musical expressiveness. This was an experimental study in junior and senior high schools conducted in cooperation with a research project under the direction of Bennett Reimer and supported by the Department of Health, Education and Welfare. The study suggested that an aesthetically consistent view of music "can be successfully translated into a course of study that produces significant measurable results in the direction desired" (125). Lewy (1971) explored the applicability of an affective taxonomy to music education. The taxonomy made it easier to state affective educational objectives with a high degree of specificity. Bullock (1973), in "A Review of Measures of Musico-Aesthetic Attitude," reviewed studies that addressed mood, interest, preference, judgment, taste, opinion, evaluation and valuation of music. In a special issue of the *Bulletin of the Council for Research in Music Education* devoted to the work of CEMREL, Madeja (1975) evaluated the CEMREL aesthetic education program.

21. Reimer went on to review the rise of the aesthetic paradigm, the need it served, and the positive effects of the aesthetic education movement: "the philosophy I articulated represented what had been growing for at least 20 years, had become by 1970 a major if not the major view of that time, and is now, in 1977, so pervasive in the thinking of our profession as to almost seem like it has always been our stance. We have been moving toward consensus, then, for some time, and we have now achieved a remarkable level of consensus.... There is little fundamental questioning of the general point of view we have come to share.... We have desperately needed the sense of unity as a profession that shared belief provides, and second ... there is still plenty of room for differences within the generality of agreement" (11–12).

22. Emphasis on the nonmusical outcomes was evident in publications of the decade. See Wolff (1978) and Haushumaker (1980).

23. Keith Swanwick's book *A Basis for Music Education* (1979), published in the United Kingdom, was clearly influenced by the aesthetic paradigm: "we have failed to notice and publicize the central core of music education, which is that music education is aesthetic education" (6).

24. Publication of Swanwick's book reflected the influence of aesthetic education in England, although it is important to note that a special edition of textbooks grounded in aesthetic education philosophy and published by Silver Burdett had been available in England for several years.

25. According to the absolute expressionist view (see Meyer 1956, 3), the meaning of a given musical work is primarily internal to that work; the expressive emotional meanings evoked by the music "exist without reference to the extramusical world of concepts, actions, and human emotional states."

26. The notion of expanding the concept of "the aesthetic" to embrace the perspectives of

disparate cultural groups (as involving different aesthetics) had been addressed by scholars in philosophy and ethnomusicology earlier in the decade. See Becker (1983) and Sparshott (1983).

27. Mark (1982) wrote: "Music educators must understand, and must be able to make others understand, that one of the fundamental components of an educational system that provides not just training but education as well as an aesthetically based music education program. Such a program helps each student develop the aesthetic sensitivity to perceive profound meaning in music, to understand and appreciate his or her own heritage and those of other cultures through music, and to lead a richer life through a choice of music that is made on the basis of educated taste. . . . In the simplest of terms, the satisfaction and pleasures of music enjoyed by a musically educated population contribute to a higher quality of life. That is the utilitarian message, which needs to be integrated with an aesthetically based philosophy when it is communicated to the society from which we expect economic and moral support" (129).

28. Reimer (1989a) wrote: "Elliott's article seems to suggest that the new ideas render aesthetic education suspect, so that we may now need a different music education philosophy than one that is based on the principles of aesthetic education. Of course, such a view would miss the absolutely essential point of aesthetic education: that an improved version of how music works (in this case how it produces affect) enables aesthetic education in music to improve concurrently. In fact, the health, growth, and vitality of aesthetic education depend on the refinements in aesthetic theorizing that are inevitable as scholarship develops. Just as aesthetic education cannot be equated with this or that methodology, it cannot be equated with this or that person's musical theory at this or that stage of its development" (26).

29. Incidentally, Reimer released an updated second edition of his *Philosophy of Music Education* the same year that these articles were published (1989). Among other minor changes, the second edition featured a section on advocacy for music education programs, perhaps reflecting his recognition of the necessity for a cohesive professional philosophy and professional unity in light of the economic strain on the public schools.

30. Gardner identified specific competencies that manifest these criteria, including linguistic, musical, logical-mathematical, spatial, bodily kinesthetic, and intrapersonal and interpersonal intelligences.

31. Paul Lehman, former president of the MENC, echoed and extended this argument as a central part of his own rationale for the importance of music in the schools: "the evidence suggests that every human being has musical ability. . . . Unfortunately, the musical ability of many people remains largely undeveloped throughout their lives. Schools should provide all citizens with the opportunity to test the limits of their potential in as many domains of human endeavor as possible. Otherwise, they will never know in what fields they could have achieved, and they will never know how far they could have gone (1987, 10).

32. See, for example, Fowler (1988, 147) and Eisner (1987, 37–41). One provocative effort (albeit highly speculative) stimulated by Gardner's work was an article on the evolution of musical behavior by Donald Hodges (1989). Hodges asked, "If music does not confer any survival benefits, why would it be provided for in our neurophysiological structures?" and "Why would it have developed to the point where it is a universal trait of our species if it were irrelevant to our existence?" Hodges observed the fundamental nature of rhythm as a life process, noting that people involved in social interactions and the presence of rhythmic entertainment in many aspects of life share rhythmic movement. He observed that there are several ways in which musical involvement may have conferred benefits for the evolution of humankind, including the facilitation of mother-infant bonding, the support of language acquisition, the de-

velopment of a unique mode of knowing, and the fostering of social organization. Regrettably, Hodges's valuable speculations had no significant influence on music education philosophy.

33. Among the most important contributions to the study of music cognition during the 1980s were those of Serafine (1988) and Sloboda (1985, 1988). The cognitive psychology of music is founded on the premise that people who respond to music do so because they form an abstract or symbolic internal representation of the music. According to Sloboda (1985), "The nature of this internal representation, and the things it allows a person to do with music, is the central subject matter of the cognitive psychology of music" (3). Inquiry into the cognitive processes by which people learn and develop musical skills and understandings has revealed much about the workings of the human mind. Notably, however, the science has so far been oriented toward understanding cognition underlying Western music, and its effectiveness at illuminating cognition involving music from different cultural traditions has yet to be realized. However, it represents an important field of inquiry.

34. See, for example, Standifer (1980).

35. See, for example, Anderson and Campbell (1989).

36. Elliott (1991a) approached music as a form of knowledge and as a source of self-knowledge. He introduced the concept of procedural knowledge (26–29) and musical performance as nonverbal "cognition-in-action" (29). Reimer (1992), in exploring "aesthetic cognition," looked at four ways of knowing—knowing of and within, knowing how, knowing about or that, and knowing why. See also Swanwick (1994).

37. Jorgensen (1994) examined the statement from the MENC National Commission on Music Education report *Growing Up Complete*. She found that evidence presented there established compelling extrinsic values for music education, with emphasis on its psychological benefits (25).

38. Although descriptions of philosophical foundations of music education in mainstream textbooks (e.g., Stubley 1992; Abeles, Hoffer, and Klotman 1984/1994) continued to focus on traditional schools of philosophical thought and aesthetic positions, there are indications in these writings that the canon was expanding at the same time, with increased attention devoted to perspectives from nontraditional areas such as pragmatism and constructivism.

39. See, for example, the *Quarterly Journal of Music Teaching and Learning* 2 (3), which focused on debating the issues surrounding philosophy in music education."

40. As Elliott (1995) says, *praxis* is derived from the Greek word *prassein*, meaning "to do." Aristotle drew a distinction in his writings between *theoria* (which he held to involve abstract, intellectual knowledge), *techne* (which he held to involve the craft or technique of making or producing something), and *praxis* (which he used to refer to practical knowledge and activity, such as that usually involved in the wider realm of human ethical and political activities or practices).

41. Karen Hanson (1999) raised questions about and challenges to Regelski's account of praxial philosophy and its application to music and music education. Regelski (2000) countered and denied Hanson's remonstrations.

References

Abeles, H. F., C. R. Hoffer, and R. H. Klotman. 1984/1994. *Foundations of music education.* New York: Schirmer Books.

Alperson, P., ed. 1987. *What is music? An introduction to the philosophy of music.* New York: Haven.

———. 1991. What should one expect from a philosophy of music education? *Journal of Aesthetic Education* 25:215–242.

Anderson, W. M., and P. S. Campbell. 1989. *Multicultural perspectives on music education.* Reston, VA: Music Educators National Conference.

Aquino, J. 1979. Reimer revisited. *Music Educators Journal* 66 (11):40–43, 84–85.

Becker, J. 1983. "Aesthetics" in late twentieth-century scholarship. *World of Music* 25 (3):65–77.

Biggs, G. B., Jr. 1971. A suggested taxonomy of music for music educators. *Journal of Research in Music Education* 19:168–182.

Blacking, J. 1973. *How musical is man?* Seattle: University of Washington Press.

Bloom, B., and D. R. Krathwohl. 1956. *Taxonomy of educational objectives, Handbook I: Cognitive domain.* New York: David McKay.

Bowman, W. 1992. Philosophy, criticism, and music education: Some tentative steps down a less-traveled road. *Bulletin of the Council for Research in Music Education* 114:1–19.

———. 1998. Universals, relativism, and music education. *Bulletin of the Council for Research in Music Education* 135:1–20.

———. 1999–2000. What should the music education profession expect of philosophy? *Arts and Learning Journal* 16:54–71.

———. 2005. The limits and grounds of musical praxialism. In D. J. Elliott, ed., *Praxial music education: Reflections and dialogues.* New York: Oxford University Press.

Brinner, B. 1995. *Knowing music, making music.* Chicago: University of Chicago Press.

Broudy, H. S. 1957. Does music education need a philosophy? *Music Educators Journal* 44 (11):28–30.

———. 1969. A philosophy of the arts in an emerging society. *Music Educators Journal* 56 (9):43ff.

———. 1978. How basic is aesthetic education, or is "RT" the fourth R? *Bulletin of the Council for Research in Music Education* 57:1–10.

Bruner, J. S. 1963. *The process of education.* Cambridge: Harvard University Press.

Bullock, W. J. 1973. A review of measures of musico-aesthetic attitude. *Journal of Research in Music Education* 21:331–344.

Choate, R., ed. 1968. *Documentary report of the Tanglewood symposium.* Washington, DC: Music Educators National Conference.

Coates, P. 1983. Alternatives to the aesthetic rationale for music education. *Music Educators Journal* 69 (3):31–32.

Colwell, R. J. 1986. Music and aesthetic education: A collegial relationship. *Journal of Aesthetic Education* 20:31–38.

———, ed. 1991. *Basic concepts in music education, II.* Niwot: University Press of Colorado.

Dissanayake, E. 1988. *What is art for?* Seattle: University of Washington Press.

———. 1992. *Homo aestheticus: Where art comes from and why.* New York: Free Press.

Editorial. 1977. The role of music in the total development of the child. *Music Educators Journal* 63 (4):59.

Eisner, E. 1985. Aesthetic modes of knowing. In E. Eisner, ed., *Learning and teaching the ways of knowing.* Eighty-fourth yearbook of the National Society for the Study of Education, part 2. Chicago, IL: University of Chicago Press.

———. 1987. Educating the whole person: Arts in the curriculum. *Music Educators Journal* 73 (2):37–41.

Elliott, C. A. 1983. Behind the budget crisis, a crisis of philosophy. *Music Educators Journal* 70 (10):36–37.

Elliott, D. J. 1986. Jazz education as aesthetic education. *Journal of Aesthetic Education* 20:41–53.

———. 1987. Structure and feeling in jazz: Rethinking philosophical foundations. *Bulletin of the Council for Research in Music Education* 95:13–38.

———. 1989. Key concepts in multicultural music education. *International Journal of Music Education* 13:11–18.

———. 1990. Music as culture: Toward a multicultural concept of arts education. *Journal of Aesthetic Education* 24:147–166.

———. 1991a. Music as knowledge. *Journal of Aesthetic Education* 25:21–40.

———. 1991b. Music education as aesthetic education: A critical inquiry. *Quarterly Journal of Music Teaching and Learning* 2:48–66.

———. 1993. On the values of music and music education. *Philosophy of Music Education Review* 1:81–93.

———. 1995. *Music matters: A new philosophy of music education.* New York: Oxford University Press.

———. 1997. Continuing matters: Myths, realities, and rejoinders. *Bulletin of the Council for Research in Music Education* 132:1–37.

Epperson, G. P. 1975. Aesthetics: What difference does it make? *Music Educators Journal* 61 (4):50–53.

Fowler, C. B. 1988. Toward a democratic art: A reconstructionist view of music education. In J. T. Gates, ed., *Music education in the United States: Contemporary issues,* 130–155. Tuscaloosa: University of Alabama Press.

Franklin, E., and A. D. Franklin. 1978. The brain research bandwagon: Proceed with caution. *Music Educators Journal* 65 (11):38–43.

Gardner, H. 1983. *Frames of mind: The theory of multiple intelligences.* New York: Basic Books.

Gary, C. 1967. The study of music in the elementary school: A conceptual approach. Washington, DC: Music Educators National Conference.

———. 1975. Why music education? *National Association of Secondary School Principals Bulletin* 59:3–4.

Gates, J. T. 1991. Solving music education's rationale problem: Music education in broad perspective. *Quarterly Journal of Music Teaching and Learning* 2:30–39.

———. 1999. Action for change in music education: The May Day group agenda. In M. McCarthy, ed., *Music education as praxis: Reflecting on music-making as human action,* 14–25. College Park: University of Maryland Press.

Gonzo, C. 1971. Aesthetic experience: A coming of age in music education. *Music Educators Journal* 58 (12):34–37.

Goodman, N. 1972. Art and understanding: The need for a less simple-minded approach. *Music Educators Journal* 58 (2):43 ff.

Gordon, R. D. 1964. Doctoral dissertations in music and music education, 1957–1963. *Journal of Research in Music Education* 12.

———. 1968. Doctoral dissertations in music and music education, 1963–1967. *Journal of Research in Music Education* 16.

———. 1972. Doctoral dissertations in music and music education, 1968–1971. *Journal of Research in Music Education* 20.

Green, L. 1997. *Music, gender, education.* Cambridge, UK: Cambridge University Press.

Hanson, K. 1999. In dialogue: A response to Thomas Regelski's "The Aristotelian bases of praxis for music and music education as praxis." *Philosophy of Music Education Review* 7:118–120.

Hargreaves, D. J., and A. C. North. 1997. *The social psychology of music.* Oxford: Oxford University Press.

Haushumaker, J. 1980. The effects of arts education on intellectual and social development: A review of selected research. *Bulletin of the Council for Research in Music Education* 61:10–28.

Henry, N. B. 1958. *Basic concepts in music education. Fifty-seventh yearbook of the National Society for the Study of Education, part I.* Chicago: University of Chicago Press.

Hodges, D. A. 1989. Why are we musical? Speculations on the evolutionary plausibility of musical behavior. *Bulletin of the Council for Research in Music Education* 99:7–22.

Howard, V. A. 1972. Symbolism, art, and education. *Bulletin of the Council for Research in Music Education* 30:1–10.

Jorgensen, E. R. 1990. Philosophy and the music teacher: Challenging the way we think. *Music Educators Journal* 76 (1):17–23.

———. 1991a. Introduction (guest editorial). *Journal of Aesthetic Education* 25:1–4.

———. 1991b. Music education in broad perspective. *Quarterly Journal of Music Teaching and Learning* 2 (3):14–21.

———. 1993. *Philosopher, teacher, musician: Perspectives on music education.* Urbana and Chicago: University of Illinois Press.

———. 1994. Justifying music instruction in American public schools: An historical perspective. *Bulletin of the Council for Research in Music Education, 120,* 17–31.

———. 1995. Music education as community. *Journal of Aesthetic Education, 29,* 71–84.

———. 1997. *In search of music education.* Urbana: University of Illinois Press.

Kaplan, M. 1966. *Foundations and frontiers of music education.* New York: Holt, Rinehart and Winston.

Keil, C., and S. Feld. 1994. *Music grooves.* Chicago: University of Chicago Press.

Kneiter, G. L. 1983. Aesthetics for arts' sake. *Music Educators Journal* 69 (3):33–35, 61–64.

———. 2000. Elliott's "new" conservatory approach: A review essay. *Philosophy of Music Education Review* 8:40–51.

Koza, J. E. 1994. Aesthetic music education revisited: Discourses of exclusion and oppression. *Philosophy of Music Education Review* 2:75–98.

Krathwohl, D. R., B. S. Bloom, and B. B. Masia. 1964. *Taxonomy of educational objectives, Handbook 2: Affective domain.* New York: David McKay.

Lamb, R. 1994. Feminism as critique in philosophy of music education. *Philosophy of Music Education Review* 2:59–74.

Langer, S. 1953. *Feeling and form.* New York: Charles Scribner's Sons.

———. 1957. *Philosophy in a new key.* Cambridge: Harvard University Press.

Lasch, C. 1984. The degradation of work and the apotheosis of art. In D. J. Shetler, ed., *In memoriam Howard Hanson: The future of musical education in America—Proceedings of the July 1983 conference,* 11–19. Rochester, NY: Eastman School of Music Press.

Lehman, P. 1987. *Music in today's schools: Rationale and commentary.* Reston, VA: Music Educators National Conference.

Lemmon, D. C. 1977. Strategy in Bennett Reimer's "A philosophy of music education." *Bulletin of the Council for Research in Music Education* 51:1–9.

Leonhard, C. 1953. Music education—Aesthetic education. *Education,* 74 (9): 23–26.

————. 1955. Research: Philosophy and esthetics. *Journal of Research in Music Education* 3:23–26.

————. 1965. The philosophy of music education—Present and future. *Comprehensive musicianship: The foundations for college education in music.* Report of the Seminar sponsored by the CMP at Northwestern University, 42–49. Washington, DC: CMP and MENC.

————. 1966. The next ten years in music education. *Bulletin of the Council for Research in Music Education* 7:13–23.

————. 1985. *A realistic rationale for teaching music.* Reston, VA: Music Educators National Conference.

Leonhard, C., and R. W. House. 1959. *Foundations and principles of music education.* New York: McGraw-Hill.

Lewy, A. 1971. Affective outcomes of musical education. *Journal of Research in Music Education* 19:361–365.

Madeja, S. S. 1975. The aesthetics of education: The CEMREL aesthetic education program. *Bulletin of the Council for Research in Music Education* 43:1–18.

Mark, M. L. 1982. The evolution of music education philosophy from utilitarian to aesthetic. *Journal of Research in Music Education* 30:16–21.

————. 1988. Aesthetics and utility reconciled: The importance to society of education in music. In J. T. Gates, ed., *Music education in the United States: Contemporary issues,* 111–129. Tuscaloosa: University of Alabama Press.

————. 1996. *Contemporary music education,* 3d ed. New York: Schirmer Books.

McAllester, D. P. 1984. The Wesleyan Symposium. In *Becoming human through music: The Wesleyan symposium on the perspectives of social anthropology in the teaching and learning of music.* Reston, VA: Music Educators National Conference.

McCarthy, M., ed. 1999. *Music education as praxis: Reflecting on music-making as human action.* The 1997 Charles Fowler Colloquium on Innovation in Arts Education. State-of-the-Arts Series, Number 3. College Park: University of Maryland Press.

McMurray, F. 1956. A pragmatic approach to certain aspects of music education. *Journal of Research in Music Education* 4:103–112.

————. 1958. Pragmatism in music education. In N. B. Henry, ed., *Basic concepts in music education,* 30–61. Chicago, IL: National Society for the Study of Education.

Merriam, A. P. 1964. *The anthropology of music.* Chicago, IL: Northwestern University Press.

Miller, T. W. 1966. The influence of progressivism on music education, 1917–1947. *Journal of Research in Music Education* 14:3–16.

Mueller, J. H. 1958. Music and education: A sociological approach. In N. B. Henry, ed., *Basic concepts in music education,* 88–122. Chicago, IL: National Society for the Study of Education.

Palmer, A. J. 1992. Leonard B. Meyer and a cross-cultural aesthetics. *Journal of Aesthetic Education* 26:67–73.

————. 1998a. Multicultural music education: Antipodes and complementarities. *Philosophy of Music Education Review* 5:92–100.

————. 1998b. The philosophical legacy of Abraham A. Schwadron. *Philosophy of Music Education Review* 6:3–11.

Phillips, K. 1983. Utilitarian vs. aesthetic. *Music Educators Journal* 69 (3):29–30.

————. 1993. A stronger rationale for music education. *Music Educators Journal* 80 (9): 17–19, 55.

Reese, S. 1977. Forms of feeling: The aesthetic theory of Susanne K. Langer. *Music Educators Journal* 63 (4):45–49.

Regelski, T. A. 1996. Prolegomenon to a praxial philosophy of music and music education. *Finnish Journal of Music Education* 1 (1):23–39.

———. 1998. The Aristotelian bases of praxis for music and music education as praxis. *Philosophy of Music Education Review* 6:22–59.

———. 2000. In dialogue: Aristotle, praxis, and music revisited—A reply to Karen Hanson. *Philosophy of Music Education Review* 8:46–51.

Reimer, B. 1962. Leonard Meyer's theory of value and greatness in music. *Journal of Research in Music Education* 10:87–99.

———. 1970/1989. *A philosophy of music education*. Englewood Cliffs, NJ: Prentice-Hall.

———. 1972. Putting aesthetic education to work. *Music Educators Journal* 59 (9):28–33.

———. 1976. Patterns for the future: Where we've been tells a lot about where we're going. *Music Educators Journal* 63 (12):22–29.

———. 1977. Philosophical monism in music education: Some thoughts in response to Douglas Lemmon's paper. *Bulletin of the Council for Research in Music Education* 51:10–13.

———. 1978. Education for aesthetic awareness: The Cleveland area project. *Music Educators Journal* 64 (2):66–69.

———. 1989a. Music education and aesthetic education: Past and present. *Music Educators Journal* 75 (2):22–28.

———. 1989b. Music education as aesthetic education: Toward the future. *Music Educators Journal* 75 (3):26–32.

———. 1991a. Essential and nonessential characteristics of aesthetic education. *Journal of Aesthetic Education* 25:193–214.

———. 1991b. Reimer responds to Bowman. *Quarterly Journal of Music Teaching and Learning* 2:88–93.

———. 1991c. Reimer responds to Elliott. *Quarterly Journal of Music Teaching and Learning* 2:67–75.

———. 1992. What knowledge is of most worth in the arts? In *The arts, education, and aesthetic knowing*. Ninety-First Yearbook of the National Society for the Study of Education, part 2, 20–50. Chicago, IL: National Society for the Study of Education.

———. 1993. Variation on a theme. *Music Educators Journal* 80 (11):10–15.

———. 1996. David Elliott's "new" philosophy of music education: Music for performers only. *Bulletin of the Council for Research in Music Education* 128:59–89.

Reimer, B., E. Crook, and D. S. Walker. 1974. *Silver burdett music*. Morristown, NJ: Silver Burdett Co.

Reimer, B., and R. A. Smith, eds. 1992. Editors' preface. In *The arts, education, and aesthetic knowing*. Ninety-First Yearbook of the National Society for the Study of Education, part 2. Chicago, IL: National Society for the Study of Education.

Reimer, B., and J. E. Wright, eds. 1992. Introduction. *On the nature of musical experience*, vii–xix. Evanston, IL: Center for the Study of Education and the Musical Experience, Northwestern University.

Rideout, R. 1987. Old wine in new bottles: More thoughts on Reimer. *Bulletin of the Council for Research in Music Education* 92:47–56.

———, ed. 1997. *On the sociology of music education*. Oklahoma City: University of Oklahoma Press.

Rideout, R., and S. J. Paul, eds. 2000. *On the sociology of music education II*. Amherst: University of Massachusetts Press.

Roehmann, F. L. 1991. On philosophies of music education: Selected issues revisited. *Quarterly Journal of Music Teaching and Learning* 2:40–47.

Schwadron, A. A. 1965. On relativism and music education. *Journal of Research in Music Education* 13:131–135.

———. 1966. Aesthetic values and music education. In *Perspectives in music education: Source book 3*, 185–194. Washington, DC: Music Educators National Conference.

———. 1967. *Aesthetics: Dimensions for music education*. Washington, DC: Music Educators National Conference.

———. 1970a. On religion, music, and education. *Journal of Research in Music Education* 18:157–166.

———. 1970b. Philosophy in music education: Pure or applied research? *Bulletin of the Council for Research in Music Education* 19:22–29.

———. 1973a. Are we ready for aesthetic education? *Music Educators Journal* 60:36–39, 87–89.

———. 1973b. Comparative music aesthetics: Toward a universality of musicality. *Music and Man* 1:17–31.

———. 1973c. Philosophy in music education: State of the research. *Bulletin of the Council for Research in Music Education* 34:41–53.

———. 1975. Research directions in comparative music aesthetics and music education. *Journal of Aesthetic Education* 9 (1):99–109.

———. 1988. Of conceptions, misconceptions, and aesthetic commitment. In J. T. Gates, ed., *Music education in the United States: Contemporary issues*, 85–110. Tuscaloosa: University of Alabama Press.

Seeger, C. 1947. Music education and musicology. In H. N. Morgan, ed., *Music education source book*, 195–198. Chicago, IL: Music Educators National Conference.

Serafine, M. L. 1988. *Music as cognition: The development of thought in sound*. New York: Columbia University Press.

Shepherd, J. A. 1987. Music and male hegemony. In R. Leppert and S. McClary, eds. *Music and society: The politics of composition, performance, and reception*, 151–172. Cambridge, UK: Cambridge University Press.

———. 1991. Music and the last intellectuals. *Journal of Aesthetic Education* 25:95–114.

Shepherd, J. A., et al. 1977. *Whose music? A sociology of musical languages*. London: Transaction Books.

Shepherd, J. A., and P. Wicke. 1997. *Music and cultural theory*. Cambridge, UK: Polity Press.

Sloboda, J. A. 1985. *The musical mind: The cognitive psychology of music*. Oxford, UK: Clarendon.

———. ed. 1988. *Generative processes in music: The psychology of performance, improvisation, and composition*. Oxford, UK: Clarendon.

Small, C. 1977. *Music, society, education*. London, UK: John Calder.

———. 1997. Musicking: A ritual in social space. In R. Rideout, ed., *On the Sociology of Music Education*, 1–12. Oklahoma City: University of Oklahoma Press.

———. 1998. *Musicking: The meanings of performing and listening*. Hanover, NH: Wesleyan University Press.

Sparshott, F. 1983. Prospects for aesthetics. *World of Music* 25 (3):3–14.

———. 1987. Aesthetics of music: Limits and grounds. In P. Alperson, ed., *What is music? An introduction to the philosophy of music*, 33–98. New York: Haven.

Spychiger, M. B. 1997. Aesthetic and praxial philosophies of music education compared: A semiotic consideration. *Philosophy of Music Education Review* 5:33–41.

Standifer, J. A. 1970. Effects on aesthetic sensitivity of developing perception of musical expressiveness. *Journal of Research in Music Education* 18:112–125.

———. 1980. *From Jumpstreet: A story of black music*. Ann Arbor: University of Michigan School of Education's Program for Educational Opportunity.

Stubley, E. V. 1992. Philosophical foundations. In R. Colwell, ed., *Handbook of research on music teaching and learning*, 3–20. New York: Schirmer Books.

Suber, C., and B. J. Stearns. 1972. Music alert: The Chicago story. *Music Educators Journal* 59 (12):33–48.

Sudano, G. R., and J. Sharpham. 1981. Back to basics: Justifying the arts. *Music Educators Journal* 68 (11):48–50.

Swanwick, K. 1979. *A basis for music education*. Windsor, Berkshire: NFER.

———. 1988. *Music, mind, and education*. London, UK: Routledge.

———. 1994. *Musical knowledge: Intuition, analysis and music education*. London: Routledge.

Tait, M. 1973. The facts of art are life. *Music Educators Journal* 59 (3):33–37.

Thompson, K. P. 1977. How the arts function as basic education. *Music Educators Journal* 63 (4):41–43.

Toward an aesthetic education. 1971. Washington, DC: Music Educators National Conference and Central Midwestern Regional Educational Laboratory.

Wolff, K. 1978. The nonmusical outcomes of music education: A review of the literature. *Bulletin of the Council for Research in Music Education* 55:1–27.

3

The Limits and Grounds
of Musical Praxialism

WAYNE D. BOWMAN

We always speak only of what we see; we don't talk about what we haven't
seen . . . What I know, I say, and nothing beyond that!

> —Russian peasant's response to Alexander Luria's persistent efforts
> to induce completion of a logical inference about matters
> not experienced firsthand; quoted in Suzanne de Castell,
> "Textuality and the Designs of Theory" (1995)

Properly speaking global thinking is not possible. Those who have thought
globally have done so by means of simplification too extreme and oppres-
sive to merit the name of thought.

> —Wendell Berry, "Out of Your Car, Off Your Horse" (1991)

Praxial orientations are relatively recent entrants to philosophical discourse in music
education, but the term "praxis" from which they take their direction can be followed
back to ancient Greek times. In Aristotelian use, praxis designated "right action,"
human activity that is goal directed and carried out with close attention to norms and
standards. Just what that means is considerably clarified by comparing praxis with
two related but distinct Greek terms, *techne* and *theoria*. The classical Greek account
of knowledge assumed a tripartite constellation: the theoretical, the practical, and the
productive.[1] Theoretical knowledge (*theoria*) was contemplative knowledge of things
unchanging and eternal, knowledge for its own sake. Productive knowledge (*techne*,
or *poiesis*), on the other hand, was theory free: a knowledge manifest in workmanlike
skill at making useful or beautiful things, and in an ability to see concrete tasks
through to successful completion. Practical knowledge (praxis) was concerned with

prudent understanding of variable situations and was situated in the sphere of human action. Accordingly, practical knowledge was centrally concerned with the moral-political idea of virtuous conduct. Since the purely contemplative life devoted to *theoria* was scarcely attainable, the cultivation of virtuous character fell primarily to this realm of practical knowledge. Perhaps we might say that the praxial realm shared with *techne* an interest in execution of tasks (in "doing") and shared with *theoria* an emphasis upon what we might characterize as mindfulness.

And yet "theoretical," "practical," and "productive" mark important distinctions. Praxis implies a more informed and deliberative doing than *techne*, and a more useful or practical kind of knowing than *theoria*. In modern usage, the word "technique" often connotes skillful yet somewhat less mindful doing than "practice." To characterize actions as "technical" is often to suggest that despite their highly skilled nature, there is something of a "mechanistic" or "artificial" aspect to their execution. On the other hand, the term "theory" and its cognates often suggest knowledge whose value is not immediately practical, or whose value is more predominantly contemplative or abstract than immediately practice related.

Hence, one might situate "practice" midway between the primarily executive sense of technique and the predominantly cerebral or contemplative sense of theory. Practical knowledge is mindful doing, action guided by attention to variable procedures, traditions, and standards. To say something is practical is to say it is somehow implicated in a consciously chosen course of action rather than being predominantly speculative or reflective; that it is concerned at once with ends and means (with "right action"), not with activity or technical execution in themselves. Practices are customary, socially embedded modes of action. To practice is to do something deliberately and attentively, attending simultaneously to one's own doing and to exemplary manifestations of that doing in others, with the intent of developing or enhancing proficiency.

Thus, we will expect praxial philosophical commitments to dispose interests in the skilled, deliberative doings of which human practices consist with "getting things right." We might also anticipate a degree of impatience or antagonism toward the two poles between which I have suggested praxis is situated: technical executive skill and theoretical abstraction. Praxial interests manifest themselves in undertakings that are intelligent but not idealistic, existing in the realm of human agency, not of metaphysical or theoretical speculation. At the same time, praxial interests extend beyond matters of mere practicality or practicability, consisting in undertakings and behaviors that are selective, critically informed, and cognitively guided.

Since variability in the ways people interpret and apply this philosophical orientation is inevitable, in this chapter I will undertake to explore some of this variability and draw a few tentative conclusions about the ground that adherents of praxialism appear to share. This is done with the further intent of clarifying the potential utility of praxialism as an orienting strategy for music education philosophy. In the pages that follow I will explore the praxial orientation from the viewpoints of three noted advocates: Philip Alperson, Francis Sparshott, and David Elliott. By probing their aims and claims I hope to shed some light on the musical values each holds, whether implicitly or explicitly, thereby clarifying the potential significance to music education philosophy of praxial commitments.

Musical Praxialism in Alperson

Music education philosophy first encountered the term "praxial" in Philip Alperson's "What Should One Expect of a Philosophy of Music Education?" (Alperson 1991). Though more extensively concerned with philosophy of music than music education, Alperson's article offers a number of tantalizing suggestions as to how a praxial orientation might differ from other strategies. It begins innocuously enough with the idea that music education philosophy should be built on a foundation provided by a philosophy of music. But its conception of the latter diverges quite sharply from convictions the music education profession has traditionally espoused, leading to some rather distinctive educational claims.

According to Alperson, music philosophy should be conceived as reasoned understanding of the "practices related to the making, understanding, and valuation of music and the social, institutional, and theoretical contexts in which such practices have their place" (Alperson 1991, 218). At first gloss, the suggestion that music philosophy should concern itself with understanding musical practices seems almost trivial. But "practices" in the sense the term is intended here involve far more than just pleasing patterns of sound. Full and proper understanding of a musical practice implicates exploration of its social, institutional, and theoretical contexts: concerns widely held to lie beyond the pale of music proper. This dramatic extension to the range of considerations that philosophies of music and music education have customarily felt obliged to explore is fully deliberate. For as Alperson sees it, comprehensiveness and inclusiveness are important measures of philosophical adequacy. Music philosophy must account for musical practice "in its widest sense" (218) in order to avoid the common error of attributing to "music," as a whole, characteristics specific to a particular musical practice.

The attempt to portray music's nature and value in strictly "aesthetic" terms is a case in point. Aesthetic doctrines as originally conceived were overly narrow in their insistence upon the purely formal determinants of aesthetic musical experience. Their insistence upon the intrinsic, self-contained character of genuinely musical value created difficulties that led to important modifications (or, as Alperson has it, "enhancements") to aesthetic formalism as originally articulated. Strict aesthetic formalism had maintained that authentically musical value arose only from the contemplative gratification afforded by attending to music's formal configurations. But this idea of an autonomous aesthetic experience rooted in refined aesthetic sensibilities was ill equipped to account for music's broad social significance and its rich meanings in human cultural life. Music's value is not restricted to contemplative satisfaction in perceiving musical form.

So, aesthetic formalism was amended to incorporate a purported capacity to speak to "the heart" and to advance the mind and to provide for ranges of meaning and value beyond those implicated by formal perception of music itself. The most significant of these enhanced aesthetic doctrines Alperson calls "aesthetic cognitivism" (which stresses the mindful nature of musical experience) and "expressive aesthetic cognitivism" (stressing feeling, or "heart," and mind). Each attempted, in its own way, to redress the insularity caused by aesthetic formalism's restriction of music's significance to formal, intrinsic, aesthetic qualities. Each also attempted to extend the range of what is considered "good" music by providing for determinants of musical value beyond strictly structural elements.

Alperson's use of the word "enhance" is crucial here. And while these strategies attempt repairs to aesthetic formalism, they do not try to reconstruct it. The formalistic and idealistic foundations are left unaltered. Whatever cognitive or expressive values music has, then, remain inextricably rooted in an adequate perception of form. Thus, these enhanced explanations of musical value retain the basic conviction that it is an intrinsic and autonomous affair, untainted by commerce with the mundane, everyday world.

Such enhancements address some of the difficulties of aesthetic formalism. However, they do not resolve its most fundamental tensions. They endeavor to show that music is useful and valuable, while maintaining a relatively strict boundary between properly musical value and value that is extra-aesthetic and therefore extramusical. In other words, aesthetic cognitivism and expressive aesthetic cognitivism represent attempts to explain how music's objective, formal qualities can be humanly useful: how they refine human mind and feeling. These strategies seek to modify the idea of music's insularity and autonomy by situating it within the broader scope of meaningful human endeavor. However, the assumptions of objectivity and autonomy remain untouched, leaving a precarious situation in which music is held to be at once valuable and of no practical value.

Why, Alperson wonders, should practical functions such as enhancing affective or cognitive experience be considered authentically musical while other functions are arbitrarily dismissed as extramusical for their instrumentality or practicality? On what grounds does one determine that some practical functions are musical while others are not? Having granted that music properly serves the practical ends of expression and insight, how is it that other functions are deemed less musical for their practicality? According to Alan Merriam, Alperson observes, music serves quite a number of important functions beyond aesthetic gratification. Those include emotional expression, entertainment, communication, symbolic representation, physical stimulation, catharsis, enforcement of conformity to social norms, validation of social institutions, validation of religious rituals, enhancing social integration, and maintaining cultural continuity and stability (Alperson 1991, 231). Construing music's value primarily or exclusively in aesthetic terms simply fails to "exhaust everything we would wish to say about the cultural importance or utility of musical practice" (232).

What Alperson proposes is not further enhancement of the idealistic, aesthetic account of music, but something bolder and more radical: an orientation that builds its account of music inductively, from functions concrete musical practices evince, rather than deductively, from one such (aesthetic) function. More directly yet, Alperson explains, the praxial philosophical turn he advocates "resists the suggestion that art can best be understood on the basis of some universal or absolute feature or set of features. . . . The attempt is made rather to understand art in terms of the variety of meaning and values evidenced in actual practice in particular cultures" (1991, 233). Its basic aim is to understand "just what music has meant to people, an endeavor that includes but is not limited to a consideration of music in aesthetic contexts" (234).

This turn toward descriptive contextualization clearly requires we judge musical worth relative to musical function. A praxial approach to music philosophy requires close attention to "the social, historical, and cultural conditions and forces in which practices of musical production arise and have meaning" (1991, 236). And yet, Alperson cautions, such contextual situatedness and relativity does not negate the possibility of truths and standards. It only requires that since "the results of human action cannot be adequately understood apart from the motives, intentions, and productive considerations of the agents who bring them into being" (236), all claims to musical truths and values be directly grounded in specific human practices.

Alperson's praxialism rejects aesthetic theory's claims to foundational status. It does not, however, go so far as to flatly deny any possible validity. Rather, the aesthetic orientation must be reconstrued as one way of construing one kind of musical practice. Musical praxialism "combines an interest in aesthetic appreciation with an interest in the productive aspect of artistic practice and the cultural (including extra-aesthetic) contexts in which the arts are created, deployed and enjoyed" (1991, 236). On this view, praxialism implicates serious consideration of "the production, study, and appreciation of music in contexts where the aesthetic qualities of music are less central" (234). It need not deny the existence of contexts in which purportedly aesthetic qualities are salient, then; but it cannot accept the idea that such qualities are constitutive of, or comprise the whole of, musically valid experience.

The potential ramifications of this determination to acknowledge the musical validity of music's many functions are significant, as can be seen in the range of concerns Alperson suggests a praxial view would consider musically legitimate. A praxial view, he says, would demonstrate concern for "psychological, sociological, and political questions" (1991, 237) and "would take the dialectic between the musical and the moral as a serious object of study" (235). Indeed, it would extend the range of musically relevant concerns to "the enlargement of mind and the development of character" (237). Such convictions diverge so strongly from traditional music philosophy, Alperson suggests, that they may even prompt some to question whether a discipline devoted to their exploration remains philosophy as such. The praxial view represents "a shift away from philosophy conceived as a foundational discipline . . . perhaps even a move from philosophy to anthropology" (236).[2]

In light of these comments, one might suggest the praxial view is not so much an alternative music philosophy as a dramatic effort to redefine the traditional bounds of music philosophical discourse. Clearly, the praxial turn draws into the "musical" fold much that conventional thought has strived to lock outside. From its perspective, whether something is musical or extramusical can be determined only in reference to the priorities and concerns of the musical practice at hand. Those who find such talk wishy-washy and prefer their philosophy definitive and absolute will probably accuse praxial orientations of philosophical irresponsibility. Although that would be excessive, it is clear that praxialism departs significantly from habitual ways of explaining music.

A praxial orientation denies that music's capacity to afford aesthetic experience is essential, or even universally relevant to the determination of its nature and value. In place of a stable and secure aesthetic foundation for all music and musical value, it offers the fluid and slippery realm of human practices. Despite Alperson's claim that this does not eliminate the possibility of truths and standards, it does appear to be precisely his position that music cannot be understood on the basis of a universal, absolute, invariant set of features.[3] The meanings and values of musical practices are plural, historically emergent, unstable, socially relative, and contextually specific. Given the problematic status of universal claims about music's nature and value, praxialism seems to leave us with ideas that are tentative and provisional, and with value claims that are changeable and perhaps ever changing. The controversies and criticisms this sparks will strongly resemble those that have long attended pragmatism, whose perspective praxial philosophy resembles in certain respects.

Any music education philosophy built on praxial foundations will have to contend with whole ranges of meanings and values traditionally dismissed as extramusical: the cultural, the social, the political, the moral, and the role musical education plays in developing character, to list only those explicitly mentioned by Alperson. This is so, Alperson implies, because a truly educational endeavor is obligated to present its subject "in all its intricacy" (1991, 237)—a clear suggestion that traditional aesthetic orientations present an unacceptably restrictive view of what music is and what its worth may be.

Precisely how music education would address praxial concerns like these is a question Alperson leaves largely unexplored. Perhaps that is because praxialism's recognition of the plurality and continuously evolving nature of musical practices makes it as reluctant to offer instructional absolutes as musical ones. Whether or not that is the case, this much Alperson makes very clear: a praxial orientation would entail very different sets of instructional arrangements and priorities than those to which the music education profession is accustomed. A praxial approach to music education would implicate goals and methods markedly more diverse, contextually sensitive, and challenging than those endorsed by aesthetic doctrines. If further evidence of praxialism challenges for the nature and aims of music education were wanted, one need only consider Alperson's assertion that on a praxial view the concept of music education would have to be tied to the concept of education through music (1991, 237).

Francis Sparshott's Praxial Orientation

Both Alperson and Elliott owe a substantial debt to Francis Sparshott, a philosopher who has had relatively little to say about music education but a great deal to say about philosophy of music and art. It is well, then, to examine some of Sparshott's reflections on music for important influences and for clues to how praxial convictions might orient philosophical discourse. In a powerful and provocative essay entitled "Aesthetics of Music: Limits and Grounds," Sparshott (1987) speculates on what music is, what purpose it serves, and what its value may be.[4]

One may approach such issues in two basic ways, observes Sparshott, though each has its problems. The deductive approach designates a particular musical or artistic practice it finds exemplary, then proceeds normatively, judging all musics in light of the assumptions and priorities inherent in that practice. The risk here is one of applying to all music assumptions and values that are only locally valid. Inductive approaches work outward from grounded observations and instances. Though these approaches promise to remain faithful to the plurality of ways music manifests itself, they fail to attain the systematic unity usually deemed desirable in a general account.

Described this way, neither alternative appears particularly promising; but we shall see shortly that Sparshott does have a clear and justified preference for the latter.

Sparshott sets out to survey some of the problems inherent in traditional attempts to explain what music is. One of the oldest such explanatory strategies focuses on music's orderliness, describing its nature and value in primarily mathematical terms. The problem with such approaches is their tendency to claim for music things that matter relatively little among those actually engaged in musical makings and doings— those who sing, or drum, or pipe, or play (1987, 37). Mathematical explanations thus fail a pragmatic test of relevance to the great majority of musical doings and discourse, unless of course one is prepared to suggest that what matters most about music is something in which relatively few people who engage in it are interested.[5] Although that is a possibility, it has little appeal from a praxial perspective.

Aesthetic explanations of music also fail this pragmatic test: for while they may adequately describe a certain range of musical practice, their validity is local, not general. Aesthetic accounts, Sparshott explains, assume the general applicability of what is in fact a normative theory of taste, one emphasizing orderliness and trained perception over other modes of musical engagement. Aesthetic accounts assume music's highest inherent value lies in "a privileged group of consumers, not themselves musicians" (1987, 40). As such, aesthetic explanations ironically underplay the engagements and actions of the people without whom music would not exist. Moreover, aesthetic accounts take an inordinate interest in questions of intrinsic musical worth, an abstract musical value presumed resident in the inner dialectics of music. As Sparshott apparently sees it, far more common than such aesthetic concerns among actual musical practitioners is a musicianly concern for getting things right in relation to specific standards of practice. As well, the rapt contemplative vigilance idealized by aesthetic accounts, and the self-denial implicit in their doctrine of object-directedness, seem to subtly denigrate music's sonorous and sensuous pleasures.

If the concept of music as aesthetic is questionable on several grounds, suggests Sparshott, so may be the idea that music is an art. For arts are unified organizations of practical skills, and music is found in cultures so disparate that there seems to be little basis for claiming any such organization. If different cultures without shared practices or common activities each have music in some distinctive sense, explains Sparshott, the claim that music is an art is difficult to sustain: "There may be arts of music (or musics) but can be no one art of music" (1987, 42). Clearly, if music is not itself *an* art, saying how it is to be considered one of *the* arts becomes a matter of significant difficulty.

Yet, whatever music is not, it is invariably something that people do. And like all such human doings, we have fairly reliable experientially derived notions of what it means to engage in musical behaviors. This means we can identify them as musical even where others may not share the same concept we do. Music is, observes Sparshott, a prevalent mode of human behavior: it is a practice. "People everywhere can be observed to sing, to drum, to blow and finger pierced pipes, to scrape and pluck strings and springs—some or all of these—in ways controlled by the intention to produce some specific sort of controlled sound" (1987, 43). But (Sparshott continues), what might it mean to call all these activities, in all their radical diversity and discontinuities, "music"? To focus on the behavioral commonalities of musically productive practices, however useful that may be, tends to exclude culturally functional aspects: aspects that may be, for a given practice, as constitutively musical as the piping or plucking. Moreover, there exist practices where things we might be inclined to call music are not considered music but instances of something else.

In short, says Sparshott, "the word 'music' covers an inherently unstable variety of practices linked functionally, and/or procedurally, and/or institutionally, in all sorts of ways" (1987, 44). And, suggests Sparshott provocatively, there may be relatively little to be said about all these practices collectively that is of any real interest or importance. In point of fact, most talk about music takes an implicitly normative stance, making unarticulated assumptions about what the nerve of the practice should be. What most people say when they talk about music is meant to hold not so much for all music, everywhere, for all times, as for music that "does what music should do or is what music should be" (44). This is how human discourse operates. Words such as "music" are not proxies for hidden essences or absolutes. Rather, they are heuristic tools, strategic devices for negotiating one's way among experiential realities that are fluid, unstable, and ever changing. As such, any use of the term "music" or claim to its meaning should be regarded as contextually specific, tentative, contingent, and temporary. The aptness or utility of any generalization about music's nature and purpose can only be determined in light of the actual interests and actions of specific musicians, publics, and practitioners. It follows, according to Sparshott, that "we should not demand of a theory that it postulate for music (however defined) a single unvarying set of determining interests, or that it demand that such interests be identifiable outside the domain of music. Some notorious difficulties . . . come from supposing that one has to choose between exclusive alternatives each of which invokes . . . interest[s] that plainly exist" (53).

Since music is human praxis—socially grounded action in which all manner of people can be seen to engage in all manner of ways—it is reasonable to expect that every kind of human interest that might conceivably find expression in that activity will in fact do so, continues Sparshott. Indeed, it would be highly extraordinary if they did not. Ignoring any such interests when attempting to explain music, designating them inherently nonmusical or extramusical, is not only overhasty but also arbitrary. Such explanations are both possible and fairly common, of course, serving as they do the desired ends of certain groups of people. But ultimately there exists no neutral ground for the adjudication of rival claims framed in this way. The validity of any given explanation of what music is, or of what its value may be, cannot be determined noncontingently. In the absence of a God's-eye point of view outside all human interests (one that permits utterly "objective" comparison of disparate or rival claims) accounting for the nature and value of music is tricky business. Identifying "the nerve of a practice," Sparshott suggests, is less a matter of discovering an inner essence than of "capturing a consensus" (1987, 53).

Sparshott conducts an impressive survey of the radical diversity of human tendencies and interests one might expect to manifest themselves in musical practices. From among these, he finds three that appear basic or foundational among humans: an interest in knowing or understanding; a tendency to transform biological necessities into broader human values; and a tendency to pattern things. Thus, for instance, repetitive physical actions have a natural tendency to exhibit rhythmic regularities in which people take interest. Such interest leads in turn to increasingly more complex and elaborate rhythmic and/or bodily activities, some of which develop into musical practices whose most prominent feature is rhythmic. Similarly, repetitive human utterances evince interesting patterns and expressive qualities that are naturally inclined to take on increasing complexity and elaboration. Such basic tendencies and interests manifest themselves in musical practices (values evolved from necessities) in which melodic or timbral expressivity is salient. At the same time, the basic human interest in exploring the limits of the knowable manifests itself in musical practices primarily designed to appeal to perception and cognition of syntactical designs and structural relations. Thus, three basic human interests or tendencies beget three distinctive kinds of music and three corresponding ways of relating to it: the conative, the affective, and the cerebral. These musics correspond in turn to three basic human ways of being (corporeal, social, and thoughtful) and to three human dispositional states (indulging, caring, and reflecting).

The extent to which music manifests each of these characteristics varies as a function of practice, of situation, and of purpose. Just as what people find meaningful and significant varies from one situation to another, so too does what they value in music. Some musical practices explicitly invoke action; some simply invite participation; some promote solidarity; some gratify contemplation; some seek to refer, describe, or characterize; some are deeply moving and expressive; some are primarily decorative; some serve explicitly utilitarian ends; and still others promise cathartic relief. But neither the nature nor the value of such practices is the kind of thing that yields gracefully to concise description or that is easily grasped by people not fluent in the particular universes of discourse in which they are situated. Such meanings are learned "only by a lifetime of immersion in them," suggests Sparshott, where they are "eked out" by hints, guesses, and such meager half-truths as words can be made to convey (1987, 56).

Because of music's profound diversity and the situatedness of its meanings, a priori, abstract accounts leave us with little more than "flaccid generalizations" (Sparshott 1987, 69). There is far more to be learned about music by attending to practices and traditions in which it is invariably embedded and from which it emerges. On this praxial view, debates as to whether the formal or relational (for instance) aspects of music are for all places, purposes, and times more important are irresolvable. Such questions are wrongheaded. There can be no impartial basis for declaring one musical practice better than another. "No doubt," observes Sparshott, "the best music is the music that best satisfies musical interests. But . . . these [interests] are radically diverse, even if we confine ourselves to interests in listening. Beyond that, there are different audiences and different occasions and different relations to music" (73). These varieties of value, purpose, and worth do not sum; their disjunction is such that they cannot be brought under a single head of "music" without doing mischief or serious injustice to one or another.

And yet, Sparshott hastens to add, "none of this should be taken to suggest that within particular classes of comparison firm judgments of relative merit cannot be made" (1987, 74). Apparently, then, although interpractice comparisons are highly suspect, determinations of musical worth may be defensible when grounded in concrete, specific musical practices—if that is the kind of thing we are interested in pursuing. Still, what of interclass comparisons? People can regularly be heard making value claims that are unqualified, global, and summative. At such times, they are not just asserting that a particular music is good in its kind, but that it is "great," without qualification. Is the notion of a greatness that lies strictly in what a music is (with utter disregard for what it does) just so much humbug, wonders Sparshott? He equivocally concludes that what people seem to mean by musical greatness is that it presents remarkable challenges to their cognitive powers and, more broadly yet, to their "moral being" (76). What he does not say, but what might follow from his arguments elsewhere, is that music seems to present such cognitive or moral challenges (when it does) because of the depth with which people learn to "live into" particular musical traditions or practices. After all, greatness is not the kind of thing people attribute with regularity to musics with which they have only passing familiarity, but rather to those that engage them most deeply. There may be grounds, then, for leaving even the issue of greatness situated within musical practices. In other words, music is not great purely for what it is, but for what it is presumed capable of doing among those whose musical interests and experiences we share.

This praxial orientation appears to relativize claims to musical significance both historically and culturally, reducing them to consensual agreements among participants in particular universes of sociomusical discourse. And as we have seen, since music consists in various practices it is less than accurate to speak of music as "an art": there are, rather, various musics, various musical arts. As well, calling music an art also tends to situate it among the so-called fine arts, a grouping that is culturally and historically specific, and to some extent arbitrary. Indeed, even conceiving of musical practice as three musical arts (corresponding to "conative, affective, and cognitive" human interests) fails to exhaust all praxial possibilities. Perhaps, reflects Sparshott, there are aspects of music's relation to human life "that the notion of an art misses entirely" (1987, 77). What, for instance, of those musics whose significance is bound up in spontaneous enjoyment of the moment—less concerned with craft and contemplation than living in the here and now? What of musics whose appreciation is predominantly a function of their social embeddedness? Perhaps we would be better served, Sparshott suggests, if we were to think of musical practices as talklike or conversationlike, as "forms of social reason" rather than "art" (78–79).

Efforts to conflate music with language have a long and troubling history, of course. But language and talking are not the same kind of things. Given the striking diversity of things we recognize as musical practices and the fact that talk manifests itself in ways that are equally diverse, perhaps the differences between music and talk are "no more important than the differences within each" (1987, 78). Both may be regarded as "improvised ways of getting from place to place in a social world" (78). Other intriguing similarities come to mind. Both music and conversation are sonorous modes of relating, for instance. And getting into the sense of music resembles the way we enter into conversation: both are learned skills whose initial efforts lead to slipping into and out of fleeting, half-glimpsed worlds, worlds that practice and fluency eventually transform into alternative realities and ways of being. As well, both music and talk are crucial determinants of our sense of relationship and community. Conversations and music are both events in which people engage each with his or her own distinctive voice; in which divergent experiences, values, and assumptions are shared with one another; and in which interpretation and misinterpretation inevitably figure significantly.

"Just as a conversation is made up of different people with different selves as well as different voices," says Sparshott, "so we may speak of a musical field that holds together people differently related. It is not so much that we all play, hear, study, the same music . . . as that we all participate differently in musical experience that is the same as languages and conversations are the same" (1987, 85). This talklike engagement in social reason is less a function of rulelike exchange than it is a messy, imprecise process of dialectical interaction. Musicing and conversing consist in sharing or voicing experiences and meanings. In both, the "voice" is intimately connected to and reflective of the self. The meanings of both are rich and radically multilayered, grasped more by hinting and guessing than literal translation. Both musicing and conversing are functions of shared habits, gradually acquired, whose success is gauged primarily by the apparent seamlessness of the experience.

Things such as voice, gesture, and inflection do not enrich conversation. They constitute it. We follow abstract reductions of such processes (reading passages like this one, for instance) only to the extent that we successfully recontextualize what in themselves are meaningless, arbitrary symbols. In conversation, voice, expression, and self merge as one. As people talk, they constantly encounter discrepancies, anomalies, and contradictions whose imaginative resolution is fundamental to the success of the process. And if Sparshott is right, much the same kind of process happens in music. One enters into and comes to exist within music much as one does conversation: as an extension of oneself, engaged with others.[6] People from different backgrounds relate to each other's musics in ways strikingly similar to conversational participants: sometimes grasping, sometimes not, first catching fleeting glimpses of promising meanings, then, progressively more and more until, after decades or a lifetime of experience, these alternate ways of being become second nature.[7]

Although these various conversations or musical practices do not sum (there being no ultimate, prescriptive, or exhaustive set of rules for conversing or being musical), neither are they mutually exclusive. Precisely because humans are social and music is a kind of social discourse, and because our minds seem to be at least enough alike to enable promising glimpses of others' meanings, we seem to have a basic sense for both music and conversation. Given basic human similarities of mind, social situation, and other tendencies and interests, that people would completely misunderstand each other all the time is no more likely than that they would succeed 100 percent of the time. This ongoing engagement in attempts to make sense of shared human sound is, observes Sparshott, one of the basic conditions of human social existence.

Being multilingual affords certain obvious advantages, as may fluency in multiple musical discourses. Knowing a variety of languages and broad conversational experience enable a breadth of purview that is essential to a full appreciation of the ways talk works. Similarly, appreciation of the radical plurality of musical practices requires a broad experiential base. But at the same time, Sparshott cautions, this wider context may impoverish, since people "for whom the music of their own place and time is all the music there is can live into that music as people of broader culture cannot" (1987, 86). For the former, their music is their world; for the latter, it is one among a number of alternatives.

There is a further irony about all this. For while on the one hand musics are radically plural and diverse—in function, in social significance, in setting, in "taste communities" to whose interests they cater, and even in ways it is considered proper to relate to music—on the other hand, people do seem to have at least some shared sense for music. Strictures about the unintelligibility of unprecedented forms are probably overdone, suggests Sparshott: "Even on a first hearing one may "catch on"; the rudiments of a new sort of order may be picked up on quite quickly. . . . One knows that people are using a human language or making music, even if one cannot specify exactly what it is one knows or how one knows it" (1987, 87). In view of the radical disparity of musical practices, the regularity and relative ease with which performers, composers, listeners, even musicologists, seem to engage differently in common experience is remarkable. There are, in Sparshott's view, "different ways of relating to music within musical understanding," none of which is "for all purposes better than all the others, and no one purpose has such privilege as to warrant exclusive authority for its viewpoint" (86).

Before moving along to David Elliott's effort to appropriate the praxial orientation for music education philosophy, a brief inventory of Sparshott's assertions and assumptions will be helpful. It is clear that the praxial orientation eschews a priori definitions and is determined to make only such generalizations about music as examination of actual human engagements, activities, and traditions will permit. This in turn leads to a conspicuously pluralistic stance, which often seems on the verge of relativism. Yet, like Alperson, Sparshott denies that praxialism is relativistic in any opprobrious way. The multiplicity of interests music serves, the plurality of ways it may be defensibly said to be, its status as a socially, historically, and culturally emergent phenomenon: each points to a fundamental plurality and relativity of music's nature and value. Yet relative does not mean arbitrary, and "many" does not mean "just any." It is clear that the praxial orientation is incompatible with the essentialist and monistic views inherited from idealism, and that it portrays a state of affairs far more complex than single-minded alternatives. But its determination to ground its theoretical speculation in experiential and empirical human realities and its willingness (indeed, its eagerness) to concede many valid ways of being musical also yield concepts of what music is and does that are richer, more interesting, and more flexible and vital than other contenders. What the limits of praxial multiplicity may be—or, indeed, whether any such limits can be determined in absolute terms—is another issue.[8]

But again, "many" does not mean "any." Although praxial reflection makes abundantly clear that music is, as Alperson (1987) observes, a "culturally unstable term" (10) covering a radically diverse range of practices and undertakings, the praxial orientation also insists that such diversity is undergirded by functional, procedural and institutional links. The concept of music, though fluid, is moored in human practices. Thus, while "music" does not designate something with an essential, immutable core, neither is it open to utterly any meaning and value one might wish to assign it. Whatever forms it takes, whatever values and functions it assumes, it is invariably situated in the social world of human relations and interactions, in practices and traditions that answer to consensually validated standards.

Elliott's Accounts of Musical Praxialism
and Educational Practice

Our discussions of Alperson and Sparshott have advanced many of the assumptions that undergird Elliott's arguments in *Music Matters*, but not all of them. For Elliott's effort moves well beyond philosophy of music into the realms of music educational practice and curriculum. At the core of his argument lies a conviction that all music everywhere consists essentially in what he calls "procedural knowledge": a know-how that is action embedded and a constitutive element in musicianship.[9] Thus, procedural knowledge, musicianship, or know-how lies at the heart of all musical practices. And yet, their specific manifestations are always situated or culture specific. In other words, while all music consists in knowledge that is procedural in nature, the specific constitution of these procedures is invariably intracultural. Music's procedural nature, we might say, is universal; but the procedures that constitute given practices are not.

To illuminate the distinction between music's universal and particular attributes (between what are sometimes designated global and local, or generic and idiomatic characteristics), Elliott employs an interesting strategic device. The term "MUSIC" is used to designate music as a "diverse human practice"—the abstract, global sense of the term subsuming all particular practices. MUSIC, then, is music in its most comprehensive sense. Saying that MUSIC is a diverse human practice is Elliott's way of saying that all musics everywhere are human practices. Yet, like musicianship (itself a universally constitutive feature of musical agency), its actual instances are always culture specific. MUSIC manifests itself empirically only in specific practices: in what Elliott labels "Music" (or perhaps more accurately in this context, "Musics"). Within each such practice there are in turn individual "audible sound events," works, or "listenables," which he designates "music." MUSIC, Music, music: universal, cultural, individual (1995, 44–45).

Now, it seems to follow that since "musicianship" is always situated relative to specific practices and traditions, there can be no MUSICianship, only Musicianship. The nature of MUSIC is comprehended only through experiences with (practice-specific) Music(s) and corresponding Musicianship(s), which in turn are truly manifest only in particular musical events. This brief sketch permits consideration of several points that eventually emerge as major themes in Elliott's philosophy. First, all Musics (MUSIC) are (is) procedural in nature, consisting in action-embedded know-how. This is true, presumably, in virtue of the definition of "practice," since practices consist in intelligent, intentional, goal-oriented doings that are executed with close attention to given traditions and standards—in short, procedures. Adherence to procedures becomes a critical component in Elliott's claim to "praxial" philosophical status, for practices (praxes) are fundamentally procedural affairs. Second, MUSIC (the collective abstraction comprised of all Musics) is multicultural in essence. This, too, is true by definition: Elliott has stipulated that MUSIC is a diverse human practice, and it thus consists essentially of multiple musical and cultural practices. In short, MUSIC is both procedural and multicultural in essence.

The upshot of these two claims for Elliott's philosophy is this. While other musical attributes may be dispensable, optional, contingent, local, or culture specific, Music's "essentially" (Elliott's word) procedural nature and multicultural "essence" obtain without qualification: they are universal. And since any experience that purports to be educational should presumably reveal what obtains for all musics everywhere (an implicit premise), two imperatives emerge for music education. First, instruction must somehow assure that music's (or Music's?) procedural nature is grasped. And second, it is imperative to approach music education multiculturally (multi-Musically) so as to assure that Music's essential diversity is illuminated and appreciated. At the risk of becoming tedious in our use of these labels, let us agree to call instructional endeavors devoted to these procedural and multi-Musical imperatives MUSIC education.

The next step would appear to be determination of what this might mean in more concrete terms, at which point the plot thickens ever so slightly because Music's nature can only be grasped through experiences with practice-specific Music. What I have called *MUSIC education*, then, can really be accomplished only through what one would probably have to call "Music education" (or, perhaps more accurately, "Musics education," since to use the singular seems to suggest inculcation in but one specific practice). In other words, access to the universal entails an inferential leap from the particular. Understanding the "essential" nature (Elliott's word) of a diverse human practice can be achieved only through engagement in culture-specific human practices.

This is admittedly a rather convoluted way to explain points that may seem relatively innocuous and straight-ahead in Elliott's exposition. But it permits clearer examination of several assumptions that are, I think, both less straight-ahead and more difficult to sustain. The first is Elliott's conviction that music's (I will abandon the cumbersome tripartite distinction, trusting the reader to infer the intended sense) nature as procedural knowledge implicates musical performance as instructional method. The second is Elliott's apparent conviction that music's praxial nature implicates an educational commitment to multiculturalism or multimusical education. Sympathies and commitments to musical performance and musical diversity are not so much my immediate concern as whether or not they are logically implicated by praxialism itself. My sense is that, practically speaking, they need not be, and that, logically speaking, they are not.[10] It will be my position here that the radical diversity of musical practice(s) is at odds with Elliott's contention that there is a single "nerve" (or two essential "nerves") necessarily and invariably shared by all of them, and that these implicate a clear set of educational practices rightfully claiming priority over all others.

Let us first examine *Music Matters*'s "performance imperative"—Elliott's apparent conviction that the only valid way to grasp music's procedural essence (that is, to develop musicianship) is to perform it, and the corollary that instruction which neglects performance fails to educate musically. "MUSIC," writes Elliott, "is a performing art. Each and every aspect of a musical work that we listen for is always the result of an individual or collective interpretation and performance of a composer's musical design, or an improvised design, or a performer's rendition of a remembered design" (1995, 91). Moreover, musical works are not physical entities, but performances: "events that are intentionally generated by the knowledgeable actions . . . of human agents . . . to be intentionally conceived as such by other knowledgeable agents (musicers and/or listeners)" (91–92). Thus, Elliott's insistence on music's essentially performed nature follows from his denial that musical works consist of physical entities, and from the fact that music could not exist without the human agents who bring it to life. Both are without question important points. But does it necessarily follow from the fact music requires human agents for its realization that music is above all else performance? We distinguish readily, for instance, among language, writing, reading, and speaking, without insisting that one mode of linguistic engagement is more truly authentic than the others. Might the same obtain for music?[11]

Other problems attend the suggestion that music only truly (or most truly) exists in performances, and that performing is thus indispensable to the development of real musicianship. For as Elliott himself suggests, music (and presumably, then, musicianship as well) is an "open" concept. One can embrace the centrality of human agency to music without taking the additional step of designating performing its quintessential modality. For better or worse, the word "performing" carries with it an abundance of culture-specific baggage, not all of it necessarily positive. At least in Western discourse, "performing" connotes fairly specific musical roles. It usually implicates non-performing others for whose edification and gratification the performance is intended. As well, it suggests hierarchical relationships some find distasteful and others find deeply disturbing. Often, it implicates physical abilities that are not widely shared or easily developed, and involvements that can lead to psychological and physical stress. It is arguable, in other words, that performing is not a universal good.[12]

It seems one can remain true to music's procedural nature and its intricate reliances upon human agency without granting place of privilege to performance as such. Other alternatives are available. There exist multiple modes of musical engagement, doing, participation, and agency. Most musical practices consist in constellations of subpractices, modes of agency, and ways of participating. And although something conveniently called "performance" is often conspicuously central, it is difficult to see how its status is any less contingent, or its value less conditional, than that of the other features of musical practices Elliott explores.

These comments are not made with a view to berating or belittling performance: for it is obviously a profoundly enriching mode of musical behavior, and Elliott is entirely justified in his alarm at the extent to which idealistic philosophy and the processes of commodification have contributed to its neglect. I only want to suggest that to turn to praxialism for unequivocal support of performance as the primary instructional means in music education may be a bit hasty. Praxial convictions rightly stipulate the mindful nature of musical doings but do not in themselves suggest one kind of doing is inherently or inevitably more valuable than others. They insist upon empirical grounding but do not appear to imply a basis for establishing any particular mode of musical engagement as more essential than others. It is doubtless true that unless someone does something musical there can be no music, but there are multiple ways of being musical—each of which would seem at least potentially justified in a claim to validity on praxial grounds.

Elliott argues persuasively that music making is a valid and valuable educational endeavor, and that musicianship must be regarded not just as an end in itself but also as a means to the laudable educational goals of self-knowledge and self-growth. These claims follow reasonably from the definition of praxis as an integration of doing and thinking. But in themselves, they do not show how one particular kind of praxis (e.g., performing) might be designated primary.[13] That conclusion seems to derive from the point that works require work doers, from convictions that making is more complex than listening, and from convictions that performing provides clearer, more overt, more reliable feedback as to the quality of one's activity than listening.[14] The unanswered question is, again, whether this serves to substantiate an indispensable educational role for performing or establishes that performing is more educationally valuable than other possibilities. That performing has these potential advantages does not necessarily establish that it serves all conceivable educational ends equally well. Again, Elliott's case for the primacy of performance need not (and does not) depend exclusively upon *praxial* validation. Since "flow" (see Csikszentmihalyi 1990) is best sustained by engagements that provide continuous and ongoing feedback as to the quality of one's achievements, performance (or, more broadly, productive activity) may be the preferred vehicle for such experience. His account of optimal experience or flow, then, provides a compelling case for performance, but this argument is psychological rather than praxial.[15]

The second major issue to be examined here is Elliott's multicultural imperative, his claim that music education is multicultural in essence. Recall that in Sparshott's view people who have but one music (their own) live into it more deeply than people whose music is but one option among many.[16] It was suggested earlier that an enterprise devoted to inculcation in one musical practice might be appropriately designated Music education. Note, thus, an interesting and ironic tension—a sense in which Music education and MUSIC education are diametrically opposed. By immersing people deeply in a given practice, Music education nurtures the kind of musical engagements that are momentous, vital, and meaningful. The only way to achieve the multicultural (multimusical) goal of MUSIC education as Elliott has defined it is by exploring and experiencing Music multiply: by exploring and experiencing Musics. Thus, MUSIC education's commitment to conceptual and experiential breadth poses a threat to the depth of engagement so crucial to Music education.[17] The more adequate to the concept of MUSIC education instruction and learning become, the less deeply are people able (instructional time and resources being finite) to live into Music. Thus, while MUSIC education rests upon education in Musics, the more Musically distributed instruction becomes, the less effectively it nurtures praxial groundedness.

These comments are not intended to discredit or disparage the ideal of multi-musical education, only to suggest that praxial convictions and loyalties do not in themselves address or answer such questions as whose, or which, or how many. Such issues are at least as political and ideological as they are philosophical and may need to be addressed by means other than an appeal to praxis. It is not so much that praxial convictions fail to resolve issues like these as that they are largely indifferent to them. Praxialism offers to empirically orient and ground music philosophy, and although that is no small achievement, its basic inclinations appear to be pluralistic and nonnormative, providing no clear basis for sustaining one practice's claim for ultimacy or privilege over others. Praxialism suggests we ground our explanations of such things as music in close observations of actual human practices. But its descriptive commitment proves a rather awkward fit to the inherently normative concerns of such an undertaking as education.

In short, it may be that praxial music philosophy's particular way of framing understandings of music's nature(s), function(s), and value(s) has a somewhat less direct relationship to questions about education than *Music Matters* appears to assume. Praxial sympathies logically implicate neither performance nor multicultural music education. They cannot serve as final arbiter in a choice between MUSIC education and Music education, since Music's multicultural "essence" is educationally binding only on those who endorse MUSIC education as a professional goal—those with the liberal intent, that is, of illuminating music's radical diversity. There are other educational alternatives in whose defense praxialism might be invoked. (Here recall Sparshott's admonition of the "notorious difficulties" that come from supposing one has to choose between exclusive alternatives, each of which invokes interests that plainly exist.) Nor does the performance emphasis endorsed by Elliott necessarily attend a commitment to praxial values, since there are (indeterminately?) many other valid modes of musical praxis (of "right doing").[18] The plurality of musical practices no more establishes which among them should be taught (or whether more than one or, for that matter, any should) than the multiplicity of intelligences decides the question of which (instructional time and money both being in limited supply) should be required of everyone.[19]

Another perspective from which Elliott approaches these issues, and the last to be examined here, is the multidimensionality of musical works. Here, the natures of musical knowing (cognition) and musically known (works) converge in interesting ways. On the one hand, since works are not to be regarded so much as things as actions and events, the kinds of understandings they entail are inherently processual, socially situated, and procedural.[20] On the other, musical works are held to consist of six dimensions, several of which are obligatory and several optional.[21] Since musical cognition (musicianship) takes five forms and musical works have four to six dimensions, the geography of musical experience is indeed profoundly multidimensional. Because neither cognition nor works are static, unidimensional affairs, Elliott argues that it is wrong to regard musics as "things."

But since Musics and musical experiences are multidimensional, and since human consciousness is such a massively distributed, parallel, and constructive affair, I think it more reasonable to speak of possibility than of essence, as Elliott is inclined to do. Any of these dimensions (and, arguably, a number of others not here accounted for)[22] may be more or less salient depending on the priorities and interests that attend a given mode of musical praxis. That none of these dimensions should be considered musically dispensable on a priori grounds (as idealistic, aesthetic accounts do) is invaluable advice. But the suggestion that some dimensions are universal, necessary, and essential, while others are contingent or optional, seems to imply the replacement of outmoded aesthetic hierarchies with new, praxial ones.

To be sure, Elliott asserts, "there is no one way to listen for all musics everywhere" (1995, 100); and (after Wolterstorff) there is "no single purpose to musical practices" (327n1); and (after Sparshott) we should expect to find in music evidence not of one single overriding human tendency, but rather of numerous human tendencies and a variety of human interests (109). But praxial convictions such as these make claims about MUSIC (about all music, everywhere) difficult to sustain. The decidedly nonnormative character of praxial convictions creates unresolved tension with Elliott's apparent conviction that there are ways of being musical that are more valid or authentic than others. If "music" and "works" are indeed "open concepts," as Elliott says, the project of designating essential and inessential dimensions seems inappropriate. If there is no "all" of music, the temptations to stipulate, a priori, a determinate number of musical dimensions, and to designate these variously essential or contingent, are probably ones we should resist.

Music is indisputably a performing art, or at least that is one way it must be construed if one takes seriously people's actual musical engagements, behaviors, and interactions. Thus, praxialism seems justified in arguing that performing music is crucial to understanding musical practices of that kind. It also seems reasonable to assert that since performing is an art (a skillful act acquired by experience and study in light of specific traditions and standards), instructional practices must avoid the reductive tendency to portray it as something less than that—as, for instance, mere technical craft. It is, however, another matter to argue that music is more fundamentally a performing art than it is any other kind of art, for it is not clear to me that such a turn is compatible with praxial convictions as I understand them. Since praxis consists in the exercise of a skill as distinct from attempts to account for it theoretically, praxialism is justified in its insistence upon the necessity of intentionality, engagement, and agency. It seems excessive, however, to claim that mindful action in music can legitimately assume but one form, or that music assumes one such form more essentially than any others.[23]

Praxialism and Music Education

Since I have hardly confined myself to exposition in the preceding sections of this essay, the conclusions I propose here will not be surprising. Still, praxial views of music and music education are relative newcomers to music education's professional discourse, and understanding what they are all about is important philosophical business. In this final section, then, let us pull together some of the strands that have emerged from my effort to understand how Alperson, Sparshott, and Elliott view praxialism.

I think at least three basic praxial emphases can be identified. These are not discrete, and there are doubtless others that warrant consideration. But three is a good round number from which to begin. The first emphasizes the nature of praxis as thoughtful action, or action-embedded thought. For short: *musical praxis is mindful doing*. While its precise implications for things like curricular content or instructional methodology may be debatable, the significance of this fundamental conviction is clear and unequivocal: praxially oriented music education must steer clear of ungrounded theory and blind execution. From this point of view, Elliott's criticisms of the speculative excesses of aesthetic approaches to music education and his insistence that musical agency be regarded as a knowing-in-action are both understandable and justified.

Second, praxial commitments stress that in order to understand musical practices one must attend to the details of what people actually do and how such doings relate to standards and traditions. In music philosophy, this promises to keep abstract generalization in check, reminding us of the pitfalls of a priori, universal claims about music's nature and value.[24] For short: *learning or describing musical praxis demands close attention to the details of peoples' musical doings.* Alperson shows the difficulties that attend unleashed speculative endeavors. And Sparshott demonstrates with remarkable vividness this conviction's sensitivity to the range, diversity, and richness of musical undertakings. At the same time, he displays something of the endless tinkering required to keep praxial ships afloat. In a general way, then, praxialism offers, as its name promises, sound practical guidance for musical instruction: skillful practices are most effectively learned by immersion in the practices themselves, with sensitive attention to how musical things of this sort are done (and taught; and learned). For guidance as to which or whose practices ought be learned, or what constitutes an acceptable degree of expertise for educational purposes, however, we may need more than praxialism appears equipped to offer. Praxialism's descriptive predilections do not serve all purposes equally well.

Third, praxial commitments acknowledge the situatedness and multiplicity of practices. Although situatedness need not and does not imply incommensurability, it does commit us to taking differences seriously and avoiding generalizations that stray too far from empirical and experiential "fact." For short, *musical praxis emerges from and is embedded in diverse yet concrete human social engagements and interactions.* Although (like Marxism and phenomenology, for instance) it stresses music's historical contingency, praxial commitments further stress music's social and cultural emergence and the centrality of human agency. These in turn implicate both pluralistic and relativistic concerns.

As suggested earlier, one way of helping conceptualize these tendencies and predilections is in terms of their affinity to philosophical pragmatism. Praxialism is pragmatic in its commitment to the openness, emergence, and socially constructed nature of musical practices, as well as its antiessentialist orientation. Like pragmatism, it regards truths less as immutable, incontestable absolutes than as socially negotiated, consensual affairs—as provisionally held beliefs, intersubjectively constructed webs of conviction whose validity lies in their utility for present needs and interests. While praxialism is firmly committed to understanding people's musical doings, it resolves to temper the effort to understand and explain with awareness that not all musical doings are the same. To commit to a praxial view, then, suggests as well a pragmatic willingness to modify one's musical claims when contradictory evidence is encountered: an inclination toward fallible belief rather than immutable concept, and a healthy distrust of the dogmatic and the doctrinaire. Pragmatic metaphors of rebuilding a ship at sea resonate sympathetically with Sparshott's characterization of music as conversation and of musics as improvised ways of getting from place to place in a social world. This pragmatic inclination is less evident in Elliott, whose arguments sometimes appear to share the essentialist character of the aesthetic views he otherwise rejects.

Another distinctive characteristic of praxially directed musical philosophy is, as we have seen, its determination to account for music's social situatedness as an integral part of what the music is. As human undertakings, musical practices are inextricably bound up in relations between and among people. This promises (or threatens, depending upon one's perspective) radical extension of the range of considerations deemed genuinely musical, implicating communal, ritualistic, moral, and even political dimensions.

At the same time, this situatedness historicizes and contextualizes anything one might wish to say about music and its value, which is to say it relativizes them in specific and limited ways. Its reluctance to confer a place of musical privilege upon a single practice or set of practices, as aesthetic accounts were often fond of doing, means praxialism is decidedly pluralistic as well. Given the perspectival specificity of musical practices, the diversity of forms and functions musical doings can assume, praxialism sees many musics where traditional philosophical reflection saw but one.

Methodologically, praxial philosophy appears to value induction over deduction, description over prescription, and empirical evidence over metaphysical speculation. It seems to advise us: "Attend closely to what people can be seen to do when they behave in ways they call musical, basing your claims about music's nature and value strictly upon what you find there. Resist the temptation to reduce the dynamism and plurality of human musical doings to lifeless, static abstractions." Since praxialism is skeptical of the notion of a foundational substrate for all music, it is also disinclined to erect value hierarchies based on such binary conceptual oppositions as objective/ subjective, sophisticated/primitive, good/ bad, profound/entertaining, authentic/corrupt, and so on.

As vital human activities, the resistance of musics to the categorical propensities of abstract thought is not surprising. On the praxial view, musics are multidimensional, fluid, polysemic, and unstable. Accordingly, efforts to reduce all musical value to aesthetic value are mistaken. Alperson and Elliott clearly differ on the nature and severity of that mistake, but both agree that it is wrong to promote its view as the whole of musical practice.[25] There can no more be a "whole" of human musical practice than there is a whole of the human condition. Music's values are not intrinsic, unconditional, or absolute, and it has no meaning outside the practices and interactions in which it is embedded. That is, *music's worth can be gauged only in reference to specific human needs and interests.* And as Sparshott shows, such needs and interests are as multiple and radically diverse as human activity itself.

We have seen a number of praxial themes whose significance for music education is both direct and immediate: the insistence that musical undertakings involve mindful doing, for instance, and the implication that musical instruction and learning must attend closely to such doings. But commitment to praxial philosophical dispositions does not provide definitive answers to all-important educational questions we might want to ask. It tells us where to look (and where not to look) for answers to questions about what a certain music is and what its values may be. But it has little to say about whose or which musical practice(s) warrant formal instruction. These are political or ideological issues, not logical or ontological ones. Such choices (and in education choice is unavoidable) need to be addressed in other ways. They draw more on one's philosophy of education than one's philosophy of music: on whether one's educational goals are liberal or conservative, on whether one believes education is more fundamentally obligated to address breadth or depth of purview, and on whether one thinks the aims of education should be reproductive or transformative. Praxialism can commend certain instructional methods for their apparent congruence with a given musical practice. But it cannot dictate the choice between Music education and MUSIC education, for instance; and it cannot tell us which practices to engage in or which musicians to observe. Put differently, praxial philosophy seems better suited to answering "is" questions than "ought" questions. It is a good tool but, like any tool, not good for all purposes.[26]

A recurrent feature of the literature explored here is a wariness of the comforting assumption that an intellectual tool (aesthetic doctrine, to take a nontrivial example) useful in one sociocultural context or for one kind of task is thereby universally valuable. Much of praxialism's strength derives from its sensitivity to difference and its inherent flexibility. However, we need to be on guard against the inclination to replace old single-purpose tools with new single-purpose tools. Elliott does us a valuable service in reminding us that different situations require different tools, and that our old tools are often of limited use for new jobs. However, in his eagerness to repudiate aesthetic doctrine,[27] he sometimes seems determined to overpower its absolutist assumptions with other quasi-absolutes, albeit multidimensional ones. His arguments sometimes appear to aspire to the same kind of authoritative stature and finality as those he rejects. What I am suggesting is that to the extent praxialism is pragmatic, it says, in effect: "If you want to know what music is or what its value is, you must look at particular instances. There is not a single essential nature and value that transcends all place and time." Where praxialism tries to beat philosophical idealism and the aesthetic ideology at their own game, it risks becoming ensnared in the very discourses from which it wants to free us. As Audre Lorde (1984) has written, "The master's tools will never dismantle the master's house."[28]

My inclination is to play a different game: to concede relativism, contingency, and potential fallibility from the outset. That musics are historically, socially, and culturally emergent does not mean they do not exist or are unimportant. It only means that they are not the kind of things that have inherent meanings or "essences." To dismantle the house of the idealist master, we need different kinds of tools: tools crafted not so much to break the back of idealism as to work through and around it, as if it were the phantom it increasingly appears to be. We need to renounce colonial propensities in favor of more nomadic ones. And I believe praxialism holds considerable promise in this regard.

But I wonder whether praxialism, as a nonnormative orientation favoring description to prescription, is better suited to music philosophy than music education philosophy. Unlike music philosophy, educational philosophy is inescapably normative. It cannot be infinitely inclusive. One must choose for instance between the liberal ideal of breadth and the conservative ideal of depth: between the kind of knowledge that comes with diverse musical experiential roots and that which can only come from deep, sustained immersion in a particular practice. It is unlikely that music education can deliver both in the same program. Perhaps *music education* need not be multicultural in essence—even if it can be shown that *music* is. Perhaps multicultural music education is a more appropriate goal in some educational situations (or praxes) than it is in others. And perhaps praxialism is not the kind of philosophical orientation that yields unequivocal solutions to issues like this.

Among the most important points to be made here is that praxialism is not a club one joins, and having joined, finds one's most important educational decisions and choices already made. The temptation to become doctrinaire is as dangerous for those who favor praxial orientations as it has proven for the aesthetic. Philosophy grounded in praxial convictions is not a competitive sport, a matter of winning or losing, of getting things fully "right" or fully "wrong." Recognizing its potential advantages does not require that it provide definitive answers to all the problems music educators face. I have suggested, for instance, that praxialism logically implicates neither performance nor multiculturalism, and that there are a number of educational choices it seems ill designed to direct. However, this does not invalidate it or compromise its value as an orienting strategy. It only acknowledges that strict rules cannot govern decisions about what we should believe and what we should do—that "is" does not lead directly to "ought." Neither does it mean that arguments favoring musical performance or multiculturalism are wholly without merit, only that they may require different evidence than praxialism is inclined to provide. There may be, praxialism suggests, more than one reasonable choice, more than one reasonable way to proceed. In real-life human endeavors (whether philosophical or musical) strictly conclusive evidence is rare, and values, meanings, and practices are seldom so monolithic as to sustain only one view or set of choices.

If I am right in this, then perhaps we might agree that praxial convictions serve music education philosophy more as a heuristic tool than a set of answers. When I am doing a job around the house or working on the car, I sometimes seize whatever tool is close at hand, as long as it looks remotely suited to the job. I've been known to use a wrench as a hammer, for instance, or a screwdriver as a chisel. In some situations, I can get away with it; in others, it only makes a mess of things. But the wrench's limited utility as a hammer does not mean it is a bad wrench. It just means one would be well advised to bring along a toolbox when the task at hand looks complex and involved.

It appears to me that praxialism holds great promise for the reorientation of music philosophy in its determination to keep talk grounded in what people do and believe when they are musical together, thus steering a middle course between extremes such as the technical and the theoretical, or idealism and nihilism. Equally important is its open mindedness: its conviction that music is many things and serves many functions. The pluralistic account of music this implicates, its recognition and acceptance of the multiplicity and multidimensionality of musics, is a welcome contrast to the awkward essentialism and universalism in which music philosophy has long been encumbered.

This can cut both ways, though. For as praxialism broadens and extends the range of musically relevant concerns, it leaves unresolved questions about the limits and bounds of musical relevance. Is everything that has anything at all to do with music to some degree a praxial manifestation? Whose contexts will be acknowledged, and whose ignored? Is the idea of praxis catholic enough to accommodate the idea of music as a form of gendered discourse, an instrument of power, a weapon, a political and economic force, and a moral undertaking? In light of these questions it is interesting to consider Alperson's suggestions that a praxial orientation to music education might be more anthropological than philosophical in the traditional sense of the word, and interested as much in the development of human character as in music itself (whatever "music itself" might mean). These suggestions are interesting at least in part because they do not appear to emerge as salient features in Elliott's appropriation of praxialism for music education. My intent here is not to weigh the merits of their respective positions, but to show that issues of praxial range are difficult to resolve in a definitive way.

Lest these remarks seem overly obscure, let me make one final effort to point out the kinds of things musical praxialism offers to clarify. It does indeed deny the musical validity of disengaged, superficial listening, though arguably not all listening need be of this kind and performing is not necessarily the only solution to the problem. It rightly insists that doing music (musicing) is not a mindlessly executive affair, secondary in importance to other modes of musical praxis. However, neither does it establish performing's inherent superiority to other kinds of musical engagement. As well, it should probably enable us to see that MUSIC and actual musical practices are radically different kinds of things. MUSIC is an abstraction, a concept, a construct, whereas musical practices are always embedded in concrete sociocultural human interactions. Musical practices cannot be described or learned except by close attention to the full range of things that attend a practice. Praxialism acknowledges and values plurality, difference, and human agency and is properly suspicious of orientations that threaten to obscure them. It cautions us against taking the particular for the general, and is concerned about the potential for induction into musical practices (training) to obscure awareness of the plurality and multiplicity of such practices. Above all, it challenges us to assure that music teaching and learning are carried out in ways that are congruent with and sensitive to actual musical practices.

I would like to advance two further observations in closing. The first arises from the is-ought distinction to which I alluded earlier. I think it may be fairly said that Elliott's argument to multicultural music education is rationalistic in character, appealing more to a sense of intellectual or conceptual obligation to an ontological given (what MUSIC "is") than to a transformative vision rooted in moral convictions (what or who we "ought" to become). Compared to the moral alternative, this ontological and rationalistic approach seems coolly dispassionate. Multiculturalism is not about cultural multiplicity in some abstract, global sense, but about multiple concrete visions and ways of being alive and being present to each other. In this light it appears that Alperson's appeal to character development taps into something that Elliott's emphasis upon knowing may not, and something that Elliott's emphasis upon self-growth suggests obliquely rather than directly. The appeal to multicultural music education, I am suggesting, must be made in language that is visionary and inspirational rather than obligational. That is one way of interpreting this essay's epigrams. Multiculturalism can be either an exploitative or liberating affair, and it has been aptly observed that its growing acceptance may have at least as much to do with the economic forces of consumer capitalism as with intellectual ideals. The point is that multiculturalism as a music educational ideal should arise from concern about peoples and oppression and understanding and sharing, rather than upon an interest in knowing MUSIC adequately. And this is so, at least in part, because nobody anywhere can know MUSIC.[29] A concern for the world's musics and cultures must be motivated by a concern for its peoples.[30] I would like to think this is a plausible extension of praxial views.

I hasten to assert that my suggestion that praxial arguments are not sufficient to music education philosophy is not motivated by a desire to discredit praxial views or sustain aesthetic ones. Indeed, the aesthetic rationale is far guiltier than the praxial of segregating music education from moral and social concerns. It seems to me the praxial turn affords a significant opportunity to reconceptualize music education as something explicitly committed to moral growth and social transformation, a move that might well permit us to do something meaningful about the ever more marginal status of music education in today's schools and today's society. However, that will require that we acknowledge the moral, social, and political ramifications of what we do, and that we begin to address such concerns as the exploitation of people by media, capital, and culture industry; the transformation of music into commodities for exchange and consumption; and the treatment of people's musical doings as mere raw materials in a fundamentally materialistic enterprise. It will also require that we stop ignoring the musics that most directly embody and reflect the culture, values, and lives of real, everyday people. It will demand that we resist the temptation to abstract, global, utopian thinking, the kind of thought that spawns, supports, and is in turn reproduced by large impersonal institutions that can operate only by detaching themselves from the problems of real people in concrete circumstances.

My last point speaks yet again to the insufficiency of praxial philosophical convictions to a philosophy of music education, and from a perspective that is, though obvious, perhaps most challenging of all. Music education is not just about music, it is about students, and it is about teachers, and it is about the kind of societies we hope to build together. So while philosophy of music education needs to address the nature and value of music and what they might mean for the way music is taught, it must do much more. It must speak to the kind of people we hope to become *through* musical education. Determinations of this kind implicate careful consideration of moral and political issues, and of philosophy of education, concerns requiring conceptual and analytical tools other than those praxialism appears to offer.[31]

Notes

Thanks to Lori-Anne Dolloff for her helpful comments and suggestions on this manuscript.

1. For the account that follows I rely heavily upon Thomas McCarthy's (1978) exploration of Jürgen Habermas. After completing this essay in spring of 1996, I found that Thomas Regelski (1996) also explored these same issues in considerably more detail. Regelski has since published another extensive (and highly insightful) treatise on the subject (Regelski 1998).

2. "Or so its critics might argue," adds Alperson.

3. I explore these themes in Bowman (1998).

4. The essay is not intended as an exegesis on praxialism per se. Yet, as will become apparent, many of its basic predilections are praxial in orientation. Sparshott (1982) includes a classic critique of aesthetic theory.

5. Plato is among those who take this view.

6. The fact that conversation and music are both aurally mediated experiences that rely on many common neurological pathways is also noteworthy. The construal of music as metalinguistic cognitive activity (here I think of the work of Harold Fiske) is not far removed from this line of thought, though Sparshott himself makes no such claim.

7. As technology continues to shrink the globe, such opportunities for understanding and misunderstanding will inevitably increase, ever extending and challenging the ways people learn to live into alternative ways of musical being.

8. The fact that Sparshott does more to illuminate diversity of musical practice than its limits almost seems to suggest that, rigorously pursued to its logical conclusion, praxialism might even eventuate in a kind of particularism.

9. "Procedural knowing" in Elliott combines the idea of know-how or "adherence to procedure" employed by Gardner (see Elliott 1995, 53, for instance) with Schön's emphasis upon its processual, dynamic, temporally emergent character. Interestingly, Schön's distinction between procedural and formal knowing (ibid., 60) suggests that "procedures" be considered formal and static.

10. This position does not contest and should not be taken to contest the value of either instructional commitment. The sole reason for seeking to distinguish between necessary and contingent claims for praxialism is to reach a more adequate understanding of what its philosophical convictions entail.

11. On this point, Alperson's position seems to differ slightly from Elliott's. Alperson stresses the necessity for music education to transmit appreciation of the "nature and significance of the skills and productive human activity that bring musical works into being, if for no other reason than the fact that the results of human action cannot be adequately understood apart from the motives, intentions, and productive considerations of the agents who bring them into being" (1991, 236). The part I have italicized seems to leave open the possibility that there might be other reasons, and that such adequacy of understanding might be imparted by means other than highly skilled performance. Note that he does not explicitly suggest exclusive reliance upon the acquisition of performance skills, only that musical appreciation be informed by appreciation of the nature and significance of such skills.

12. These points are considered more extensively in the other essay I have contributed to this volume.

13. "The challenges involved in making music well are more complex than those involved in listening alone" (124).

14. Elliott draws his accounts of flow from Csikszentmihalyi (1990).

15. Note that "flow" bears a strong resemblance to many of the claims advanced by advocates of "aesthetic experience" over the years. Consider, for instance, Walker (1981).

16. Also quoted by Elliott, whereupon Elliott observes (ironically, in view of his claims to music's and music education's multicultural "essence"), "Musical breadth is not necessarily a virtue" (211).

17. Elliott is well aware of this, as evidenced by his insistence that music education should favor depth over breadth (134). But even this passage goes on to assert that since MUSIC consists in multiple practices, "music educators have a fundamental responsibility to induct children into a variety of practices."

18. Conventional categories such as listening and composing are only the most obvious. What I intend to imply by this suggestion of indeterminacy is that the range of potential musical modes of praxis is neither fixed nor static.

19. A further question demanding critical attention is how well the ideal of multiculturalism is served by multimusicality, since these ideas differ in important ways. Where music is not considered coextensive with culture per se, a multimusical education will not in and of itself be multicultural.

20. Musical cognition (musicianship) integrates procedural, formal, informal, impressionistic, and supervisory forms of knowing, says Elliott.

21. All musical works consist in (a) performances or interpretations of (b) musical designs that evince (c) standards and traditions of practice conveying (d) cultural or ideological information. Additionally, they may incorporate (e) expressions of emotion and (f) musical representations (cf. 199).

22. One interesting omission is a specifically corporeal or bodily dimension. It might be

further argued that the so-called cultural or ideological dimension generically designates a host of distinctive dimensions. What grounds can there be for suggesting that musical works consist in only these dimensions? Does calling a dimension "musical" design beg the question? Might musical practices be conceived that are not design based (that prioritize process to product, for instance)? Although these are vexing issues, the fact that construing music multidimensionally provokes them is clear evidence of its fruitfulness.

23. Alperson (1992) discusses, for instance, the idea of music as a decorative art. Recall as well Sparshott's suggestion that music be considered a conative art, an affective art, or a cognitive art—indeed, his highly provocative suggestion that some musical practices may not even be predominantly artlike.

24. There is irony, as we have seen, in the centrality a universal abstraction such as MUSIC seems to assume in Elliott's avowedly praxial orientation; for part of what is distinctive about praxis is its misgivings about theoretical abstraction. Is MUSIC indeed a "diverse human practice," or is it rather a theoretical construct of the kind that so pervades aesthetic accounts of music?

25. Unlike Alperson and Sparshott, Elliott seems to hold that the aesthetic orientation is not just defective or partial, but wholly unacceptable and totally wrong.

26. More accurately, Elliott attacks Bennett Reimer's particular version of the aesthetic doctrine.

27. What I am suggesting here is that at times it appears Elliott unwittingly helps perpetuate the tradition he wants to repudiate by accepting its vocabulary and frame of reference.

28. Though they might both be incensed at the suggestion, it sometimes appears that Elliott and Reimer occupy not so much different houses as different rooms in the same house. I do not intend this as criticism of Elliott but as a caution: opposites share a common ground. A more radical critical strategy would attempt to undercut the received frame of reference.

29. Here I have in mind Wendell Berry's point expressed in the epigram to this essay. That point is also made powerfully in Berry (1991b): "You can't think about what you don't know, and nobody knows this planet." Further yet: "You can't do a good act that is global. . . . . A good act has to be scaled and designed so that it fits harmoniously into the natural conditions and given of a particular time." These statements appear on p. 4.

30. Two unrelated parenthetical comments. First, such concerns ought to be directed not just toward the ethnic or the exotic (and the curious preoccupation with "authenticity" these interests inevitably spawn) but toward the many musics and peoples very close to home about which professional discourse in music education is disconcertingly silent. Second, it might be argued that Elliott's emphasis upon performance also suffers somewhat for its predominantly rationalistic (knowing or thinking) foundation, however laudatory its intentions may be.

31. An argument to performance might be expected to appeal to more of the bodily, the participatory, the playfulness, and the joy that seem to figure so centrally in people's musical experiences.

References

Alperson, P. 1987. Introduction: The philosophy of music. In P. Alperson, ed., *What is music?* New York: Haven Press.

———. 1991. "What should one expect of a philosophy of music education?" *Journal of Aesthetic Education* 25 (3):215–242.

———. 1992. The arts of music. *Journal of Aesthetics and Art Criticism* 50 (3): 217–230.

Berry, W. 1991a (February). Out of your car, off your horse. *Atlantic Monthly*, 61–63.

———. 1991b. Nobody loves this planet. *Context, 27*, 4.

Bowman, W. 1998. Universals, relativism, and music education. *Bulletin of the Council for Research in Music Education* 135:1–20.

Csikszentmihalyi, M. 1990. *Flow: The psychology of optimal experience*. New York: Harper and Row.

de Castell, S. 1995. Textuality and the designs of theory. In W. Kohli, ed., *Critical conversations in philosophy of education*. New York: Routledge.

Elliott, D. J. 1995. *Music matters: A new philosophy of music education*. New York: Oxford University Press.

Lorde, A. 1984. *Sister outsider*. Freedom, CA: Crossing Press.

McCarthy, T. 1978. *The critical theory of Jurgen Habermas*. Cambridge, MA: MIT Press.

Regelski, T. 1996. Prolegomenon to a praxial philosophy of music and music education. *Finnish Journal of Music Education* 1 (1):23–39.

———. 1998. The Aristotelian bases of praxis for music and music education as praxis. *Philosophy of Music Education Review* 6 (1):22–59.

Sparshott, F. 1982. Aesthetic this and aesthetic that. In Sparshott, F. *The theory of the arts*. Princeton, NJ: Princeton University Press, 467–486.

———. 1987. Aesthetics of music: Limits and grounds. In P. Alperson, ed., *What is music?* New York: Haven Press, 33–98.

Walker, E. 1981. Hedgehog theory and music education. In *Documentary report of the Ann Arbor symposium*, 317–328. Reston, VA: Music Educators' National Conference.

4

The Nature of Music
and Musical Works

CONSTANTIJN KOOPMAN

David Elliott's *Music Matters* constitutes a milestone in the progress of the philosophy of music education. He not only brings together a wealth of findings from musicology, philosophy, and psychology but, more important, he elaborates a new conception of the nature and value of music. In this chapter I analyze the structure of Elliott's conception. I discuss the most prominent characteristics of his views on the nature of music and musical works, and I evaluate their pros and cons.

Music as a Practice

Elliott (1995, 39–45) conceives music as "practices." Music is to be seen, in the first place, as an activity, as something people do. Central to musical practices are the activities of "musicing" (making music) and listening. Besides (1) musicing, the creative side of musical practices is constituted by the dimensions of (2) the agent, the "musicer"; (3) the thing achieved, the music; and (4) the entire context in which musicers operate. These four dimensions are complemented by four other dimensions of listening: (1) the doing of listening; (2) the listener; (3) "listenables" (i.e., sounds to be listened for); and (4) the context in which listening takes place.

Each of these eight dimensions involved in musical creation and musical reception can be approached from four viewpoints: (1) head-on, as the outcome of systematic action on its own; (2) in back, in terms of motivated action, (3) in front, as goal-directed action, and (4) around, as action in a context of similar actions (1995, 40–41). So, Elliott presents music as a complex phenomenon that depends on the interlocking activities of musicing and listening.

This view has great benefits. It provides a broad framework that in principle can accommodate every musical action or musical product within every tradition. Music, says Elliott (1995, 44–45), consists of a wide variety of *Musics*, or "musical practices," which all conform to the basic eight-part framework.

Elliott distinguishes between MUSIC (the overarching term for the world's many musical styles or practices); Music (one of these many specific practices that constitute MUSIC), and music (the sound events achieved in musical practices).

Thus, Elliott's framework is comprehensive; it is also flexible. Elliott's conception can deal with traditions that diverge widely with respect to their structure. Practices focusing on diverse functions (e.g., religious, social, or political) or on a specific dimension (e.g., musical works, the person of the musicer, or improvisation) all are studied fruitfully within the framework set out by Elliott. Therefore, Shusterman's (1992) positive evaluation of the conception of art, in general, as a practice, seems to fit quite well with Elliott's conceptual framework of MUSIC.

There is much truth in the view of art as a practice. Indeed, in terms of philosophy's traditional aims, the concept of art as historically defined sociocultural practices is probably as good as we can get. Because of its scope, flexibility, and potential art-historical substance, it seems to be the culmination of philosophy's attempt to theorize art by fully capturing the content of this concept and differentiating it from other things. In faithfully representing how art's objects and activities are identified, related, and collectively distinguished, it best realizes the dual definitional goals of accurate reflection and compartmental differentiation (Elliott 1995, 43).

However, the advantages of comprehensiveness and flexibility can be had only at the cost of serious limitations. In itself, Elliott's basic framework of the interlocking activities of musicing and listening is empty; it defines a number of dimensions of these activities but does not comprise a notion of what they consist in. What are the distinctive characteristics of engaging in musical activities? What values do these activities involve? Elliott's framework does not provide an answer to such questions. In other words, a substantive view of the nature of music is not included in Elliott's initial conception of music as a practice.

At this point the philosopher of music education who starts from a practice-based view faces a "trilemma." In view of the fact that music is an enormously diverse practice, what should one do? First, one might try to come up with a theory of music's nature covering all practices that constitute the diverse practice called MUSIC. While acknowledging the huge differences between practices, one could then attempt to define a core that can be found in every one of them.

Second, one might try to provide a substantial account of a single practice or a limited number of them. Holding to the view that no single account of the nature of music can satisfy all practices, but the question what music is can only be answered within the context of a specific practice, one tries to define the constitutive characteristics of a single practice or a group of related practices. Finally, one might give up completely the ambition of developing substantive theories of music, holding that even within individual practices there is no nature, essence, or set of constitutive characteristics to be fixed. Thus, one refrains from developing a substantive theory on the nature and value of music and contents oneself with analyzing and clarifying (parts of) specific musical practices.

The position Elliott takes with respect to this trilemma is not completely clear. When criticizing aesthetic conceptions of music, he suggests that there is no single way of responding to music and no single purpose or function valid for music all over the world (1995, 33). This points to the second or third path the trilemma offers. However, for the major part of his book Elliott follows the first path, developing a substantial theory of the diverse practice of MUSIC as whole.

Elliott's views on the nature of music and musical works have three major characteristics: it views music as an essentially cognitive activity, it heavily prefers musicing to "merely" listening, and it views a musical work as a multidimensional achievement rather than as an object.

In the next sections of my essay I analyze and evaluate these characteristics. It is important to note that the views I offer below are contingently related to Elliott's basic framework of the musical practice I summarized above. That is, Elliott's substantive views of the nature of music do not necessarily follow from his initial framework. They are one of a number of ways the empty shell presented by the praxial framework can be filled in. So, while his basic conception of music as a practice appears to be solid, this does not guarantee that his further ideas about the nature and value of music are equally compelling. They have to be assessed independently.

Music as Cognition: Knowledge-in-Action

Elliott's substantial view of music is dominated by the idea that music is essentially a cognitive activity. Key notions in his account are those of thinking-in-action and knowing-in-action. In Elliott's view, musicing and listening are not correctly viewed as activities in which mental thinking and physical action alternate rapidly, the mind guiding the activity of the body. Rejecting the dualist view that conceptualizes mind and body as two distinct entities, he holds that in music—as in many other activities— thinking and acting cannot be separated. Our thinking and knowing is in our very actions. Thinking does not proceed before or parallel to action, but it is realized in action itself. Thus, thinking and moving with the body are two aspects of one and the same activity.

Elliott complements his view of musicing and listening as knowing-in-action with an account of the various kinds of knowledge involved in musical activities (1995, 53–68; 96–101). *Procedural knowledge*, or knowledge-how, is by far the most important of the five categories he distinguishes. Musicianship and "listenership" (Elliott's term) are not a matter of verbal knowledge. Rather, they are to be characterized as procedural knowledge (or knowing-how) to make music musically and to listen musically. Central to music is the knowledge that enables one to act adequately when engaging in music. Propositional knowledge, or *formal knowledge* (as Elliott calls it), is only secondary. Facts, descriptions, and theories on music can guide musicing and listening. But music is not primarily a matter of dealing with musical concepts and facts; rather, it is about engaging in musical activities. Formal knowledge must be converted into procedural knowing-in-action if it is to be relevant to the core of music. Besides formal knowledge, three other kinds of knowledge "contribute to the procedural essence" of music making and listening: *informal knowledge*—the savvy or practical common sense developed by people who know "how to do things well in specific do-mains of practice"; *impressionistic knowledge*—intuitional knowledge of what counts in a particular musical situation; and *supervisory knowledge*—meta-knowledge that allows us to regulate our musical thinking.

The central place Elliott gives to the concepts of thinking/knowing-in-action and procedural knowledge are among the main assets of his philosophy. Until recently, philosophers of education, especially in the British tradition, have distinguished be-tween subjects that provide formal knowledge and those that develop limited skills in relation to a specific end or function. The term "education" is frequently reserved for school subjects that provide formal knowledge, the acquisition of skills being re-ferred to as training.[1] Education in the liberal tradition involves the development of a broad cognitive perspective by acquiring, digesting, and reflecting on diverse kinds of formal knowledge.

Music presents a hard case for the division between formal knowledge and train-ing. As a physical activity, making music would at first seem to belong to the domain of skills. But because of its status as one of the fine arts, it is assigned to liberal edu-cation rather than to training. Thus, music education is often focused on formal knowledge about music, the critic and the musicologist becoming the model for lib-eral music education. While listening to music becomes a means of acquiring a cog-nitive perspective on music, musicing conceived as a mere skill can disappear entirely.

With Elliott's philosophy we can go beyond intuitive doubts about this erroneous conception of music education. He points out that instead of being merely a "skill," musicing constitutes a highly intelligent activity—as does listening. The concept of knowing-in-action opens our eyes to the inadequacy of the simple distinction be-tween formal knowledge and skills. Music does offer a highly complex form of knowl-edge, but this knowledge is not to be found in the way we reflect on music; rather, it is manifested in the activities of musicing and listening. As Elliott's view allows us to see, the fact that (in music education) making and listening to music are more im-portant than abstract reflection is no reason to take music less seriously than other subjects. Like other subjects, music involves a complex set of knowings, but its na-ture differs crucially from other subjects where formal-verbal knowledge dominates.

Cognition and Value

Elliott's views about the value of music are based on the view that music is essentially cognition. In this he follows Csikszentmihalyi's theory of self-growth and optimal experience. According to Csikszentmihalyi, human beings have a fundamental drive to order and strengthen the self and gain self-knowledge. Taking up challenges that match and extend our powers of consciousness can allow us to attain these goals. When dealing successfully with cognitive challenges, information we receive from outside is congruent with our self-goals; this leads to an experience of intense enjoy-ment. Csikszentmihalyi refers to this phenomenon as "optimal experience" or "flow" (as cited by Elliott, 113–114). According to Elliott, music is a unique and important way of achieving the values of self-growth, self-understanding, and the concomitant values of optimal experience (enjoyment) and self-esteem. Dynamic musical prac-tices provide both necessary conditions for achieving continuous self-growth: multidimensional musical challenges of increasing complexity and the possibility of increasing levels of musicianship required to meet these challenges (121).

This view of the value of music is a cornerstone of Elliott's philosophy, as evidenced by its incorporation into his concept of music:

> *MUSIC is the diverse human practice of overtly and covertly constructing aural-temporal patterns for the primary (but not necessarily the exclusive) values of enjoyment, self-growth, and self-knowledge. These values arise when musicianship is sufficient to balance or match the cognitive challenges involved in making and/or listening for aural patterns regarded significantly, but never exclusively, as audible designs.* (128; italics in original)

Elliott's account of value certainly has something to recommend itself. It captures several characteristics of musical practices in which people continuously aim at improving their musicianship. Intense concentration, a feeling of buoyant satisfaction, and loss of self-conscience are indeed major features of rewarding musical experiences. However, as a general explanation of the specific value(s) of music, Elliott's account is unconvincing for several reasons.

One of the first points is that whereas Elliott repeatedly contends that musical engagement promotes the prestigious value of self-knowledge, he fails to substantiate this claim. What he provides is essentially a psychological account about the conditions under which the self expands and is strengthened. Elliott suggests that there is a logical connection between self-growth and self-knowledge, in the sense that the first entails the second. But there is reason to doubt this connection. Self-knowledge is the possible outcome of self-conscious reflection on one's acting within a practice, rather than an automatic result of action itself. People may be very successful artists or scientists while demonstrating a remarkable lack of self-knowledge. Moreover, it seems that self-knowledge is as likely to result from our unsuccessful actions as from our successful ones. Therefore, there is no reason to link self-knowledge to the challenging activities described by Csikszentmihalyi. On the contrary, there is reason to think the opposite. Elliott states that a salient feature of the optimal experience resulting from these activities is the loss of self-consciousness. This suggests that challenging musical activities hinder rather than stimulate self-knowledge.

A second point is that Elliott's theory covers only a limited number of musical practices and cannot therefore be considered a general theory of musical value. Most musical practices do not seem to center around the kind of significant challenges Elliott has in mind. Listening to music, singing in a choir, or playing an instrument—all these can be very worthwhile without testing our musical capacities seriously. To be sure, music is always a form of cognition so complex that we are only beginning to understand its many dimensions. But this does not imply that musical activities always or even in a majority of cases involve the type of cognitive challenges explained by Csikszentmihalyi's theory. As with other highly complex activities, such as orienting oneself within an unknown environment or formulating correct sentences, people are able to listen or make music without having to perform at the limits of their capacities. Thus, the scope of Elliott's theory appears to be much smaller than he suggests; it seems to include only those musical practices in which musicians continuously work at developing their musicianship.

In the third place, there is no reason to believe that the enjoyment one derives from musical activities is exclusively or even primarily a function of the magnitude of the cognitive challenge they involve. To make the best of some mediocre work written in a complicated idiom may present a musician with a formidable challenge, but is there any guarantee that a successful performance of it will give him more satisfaction than a new rendition of an absolute masterpiece he has had on his repertoire for many years? Even in the case of highly demanding musical practices, value derives in the first place from the nature of that in which one is being engaged, rather than the way one is being engaged in it. That is, the values of music are to be found primarily in the nature of dwelling and acting in the world of sound, rather than in one's functioning at the height of one's cognitive capacities when doing so.

This leads to the central problem of Elliott's position: its failure to mark out music as a practice with a distinctive value. According to Csikszentmihalyi's theory, every practice involving progressive challenges can yield the values of self-growth, self-knowledge, and enjoyment. If so, why engage in music and teach it at school? If the same values can be had by climbing a mountain, playing tennis, doing science, or doing meditation exercises, what is left of the special status of music? Elliott counters that music is a unique kind of cognition, consisting of the construction of aural-temporal patterns and involving six dimensions (see the section entitled "Cognition and Feeling"). But his argument misses the mark. For according to his explanation, it is not as a specific type of cognition but as a cognitive challenge that music has its value. In other words, the fact that music is a unique kind of cognition is not relevant to the theory of value endorsed by Elliott. The theory is simply too crude to present an answer to the question why musical practices rather than all other kinds deserve a special place in our lives. If we want to explain the distinctive values of music, we should inquire more precisely into the characteristics that make music unique, or at least special, and we should try to establish which particular goods they bring about.

In summary, Elliott's theory of musical value faces a number of serious criticisms. Apart from the fact that his claim that music provides self-knowledge is unwarranted, Elliott's account is by far not as inclusive as he takes it to be. It applies only to a limited number of practices in which people act at the limits of their musical abilities. The conception of cognitively challenging practices may provide a model for some kinds of music education, but it does not lead to a global account of the values of music as a diverse practice.

Again, Elliott fails to establish a distinctive value for music. The values he takes music to provide can be found in a large number of other activities. Elliott looks for value at the wrong place. The distinctive values of music are to be discovered in the specific characteristics of music itself, rather than in its presenting cognitive challenges.

Cognition and Feeling

Another limitation of Elliott's cognitive conception of music—which is also related to his unsatisfactory explanation of musical value—is his disregard of the role of feeling in music. The only kind of feeling that features in his theory of the nature of music is the enjoyment gained by performing successfully in cognitively challenging musical practices. This account can do no justice to the richness, both qualitatively and quantitatively, of feeling in music.

Let me first make clear that feeling, as I use the term, is not to be equated with emotion. The latter notion involves the presence of some cognitive content. If I am sad, I am sad about something, for instance the death of my dog. And if I am so, I know that my dog is dead. In general, to be sad entails one's having a cognitive awareness of some adversary state of affairs. An emotion may be said to have a cognitive component and a feeling component.[2] Feeling is a much broader concept. It comprises the whole range of our subjective awareness. Without embracing Susan Langer's (1957) view of the role of feeling in music, we may adopt her definition of feeling as "everything that can be felt" (15). Although this definition is, of course, circular, it has the advantage of taking into account the broad variety of phenomena the notion of feeling can cover; it does not restrict the notion in advance to, for example, bodily sensations. Feeling includes awareness of tension and release, smoothness, surprise, satisfaction, uneasiness, balance, harmony, closure, chills, and so on. Furthermore, it includes countless other subjective phenomena we have not given names. Feelings can be (but need not be) incorporated into emotions. Whereas emotions emerge occasionally, feeling goes on all the time. Thus, from the fact that the expression of distinct emotions is often absent from music, it does not follow that feeling plays only a modest part in it.

On the contrary, feeling is vital to musical engagement in several ways. First, it plays a crucial role in cognizing musical form. Constructing musical patterns is not simply a matter of "cold" cognition but, as an increasing number of scholars are beginning to acknowledge, is accompanied and informed by feeling. Availing herself of the findings of prominent theorists like Goodman, Dewey, Arnheim, Langer, and Dufrenne, Stokes (1994) argues that at least eleven cognitive processes operate in art on the basis of feeling. Feeling plays an indispensable part in the perceptional processes of discrimination, comparison, classification, abstraction and weighting, in the formation of schemata or percepts, and in processes of musical understanding such as problem setting and solving, synthesis, judgment, intuition, and interpretation. Thus, feeling is not merely the passive aspect of musical experience, but plays an active role.

However, feeling is not merely instrumental to grasping musical form, expression, and representation. It is also a good in itself. The enormous variety of feelings we go through when musicing or listening accounts for a major part of music's value. While in everyday life our feelings come and go in a haphazard way, in music our feelings are organized in systematic ways. One of the greatest assets of listening to or performing a great piece of music is the way feelings are developed in cogent ways from moment to moment. Different kinds of feelings are carefully balanced; climaxes and episodes of repose are brilliantly structured. Engaging in music is somewhat like undertaking a well-organized journey through a marvelous country: we have a wealth of both cognitive and feeling experiences, brilliantly attuned to each other.[3] Moreover, feelings are not merely juxtaposed like static entities, but are continuously in a process of transformation. One kind of feeling grows out of another, which in turn develops into a third kind of feeling, and so on. We can say that a musical composition is not merely a composition of sound structures; it is also a composition of feeling responses as well as cognitive responses. In organizing sound, the composer also organizes a complex experience available to anyone who listens carefully and who has the appropriate cultural background. Structured sound and structured experience are two sides of the same coin.

Feeling always features in our musical experience. This is the case even with music that tries to break away from it. As a reaction to romantic and postromantic expressionism, leading composers of the twentieth century such as Stockhausen, Boulez, and Xenakis have tried to expel every consideration of emotion and feeling in general from their compositions. But even in this "objectified" music, feeling has not been extinguished. Though, clearly, such music does not express or invoke specific emotions, when listening to it one cannot help developing feelings like those of roughness and smoothness, spaciousness and narrowness, friendliness and hostility, tension and release. Feeling, it seems, cannot be banned from music. As Malcolm Ross (1984) succinctly puts it: "Sensuous forms make us feel" (75). Feeling occurs naturally as we perceive sound structures. Engaging in music is always a response in which cognition and feeling go together and inform each other.

The role of feeling in music is so crucial that it cannot be omitted from a well-balanced theory of music's nature. An adequate understanding of feeling also presents a precondition of an adequate account of music's values. In a brilliant essay on the value of listening to music expressive of negative emotions, Levinson (1990, 322ff.) distinguishes no fewer than eight rewards: apprehending expression, emotional catharsis, savoring feeling, understanding feeling, emotional assurance, emotional resolution, expressive potency, and emotional communion. These rewards are not specific to negative emotional responses to music. With the possible exception of emotional catharsis, all of them can just as well be said to apply to music expressive of positive emotions and emotions to which the positive-negative distinction is irrelevant. More importantly, claims about savoring feeling, understanding feeling, reassurance about our feeling capacities, a sense of resolution (i.e., mastery and control) and potency with regard to these capacities, and a sense of communion of feeling (as the result of our empathetic response to music) can be applied to all sorts of music that do not express any specific emotion.

A full theory of the nature and value of music should give both cognition and feeling and their complex interrelationships their full due. In this respect Elliott's conception of the nature of music is incomplete. Whereas his account of the cognitive side of music is strong and detailed, feeling is neglected.

Music as a Performance Art

Many music educators treat musicing and listening as equally important activities. However, Elliott strongly favors musicing, particularly performing. In his view, listening is an independent activity that should be allowed at most a marginal place in music education. He gives three kinds of arguments for putting performance at the center. First, he repeatedly states that music is a performance art. Music is an interpretive and social art in which "people join together in the communal and ritual actions of listening, watching, and participating empathetically as music makers bring forth unique musical events and experiences." Merely listening to music, especially recorded music, leads to the illusion that music is a collection of autonomous sounds alone. It promotes the erroneous view that music is a collection of objects to be consumed asocially (1995, 102–103). Second, Elliott argues that listening is inferior to performance. Whereas performing engages the whole person, listening anesthetizes part of the self (1995, 103). Instead of developing the mind, it leads to passive consumption of musical works. However, there is another, active type of listening, which is a part of performing. The expert musician's listening know-how is completely embedded in his singing or playing. Thus, listening and musicing are intimately related and listenership and musicianship are two sides of the same coin (103).

This leads to the third argument: listening can and should be trained in conjunction with musicing. The best preparation for listening is full participation as a performer in musical practices. Moreover, the level of students' musicianship is manifested most clearly in their performance activities. Answers given to verbal questions after listening sessions yield a far less reliable picture.

To assess Elliott's first argument—that music is a performance art—we need to distinguish three different claims: that in order to be fully realized music must be performed (somewhere, somehow); that music *is* in fact a social art that centers around performing; and that music *ought to be* a social, participatory art.

Although the first claim applies to the overwhelming majority of musical practices, we should be aware that there are also genres of music that do not feature musical performance. Computer music is the most prominent of these. By manipulating sound processors, composers can create definitive musical works without the intercession of any performer. Another, more controversial kind of nonperformed music is found sound, of which Stan Godlovitch (1998, 112ff.) identifies two types. With ambient found sound, a composer designates sounds emanating from the environment as music. With prepared found sound, a particular arrangement is made that leads to sound events. For example, in his *Drip Music*, George Brecht requires an empty vessel to be put beneath a source of dripping water. Although there is a causal linkage between the person who makes such an arrangement and the sounds that result from it, he or she is obviously not the performer of the sounds.

If we now turn to the second claim and ignore the rather atypical cases in which music does not get performed at all, there is no doubt that many musical practices, though performance-based, do not center around the very activity of musicing at all. In present-day society, music is not usually an activity in which people participate by performing. Most music we encounter comes to us via mass media: radio, television, the CD player, and so on. Indeed, as Adorno (1932/1978) observed, music in our society has often had the status of a commodity. Music is something that is always readily available in our society. Often the fact that a group of musicians once came together in order to perform a work and have it recorded has completely faded into the background. The sounds have indeed acquired an existence independent from the act of performance. Elliott suggests that only direct participatory musical practices are real and that musical practices in which music is consumed as a quasi-object rest on an illusion. But there is no good reason whatsoever for thinking this. Ontologically, listening to prefabricated music is as real as engaging in a performance happening.

In holding that music *is* a performance practice, Elliott suggests that, in spite of its many varieties, music has a timeless essence as a performance-centered practice. But because contemporary musical practices show that there is no such essence, his point is better interpreted in terms of the third claim: music *ought to be* a social, participatory art. Elliott's statement about music as a performance practice cannot be sustained as a descriptive claim about the actual nature of music as a diverse practice, but it might be defended as an evaluative claim about what is most worthwhile in musical engagement.

Thus, we arrive at his second argument, that performing is far superior to listening as a self-sufficient activity. Indeed, a plain comparison between the two activities leads to the conclusion that performing is generally more rewarding than listening. Making music is a richer, more intense experience. Although this is an empirical fact, it is not easy to give a full explanation of why this is the case. Among other things, it has to do with the satisfaction of expressing oneself, the integration of creating and perceiving (and feeling) what one creates—as opposed to merely perceiving—and the autotelic experience described by Csikszentmihalyi. However, Elliott's claim that, while performance partakes of the whole self, listening anesthetizes part of it, is grossly overstated. Listening (even listening to records) can be a holistic experience in its own right. When we are absorbed in a masterwork, we use all our mental and bodily faculties: cognition, feeling, and motor systems equally contribute to a unified response.

Elliott's suggestion that listening to records automatically leads to passivity is therefore unwarranted. It ignores the practices of music lovers who attend to recorded music with deep concentration and derive an immense satisfaction from this. Besides, Elliott tends, in arguing for a monopoly for musicing, to create a false dilemma between listening to records and active performance. When attending concerts or more informal occasions of musical performance, listeners are in direct contact with the performers and can get a good sense of the performance acts. Elliott rightly points out that a number of aspects of a music (e.g., the relationships between the movements of performers and their production of the music) can only be known by those who have performed (1995, 174–175). But his suggestion that listening to music is analogous to watching the moves of a chess game while not knowing the game can hardly be meant seriously. Experienced listeners *do* know the musical game. In spite of all the differences between performing and listening, these activities share the most important thing: the experience of dwelling in the world of sounds. Thus, listening is a fully realized form of musical engagement, not merely an ersatz kind of musicing.

This leaves Elliott's position that performance is usually richer and more intense, and thus preferable to listening, practically unaffected. However, we now come to a number of benefits that belong exclusively to listening. We have a much wider scope and are much more flexible as listeners than we are as performers. In some genres, such as computer music and found sound, we can only relate as a listener, never as a performer. Furthermore, if we restrict ourselves to performance-based music, it is clear that the quantity of musical works we are able to listen to in our life is many times larger than the number of works we will ever be able to perform. As performers we are subject to several limitations. In the first place, we can become proficient in only a limited number of styles. Reaching the performance level required for playing pieces common to a particular kind of repertoire costs the average musician several years. Each new piece can be acquired only by time-consuming practice, and, once we have mastered the piece, we usually have to continue rehearsing it if we want to retain the appropriate level of execution. Besides, there is the problem of virtuosity. For many musicians, amateurs and professionals alike, large parts of the repertoire remain beyond reach because of the heavy demands they make on the performer's technique.

The listener is much more flexible. The musical enthusiast can easily familiarize himself with a wide variety of traditions: classical, avant-garde, pop, jazz, and non-Western (e.g., Indonesian gamelan, Indian raga, or pygmy polyphony). Within these traditions he or she can focus on various genres. The fact that different traditions and genres use different instruments and different techniques poses no problems to listeners. Virtuosity causes listeners no worries; rather, virtuosity provides an additional source of musical enjoyment. Clearly, the freedom and scope that listeners have—in comparison to people who approach music only as performers—is tremendous.

But also within the limits of one particular tradition, listeners have opportunities not available to performers. When attending to complex works, listeners can freely divide their attention among the various parts. Performers must concentrate maximally on the individual parts for which they are responsible. If a performer is a good musician, he or she will, of course, listen to other parts; but performers are not in a position to divide their attention as they wish. Therefore, listeners have a better view of the work as a whole.

It now becomes clear that Elliott's third argument in favor of performing—that listening is best learned through performing—is only partly true. Surely, performing usually involves a high level of concentrated listening that is never guaranteed in listening activities. And certainly, performing leads the pupil to become aware of many aspects the listener is likely to pick up much less easily. But performing music cannot possibly teach us to listen to music in a way in which we freely divide our attention among the various parts and the way each of them contributes to the whole. And given the limited time the music educator has, listening is the most effective way of coming to know a wide variety of traditions, styles, and genres.

In view of the fact that the majority of music in present-day Western society is made to be listened to, instead of being performed, teaching pupils to become critical listeners is a major task of music education. Music education cannot ignore the present situation, in which music is constantly being poured out upon us, and shut itself up in idealized musical practices in which music is performed for its own sake or, in Elliott's words, for the sake of self. Music educators should prepare their pupils to deal effectively with their sound environment. Educators should protect students from getting benumbed by the continuous presence of musical noise in everyday life, make them aware of the multifarious uses and misuses of music, and provide them with strategies for selecting fine music and saving it from becoming trivialized.

In sum, Elliott's philosophy rightly emphasizes the fact that musicing (especially performing) and listening are not just two similar ways of relating to music. He correctly argues that performing music is usually more rewarding and that performing should be given plenty of room in music education. However, he erroneously denies listening (as a separate activity) any significant part in the classroom. In doing so, he ignores two facts: that in Western society, dominated as it is by mass media, listening is a prominent way (if not the most prominent way) of relating to music; and that teaching pupils to become critical listeners—listeners who are able effectively to se-

lect and deal with the valuable part of the tremendous supply of music in Western society, but also know how to resist the large supply of music that is worthless or potentially harmful—cannot be done by having them perform within a limited number
of practices.

The Musical Work

Opposing what he considers to be the "aesthetic" conception of the musical work, Elliott works out an alternative theory. He holds that the aesthetic conception of the musical work suffers from two serious mistakes: it views the musical work as an ideal
object, and it considers musical structure (i.e., musical form) to be the only significant dimension.

In Elliott's alternative conception, a musical work is an achievement, rather than
an object, and it features as many as six dimensions. Besides form, the aspects of performance-interpretation, standards and traditions of practice, expression, representation, and cultural-ideological information are vital to fully appreciating a musical work.

The problem with Elliott's alternative conception of the musical object is that it
fails to solve the ontological problem of what kind of entity a musical work is. What
does it mean to say that a musical work is an achievement? Elliott's small passage on
the ontology of musical works (1995, 201) sheds no light on this question. On the
contrary, in this passage he intermingles questions about definition—what characteristics are essential to (or, alternatively, constitutive of, or definitive of) a musical
work?—and questions about ontology—which mode of existence does the musical
work have? Without distinguishing between these two different kinds of questions,
he alternates ontological statements (that the musical work is neither an object nor a
score) with the rather definitional propositions that six dimensions make up the
essence of a musical work and that the essence of music is not to be found in a special relationship between musical sounds and time.

To be sure, philosophers in past decades have come to realize that questions of
ontology and definition are interrelated in complex ways. This does not mean, however, that these two kinds of questions can simply be lumped together. Therefore, the
question remains: if music is to be defined as an achievement featuring six dimensions (definition), what kind of entity is it (ontology)?

Much more convincing is Elliott's concept of the six dimensions of musical
meaning in a musical work. This is, indeed, one of the major contributions his book
offers to the philosophy of music education. Elliott rightly dismisses the view of aesthetic educators, such as Bennett Reimer (1989), who claim that musical form is the
only relevant dimension and that responding to expression and representation (i.e.,
hearing musical patterns as being expressive of emotions and ideas) is nonmusical.
Because attending to content can contribute significantly to one's appreciation of the
music *qua* music, there is no reason for denying the expressiveness and representation of the status of musical experience. Elliott's succinct discussion of the dominant
views of expressiveness and representation presents an excellent introduction for
those who are not at home in the field. The same goes for his survey of cultural-

ideological information. All in all, Elliott's viewpoint appears to take into account all relevant aspects of a musical work:

- the intramusical aspect: properties of musical "design" or structural elements;
- the intermusical aspect: "standards and traditions of practice" wherein a musical piece embodies specific style features and, therefore, its relation to other authoritative works in its style tradition;
- the extramusical or referential aspect: the relationship musical form establishes with phenomena beyond the so-called purely musical realm through expression of emotions and representations;
- the contextual aspect: the cultural-ideological import a musical work manifests by virtue of being created in a particular society, place, historical time, and so forth.

However, we may ask whether another dimension, which Elliott calls "performance-interpretation," should be viewed as a part of the meaning of a musical work. By posing this question I do not mean to underplay the importance of performance. The issue is purely conceptual: should a concept of the "musical work" be taken to include a particular performance-interpretation as one of its dimensions, or should we conceptualize a musical work and a specific performance-interpretation of that work as separate but related entities?

In contrast to Elliott's view, the latter view seems preferable, at least for a majority of musical works. Usually we make a distinction between a musical work that outlives a number of performances and a particular interpretation of the work. This is clear with works in the classical tradition. For example, we distinguish between Ravel's *Bolero* and the many performances that have sounded and been recorded of this magnificent musical work. The very fact that we speak of various performances of the same composition testifies that a single performance should not be conceptualized as a dimension of the musical work. This is not to say that performance is irrelevant to the concept of the musical work. Indeed, as Levinson (1990, 73ff.) argues, specific means of performance or sound production are integral to them. The character of a musical composition is, in part, a function of how its sound structure relates to the potentialities of a certain instrument or set of instruments designated to produce that structure for audition. Furthermore, our conception of a musical work is influenced by the performance traditions that have developed with regard to this work and similar compositions. For instance, "authentic" performance traditions making use of period instruments have significantly changed our understanding of many baroque and classical works.

In contrast, Elliott suggests that a *single* performance is a constitutive dimension of a musical work. This would mean that a new musical work comes into existence every time the score of the *Bolero* is performed. Clearly, this runs counter to our linguistic habits; traditionally, we make a distinction between a musical work and a specific realization of that work . This is the case not only with classical music but also with pop music, folk songs, national anthems, dance music, religious chant, and so on. While these kinds of works are usually not so strictly codified as works in the classical tradition, Levinson (1990) suggests that there is still a specific sound structure, often in conjunction with a specific performance-means structure, that remains relatively stable through various performances. Only in the case of free improvisation (e.g., some kinds of jazz) is it difficult or impossible to separate a performance from the work. But even with jazz, successful performances may often lead to the crystallization of a global sound-and-performance-means structure that is realized several times.

Therefore, for reasons of clarity, it is better to distinguish between a work and a performance of a work than to conceptualize a performance as a dimension of the work. In many cases we cannot dispense with the distinction between a performance and that which transcends a specific performance—that is, the work. In the case of freely improvised music, we could simply speak of an improvisation or an achievement. If so desired, one could also refer to the product of the improvisation as a work or piece in a secondary sense of the term, which includes the performance. But this should not lead us to ignore, as Elliott does, the more usual sense of "work," which does not comprise a particular performance as one of its constitutive aspects.

Another point I wish to raise with respect to Elliott's five other dimensions of musical meaning—design, expression, representation, standards of practice, and cultural-ideological meaning—is that these do not all operate at the same level of musical experience. When absorbed in a musical work as listeners or music makers, we immediately respond to the formal, expressive, and representational features of a musical work: that is, we are directly aware of the characteristics of musical design, the expressive content, and also (to a certain extent) the representational content of a piece. However, this is not the case with "standards and tradition of practice" and "cultural-ideological information." While these two dimensions are vital to a comprehensive understanding of a musical work, they do not feature in our phenomenologically immediate experience of a musical work. It is only through reflection upon the practice that they come to the fore.

Let me make clear what I do and do not mean by the phrase "phenomenologically immediate experience." When saying that musical experience has an immediate character, one does not have to deny that all musical experience is mediated by culture-specific beliefs and experiences. But from a phenomenological viewpoint, when we are absorbed in musical sound structures, our experience is characterized by a sense of immediacy. We have a direct experience of musical form and its emotional or representational content, without our being aware of our culture-specific beliefs. Since it is this phenomenologically direct experience, rather than conscious reflection, in which the principal rewards and values of music reside, it is important to single out the dimensions that feature in this experience. These dimensions— musical form, expression, and representation—should constitute the focus of the concerns of music educators. It is by developing a sensitivity toward them that our ability to experience music deeply is being promoted.

Understanding of standards and traditions of practice and of cultural-ideological information is secondary from the perspective of value. Knowing about standards and tradition is crucial if one is to participate successfully in a musical practice. But dealing with such knowledge is not a goal in itself. Rather, its value resides in the fact that it contributes to our becoming a competent listener or musicer and thus to our ability to have satisfying musical experiences.

The relationship of cultural-ideological information to musical experience is a very interesting one. This information functions in two ways. First, musicologists can study the ways in which "the nature of a musical work" has been determined by a particular society. Elliott gives various examples of these, including the social and cultural background and implications of Bach's oeuvre (1995, 186–188). However, as interesting as these studies may be, their consequences for musical experience are limited. Consider the fact that Mozart composed his Symphony No. 36 in C Major K. 425 "Linz" because he had no earlier symphony at hand for the concert he gave in Linz in 1783. Does knowing this really affect the way we engage with this piece? Does knowing that Beethoven dedicated most of his works to Viennese noblemen make me appreciate more fully the quality of his oeuvre? Cultural-ideological information contributes to our musicological understanding of music rather than to the quality of our direct musical experience.

But at another level—the level of value—cultural-ideological meanings can indeed deeply affect our attitude toward and hence our experiences with musical styles. For those sensitive to this dimension, each style evinces a specific pattern of values that they may find attractive or repellent. According to such evaluations, one's ability to respond openly to music is likely to be facilitated or impeded. Often the affirmation or rejection of a musical style operates unconsciously. For instance, someone with a working-class background may feel uncomfortable when confronted with classical music. He may feel that this is not music for him and consequently refrain from giving attention to it. Music educators cannot remain passive when their pupils try to evade certain traditions or styles. Though it is not precisely known how strong the barriers of cultural-ideological meanings can be, they should do as much as they can to level them. We cannot remain indifferent to the fact that different groups in our society tend to cling to their own musical traditions. Only if we succeed in liberating musical appreciation from narrow ideological constraints will multicultural music education have any chance of success. In our society, education's success depends on whether it is able to integrate individuals from different cultural backgrounds. Here music education is of vital importance, because it is precisely the power of music that it can unite people of different groups in a smooth way.

The most important point is that constructing cultural-ideological meanings—just like dealing with knowledge about standards and traditions of practice—is not the core value of musical practices. The heart of musical practices is focusing on musical engagement for its own sake, rather than serving some purpose beyond music; it is the phenomenologically direct experience in which we recognize and feel a particular musical form with (possibly) an expressive or a representative content. Thus, there is a difference, with respect to both status and value, between the dimensions of design (form), expression, and representation, on the one hand, and cultural-ideological information and standards and traditions of practice, on the other.

Next, we can assess the differences among the dimensions of design, expression, and representation. Although musical form is the substance of the musical work, expression and representation are embodied in form. Thus, musical form is a necessary condition for the existence of musical experience, but expression and representation may be (and often are) absent from musical works, as Elliott also observes. And though expression often puts a strong mark on musical works, music's power to represent phenomena is relatively poor. Thus, it is understandable (though not entirely correct) that Levinson (1998, 99ff.) relates the value of musical works to the dimensions of form and expressive content, while leaving out representational content.

So, although musical structure, expression, representation, standards and traditions of practice, and cultural-ideological information are all relevant dimensions of a musical work, we should not put them all in one box. There are important differences with respect to their status and the extent to which they contribute to the value of music. Elaborating on Elliott's conception of musical dimensions, we should study these differences more thoroughly, so that we can give each of them its appropriate weight in music education.

Conclusion: The Claim to Universality

Elliott's account of the nature of music and musical works constitutes a most valuable contribution to the philosophy of music education. It provides a fine analysis of a number of core concepts in music, particularly music as musical practices, the musical work, listening, musicing, and musical knowledge.

Because discourse in the philosophy of music education is better served by exploring problematic issues than by merely repeating the strengths of current theories, I have given much attention to discussing the issues I did not find resolved satisfactorily in Elliott's philosophy. In the preceding paragraphs I questioned Elliott's cognitive account of musical value, his exclusive focus on cognition at the cost of feeling, his neglect of listening as an independent way of engaging in music, and the inclusion of performance in his otherwise lucid conception of the musical work.

To conclude my discussion, I will comment briefly on the claim to universality that Elliott makes for his philosophy. Does Elliott's conception of the nature and value of music and musical works do justice to the diverse practice of MUSIC as a whole? There is no unequivocal answer to this question. As I said at the beginning of this essay, Elliott's basic conception of music as a practice, which centers on musicing and listening, appears to be universally valid, indeed. Music is always an activity that entails the action and interaction of a group of humans. As Christopher Small (1998) shows, even the solitary herdsman who plays his flute at night is related in multiple ways to and is, in fact, a part of the musical practices of the cultural group in which he grew up.

Furthermore, Elliott's account of music as knowing-in-action, and of five dimensions of musical knowledge, may very well have universal validity. Any kind of musicing or listening in whatever practice appears to center around knowledge that is embodied in action. And besides procedural knowledge, the types of knowing he calls formal, informal, impressionistic, and supervisory are likely to feature in every practice.

As with knowledge, a general account of the role of feeling in musical experience—which, unfortunately, does not feature in Elliott's philosophy—may have considerable claims to universal validity. It seems to be a general fact about music that sensuous forms make us feel, as I mentioned earlier, and, together with musical cognition, these feeling responses are constitutive of our musical experience.

However, it should be stressed that questions about whether a theory of some aspect of music can be universally valid are empirical ones that can be solved only by gathering data from musical practices in all sorts of cultures around the world.

However, one need not have much ethnomusicological expertise to see that Elliott's conception of music exhibits a number of characteristics that are definitely not universal: music is seen as a practice centering around cognitive challenges, as aiming at expert performance, as having no function beyond musicing itself, and as being valuable to the individual (in terms of self-growth, self-understanding, and autotelic experience), rather than to the social group.

Whereas Elliott's conceptions of music as social practices and musical cognition appear to have universal import, his philosophy as a whole is best considered a philosophy of musical practice in the Western world. There is nothing wrong with this. Indeed, it is questionable whether a philosophy of music education is possible that, on the one hand, is universally valid and, on the other hand, is sufficiently specific to allow effective pedagogical action. Musical practices around the world are so diverse with respect to their uses, functions, and values, as well as their specific ways of musicing and listening, that a comprehensive theory of musical practice intending to go beyond the most general level seems doomed to endless enumeration.

In restricting oneself to Western culture, one can put aside many specific functions and values of music that are not current in present-day Western society (e.g., worshipping ancestors, celebrating the harvest, healing physical injuries) and concentrate on the still enormously diverse practices that are prominent in our society. This does not mean excluding multicultural practices. We should keep in mind, however, that multicultural approaches to music are a typically Western phenomenon. First, in many cultures and cultural groups, the value of multicultural engagement is absent. Second, when dealing with music from other cultures, we adapt it to our own Western purposes. Often, we do not use music in the same way as people do who belong to a specific culture. We engage in it to enjoy it for its own sake, to learn about other cultures, or to broaden our horizons.

There is no point in blaming philosophies of music education for not having universal validity. Why should a philosophy of music education be valid in Laos, Ghana, and Bolivia, as well as in Europe and North America? If we are able to devise a philosophy that is suitable for educating children (and adults) in an open, Western society, then we have done a great job. I think David Elliott has made a splendid contribution toward attaining such a philosophy.

Postlude: Implications for Educational Practice

From the above discussion we can derive various suggestions for adjusting the practice of music education as envisaged by Elliott. First, music education should not place all its bets on practicums. Though they are crucial to the development of pupils' abilities to make music, an exclusive focus on practicums fails to do justice to the diversity of musical roles one can take nowadays. As I stated previously, listening as a self-sufficient activity has important advantages over musicing: it allows for an end-lessly broader musical scope and for more freedom in attending to the various parts of complex works. Because of this, listening—as an active and independent way of relating to music—deserves a substantial place in the music curriculum. Besides ig-noring the values of listening per se, a curriculum focusing exclusively on practicums closes the pupil off from the outside world. Music education should be open to the many uses and misuses of music in contemporary society. This means that students should learn how to deal with music in multiple situations. Stimulating pupils to be-come critical musical agents is one of the music educator's major tasks.

A second suggestion for broadening the scope of the music curriculum is not to lay the emphasis so strongly on music as a cognitive challenge. Music educators should bring music to life in all its richness and versatility. This means that, apart from focusing on cognitive tasks, music educators should give ample room to such prominent aspects as play and feeling.

More than any of the other art forms, music is an art of play. This applies to acts of both composing and performing (it is not an accident that we speak of "playing" an instrument). Furthermore, when listening to music we appreciate the way the com-poser and the performer play with the sounds. Apart from being a pleasure in itself, musical play is a potent motor for learning. By accentuating music as play, rather than as a cognitive challenge, teachers relieve psychological pressure on children. Musi-cal learning will become more relaxed, and pupils will not get the impression that music is only for the more talented.

I argued also that, besides involving a high form of cognition, musical experience is thoroughly affective. Feeling in music both supports musical cognition and consti-tutes a value of its own. Music cultivates our capacity of feeling, not only by enhanc-ing our awareness of the endless shades of feeling, but also particularly by directly intimating to us a treasure of unique episodes of affective life. Every musical work acquaints us with a new course of feeling we have never experienced before. A major task of music education, then, is to support people in discovering the rich domain of feeling life presented by music.

My third suggestion is a plea for focusing our efforts rather than widening them. Music education should concentrate on those dimensions of musical works directly related to musical experience. When listening to music, we attend to a sensuous form, which often manifests an expressive content and occasionally also a representational one. Therefore, form in particular, but also (if present) expression and representation, should be the main targets of the music educator. The performance-interpretation di-mension, which crucially determines the quality of musical experience, is the fourth dimension of a musical work that demands special attention. The other two dimen-sions of a musical work—standards and traditions of practice and cultural-ideological information—should take a less prominent position. While basic knowledge about them is indispensable for an adequate intellectual understanding of the nature and the context of musical practices, they do not directly contribute to the quality of musical experience as such. When being immersed in the music, we are attending to the form, the expressiveness, the representation, and the interpretation of the musical work, not to the cultural-ideological background or the specific standards and traditions of the practice at hand. Accepting the premise that the major value of music resides in direct musical experience, rather than in reflecting on musical practice, I conclude that the former dimensions should take priority over the latter in the music curriculum.

Notes

1. See, for example, Peters (1966, 33–34).

2. Levinson (1990, 313) observes that, in addition to affective and cognitive components, a case can be made that emotions have behavioral and physiological components as well.

3. Elliott also uses the metaphor of a journey in relation to musical experience (141). But, typically, he passes over the aspect of feeling, characterizing music listening as a mindful journey.

References

Adorno, T. W. 1932/1978. On the social situation of music. *Telos 35* (Spring):129–165. (Originally published in German.)

Csikszentmihalyi, M. 1990. *Flow: The psychology of optimal experience.* New York: Harper and Row.

Elliott, D. J. 1995. *Music matters: A new philosophy of music education.* New York: Oxford University Press.

Godlovitch, S. 1998. *Musical performance: A philosophical study.* New York: Routledge.

Langer, S. K. 1957. *Problems of art.* New York: Charles Scribner's Sons.

Levinson, J. 1990. *Music, art, and metaphysics.* Ithaca: Cornell University Press.

———. 1998. Evaluating music. In P. Alperson, ed., *Musical worlds,* 93–107. University Park: Pennsylvania State University Press.

Peters, R. S. 1966. *Ethics and education.* London: George Allen and Unwin.

Reimer, B. 1989. *A philosophy of music education* 2nd ed. Englewood Cliffs: Prentice Hall.

Ross, M. 1984. *The aesthetic impulse.* Oxford: Pergamon Press.

Shusterman, R. 1992. *Pragmatist aesthetics.* Oxford: Blackwell.

Small, C. 1998. *Musicking: The meanings of performing and listening.* Hanover, NH: Wesleyan University Press.

Stokes, A. 1994. Thinking and feeling in music. *Quarterly Journal of Music Teaching and Learning* 5 (3):37–48.

5

Understanding Musical Understanding

WILFRIED GRUHN

"Understanding" is a common—and commonly misunderstood—concept in music education. True, music education aims to develop a "better understanding" of the musics people make and/or listen to. But what does this mean? To answer, we must overcome two barriers. First, we must develop a deeper understanding of "understanding"; second, we must confront what we mean when talking about "music education." To do so, let us examine some discussions—real and hypothetical—that have been opened (or could have been opened) by *Music Matters*.

In North America, Elliott's praxial philosophy has been received as a basic contribution to the philosophical foundations of music education. In sociological terms, for example, Elliott's ideas have been praised for their sociological values: "At no other time in our professional history did we have a view of music education that is as people-focused and as action-oriented as that presented in *Music Matters*" (McCarthy 2000, 3). Also, the Aristotelian, "praxial" tenets of this philosophy have renewed debates about the mind—body controversy and the reductionist mind—brain antinomy. In short, Elliott has opened a substantial philosophical discourse on different models and aspects of the human being. For example, Regelski (2000) complains that Elliott's book "is based on materialist reduction of mind to brain and an equating of human consciousness with 'self'" (69). With regard to practical applications, Bowman argues that the praxial philosophy is too strongly based on cognitive qualities: it is "cognitively substantive: because [music] entails thoughtful engagement, because it is mindful" (2000, 46). Thus, it "neglects a corporeal, somatic, or visceral dimension" (47).

On the other hand, the impact of *Music Matters* has been described as innovative because it is "a work of and about change" in comparison with and in opposition to traditional philosophy: "It is revolutionary for its full frontal assault on the assumptions of 'Music Education as Aesthetic Education' and for its advocacy of performance as a central means of knowing and doing music" (Paul 2000, 12).

Although extended discussions of these points could happen in Europe as well, the situation here is different. The idea of "action theory" is widely accepted as an appropriate method of teaching and learning. However, music in Germany's public schools is not split into instrumental and vocal programs. Instead, music education is always "general music," with a focus on introducing students to the cultural heritage and the actual musical life of today. Music education in secondary schools is not usually performance oriented; it is more often based on traditional music history and theory. The main goal is to "open" all students to compositions of the past and present; all students (it is assumed) should become acquainted with classical string quartets, symphonies, songs, operas, masses, cantatas, and so forth, as well as works of jazz, pop, rock, commercial musics, film music, and so on. In regard to teaching and learning these musics, applied methods and conceptions of music pedagogy in Europe are extremely diverse; they depend on the conditions and cultural policies in each country.

Thus, in Europe, the "action tenets" of praxialism have not aroused the reactions or debates we have seen lately in North America and the United Kingdom, where the two major philosophical paradigms (music education as aesthetic education and praxialism) have been juxtaposed and cross-examined.

Let us now consider how teachers elsewhere (beyond Europe, the United Kingdom, or North America) might receive the tenets of praxialism. Imagine a situation where students attend a singing class in (say) India. How would music teachers in that cultural context feel about the praxial philosophy? In my view, they would not see any theoretical problems in praxialism because learning how to sing a *rag* always depends on studying with a guru for a long time. The student listens intensely to the guru, learns to imitate him, learns all details and nuances of a song by rote, and finally becomes independent of the guru. How? By gradually creating his or her own way of interpreting and performing the *rag* (far beyond a mere imitation of the guru's style).

Of course, at the center of such music teaching and learning is a process wherein the guru's student actively constructs a personal, mental representation of the *rag* (in all its rich acoustic detail) based on the model presented by the guru in situ. Indeed, the guru's intent is to develop the student's ability to hear, grasp, and express the emotions evoked and mediated by the *rag* in his or her own artistically unique and characteristic manner. One's ability to mediate the musical emotions expressed by the musical details of the *rag* is the core of one's understanding of the *rag*. This understanding is reflected by one's performance of the *rag*. In other words, the strongest knowledge of a *rag* is reflected in and by the quality of a person's interpretive performance. This view comes from tradition and reflects everyday practice; it is not formulated as a theoretical conception.

Because music education differs across cultural contexts, the concept of musical understanding differs to the degree musical cultures and contexts differ. So, in our quest to understand the nature of musical understanding, we need to examine the biologically and neuronally determined conditions of human understanding.

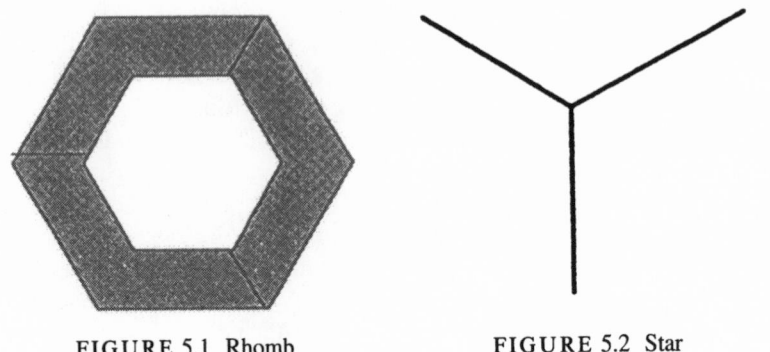

FIGURE 5.1 Rhomb   FIGURE 5.2 Star

Neurobiological Features of Understanding

Let us begin this part of our discussion with cognition. The phenomenon of cognition is a process by which one *recognizes something to be something*. That is, in the act of recognition we perceive sensorial data that we then decode and interpret *as* something. Sensory input never duplicates reality. Sensorial data perceived via senses (e.g., eyes and ears) does not mirror reality in a one-to-one relation. The human mind adds information from personal learning and experience to recognize, identify, or understand something to be something. (So, whatever we take in with our senses is, in fact, "under-represented" without attention and knowledge from an individual, interpretive, human perceiver). In acts of perception we "attribute" functional, pragmatic, or culturally defined meanings to a sign or symbol that is mediated by sensorial stimulation. Again, however, sensorial stimulation is not identical with what we perceive or recognize.

For clarification I offer examples: In Figure 5.1 we easily recognize a gray disc of a rhomb with an inner hole. In Figure 5.2 we see three lines forming a star. However, as soon as we put the star into the hole of the rhomb (see Fig. 5.3) we recognize the same lines as something quite different: a cube. In these examples, the mind adds information (from our former experience) to the objective data and constructs this information we call a cube. That is, we recognize the rhomb *as* a cube. But the cube is not on the paper; it only exists in our minds.

Figure 5.4 illustrates the interactions that occur among perception, cognition, representation, and interpretation. The question now is this: how does an "object" (i.e., any sensory information) acquire meaning, which then becomes associated with the object *as* its meaning? This can only happen in a communicative context where participants exchange information. In a social and cultural setting, a child (for example) perceives pictures, sounds, words, objects, and so forth. "Just" through the "normal" processes of being actively engaged in perception, a child learns to cognitively-psychologically associate meaning with demonstrated and perceived objects. Neurologically, these processes depend on a physiological process by which one develops mental representations. The concrete neurological substrate of the development of representations is bound to the growth of synaptic connections (synaptogenesis) between neurons in the brain.

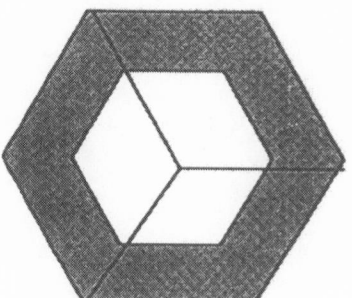

FIGURE 5.3 Cube

An infant growing up in a particular cultural context perceives information (pictures, sounds, words, and objects) that fulfills a special function in his or her communication and social life. The function is conceived implicitly as meaning and is acquired when a functionally correct use has been established and can be observed. (Normally, humans neither define uses nor receive verbal or theoretical instruction about such uses.) Correct application is a function of participating in a communicative, cultural context. Infants observe, practice, and—by repetitions and reinforcements of functionally appropriate uses—develop the meanings of particular words, signs, and actions. Meaning depends on one's interaction with and participation in a communicative "play"; according to Wittgenstein (1953), acts of speaking may be considered "linguistic play" or *Sprachspiel.*

Let us now reconsider the processes outlined above in terms of their neurological equivalents. The mind perceives sensorial data. The perceived stimuli activate very specialized neurons tuned to specific incoming stimuli. When neurons fire they activate related neurons within an already functioning cell assembly (which develops through earlier stimulation and activation). These neurons transmit an electrochemical impulse to other cell assemblies associated with certain stimuli (also because of connections developed earlier).

More specifically, the transmission path consists of axons that send out electric impulses; they end at synaptic spines of dendrites that carry these impulses and activate other neurons. Chemical neurotransmitters help impulses to pass synaptic gaps and regulate activation propagation by exciting or inhibiting electrical activity. Thus, synaptic density is important for information processing.

Neurological research has shown that shortly before and during the first year after birth synaptogenesis peaks and gradually decreases toward a mature level (Huttenlocher 1979, 1990; Huttenlocher and Dabholkar 1997). This process develops under genetic control; however, neural stimulation enhances and facilitates synaptogenesis.

Mental representations can develop only within the gross wiring of the brain. These representations can be described in terms of synaptic density and neuronal connectivity. In regard to music, perceived and performed sounds actively support the growth of synaptic connections. These connections form larger units (cell assemblies) that interact with one another. Such interactions establish more neural networks. The stimulation of neurons by incoming information (e.g., musical sounds) activates the highly interconnected structure of a neural network.

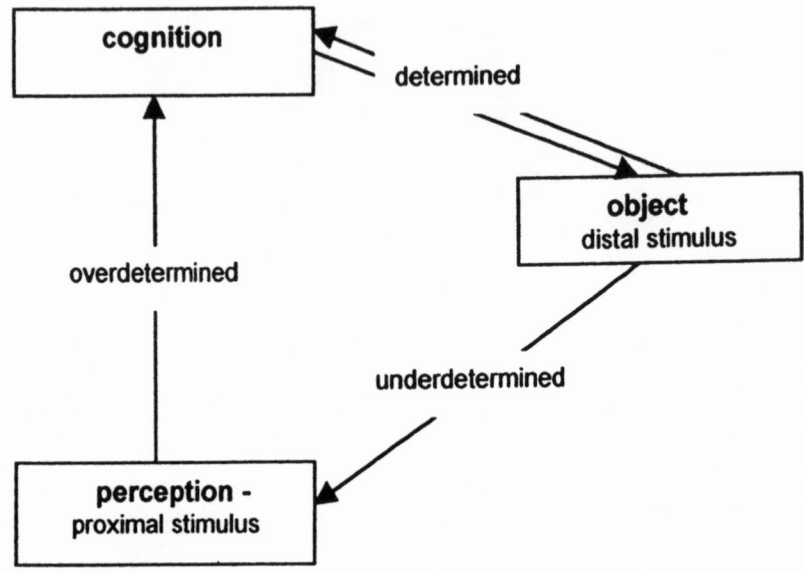

FIGURE 5.4 Perception and Cognition

What I have just outlined can also be described as the activation of mental representations: that is, our cognition of *something-as-something-meaningful* refers to the
activation of mental representations and the linking of these representations with
other representations (e.g., cell assemblies and networks).

Put another way, the more a person develops representations, the more his or her
cell assemblies can be activated and, consequently, the more complex and differentiated his or her understanding can become (because the brain has more options for
connecting neurons and forming more extended neuronal nets). With respect to the
concept of understanding, this means that one gains multiple opportunities to recognize something *as* something; one develops a broad range of interpretations and meanings. As mentioned earlier, meanings are gained through experiences of cultural participation and communication.

The next questions are how do we develop mental representations? and what supports the growth of neural networks and synaptic strength?

In general, the growth of synaptic connections is under genetic control. But this
is reinforced by sensorial stimulation. In language acquisition, for example, the phono-
logical or aural-oral loop is extremely important. That is, what we articulate orally is
immediately controlled aurally. Aural feedback initiates an oral change of sound production as long as it matches the intended and mentally imagined sound. Our aural
system tests our oral sound production, which then produces new aural information,
and so forth (Brodsky et al. 1999). So, cross-modal activity is central to the development of mental representations—or, to turn it the other way around, representations
need activities to stimulate a neuronal loop.

It is important to note that young children reveal a highly significant interaction
between body movement and voice production. In a long-term study (Gruhn 2002),

one- to-three-year-old infants performed a more consistent beat in their babble and singing and were more accurate in their tonal and rhythm patterns when they also performed a smoother flow of movement and when their movements were coordinated more precisely. In another experiment, Bangert et al. (1999) demonstrated that for subjects who played the piano, mere listening to a piano activated not only the frontal and temporal regions of auditory information processing, but also the motor cortex. This did not occur when the relationship of keys and tones was irregularly changed after each trial.

This indicates that the musical brain develops a local map of motor activities in parallel with a sound map. So, even when a professional pianist reads notation or moves his or her fingers on a silent keyboard, these actions cause a similar (or the same) auditory activation as when the sound is present. Obviously, a cross-modal structure is operating in these cases, based on a link between auditory and motor brain areas where representations in one region can immediately stimulate other representations in another region. The same mechanism appears to produce both activations.

In view of this research, and the general observations of educators, there seems to be strong evidence that corporeal activities and practical experiences enhance and stimulate the development of genuine mental representations. Here I would like to introduce the distinction between genuine representations and symbolic representations, depending on what is represented. In music, it is primarily the sounds directly associated with the corporeal movements that produce these sounds (e.g., muscle tension, posture, finger movement, and breath). This is what I call genuine representation; "symbolic" indicates a referential representation. In the latter, something like a sign, word, or picture substitutes for a real entity or phenomenon. Therefore, we must differentiate between the represented sound of a tonic, the word "tonic," and the notation of a tonic chord.

All types of representation interact and refer to one another but differ in the way they develop. Genuine representations of music can only be achieved by musical doing: performing (by means of scores and improvisations), composition, and listening. By these means we develop genuine knowledge *of* music (i.e., of musical sounds), and this is always procedural. However, symbolic representations come from declarative (or formal-verbal) strategies when we gain information about something.

For genuine musical representations, Jeanne Bamberger has introduced the distinction between figural and formal representations (Bamberger 1991), depending on different features that students focus on. Figural representations refer to a series of actions or single elements in time, one after the other. Formal representations demonstrate a much more abstract representation of a general category of sound. Figure 5.5 offers a general hierarchy of different types of representations.

Praxialism and Musical Understanding

Elliott's praxial philosophy is very much in accordance with the neurobiological foundations of musical understanding I have outlined above. The key word introduced into this context by Elliott is "musicing," which describes the processes of music making (in all its forms: improvising, composing, arranging, and conducting)

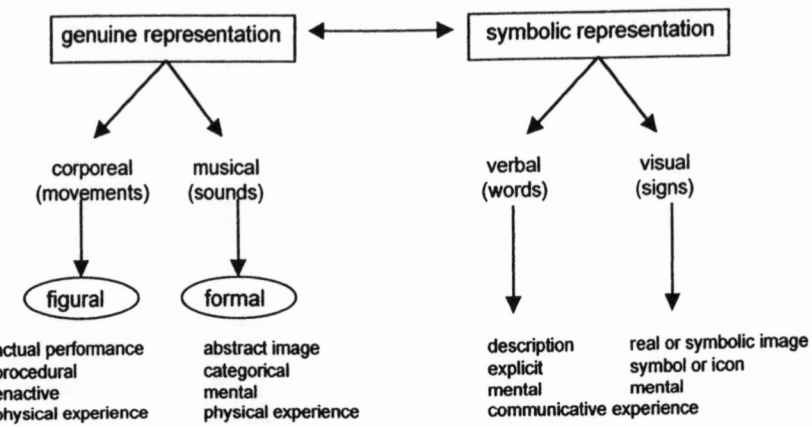

FIGURE 5.5 Types of Representations

and the manifestation (in a literal sense of the Latin root *manus* = hand) of musical reflection in performance.

For Elliott, music lives as "something people do" (1995, 49). Its basic reality "is not works nor the composition of works but music making" (Wolterstorff, cited in Elliott 1995, 49), which is "a particular form of intentional human action"(50) that comes into existence through actual musical doing. Since action is a nonverbal form of thinking and knowing, which is intentional in nature, musical performing (improvising, conducting, and so forth) can be defined as "to act thoughtfully and knowingly" (50).

This seems plausible and intelligible. At the same time, it makes clear what is *not* "music in education." Music cannot be seen as an object—a kind of untouchable piece of art documented by an Urtext edition, a CD, or a score that we can analyze and explain structurally in terms of music theory. Insofar as music becomes concrete through intentional actions, our reflections (thoughtfulness and genuine musical knowledge) can no longer be separated from performing, improvising, and so forth. Rather, as Elliott rightly says, "a person's performance of a given composition is a robust representation of his or her level of musical understanding of that work" (59). In performance one articulates a composition according to one's degree of understanding. Therefore, the development of musical knowledge is (or ought to be) procedural in essence (54).

This view receives parallel support from a comparison with language acquisition. Infants learn language by participating in a communicative process. In the babble stage, they actively practice vocal sound production whereby phonemes are preferred that are predominantly produced in the perceived language. They listen to all kinds of speech that adults use to talk to them. Through these interactions, they acquire a language making-and-listening vocabulary and develop patterns of well-formed sentences. Infants start with short, one- and two-word sentences and articulate what they think or want to express.

What is important to note about this stage of development is that infants do not simply imitate what they hear: they do not imitate infant-directed speech (motherese) and they do not imitate syntactically complex sentences. Furthermore, infants do not imitate syllables that have no meaning to them, and they do not create sets of curious sounds. Rather, infants articulate their thoughts according to their level of linguistic competence. Infants say what they think and what they understand. Finally, infants do not understand grammar, letters, or rules—they do not have access to these kinds of explicit, formal-verbal, grammatical knowledge; they develop only implicit, procedural knowledge of how to pronounce meaningful expressions.

Understanding, therefore, precedes speech. This is what Heinrich Jacoby pointed out in 1925 when he stressed that children learn to speak their language because their parents provide them (before and after birth—see Woodward's chapter in this book) with an acoustic model of correct pronunciation. Children do not acquire speech by learning to avoid wrong pronunciations on the basis of adult instructions about how to form their lips and move their tongues and such.

Musical understanding can and should develop the same way. However, in daily life there are profound differences between the acquisition of speech and that of music. Whereas language competence manifests itself in the "performance" of language in an expressive and communicative way, musical competence culminates in the reproduction of compositions. In language we articulate our own thoughts; we discuss, communicate, and come to terms with other ideas. In music, however, we often produce products (works and compositions) notated by others—and often by others from long ago. Music students practice hard to become excellent in technical skills and to achieve flawless executions of technically difficult passages. Affective expression, then, functions as a supplement to performance—it transforms a brilliant technical execution into a musical performance. However, a wrong note is often considered worse than a meaningless or inadequate expressive gesture.

People are usually said to have achieved mastery of a language when they can express what they think and feel in appropriate (if not elegant) terms. Transposed to music, we can say that music education should enable learners to participate in musical communications, to "speak" music musically—to express musically what they think and feel musically by means of improvising and composing. In language, we "improvise" with words and thoughts every day; we "compose" our texts and speeches.

In music, improvising and composing are often considered the special gifts of experts. This is because of the traditions, myths, and expectations of Western aesthetics and a classical music culture that regulate the conditions of concert life. Music, in this classical context, functions as "exceptional"—something best left to experts— whereas, in fact, it should be accessible to all humans.

If you agree, then it follows that to understand music, music learning should be as procedural as speech learning, and that music learning has ends and advantages for social survival similar to those of other forms of human communication. Once a basic procedural musical competence has been developed, teachers can teach artistic values much more deeply and appropriately (just as we move on in language development to enable children to read, understand what they read, understand and recite poetry, analyze novels, talk about dramas, and so forth).

Understanding a particular language procedurally is a prerequisite for understanding any art form (e.g., a story, joke, poem, drama, or novel) produced in that form and style of discourse. Understanding a particular piece of music procedurally is basic to understanding the meaning and style of that piece. True, one can enjoy the surface sound of an unfamiliar language. However, we must keep in mind that there are at least two basic and different levels of language: the use of colloquial language and the use of language as a means for creating art.

This is not necessarily different in music. However, we must realize that the first (i.e., the colloquial use) is not common in musical practices any more. In our Western culture—not in all cultures—the social and communicative functions of music have been replaced by music as an art, in the aesthetic eighteenth-century sense of the word. Furthermore, because instrumental music is not always referential in the way language is, we use the term "understanding" differently. "Understanding music" commonly includes being touched by its expressions of affects and emotions, or being able to explain musical grammar in terms of music theory. However, if we agree that music has equivalents to colloquial languages, and that colloquialism is a kind of improvisation, then it may also be true that musical competence (i.e., understanding in the sense I have described) is a prerequisite for understanding musical forms (e.g., a concerto, symphony, opera, or song).

The praxial view of musical understanding and learning is concerned primarily with a basic musical capacity analogous to the ability to speak and understand a language. This basic musical competence might be related partly to what Gordon (1980/1997) calls "audiation," if what we mean by audiation is the activation of mental representations and the attribution of meanings to sounds.

As I argued earlier, mental representations are stimulated by actions. These representations can be activated while listening, performing, mentally imaging, moving or dancing to, composing, improvising, and conducting music.

A praxial approach to developing musical understanding integrates so-called practical and mental skills; it brings together doing, making, feeling and thinking; and it complements action with reflection, which Elliott describes as "reflection-in-action."

Consider the example of a choral rehearsal. The main concern of *poeisis* during a rehearsal is to sing the proper notes, hit the correct pitches, stay in tune, and keep the right tempo. Then, the choir is well prepared for performance. It may make a concert recording as a product of all the efforts put into the rehearsals. But this is not the only thing that happens. In addition to the sonic-expressive musical details, the singers must feel socially responsible for attendance, for learning their parts, for participating in producing a balanced sound, for contributing to an interpretation, and so forth. And because of their praxis as choral singers, they make use of what they already understand about singing in an historical context and creating interpretations according to the different genres and styles they are singing (e.g., Renaissance polyphony, jazz), which have been formulated by historical performance practices (*Aufführungspraxis*). So praxis includes cultural knowledge developed in a social context; praxis includes *poeisis* but exceeds it by the formation of attitudes (see Fig. 5.6).

Understanding as Part of Music Learning

In his praxial approach, Elliott refers to Donald Schön's work (1987) in terms of *knowing-in-action* and *reflection-in-action*. His description makes clear the different natures of implicit and explicit knowledge.

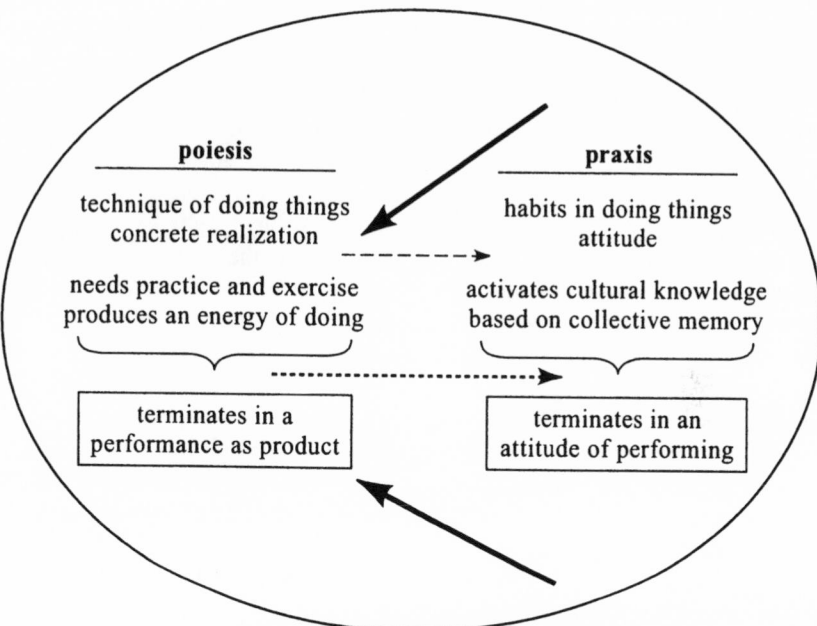

FIGURE 5.6 Poiesis and Praxis

Like knowing-in-action, reflection-in-action is a process we can perform without being able to say what we are doing. Skillful improvisers often become tongue-tied or give obviously inadequate accounts when asked to say what they do. Clearly, it is one thing to be able to reflect-in-action and quite another to be able to reflect *on* our reflection-in-action so as to produce a good verbal description of it; and it is still another thing to be able to reflect on the resulting description. (Schön 1987, 31)

With this, Schön refers to different levels of reflection, the first of which is most important to knowing-in-action. This kind of knowledge is intuitive and immediately tied to action, or becomes relevant through action. "What distinguishes reflection-in-action from other kinds of reflection is its immediate significance for action" (Schön 1987, 29). Acting and reflecting interact in this process; one is the manifestation of the other; they are fully and inseparably integrated. In improvisation, musicians feel where the music is going (Elliott's "impressionistic musical knowledge") and react spontaneously: "Each player makes on-line inventions and responds to surprises triggered by the inventions of the other players" (Schön 1987, 30). Performance integrates practical aspects of reflection; the reflection, then, directs and influences the performance.

If we consider music learning, we must look at the starting point for musical understanding. The question here is whether learning is sequential in essence or responsive to random stimulation. Elliott looks at musicianship in a top-down manner, as ten kinds of musical knowledge (five kinds of music-making knowledge plus five kinds of "listenership" knowledge) in a systematic order: "But while musicianship is procedural in essence, four other kinds of musical knowledge contribute to this essence in surrounding and supporting ways" [the same holds for listenership, which is always included in musicianship, says Elliott] (1995, 54). In contrast, Gordon's "learning theory" looks at musicianship from the bottom up. The sequential order of developmental steps is of vital importance. Children normally start with concrete— conscious or unconscious—actions. They interact with the environment and tend to keep homeostasis with respect to their needs and emotions. These very first types of intentional actions are widely documented as the sensorimotor phase in cognitive development (Piaget 1947). In continuing and elaborating the Piagetian cognitive approach, Aebli (1980/1981) equated doing (acting) and thinking because they stem from the same epistemological source. In doing things, humans fulfill plans and follow intentions. Thoughts are compensated actions.

Children start with actions to develop genuine musical representations: they sing and move and listen. Listening gradually becomes a form of compensated singing. In listening, we respond to music and follow its progression tacitly in our mind. The formation of attention and attraction to musical sounds through listening provokes actions by means of imitation and exploration. These activities stimulate the development of musical representations: types of *knowing-what*, instead of *knowing-that* or *knowing-about*. Mental representations form neural networks of a higher level. In this process, the aural-oral loop plays an important role. This sort of musical competence is (as Elliott says) dominantly procedural and implicit. If this kind of knowing is established, then it makes sense to associate words and symbols with what is already developed in the mind musically. This, finally, leads to explicit knowledge, which is mainly verbal. By this, one can define, explain, notate, transcribe, analyze, and reflect on what is known about a particular work or a particular kind of music; one can communicate verbally with others—musicians and nonmusicians—about a style or piece of music.

Through procedural knowing-in-action we can communicate musically with other musicians without verbal discussions about what is going on in the moment when we interact musically—that is, improvise or perform music (see Fig. 5.7). So, again, Elliott's model is supported by music learning perspectives. However, I would suggest that Elliott should place more stress on the sequential order of music-learning activities that call for action and praxis as the first steps in music learning (the goal of which, then, is musicianship). This can be seen as an attitude rather than a readiness. In musicianship, at any level, reflection and action are integrated to their full extent. But for learners at beginning stages, procedural strategies precede reflective actions.

Music Matters and a Change of Paradigms

In chapter 3 of his book, "Musicing," Elliott begins to explicate his approach to music learning with a focus on performing (his subsequent chapters explicate his approach to learning listening, composing, arranging, and so forth). To him, learning to perform is a process by which one is critically reflective in action. Performing means "acting thoughtfully and knowingly" (1995, 50). It is not acting mechanically; it is not "just sound producing"; rather, performing is interpretive and "thought-full" (in all senses

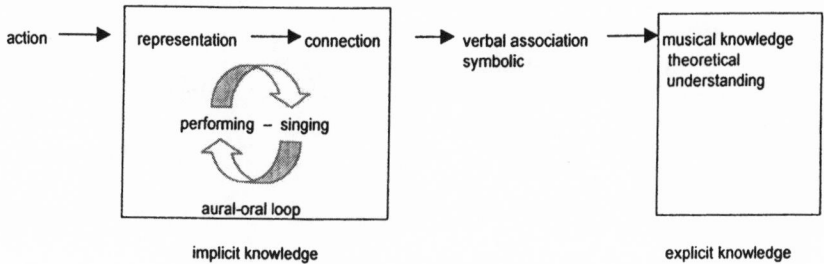

FIGURE 5.7 Implicit and Explicit Knowledge

of the word "cognition," which includes feeling). To Elliott, *performing musically embodies and demonstrates "musical understanding" in the sense of musicianship-and-listenership.*

By "musicing" (of whatever kind), one *does* his or her understanding. The quality of this process demonstrates the level of one's musicianship. In chapter 4 of *Music Matters* ("Listening"), Elliott extends the same theoretical and philosophical approach to listening, which is the other side of the coin of musicing.

We know from learning theory that through listening one collects a repertoire of auditory patterns and in this way develops mental representations. Previously established mental representations are the prerequisites for mental activation, which is needed in performance. In short, listening and performing are linked together, as Elliott says: "all forms of music making and music listening depend on practice-specific forms of musical knowing (both tacit and verbal) that musical practitioners and listeners learn informally and formally" (83).

However, musical works are not only performances. The outcomes of a musicer's intentionally generated actions are less than a musical "work," in its emphatic meaning. A work of art represents neither what is written down in a score nor what is physically executed in a particular moment and situation. Instead, the essence of a work is what it has in common with all thinkable interpretations (which one actual performance is one part of), which is why we can recognize it as one interpretation of that score. A work, therefore, can be abstracted from a single performance, of which a score is only the cause. For this reason, I would suggest to Elliott that he differentiate between listening as a learning activity and listening to musical compositions as a means of understanding, which is fully achieved by an amalgamation of the listener (subject) and the aesthetic object. This process is described by Eggebrecht (1977) as the process of aesthetic identification.

Through learning activities, one develops the ability to give an intrinsic or genuine musical meaning to perceived sounds, whereas listening to works includes (1) identifying a potential intention, (2) merging with the aesthetic presentation, (3) reflecting on the experienced emotional effects, (4) considering the impact of a performance practice and the historical and cultural traditions of reception, and, then, (5) generating multiple interpretations of possible ways of understanding.

Nevertheless, this example demonstrates that learning is a sequential process based on the crucial issue of what comes first and what follows. The elaboration of interpretations needs to first give musical meaning to sounds. When listeners can hear music without relying on perceiving sound, they are ready to listen for interpretations. Of course, it is absolutely true (as Elliott says) that music cognition is not an aural "photocopy" of acoustic materials (Fiske 1992); "music listening is a matter of minding" (Elliott 1995, 87). This has to be developed by informal and formal instruction; it is not a natural gift, but a cultural value in which students must be educated.

Conclusion

David Elliott's contribution to a better understanding of the processes discussed above is profound. His book opens a window into a new philosophy of music education that is no longer limited to practicing executive skills, or memorizing rules of music theory, or collecting verbal knowledge about musical concepts and structures. Instead, his message is to stop the traditional separation of action from reflection and to reconcile doing and thinking, body and mind. Action becomes a mode of reflection that turns it into reflection-in-action. In the praxial philosophy, when an instrumentalist practices to move his or her fingers fast and correctly and when the player stops and reflects upon what he or she did are no longer two separate phases. Practice consists of actions and reflections at the same time—as Elliott says, the mind is in the body as the body is in the mind (51, 103).

The praxial philosophy brings music education back to its roots: teaching and learning the conditions of music making and listening, together, for a better understanding of culturally emergent and historically mediated musical products (i.e., all musical works). By musicing, one learns music musically, as one learns a language by speaking and communicating (instead of being mute and memorizing a vocabulary).

From my point of view, the crucial value of *Music Matters* is that it conceives and anchors music education philosophically as a cultural process aimed at immanent understandings of the inherent neurobiological processes involved in music making and listening. Consequently, it guides teachers to develop musical skills, understandings, and attitudes that are necessary for students to participate in a musical culture and for appreciating and understanding our cultural heritages.

References

Aebli, H. 1980/1981. *Denken: Das ordnen des tuns*. 2 vols. Stuttgart: Klett-Cotta.

Bamberger, J. 1991. *The mind behind the musical ear*. Cambridge, MA: Harvard University Press.

Bangert, M. W., D. Parlitz, and E. Altenmüller. 1999. Neuronal correlates of the pianist's "inner ear." *Proceedings of the Conference on Musical Imagery*. Oslo.

Bowman, W. 2000. A somatic "here and now" semantic: Music, body, and self. *Bulletin of the Council for Research in Music Education* 144:45–60.

Brodsky, W., A. Henik, B. Rubinstein, and M. Zorman. 1999. Inner hearing among symphony orchestra musicians: Intersectional differences of string-players versus wind-players. In S. Won Yi, ed., *Music, mind, and science*, 370–392. Seoul: National University Press.

Eggebrecht, H. H. 1977. Theorie der ästhetischen identifikation. *Archiv für Musikwissenschaft* 34:103–116.

Elliott, D. J. 1995. *Music matters: A new philosophy of music education*. New York: Oxford University Press.

Fiske, H. 1992. Structure of cognition and music decision-making. In R. Colwell, ed., *Handbook of research on music teaching and learning*, 360–376. New York: Schirmer Books.

Gordon, E. E. 1980/1997. *Learning sequences in music*. Chicago, IL: GIA.

Gruhn, W. 2002. Phases and stages in early music learning: A longitudinal study on the development of young children's musical potential. *Music Education Research* 4 (1): 51–71.

Huttenlocher, P. R. 1979. Synaptic density in human frontal cortex – developmental changes and effects of aging. *Brain Research* 163 (2):195–205.

———. 1990. Morphometric study of human cerebral cortex development. *Neuropsychologia* 28 (6):517–527.

Huttenlocher, P. R., and A. S. Dabholkar. 1997. Regional differences in synaptogenesis in human cerebral cortex. *Journal of Comparative Neurology*, 387 (2):167–178.

Jacoby, H. 1925/1984. Voraussetzungen und grundlagen einer lebendigen musikkultur. In H. Jacoby, *Jenseits von "musikalisch" und "unmusikalisch,"* ed. S. Ludwig, 30–73. Hamburg: Christians Verlag.

McCarthy, M. 2000. Music matters: A philosophical foundation for a sociology of music education. *Bulletin of the Council for Research in Music Education* 144:3–10.

Paul, S. J. 2000. The sociological foundations of David Elliott's "music matters" philosophy. *Bulletin of the Council for Research in Music Education* 144:11–20.

Piaget, J. 1947. *La psychologie de l'intelligence*. Paris: Armand Colin.

Regelski, T. A. 2000. Accounting for all praxis: An essay critique of David Elliott's *Music Matters*. *Bulletin of the Council for Research in Music Education* 144:61–88.

Schön, D. A. 1987. *Educating the reflective practitioner*. San Francisco, CA: Jossey-Bass.

Wittgenstein, L. 1953. *Philosophical investigations*. Oxford: Blackwell.

6

Music and Knowledge
in Bodily Experience

HEIDI WESTERLUND AND
MARJA-LEENA JUNTUNEN

As educators, we often "read" our students' body language to glean a sense of how they feel, or whether they understand us. Body language can inform us silently and unconsciously; it can help us draw conclusions about students' experiences. Educational behaviorists once claimed that since it is impossible to know what happens in a student's mind, teachers should only be concerned with what students do "overtly"—how they behave—their responses to educational acts.

There is a grain of truth in behaviorism in the sense that observable human action should be taken seriously. Action is not only an end product of thinking. Elliott addresses this when he argues that musical performing is not an outcome of something we call "mental" acts; instead, we think through and in our actions of performing and improvising music (and so forth) and in our covert (internal) acts of listening to music. Elliott's concept of "thinking-in-action" (as a music maker and a music listener) is central to his combinatory concept of musicianship-listenership. This suggests an epistemological turn to musical know-how wherein "knowing" means constructive musical doing as a music maker and a listener, not just as a maker.

Following Elliott, our starting point is that the development of musicianship happens in action, through action, and within action. However, we also argue that the human body plays a crucial but (unfortunately) a taken-for-granted and opaque role in the development of agency. This is not a bracing new idea. In the first half of the twentieth century, Emile Jaques-Dalcroze (1865–1950) focused on the musical body in education.

In this chapter we consider the musical mind and body within a naturalist framework of holistic duality, but without dualism (Roth 1998, 153). In this duality, a human organism is a functional whole; the mind and body are inseparable, though there are different aspects to this singleness (Benson 2001, 5; Dewey 1958, 285; Velmans 2000; Williams and Bendelow 1998). The feeling, sensing, and experiencing body is engaged with musical sounds and their consequences in many ways, whether we are aware of it or not. Along with Jaques-Dalcroze (and many pragmatist theorists such as John Dewey and Richard Shusterman), we argue that the body is not only an instrument through which musical thinking takes place; the body can be taken as a conscious and explicit object of transformation. Jaques-Dalcroze's idea of bodily transformation and, therefore, of better musicianship, was ahead of its time in many ways. The transformative and experiential view is easily lost even in contemporary cognitive approaches that, for example, Elliott has applied in *Music Matters*.

The Absent, Transparent, and Instrumental Body

For Dalcroze, the issue of the body in relation to musical understanding was a practical one. He became concerned when he observed that his students in the Conservatory of Geneva performed and composed correctly but without revealing any of their musicality. The musical, physical, and emotional problems of his students led him to dispute the philosophies and teaching methods of his time (Jaques-Dalcroze 1935). Music educators today still ask many of the same questions. Why are details of music theory taught as abstractions? Why does the study of music history fail to reflect the movement of peoples, societies, or individuals? Why do students seem to perform without understanding, read music without comprehension, and write music they cannot hear? (Choksy et al. 1986, 30; Dutoit-Carlier 1965, 312–313; Jaques-Dalcroze 1920/1965, 5–11). Jaques-Dalcroze found many faults in music education during his time, especially in regard to the limited accomplishments of the future professional musicians he was teaching and in the weak motor abilities of his students (Bachmann 1991, 78).

These kinds of issues can be related to the more general disembodiment of experience in relation to knowledge in Western culture. Charles Taylor (1989) traces the disembodied human being back to Plato, for whom reason, in contrast to passion, was the capacity of seeing, grasping, and understanding. Plato created dualities (e.g., the soul against the body; the eternal against the changing). Descartes reinforced these dualities. In his famous statement "Cogito ergo sum" (I think, therefore I am), "knowledge" means the correct representation of things, which Descartes separated from the so-called nonintellectual senses of touching, smelling, tasting, and hearing. The Cartesian "mechanical eye," as Levin (1988) calls it, observes the world "outside"— withdrawing from the flesh of the world (106). Confidence and rationality are achieved by the power of the godlike ego, *cogito*, or the mind, by disengaging our "selves" from the material world (141). Within the Cartesian frame, music is viewed as patterns of permanent, ideational structures to be cognized, rather than something to be done, felt, or experienced. In this view, we do not experience in and through music, but rather, cognize it "out there."

When the concept of the modern Cartesian self was advanced by Locke and other Enlightenment thinkers, the self became what Taylor (1989) calls the "punctual" self (161). The punctual self is self-centered in its omnipotent power to construct the world. Similarly, Charles Varela (1992) maintains that in modern individualism matters of truth, reality, and meaning have been transposed to the individual mind. Hence, everything of value (such as individuality, authorship, or agency) is removed from the phenomenal world of visible physical objects. In this paradigm, the body and its movements became unproblematic. Movements were assigned to the phenomenal realm of mechanism and determinism. In consequence, even intersubjectivity is not a matter of the existence of other things and bodies. According to Taylor, Protestant versions of this modern conception of the human being valued detachment from purely personal enjoyments. Taylor explains that in Protestant views, "the lived experience of the passions teaches us nothing; it can only mislead. Our passions should in the end function only as cold disengaged understanding shows us they ought to" (1989, 283). Under such institutional conditions, sense and flesh developed a bad name. Flesh became corruptible, spirit incorruptible, as John Dewey once said (1958, 249; 1934, 21).

These disembodied conceptions of the human being have been repeated over and over in Western aesthetics. Lydia Goehr (1994) argues that in the Western view art music (as well as philosophy) has searched for the transcendental—the a priori precondition of any experience. Music is not only against the world; it is also not of the world. In Western aesthetics, the transcendental relationship with music is sanitized from what Goehr calls the "dirty hands" and the "real world" of human craft, participation, behavior, feelings, usefulness, functionality, practicality, and interestedness. In this view, art and aesthetics involve the transcendental conceived as truth, knowledge, civilized thought, contemplation, control, distance, abstraction, self-expression, individuality, nonpracticality—music for music's sake, and so on (Goehr 1994, 103).

Jaques-Dalcroze was among those who tried to break the modernist paradigm in music education. He wrote that when the unity between matter and spirit was broken, rhythm could only find refuge in the architecture of cathedrals. Music forgot its origin—which is in the dance—and people lost the instinct for expressive and harmonious movements in art and everyday life (Jaques-Dalcroze 1921/1980, 188).

However, it is not correct to say that this disembodied conception of human beings applies to all Western music. There has always been room for musical practices that have been organized around a sensibility in which the needs, emotions, and passions of the participants resonate with the artistic material. Henry Giroux (1992) argues that this phenomenon, which he calls "a productive moment of corporeality," is found, for instance, in rock music (191–192). Similarly, Richard Shusterman (2000b) has disputed that rock involves "overcoming resistances like 'embarrassment, fear, awkwardness, self-consciousness, [and] lack of vitality'" (184). From the viewpoint of the body, says Shusterman (1997, 111; 2000b, 184), the basic characteristics of rock and African American music (e.g., active, excited, communally impassioned engagement) contrast sharply with the passivity of the Western aesthetic attitude of disinterested and detached contemplation.

Without claiming that all music education today is uncritically repeating modernist thought, the normative power of modernist thinking often reinforces these old dualities. As Levin (1988) argues, the disembodied experience and individualistic conception of the human being is not only a philosophical construction, it is alive in Western culture (96). Music has been widely (and very nearsightedly) accepted as a matter of cognitive understanding, or special intelligence, instead of a flesh-and-blood experience in which there is a continuum between various aspects of experience. For instance, some writers suggest that pop music's challenge to the controlled and transparent body is a primitive excitement rather than a proper attitude toward music. In practice, this unfounded idea often means (for example) that in music education rock loses its passionate expressiveness.

Traces of this line of thinking can also be found in Elliott's notion of musical agency. In spite of Elliott's strong attempt to overcome dichotomies (such as mind versus body; subject versus musical object), he suggests a dichotomy between pleasure and enjoyment:

> When biological and social needs intrude into consciousness, the result is disorder. Order is restored in consciousness by satisfying these needs. When consciousness tells us that our biological needs or social expectations are satisfied, we experience pleasure. Pleasure can occur with little or no conscious effort; enjoyment cannot. Pleasure can be stimulated electrically and chemically in the brain; enjoyment cannot. Enjoyment results not from satisfying basic biological and social needs but from moving forward in psychological growth and complexity. Enjoyment arises only from unusual investment of our conscious powers. (115)

For Elliott, conscious powers appear as the "ghost in the machine"—a social and biological machine. Although pleasure does not need to be our primary aim in education, it is involved with objects of interest that promote growth, such as learning music. And as musical practices do involve social expectations—we do teach and learn them in various ways.

As historical constructions show, there is no ontological ground (other than historical and cultural contingency) for our belief that music can be reduced to inward, mental, dispassionate matters, or even a special intelligence. Our bodily and nonbodily involvement in music is a normative question instead of an ontological one. Dewey (1958) tried to debunk such biased dualisms by employing the term "body-mind."

Toward a Holistic View of the Human Being

Like Jaques-Dalcroze, Elliott is interested in developing musicianship defined as embodied action. In his definition of embodied musical action and knowledge, Elliott leans on Gilbert Ryle's behaviorism. Ryle (1949) tried to replace mental terms with the term "dispositions"; he attributed mental states to any system that has appropriate behavioral dispositions. Musical thinking is evidenced in musical action that follows certain rules. There is, therefore, no need to talk about mental states that refer to the musical object as such. It is the ability to think while acting that counts (59). This argument seems to serve Elliott's purposes. Elliott also employs categories of knowing developed by Bereiter and Scardamalia (1993): formal, procedural, informal, impressionistic, and supervisory knowledge. These categories defend the apprenticeship tradition and are, as Schrag (1992) writes, descendants of the Rylean dichotomy of knowing-that versus knowing-how (283). In the apprenticeship tradition, the main interest is in illustrating how acquisition of practical know-how happens by models and demonstration. By applying Dennett's materialism, Elliott (1995) then deduces a view in which "the body is in the mind," and the mind is nothing but the physical brain (51), which "scans acoustic waves for musical information" (83). The apprentice's brain is working with the "norms, rules, and ideas" (cultural memes) that are passed on through generations (111).

As a result, instead of embodied mind and knowledge, Elliott seems to have a "theory for embrained knowledge," as Pentti Määttänen (2000) suggests. The human brain-mind is viewed from a third-person information perspective instead of an experiential one.

The whole question of mind and body can, however, be set another way. According to Max Velmans (2000):

> the *proximal* causes of consciousness are to be found in the human brain, but it is a mistake to think of the brain as an isolated system. Its existence as a material system depends totally on its supporting surround, and the contents of consciousness that it, in turn, supports arise from a reflexive interaction of perceptual processing with entities, events and processes in the surrounding world, body and the mind/brain itself. (229–230)

Moreover, we do not experience this world as being inside our brains (230). Furthermore, all experiences should not be likened to thoughts, as Descartes did (247). There is therefore no need to reduce the body and mind to the material brain in order to avoid Cartesian dualism and transcendental idealism. What we need to do is to examine music and learning as experience in which the body is engaged in various ways.

According to Dewey's nonreductionist naturalism, the human organism is not simply a sum of its parts. The organism as a whole thinks with the brain while interacting in a context and situation; in this process, the brain is just an organ for thinking (Dewey 1972, 108). Similarly, it is the human being that runs with the legs, and not the legs that run (Määttänen, 2000; Määttänen and Westerlund 1999). Along with Dewey, Maurice Merleau-Ponty (1945/1962) also argued that it is our lived body itself, not an intellectual mind, that finds its way around the room. This embodiment is always lived through from the first-person perspective. My embodiment and physicality is fundamentally conditioning my experience and sense of self. In the experience of the human organism, all senses are inseparable and interacting.

Jaques-Dalcroze believed that it is "the sixth sense" (*le sens musculaire*) that controls the multiple qualities of movements (Jaques-Dalcroze 1920/1965, 140–141). This kinesthetic sense—as it is called today—combines moving and sensing, and it works on a subconscious level.

Yet, our lived bodily experiences are not subjective and inward; they are developed in the social and material environment, in relation to various practices and other bodies. In experience, we are engaged in human habits that direct life, as Dewey and other pragmatists have maintained. In anthropology, as well as in music education, Blacking was one of the first to point out the cultural and social aspects of bodily experience. He held that feelings, and particularly fellow-feelings expressed as movements of bodies in space and time, often without verbal connotations, are the basis of mental life (Blacking 1977, 21). Blacking's point is that the human body is not only executing tasks that the autonomous individual mind gives to it. The body is an instrument for being a social human being as well as an expression of it. The body both generates and expresses imposed sociality.

Also, Jaques-Dalcroze acknowledged the social aspect of the body. Long before Blacking, he emphasized that music, and the rhythms of the human body embedded in it, has been the basis of human emotion down through the ages (Jaques-Dalcroze 1930/1985, 7). According to him, "each nation has its own particular motor rhythms, expressed in everyday life by certain ways of carrying out the various tasks required by climate, environment, and social conditions" (223). Jaques-Dalcroze believed that every artistic action is a product of its time and culture (239). Music from a certain period of time reveals the entire mental state of the period and response of the bodily movements imposed at that period by social conventions and necessities (7). On the other hand, he claimed that the rhythmic character of the music of a country would conform to the physical aptitudes of its inhabitants (Jaques-Dalcroze 1921/1980, 45).

Culturally maintained habits do not always lead to improved experience. Dewey, a contemporary of Jaques-Dalcroze, defended F. Matthias Alexander's view that many of the physical and mental ills that people suffer result from disharmony between our more advanced intellectual behaviors and our more basic bodily functions (Shusterman 1994, 137). Jaques-Dalcroze used the expression *a-rhythm* to refer to the same problem.[1] Alexander was after better somatic awareness and a new attention to bodily experiences offering a concrete method for such reflective education (Alexander 1932/1987). Shusterman (1994) writes, "This insistence on thinking through the body, to achieve more conscious control and more acute perception of its condition, clearly distinguishes Alexander's approach from standard physical culture and body building" (137). Neither Dewey, Alexander, Jaques-Dalcroze (1921/1980, 5), nor many of their contemporaries thought that bodies were tabula rasa that a society just stamped with its symbolic imprint. They recognized that body-functioning influences the mind, and vice versa, in a heterogeneous way. This implies, for example, that by becoming consciously aware of one's otherwise subconscious movements, it is possible to prevent oneself from doing unnecessary habitual movements and, thus, to improve body functioning.

Similarly, by learning new social habits consciously (e.g., musical expression and dance), we can improve our psychophysical existence. The body needs cultivation and habituation. Moreover, action in music education can develop morality, which comes from the sensibility of the body, rather than being channeled exclusively through the socially constituted being. Levin (1988) calls this "organismic bonding" or, after Merleau-Ponty, "initial sympathy" (332). In these views, we "move" from phenomenologically embodied notions (such as the body-subject and body-image) to social habits and the disciplined body (e.g., Blacking). More important, we see body awareness techniques in terms of constructive conscious control (e.g., Alexander, Eutonie, Feldenkreis), therapy, and, finally, transformation of the whole body-mind (see Jaques-Dalcroze, Dewey, and Shusterman).

In his search for a closer connection between body and mind, Jaques-Dalcroze (1930/1985, 58) shared the goals of Dewey, Alexander, and, later, Shusterman (2000a, 138–144), with his "somaesthetics." Jaques-Dalcroze's goal was to establish a system of music education in which the body is the intermediary between sounds and thought, where there is communication between feeling and understanding, and between sensations that inform the mind and those that recreate sensorial means of expression (Jaques-Dalcroze 1921/1980, 4–5). He emphasized the principle that the "body is an inseparable ally of the mind; body and mind should harmoniously perform their diverse functions, not only separately but simultaneously" (Jaques-Dalcroze 1921/1980, 109). By harmonizing the functions of the body with those of the mind, it would be possible, as he argued, to ensure "free play and expansion to imagination and feeling through the state of satisfaction and joyful peace that follows" (1930/1985, 6). A change in mental state (e.g., bad news) affects body functioning (e.g., causes the diaphragm to contract), thus disrupting the balance.

This balance of the body-mind can be reconstructed by certain exercises (e.g., in relaxation), says Jaques-Dalcroze (1930/1985, 5; 1921; 1945/1981, 157). These exercises, for instance, improve the ability to solve the problem of unexpected information without losing the flow of movement. Hence they prepare the musician to interact smoothly, without interruption, in changing musical situations.

The theoretical and practical implications of Jaques-Dalcroze's view are that there is no experience, emotion, or body that is separate from various ways of acting, attitudes of appropriate experiences, emotions, or social "bodies." The body is an experiencing, relational, and actively transforming body. Body is intended, as well as unintended, in empowered agency. The experience of the relational body-mind cannot be examined as something that happens only inside the skin and behind the eyes. Consequently, in addition to developing students' skills and know-how in relation to a preexisting practice and its cultural context, the challenges for music educators include enhancing the perspectival, lived experience of students in relation to possible practices.

Transformation through Music

Music has several values and tasks in education. Jaques-Dalcroze underlined that music education is *pour la musique* and *par la musique*: for and through music. He seems to have understood the importance of combining both the third- and first-person perspectives in music education. He maintained that music is the most powerful means of education and can strengthen the communication between the senses, muscles (body), and mind (Jaques-Dalcroze 1921/1980, 54). Through rhythm, according to him, it is possible to bring together the mind, body, feeling, music, and all forms of arts in a conscious human experience (see also Juntunen 1999, 67–69, 144). For Jaques-Dalcroze, the teaching of rhythmic movement, although based on music, is not solely a preparation for musical studies; rather, it is a more profound education of general culture (1930/1985, 102).

So, the relationship between the body and music that Jaques-Dalcroze sought is different from a stimulus-response relationship between the object and experiencing subject. Such causal effects of musical sounds on the felt body have been described by Reimer (1995), for example, as "faster or slower heartbeat or breathing, shivers, chills, tingling, sweating, a feeling of being 'high' or of 'floating'" (3). It is noteworthy that these feelings are subjectively located and felt in different parts of the body and not in the brain, as Velmans writes (2000, 129). Another kind of relationship between the body and music has been described by Swanwick (1992), who acknowledges the connections between feeling, gestural movements, imagination, and musical sounds. In his research, children described music in terms of postural metaphors and emotional labels (90–91). Swanwick's results have a connection to Jaques-Dalcroze's ideas that music depends on movement that finds its nearest prototype in our muscular system, though Swanwick seems to relate the body and movements to the structures of music. According to Jaques-Dalcroze, "All the nuances of time—all the nuances of energy—can be 'realized' by our bodies, and the acuteness of our musical feeling will depend on the acuteness of our bodily sensations" (1921/1980, 60; cf. Swanwick 1992, 90). For example, concrete bodily performance of musical phrases clarifies and strengthens musical experience. An educative bodily involvement with music changes thinking-in-action and leads toward better experience. Thus, Jaques-Dalcroze emphasizes embodied and transformational *agency*, instead of plain bodily reaction, as causal response.

In his view of agency, Elliott (1995) states that "if the body is in the mind, then it makes perfect sense (as Dalcroze, Orff, and Kodaly specialists maintain) that the kinds of moving involved in music making are essential to improving musical understanding" (103). However, as explained earlier, the importance of the body in musical experience becomes transparent in these approaches. Movement involved in music making also increases so-called bodily knowledge. "Bodily knowledge" refers to improved knowing *in* and *through* the body, which, in turn, has a direct connection to senses and bodily awareness, as well as to abilities, skills, and action. It also has direct connections to embodied pleasure (Shusterman 2000a, 138–141). In embodied musical agency, the body and the mind function as complex interacting allies of the experiencing and acting organism as a whole.

Jaques-Dalcroze's challenge was to develop our psychophysical beings within and through music and action. Like Jaques-Dalcroze, Elliott also acknowledges the possibilities of music education for improving the more general goals of the self (1995, 114–122). In Dalcroze exercises, our senses, body, mind, and emotions fuse with music to create one experience. The most significant and far-reaching innovation that Jaques-Dalcroze brought to the teaching of music was to incorporate meaningful rhythmic movement experiences for purposes of facilitating and reinforcing students' understandings of musical concepts, thus bringing awareness to the physical demands of an artistic performance. The bodily experience of music opens the doors of hearing, feeling, understanding, reproducing, remembering, and inventing (Juntunen 1998). Central in the bodily experience is the constant interaction of rhythmic movement, aural perception, and improvisation. In the bodily exploration of music, movement is spontaneous and joined to cognitive conceptual responses involving locomotion and gesture. Exercises bring awareness to students' physical responses to music so that the body and the ear form a dynamic partnership. In this partnership, listening inspires movement, while moving guides and informs listening (Juntunen 1999).

One characteristic of Jaques-Dalcroze's pedagogical views, which contemporary music educators call "eurhythmics," is the evoking of sensations that create mental images (1930/1985, 108). The time, energy, and space used to express music in movement are recorded in the muscles and brain as kinesthetic images (1921/1980, 152). Jaques-Dalcroze believed that music students should continually cultivate a memory bank of aural, visual, and kinesthetic images that can be recalled at any time while engaged in music.

Before any scientific studies of music learning, Jaques-Dalcroze seems to have been aware that we learn in different ways and by the combination of various senses (1930/1985, 53, 99). Even though we may have different intelligences, of which musical intelligence is one, "they can be fashioned and combined in a multiplicity of adaptive ways by individuals and cultures" (Gardner 1983, 9) and can be developed with an assist from another. Moreover, "the intelligent body" does not exist or develop alone but in relation to other people and the environment within "organismic bonding." Our lived bodily involvement is not just a compartment for our many intelligences. Jonathan Matthews (1994) even argues that "if the active body is not actually or imaginatively involved in the learning process, learning doesn't simply occur" (130).

Jaques-Dalcroze believed that the result of his approach—in addition to an excellent physical development—would be a certain intellectual quickening (1921/ 1980, 99). He was convinced that the power of his approach was in "transforming the mind along the lines of greater self-possession, stronger power of imagination, [and] more constant mental concentration" (104). As a student feels himself or herself delivered from all bodily embarrassment and mental obsession of a lower order, he or she will feel a profound joy, which Jaques-Dalcroze looked upon as the most powerful of all mental stimuli. In this respect it can be argued that Dalcroze exercises also influence various capacities needed for academic learning and schoolwork, such as paying attention, becoming aware, recalling, concentrating, and so forth (Bachmann 1991, 87; Caldwell 1995, 63–66).

Conclusions

Despite his similar interest in developing musicianship, Emile Jaques-Dalcroze could challenge David Elliott's view of music education in many ways. The differences between their conceptions of the human being go in Jaques-Dalcroze's favor, not least of all because of Dalcroze's inclusion of the therapeutic possibilities of music. The enjoyment of one's own skills, the pleasure of flow, as defined by Elliott, are not the only pleasures, though they are important ones in musical engagements. Through the ages people have used sounds to generate communally enjoyed situations in which individual experience intersects with sensibilities, ethics, and artistic expression in a productive and transformative sense. Music as information and representation of communal interests abstracts the body and bodies into mere biological antennas for culturally loaded impulses. In the Dalcrozian framework, the whole human being is transformed through music within musical practices. Music education thus serves various musical and so-called nonmusical goals of the individual, as well as of the larger society. Instead of building up unnecessary demarcations between bodily pleasures and more intellectual enjoyments—between various senses, intellects, or art forms—the relational body-mind in action should be the nexus of music education. "Knowledge" means *any* transformation in the experience of body-mind.

In conclusion, a more holistic view of the human being would allow music educators to expand their vision of music's values and the practical possibilities we can develop to achieve these values.

Notes

An earlier version of this chapter by Heidi Westerlund and Marja-Leena Juntunen was published as "Digging Dalcroze, or, Dissolving the Mind-Body Dualism: Philosophical and Practical Remarks on the Musical Body in Action," *Music Education Research* 7 (2):203–214. Reprinted with the permission of Taylor and Francis, http://www.tandf.co.uk/journals.

1. Jaques-Dalcroze wrote, "A-rhythm is a malady usually caused by the inability of a man to control himself, from a predominance of intellect over nervous functioning" (1921/1980, 52).

References

Alexander, M. 1932/1987. *The use of the body*. London: Victor Gollancz.

Bachmann, M.-L. 1991. *Dalcroze today: An education through and into music*. Trans. D. Parlett. New York: Oxford University Press.

Benson, C. 2001. *The cultural psychology of self: Place, morality, and art in human worlds*. London: Routledge.

Bereiter, C., and M. Scardamalia. 1993. *Surpassing ourselves: An inquiry into the nature and implications of expertise*. La Salle, IL: Open Court Publishing

Blacking, J. 1977. Towards an anthropology of the body. In J. Blacking, ed., *The anthropology of the body*, 1–28. London: Academic Press.

Caldwell, J. T. 1995. *Expressive singing: Dalcroze eurhythmics for voice*. Englewood Cliffs, NJ: Prentice-Hall.

Choksy, L., R. M. Abramson, A. E. Gillespie, and D. Woods. 1986. *Teaching music in the twentieth century*. Englewood Cliffs, NJ: Prentice-Hall.

Dewey, J. 1934. *Art as experience*. New York: Perigee Books.

———. 1958. *Experience and nature*. New York: Dover.

———. 1972. *The early works: 1882–1898*. Carbondale: Southern Illinois University Press.

Dutoit-Carlier, C-L. 1965. Le createur de la rythmique. In F. Martin, ed., *Emile Jaques-Dalcroze: L'homme, le compositeur, le createur de la rythmique*, 305–412. Neuchatel: Editions de la Baonniere.

Elliott, D. J. 1995. *Music matters: A new philosophy of music education*. New York: Oxford University Press.

Gardner, H. 1983. *Frames of mind: The theory of multiple intelligences*. New York: Basic Books.

Giroux, H. A. 1992. *Border crossing: Cultural workers and the politics of education*. New York: Routledge.

Goehr, L. 1994. Political music and the politics of music. *Journal of Aesthetics and Art Criticism* 52 (1):99–112.

Jaques-Dalcroze, E. 1920/1965. *Le rythme, la musique et l'éducation*. Lausanne: Fœtisch.

———. 1921. Définition de la rythmique. *Le Rythme* 7 (8):1–8.

———. 1921/1980. *Rhythm, music and education*. Trans. H. Rubinstein. London: Dalcroze Society.

———. 1930/1985. *Eurhythmics, art and education*. Trans. F. Rothwell. New York: Arno Press.

———. 1935. Petite histoire de la rythmique. *Le Rythme* 39 (3):18.

———. 1945/1981. *La musique et nous: Note sur notre double vie*. Genève: Slatkine.

Juntunen, M.-L. 1998. Dalcroze-rytmiikka ja muusikkous. [Dalcroze eurhythmics and musicianship]. *Finnish Journal of Music Education* 2 (1):86–95.

————. 1999. *Dalcroze-rytmiikka: kehollisuutta korostava ja muusikkoutta kehittävä musiikkikasvatuksen lähestymistapa.* [Dalcroze eurhythmics: an approach to music education with an emphasis on the embodiment and the musicianship.] Ph.D. diss., University of Oulu, Finland.

Levin, D. M. 1988. *The opening of vision. Nihilism and the postmodern situation.* New York: Routledge.

Määttänen, P. 2000. Elliott on mind matters. *Bulletin of the Council for Research in Music Education* 144:40–44.

Määttänen, P., and H. Westerlund. 1999. Tradition, practice, and musical meaning: A pragmatist approach to music education. In F. V. Nielsen, S. Brändström, H. Jørgensen, and B. Olsson, eds., *Nordisk musikkpedagogisk forskning* 3:33–38.

Matthews, J. C. 1994. *Mindful body, embodied mind: Somatic knowledge and education.* Ph.D. diss., Stanford University.

Merleau-Ponty, M. 1945/1962. *The phenomenology of perception.* Trans. C. Smith. London: Routledge and Kegan Paul.

Reimer, B. 1995. The experience of profundity in music. *Journal of Aesthetic Education* 29 (4):1–21.

Roth, R. J. 1998. *Radical pragmatism: An alternative.* New York: Fordham University Press.

Ryle, G. 1949. *The concept of mind.* London: Hutchinson's University Library.

Schrag, F. 1992. Conceptions of knowledge. In P. W. Jackson, ed., *Handbook of research on curriculum,* Project of the American Educational Research Association, 268–301. New York: Macmillan.

Shusterman, R. 1994. Dewey on experience: Foundation or reconstruction? *Philosophical Forum* 26 (2):127–148.

————. 1997. *Practicing philosophy: Pragmatism and the philosophical life.* New York: Routledge.

————. 2000a. *Performing live: Aesthetic alternatives for the ends of art.* Ithaca: Cornell University Press.

————. 2000b. *Pragmatist aesthetics: Living beauty, rethinking art.* 2nd ed. New York: Rowman and Littlefield.

Swanwick, K. 1992. What makes music musical? In J. Paynter, T. Howell, R. Orton, and P. Seymour, eds., *Companion to contemporary musical thought,* 1:82–104. London: Routledge.

Taylor, C. 1989. *Sources of the self: The making of the modern identity.* Cambridge: Cambridge University Press.

Varela, C. 1992. Cartesianism revisited: The ghost in the moving machine or in the lived body; An ethnogenic critique. *Journal for the Anthropological Study of Human Movement* 7 (1):5–64.

Velmans, M. 2000. *Understanding consciousness.* London: Routledge.

Williams, S. J., and G. Bendelow. 1998. *The lived body: Sociological themes, embodied issues.* London: Routledge.

7

Listening Reconsidered

ROBERT A. CUTIETTA AND SANDRA L. STAUFFER

The music industry measures music "listenership" (Elliott's word) by the billions of dollars. In 1999 sales of all music formats worldwide were 3.8 billion units, with compact discs accounting for 65 percent of that market (Masson 2000). In the same year, over $1 billion in revenue was generated collectively by popular touring acts and artists who performed over six thousand concerts ("Tour Attractions" 2000). In 2000 consumers in the United States alone spent $14.3 billion on CD recordings (Recording Industry Association 2000). In the same year, approximately 32 million concertgoers attended performances by over twelve hundred symphony orchestras in the United States (American Symphony Orchestra League 2001), and 40 million American adults tuned their radio dials to country music stations (Country Music Association 2000). Music listening is, apparently, alive and well.

Historically, music listening became a part of music education curricula when broadcasting and recording made both live and recorded performances widely available to school students (Mark and Gary 1992). Today, publishers of music series books for elementary and middle school students produce CD packages that include recordings of songs, accompaniment tracks for group singing, and hundreds of selections intended specifically for music-listening experiences. Similarly, instrumental music method books and materials now include recordings designed with the specific intention that students listen and play along. Orchestras mount young people's concerts, and opera companies and other musical ensembles broadcast performances on public radio and television in order to develop future audiences, otherwise known as music listeners.

David Elliott challenges music educators to consider music listening from a different paradigm and to change our definition of listening, including what music listening is and how expertise in listening develops. Elliott describes music listenership not only as listening to live or recorded performances, but also as listening *while* one is performing. The most expert form of listening, he claims, is listening within the act of making music.

In this chapter we examine the following questions: Where does Elliott place music listening in the context of the praxial philosophy he articulates in *Music Matters*? What are the implications of his writings about music listening for music educators and music students? What other models and thinking can contribute to the professional dialogue about music listening?

Music Listening and Praxial Philosophy

Throughout *Music Matters*, Elliott emphasizes actions—specifically, the actions of making music, which he labels "musicing." If music-making actions include, as Elliott suggests, "performing, improvising, composing, arranging, and conducting" (1995, 40), where does listening fit? The answer lies in Elliott's definition of music as "a multidimensional human phenomenon involving two interlocking forms of intentional human activity: music making and music listening" (42). So critical and complex is the relationship between music making and music listening that both are required for a musical practice to exist.

Elliott describes music listening as a specific kind of human action that is distinct from the action of music making. While music making is overt and observable, music listening is covert and (largely) not observable. The action of music listening, then, is a "form of thinking-in-action and knowing-in-action" (80) in which one is processing musical information, or thinking musically. Furthermore, the actions of music making and music listening occur in sociocultural contexts that musicers and listeners share. In Elliott's words:

> By calling this a praxial philosophy I intend to highlight the importance it places on music as a particular form of action that is purposeful and situated and, therefore, revealing of one's self and one's relationship with others in a community. The term *praxial* emphasizes that music ought to be understood in relation to the meanings and values evidenced in actual music making and music listening in specific cultural contexts. (14)

Just as music making is a context-dependent art, music listening is "a *context-dependent* process" (81) in which the mutually held beliefs and understandings in a particular community of music listeners and music makers frame that specific musical practice. These points form the underpinning of Elliott's writings about music listening. Briefly stated, (1) music making and music listening are human actions that together constitute musical practices; (2) music listening is a covert form of thinking and knowing in action; and (3) both music making and music listening (and therefore music practices and music) are culturally situated actions.

Within the context of each musical practice, listening occurs in two different ways: listening inside the act of making music, and listening outside the act of making music. In the "inside listener" (our term) category, the listener and maker are one and the same individual. "Music makers," Elliott writes, "listen for what their thoughtful actions produce and for what other musicers do and make" (78). Inside listeners include the soloist listening to himself or herself playing while practicing alone, rock band members listening to each other as they perform, the young composer listening to his or her music as it unfolds, and the conductor listening to an ensemble as he or she leads it in a concert. For inside listeners, the action of listening is embedded in the action of making music, or "musicing," as Elliott defines it.

In contrast, "outside listeners" (our term) are not actively engaged in music making during the act of listening. Instead, they are listening from the perspective of observer. Elliott notes that "each musical practice usually includes (or attracts) a group of people who act specifically as listeners or audiences for the musical works of that practice" (78). Audience members, however, are not the only members of the outside-listener category. Elliott describes listeners in any musical practice as listening "for the musical products of that kind of musicing" (41). The products of a musical practice may include live and recorded performances. Outside listeners are those who listen to recorded performances in the comfort of their homes (or elsewhere) or audience members at live performances.

The various kinds of listeners, then, may be grouped as shown in Figure 7.1. Musicer A is the individual who is actively making music and simultaneously listening to the product of his own musicing (and that of others, if he or she is an ensemble member). When musicer A performs for individuals who are not fellow collaborators in the act of making music, a second group of listeners is engaged—audience members. Still another group, listeners, actively attends to recorded performances by musicer A or other music makers. Musicer B, a new kind of listener born in the twentieth century, is the individual who actively makes music within the context of recorded performances by others. Musicer B might be the young jazz musician practicing or improvising with a recorded accompaniment track, a group singing along with a karaoke machine, or even a driver singing along with a favorite song on the car radio. For musicer A and musicer B, both music making and music listening are operative and occur simultaneously. Audience members and listeners are listening as well, but they are not actively making music simultaneously with the action of listening.

Listening expertise may vary significantly among the members of any single category of listenership represented in Figure 7.1. Differences in listening expertise, according to Elliott, are related to an individual's expertise as a music maker. A proficient concert soloist, for example, is likely to be a more proficient listener than a novice music maker on the same instrument, though both are members of the musicer A category in Figure 7.1. Similarly, the audience member attending a concert to listen to a favorite piece of music is likely to have more listening expertise than the audience member encountering that same concert experience for the first time.

But another distinction regarding listening expertise can be drawn. In *Music Matters*, Elliott implies that individuals who have crossed the horizontal axis of Figure 7.1 (our representation) into the realm of "musicer" have an advantage over those who have not. The inside listeners, or musicer A and musicer B, are music practitioners, and the more experience of making music that one has, the more insider knowledge one has available when engaged in the action of listening from the audience or listener perspective. The listener or audience member who has also been a musicer, particularly a musicer in the same practice, listens with more expertise than the listener

LISTENING in a . . . Live Concert . . . Recorded Context

	Live Concert	Recorded Context
Inside the Act of Music Making	Musicer A	Musicer B
Outside the Act of Music Making	Audience Member	Listener

FIGURE 7.1 Types of Music Listenership

or audience member who has not been a musicer *because of the knowledge acquired through music making.*

A caveat merits consideration here. "Audience" is a culture-specific term we have come to associate with those attending a live performance, usually a performance of Western music. "Listener," as we have used it here—one who listens to recorded music without making music at the same time—is also culture-specific. Because both are so situated, neither may hold much meaning outside of Western music practices.

Still, all forms of listenership are (or can be) listening-in-action and knowing-in-action. According to Elliott, listeners can be said to "know" if, "upon hearing the initial patterns of [a] piece, they believe certain sound patterns will follow that do in fact follow," "they can detect variations, errors, or omissions in [a] performance" of the piece, or "they know how to sing, whistle, or hum along accurately" (79). In other words, expert listeners know how musical patterns unfold; they have "style-specific cognitive processes" (79).

Cognition figures prominently in Elliott's writing about listening. Listening differs from hearing, which may be a washover experience or one of simple identification only (e.g., "I hear the train"). Evidence that an individual is indeed listening to music is that he or she is, at the very least, consciously attending to musical sounds. Furthermore, the focus and direction with which one listens to and for something in music implies intent, and intention is yet another critical element in the covert act of listening. In Elliott's words,

> intelligent music listening requires that we employ our powers of consciousness deliberately to achieve an intention. In music listening, "getting something done" is a matter of thinking and knowing in relation to auditory events. . . . Music listening requires us to interpret and *construct* auditory information in relation to personal understandings and beliefs. (1995, 80–81)

What listeners construct are "the complex physical events we experience as musical sound patterns" (83). Music listening, then, is not merely perception or processing. Music listening is a form of cognition in which one is thinking musically.

Elliott on Listening and Ways of Knowing

Elliott expends considerable effort in describing the act of listening. He states that listening is "a covert (or internal) form of thinking-in-action and knowing-in-action that is procedural in essence" and "that at least four other kinds of musical knowing contribute to the procedural essence of music listening in a variety of ways" (81).

We would like to argue that Elliott's philosophy actually implies several ways of knowing and types of knowledge that may be arranged hierarchically on two levels. This rearrangement of ways of knowing and types of knowledge may be more logical and useful for music educators.

First and foremost, Elliott makes a clear distinction between learning that is verbally based and that which is not verbal, or procedural, as illustrated in Figure 7.2. In verbally based learning, all musical sounds and knowledge are mediated through words. For example, music may be explained to the learner, or the learner may read or hear verbal descriptions about music. A listener may also reason about music verbally, respond to questions about music verbally, or discuss music verbally with others. In other words, knowledge can be acquired and shared through verbal means, and knowledge can be remembered and utilized verbally, including knowledge about music.

When musical knowledge is learned through words, knowledge itself is fundamentally verbal, not musical. The words act as mediators between the music and the learner. When knowledge is only verbal, the learner cannot have direct understanding of the music because the learner does not have direct contact with the music. Although one would be hard pressed to completely discount the value of verbal learning in music listening, it is equally obvious that verbal knowledge is woefully incomplete without direct experiences of music. One cannot learn about music through words alone.

To benefit from verbal ways of knowing, one must have knowledge of the language used, including understanding of the language's rules, syntax, logic, and etiquette. These language rules, often unwritten and unconscious, allow one to utilize the language. As obvious as this seems, it is an important concept to appreciate in order to understand Elliott's next mode of learning or way of knowing music.

Elliott contrasts verbal ways of knowing with nonverbal ways of knowing. Of these, the most important in his writing is the procedural knowledge that is acquired and used when engaged in music making and listening. This type of knowledge is the musical "sense" that enables a person to make musical sounds. For music makers, procedural knowledge includes performing patterns appropriately, sensing the common beat, performing in tune, and other acts of making music that help the musicer develop understanding of the unwritten syntax of music. For music listeners, "the procedural essence of music listening consists in such covert, nonverbal acts as constructing coherent musical patterns, chaining musical patterns together, making same-different comparisons among and between patterns, and parsing musical patterns together" (85), as well as other, similar covert cognitive actions. Procedural knowledge is unmediated; the listener is in direct contact with musical sounds and with thinking musically.

According to Elliott, procedural knowledge is also the most important manner in which to learn. Although he states that "the procedural dimension of listenership and

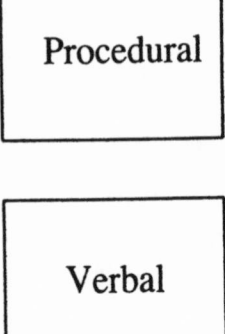

FIGURE 7.2 Ways of Knowing Music

the procedural dimension of musicianship are two sides of the same coin" (86), he also implies that procedural knowledge acquired through actively making music is essential to developing listening expertise. "Without developing some competency in the procedural knowings that lie at the core of musical practices and musical works, and a first hand knowledge of the circumstances in which these knowings apply, a listener's perspective of and relationships with music will remain moot in the most essential regard" (57).

Elliott's praxial philosophy implies, then, that we experience music directly through the procedural ways of knowing (including both listening and making) and indirectly through verbal ways of knowing. All other types of music knowledge evolve from these two foundations, as shown in Figure 7.3. Formal, informal, impressionistic, supervisory, and technical knowledge (the last element is our addition) are acquired best, and perhaps only, through one of the two basic ways of knowing. According to Elliott, any type of listening that rises above the novice level must involve all types of knowledge and ways of knowing.

Formal knowledge grows directly out of verbal learning and includes theoretical and historical information, as well as labels or terms related to music. Since formal knowledge is verbally based, it is the only type of knowledge that can be acquired without direct contact with music. One may verbally learn the rule that "a flatted seventh scale degree is characteristic of jazz styles." But formal knowledge can also be derived from procedural modes of knowing when musicers or listeners are engaged in musical problem solving. For example, a musicer or listener may recognize that "flatting the seventh" in a scale sounds more stylistically correct in a jazz tune than in a pop tune and only later verbally "discover" the rule that applies.

Just as formal knowledge grows directly out of the verbal learning mode, technical knowledge grows directly out of the procedural learning mode. By technical knowledge, we mean, for example, the mechanics of how to perform. To play the trumpet, one must learn correct fingerings, how to "buzz," breathing techniques, and so on. One can read about how to play the trumpet (verbal knowledge), but actually playing the trumpet leads to technical knowledge about trumpet playing, just as reading about the history of a musical work leads to knowledge of music history. We argue

Ways of Knowing   Types of Musical Knowledge

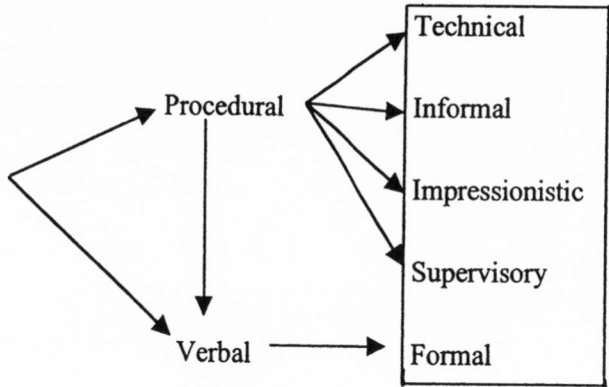

FIGURE 7.3 Types of Musical Knowledge

here that technical knowledge is a component of procedural knowledge, but not its equivalent. In Elliott's writing, procedural knowledge is a more global construct and includes but is not limited to technical knowledge.

The remaining types of knowledge (informal, impressionistic, and supervisory) are, according to Elliott, "non-verbal and situational" (101). In other words, because informal, impressionistic, and supervisory knowledge are acquired through the act of making music, the listener must have sufficient use of procedural knowledge *from the perspective of the music maker* to make meaningful use of these ways of knowing as a listener.

Informal knowledge involves "knowing how to listen critically—in relation to authoritative principles of musical interpretation and performance" (Elliott 1995, 98). Elliott asserts that listening expertise associated with informal knowledge can be gleaned only from the insider perspective described earlier. Because informal knowledge has to do with reflective music making, one must be an active, goal-directed music maker within a musical practice to acquire and use informal knowledge as a listener. Informal knowledge allows the concert violinist to negotiate and make explicit in performance the subtle differences between the music of Mozart and Beethoven, yet the same technically proficient violinist may be unable to negotiate the larger difference between Beethoven and bluegrass because he or she lacks informal knowledge about the latter musical practice. From the listener's perspective, informal knowledge is, for example, what makes the music of P. D. Q. Bach humorous. While the novice music listener may laugh at the obvious slapstick comedy involved, the listener with informal knowledge chuckles because "that's not how it's done."

Impressionistic knowledge is what is used to develop "a refined emotional sense or feel for what is musically appropriate, original, and artistically significant in the music one makes or listens for" (Elliott 1995, 98). The "educated feelings" or "cognitive emotions" of impressionistic knowledge arise from and are developed within musical practices and lie at the root of musical judgments about what is good and bad, or artistically appropriate or inappropriate. Through "the actions of natural music problem solving" (99), the student develops a refined emotional sense of what works and what doesn't work. Once attained, impressionistic knowledge can be used in listening experiences outside of music making. But impressionistic knowledge must first be attained, Elliott claims, through the act of making music.

As noted earlier, Elliott describes music listening as thinking-in-action that requires focus and attention directed to the details of musical sound. It is not a washover experience. Supervisory knowledge is the means by which both musicers and listeners "monitor and direct their listening in relation to the several dimensions of meaning or information that musical works evince" (100). Listeners who function above the novice level possess cognitive awareness that allows them to monitor and redirect their own thinking during the act of listening. In effect, supervisory knowledge is "the ability to continuously retarget one's attention forward to new details or problems in the music one is making or listening for" (100). Elliott notes that "the primary way" to acquire supervisory knowledge is in the context of making music, and "a second way . . . is to encourage students to reflect verbally about what there is to interpret, express, and listen for in specific works" (101).

Throughout his writing, Elliott implies that the skilled listener must acquire all types of knowledge in order to attain more than a rudimentary level of listening skill. All musicers are listeners; they listen during the act of music making. Elliott also implies that all listeners must be musicers to attain the insider perspective and to attain expertise in listening, as he defines it. The larger implication for music educators is that all learners must first be music makers if the goal of instruction is to increase listening skills. In short, Elliott proposes that one cannot be more than a novice listener without first being able to make music at a meaningful level. In his words,

> to educate music listening beyond a novice level requires that music students be inducted into and immersed in musical practices through meaningful music making. Listening artistically for the music one is making oneself (and with others) enables a student to understand how different aspects of musicing and listening relate to one another. . . . Learning to listen deeply and intelligently for the music of a particular practice requires that students learn music from inside musical practices, from the perspective of reflective musical practitioners. (101)

Questions and Commentary

A fundamental tenet of Elliott's theory is that essential musical understandings can be acquired only through the process of making music, and knowledge gained in and through music making is prerequisite to achieving listening skills beyond the novice level. A second fundamental premise of Elliott's theory is that musical experiences are grounded in cultural contexts, and, therefore, musical meaning is embedded in the cultural context and can be deciphered only by a listener who is likewise embedded in the culture. In other words, one cannot have essential knowledge about a given musical practice unless one is immersed in the cultural context of the music.

These arguments appear sound, as presented individually in the theory. However, the implications of how these two ideas interact are not fully explored for the act of listening, and this interaction possesses some intriguing questions.

Perhaps the best way to envision the interaction of music making and culture is to plot each as a continuum on a graph. This proposition is presented in Figure 7.4. The horizontal axis represents the degree of a listener's involvement in music making. The listener with no involvement in music making is at the left end of the continuum, and the listener who is deeply involved in music making is at the opposite end. The vertical axis represents a listener's involvement in (and understanding of) the culture that surrounds and is part of a musical practice. A listener who is not in the culture would be located at the bottom of the axis. A listener who is totally immersed in the particular culture of the musical practice would be at the top of the axis.

Let us examine four potential listeners represented in Figure 7.4. Listener 1 has a high degree of music-making skill and is simultaneously embedded in the culture of that musical practice. This represents the optimum scenario for advanced listening, in Elliott's view. Listener 1 perceives and understands the music at the highest possible level. Listener 2, in contrast, is not a music maker and also is not involved in the culture of the musical practice. Listener 2 can make little, if any, sense of the music being heard.

These two scenarios are very clear. However, the picture becomes less clear when we examine listeners 3 and 4. Listener 3 is an active music maker but does not know the musical culture. While listener 3's level of perception of the music may be high, essential meanings will always be missing. Listener 3 might be, for example, a highly experienced and expert classical musician listening to zydeco. This listener may perceive musical information at a high level but without nonverbal and verbal knowledge of this particular musical practice (or music culture). This kind of music remains for listener 3 essentially meaningless.

Conversely, listener 4 is totally embedded in a musical culture but lacks the types of knowledge that can only be acquired through music making. This listener can extract the cultural meanings of the music but may have difficulty with the musical information. To put a face on this listener, imagine a young person involved in the hip-hop music scene. Hip-hop music presents an interesting challenge for praxial theory in that it has very few actual music makers, but an extensive musical culture (of mostly listeners) attached to it.

One of the implications of Elliott's theory is that listener 3 is a superior listener to listener 4 by virtue of his or her music-making skills and is therefore able to make more sense of the sounds. However, it can be argued that the cultural experience of listener 4 allows him or her to extract more cultural information and meaning from the music than listener 3. Thus, listener 4 would be the better listener, because the perception of listener 4 is richer in meaning when compared with listener 3. Listener 3 is unable to extract meaning from what is being heard and actually may apply culturally inappropriate meaning.

An important question, then, is how was the knowledge of listener 4 developed? Listener 4, by being involved with the culture, may have had extensive listening experience to musical works within a specific musical practice. But according to praxial theory, repeated listening embedded in the proper cultural context would not necessarily increase listening skill past the novice level without music-making experiences as well.

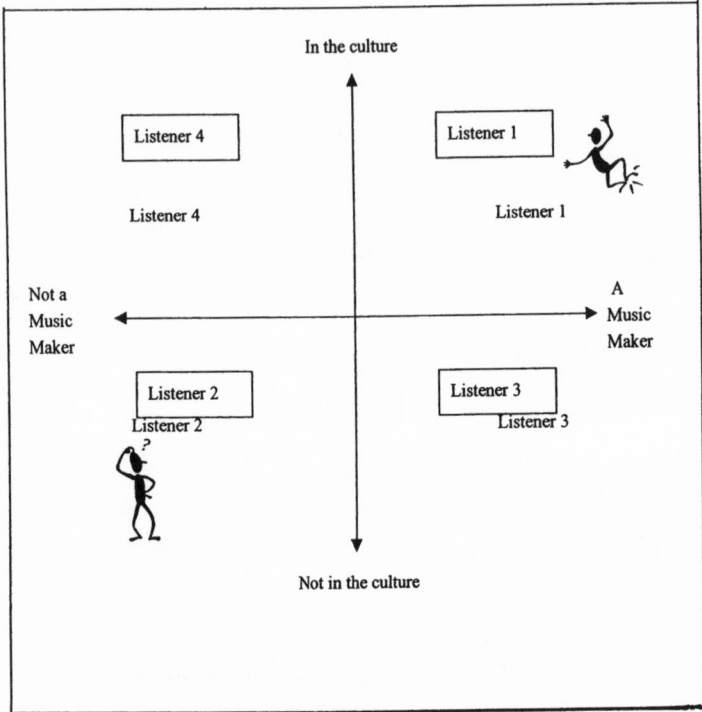

FIGURE 7.4 Music Making and Cultural Context

This seems contrary to common experience. How is it that non–music makers who are deeply grounded in a musical culture (such as opera fans, Dead Heads, hip-hoppers, or country music fans) are able to develop levels of listening skill not accounted for in praxial philosophy? Can it be that certain interactions between culture and music making create unpredicted consequences?

The relationship between culture and music making as it relates to the act of listening needs to be explored in greater detail within praxial theory. Intense musical cultures, especially those of youth and popular cultures, should be examined in search of individuals who are not necessarily music makers, but who exhibit sophisticated listening skills not accounted for by praxial theory.

Therefore, the first set of questions we pose is: What is the relationship between culture and music making in praxial theory for individuals who are primarily listeners within various musical practices? What are the implications of this relationship for learning to listen?

At the core of the praxial theory is the assertion that music making is the only way to acquire certain types of musical knowledge. Elliott states that "to understand and appreciate an intelligent performance, a spectator (or audience member) requires the same kinds of knowledge as the performer, including a reasonable level of procedural knowledge in performance of that nature" (56).

If Elliott is correct, one would assume that musicians who had performed a work would have more finely attuned responses when listening than those who had not. But

Frederickson (1999) found no significant difference in perceptions of tension in a wind ensemble work between musicians who had performed the piece (high school and university ensemble members) and those who had not (high school band members who had not yet learned the work and college choral ensemble members). Elliott would attribute the finding of no difference to isotropy, or the ability of music makers to carry forward their musical knowledge to the listening experience. Because all the musicians were experienced performers in Western art music traditions and therefore could be assumed to have "a reasonable level of procedural knowledge," their perceptions of musical tension as listeners were similar, regardless of the fact that some had performed the work and some had not. At this level of musical expertise, performing the specific musical work was not a sufficiently powerful experience to make a difference in listeners' perceptions.

Other researchers have shown, however, that repeated listening to music (not performing) does effect a change among listeners, particularly with regard to music preferences. In an extensive literature review, Finnäs (1989) found that preferences for "somewhat complex music can be increased by repeated listening" (77). Hedden (1981) noted, following a similar review, that "sheer repetitions may be sufficient to bring about affective shifts" (24).

Repeated listenings apart from music making do make a difference (at least) in listener preferences, and an individual who is listening more frequently may also be acquiring listening skills of some kind. Repeated listenings within a certain musical practice may give listeners, including individuals who are primarily listeners and not music makers, access to what Elliott describes as informal, impressionistic, and supervisory knowledge. For example, individuals who are fans of a particular style listen with intention and intensity to the point that they can readily identify (and often reject) crossover recordings. Opera and musical theater devotees recognize that singers in one genre are out of their element in the other. Regular listeners to popular music genres excel in identifying artists and musical works when only two-second snippets are provided to the listening audience. Karl Haas, whose radio broadcasts in earlier decades reached thousands nationally, frequently reported that truck drivers were among his most regular, inquiring, and informed listeners. In Elliott's language, these listeners possess sufficient informal, impressionistic, and supervisory knowledge to make critical judgments. They listen with intention, and they are indeed listening to and listening for. They are listening in the company of a culture of other listeners and operating within a musical practice.

On a practical level, radio stations know that they must balance the number of playings of a song such that they increase familiarity without oversaturating the listener. We would venture to say that everyone reading this could cite an example of an individual who is an acute music listener but not a music maker. How can this be if performance is the only route to expertise in listening? How can we account for music-learning expertise evidenced by familiarity and a listener's ability to discriminate through repeated exposure? One answer may be that performance or music making is not the only route to listening expertise, but simply the most efficient route. Through performance, listening skills may be enhanced quickly, but given ample effort and dedication, listening skills may be developed to sophisticated levels through other means, including repeated listening.

Therefore, the second set of questions we pose is: Can praxial theory allow for the development of music listening skills through repeated listenings of music without the need for music making? If it cannot, how does it address the changes that take place in listening ability through repeated listenings?

Elliott defines procedural knowledge broadly throughout *Music Matters*. Procedural ways of knowing include not only performing, but also the overt acts of composing, improvising, and moving, as well as covert acts of thinking-in-action and knowing-in-action, as described above. With regard to movement, Elliott notes that "the kinds of moving involved in music making (including conducting) are essential to improving musical understanding, which . . . is essentially procedural" (103).

An ensemble director intends to shape the music making of ensemble members and communicates that intent nonverbally through movement gestures, otherwise known as conducting. The conductor might be described as successful to the extent that ensemble members follow the intentions communicated in his or her movements. The point here is that the conductor's movements are specifically and purposefully directed to achieve an intention in the act of music making. The conductor is "making music" (in a form of procedural knowledge) through movement. But what of other movements? Is moving in response to music or movement coordinated with music procedural knowing as Elliott defines it? Do other kinds of moving achieve musical intentions? And what does moving have to do with the act of listening or developing listening expertise?

Elliott holds that "learning to listen critically, with strategic judgment, develops from listening to *one's own efforts to make music well*" (1995, 98; italics ours). How does this idea apply for one kind of expert mover and listener—a ballet dancer? One might describe a prima ballerina's movements as musical and the dancer herself as a listener, because she is performing within the context of music made by others. But the gesture of her arm through the air, for example, does not itself create musical sound, though the same gesture may indeed shape music when the dancer performs with musicians who watch her movements and respond with differences in their playing. Even so, is the intent of the dancer to shape the music via movement, and has the dancer learned to listen expertly by her "own efforts to make music well"?

The same question holds for mover-listeners in earlier stages of development or expertise. For example, we recently watched a two-year-old child respond spontaneously with swaying and shuffling movements to tempo changes in a recording of Vivaldi's "Spring" Concerto from *The Four Seasons*. His giggling caused an adult to play the music again, and eventually the child learned to "request" the music by randomly pressing buttons on the sound system. Several days later, he began to change movements a few moments *prior to* the tempo changes in the same piece. How did this two-year-old child, who appeared to be "listening for," learn to anticipate and respond to changes in the music?

The movements of the ballerina and of the child differ from the movements of a conductor in that the conductor uses specific movement gestures to shape the collective performance of a group of musicians actively engaged in making music, while the two-year-old child and the ballet dancer move with music or to music but are not usually shaping, directing, or "making" music by virtue of their movements. Yet their movements appear to focus listening and contribute to "knowing" about music.

We recognize that our examples are embedded in Western art music traditions, but "conducting" is also a practice-specific term. In some cultures and musical practices, music and movement occur in tandem, with movers giving impetus to the musicers and vice versa. When the mover is performing with live music makers who are sensitized and respond to the nuances of movement to the extent that music is changed, then moving is similar to conducting. Conversely, some movers are moving *to* the music; they do not intend to make music, nor does the music change by virtue of their actions.

The point here is that Elliott asserts that "the kinds of moving involved in music making" are those that advance listening skills. We can think of examples of moving that appear to advance listening skills, or be related to the development of listening skills, but in which the mover is not a music maker. In some instances, movement may support learning in the way that one form of intelligence or way of knowing supports another (Gardner 1988). Movers may be engaging in thinking-in-action; and even when thinking may be concentrated on movement and moving, listening skills may be advanced. Conversely, several researchers (Cheek 1979; Moore 1984; O'Hagin 1997) have found that focused attention to non-music-making movements, within a music-learning environment, do enhance musical skills. In a review of literature at least one author implies that moving, like repeated listening, may be a less efficient way of learning about music, but effective nonetheless (Lewis 1989).

Although it may be more experiential than procedural, moving without actually performing music may be a powerful way of acquiring listening expertise. Elliott states that one must make music to acquire informal, impressionistic, and supervisory musical knowledge. We posit that non-music-making movers may indeed be "listening to" and "listening for," and that their direct and indirect listening and moving experiences may be a gateway to musical knowledge and listening expertise as well.

The third set of questions we pose is: Is physical response or movement procedural knowing, as described in praxial philosophy, if no musical sounds are produced or if there is no intent to make music by the mover? How does praxial philosophy account for musical knowledge and listening expertise past the novice level acquired through moving and movement responses? Is there room for ways of knowing that are not directly musicing in praxial philosophy, including movement?

Elliott's discussion of emotion and music emerges first in his descriptions of impressionistic ways of knowing. Impressionistic knowledge "is a matter of cognitive emotions or knowledgeable feelings for a particular kind of doing and making" (1995, 64). Later Elliott says that impressionistic knowing "involves educated feelings for particular kinds of musicing and listening" (98). Throughout *Music Matters*, Elliott ties the concept of educated feelings to the listener's engagement in a musical practice and beliefs about that musical practice. "A fundamental part of the challenge, enjoyment, and human significance of musicing and music listening," he writes, "concerns the cultural-ideological nature of these forms of action and the cultural-ideological information that musical works convey" (185). When the listener is an enculturated member of a musical practice, then "music listening may also involve cognition of musical expressions of emotion and/or musical representations" (184).

By stating that "thinking and feeling (cognition and affect) are interdependent" (1995, 65), Elliott rejects dualistic concepts of emotion and intellect in favor of current mind-brain models of integrated consciousness. In short, there is no thinking without feeling and no feeling without thinking. But Elliott goes one step further by strongly tying the acquisition of cognitive emotion to making music. Recall that the discussion of emotion occurs primarily in the context of impressionistic ways of knowing, which, according to Elliott, are acquired through making music. He says that "the development of impressionistic musical knowledge depends on coaching students to make appropriate appraisals regarding the standards and traditions of practice that apply to musical works that students themselves are learning to interpret, perform, improvise, compose, arrange, and conduct" (99). In other words, emotion is cognized through engagement as a music maker, and "developing [the] refined emotional sense" (98) that Elliott describes as characteristic of competent listeners depends on students participating in music and on teachers coaching them to make judgments about their own performances.

We have no doubt that making music contributes to "cognitive emotion," as Elliott claims. But to discuss music listening and the responses musical practices evoke among listeners in these terms only seems limiting and even counterintuitive. Emotion may be the reason we listen in the first place. Music can attract the attention of the individual to the point that the music is conscious in that person's experience. At the moment of consciousness, the individual shifts from "hearer" to "listener"—a shift of consciousness that may be triggered by emotion. In other words, music may come into consciousness *because* emotion is enacted.

It is also possible that music can arouse emotion to the point that the listener wants to return to the experience of listening or the music itself. Even listening to music outside of practices with which one is familiar may engender emotional response, and although the response may be entirely different from that of the listener with enculturated understandings of the meanings of the music, we would be hard pressed to say emotion is not present. Here we agree with Elliott in part: the *specific* emotional meanings and referents (all part of "cognitive emotion") are learned through engagement in the musical practice, whether from the perspective of the listener or from that of the musicer. But it may be emotion or emotional response of a different nature that, in part, brings the music to the consciousness of listeners both inside and outside the practice.

Elliott does not deny that listening to music can be an emotionally satisfying experience. He notes, "The actions of music making and music listening often give rise to experiences of positive or satisfying affect" (1995, 109), and ties his discussion to Csikszentmihalyi's model of optimal experience or "flow" (1990). In the flow model, one reaches optimal experience through concentrated and directed effort in which the tension between skill and challenge is such that the individual is completely absorbed by and focused on the goal. Achieving a "positive or satisfying affect" requires concentrated effort. Elliott claims, then, that "intelligent music listening consists in deliberate acts of informed thinking in relation to performed or improvised patterns of musical design that, in turn, evince histories and norms of musical practice" (1995, 184); hence, cognitive emotion. But is that the sum total of the emotional experience of music listeners?

Elliott's concept of cognitive emotion is tied strongly to making music and the flow model. But individuals come to and return to the music they choose for social, cultural, intellectual, and emotional reasons that may have nothing to do with music making per se, and other models of emotion and affect could be considered (e.g., Damasio 1994, 1999). People participate in musical cultures for various reasons, including reasons that may have to do with emotion at a deep level. Elliott says that listeners are listening to and listening for. In our experience, listeners also choose what and when, and they may also choose how. Some of that choosing may have to do with emotion.

The fourth set of questions we pose is: How does praxial philosophy account for responses to music that are evident but not related to the cognitive focus of "listening for" something? Are all emotional responses "cognitive emotion," as defined by Elliott, or are other kinds of emotional response part of the listener's experience? What do other theories of emotion and brain function have to say about music and listening, and is there room for them in praxial philosophy?

Basic to praxial theory is the idea that music making leads to expert listening. Elliott states that "moving beyond a beginning level of listenership requires that students develop their musicianship by entering into the multidimensional nature of music as a reflective, artistic endeavor." The road to expert listening is described as "progressive problem solving [that] requires student listeners to take more and more dimensions and details of musical works into account during their efforts to make and listen for music artistically" (1995, 104).

This road map points to a learning process that places the student's cognitive effort directly at the center of learning to listen. Elliott asserts that it is through students' reflective practice and performance that listening skills are developed, and he describes reflective practice as a "problem-solving and problem-finding" process in which learning ultimately rests with the learner. There is no reason to suspect that reflective practice is any more or less powerful in music learning than in other domains. However, we fear that Elliott has not adequately addressed the unique difficulties one encounters when attempting to apply reflective practice strategies to the discipline of music, specifically in school settings.

The overriding impression we get from reading *Music Matters* is that music making leads to enhanced listening skills. We disagree. Music making *can* lead to improved listening skills, but the relationship is by no means automatic or guaranteed. We can recall examples of students practicing a piece of music repeatedly with a glaring error that is continuously missed. We have heard students in practice rooms playing a blues pattern for twenty minutes or more while something else seems to be going through their minds. We know college music majors who do not remember hearing a single note of their senior recitals. Listening during music making is not a given and sometimes seems to be the exception.

The tone quality, the tempos, or the mistakes that they hear in a recording, but that they did not perceive while performing, often surprise students who hear tapes of their performance. Kepner (1986) convincingly demonstrated the inability of experienced high school musicians to listen to themselves while performing. The students in his study repeatedly missed glaring errors in their own performances. Kepner explains this phenomenon by proposing a sensory-blocking theory that suggests that a student who is playing an instrument is presented with so much sensory information (e.g., visual note reading, kinesthetic fingerings and embouchure, maintenance of beat, visual translation of dynamic markings, and maintenance of rhythms) that a type of "sensory overload" occurs, leaving little sensory ability left for the act of listening.

We believe that Kepner has in fact exposed an important limitation to implementing a praxial theory for the development of listening skills. The procedural difficulties inherent in musical performance require extensive cognitive efforts themselves, as well as the cognitive effort required for focused listening. What is missing from Elliott's work is an acknowledgment that the reflective-practice model of teaching may be harder, much harder, in music than in other disciplines. The student studying poems by Browning is not struggling to achieve motor skills. Likewise, students studying math or science are much better able to concentrate on their thinking and reflection without the distractions of physical performance.

Elliott offers suggestions to music teachers who wish to develop listening skills in their students. He points out that the teacher's "role is principally one of mentoring, coaching, and modeling for music students conceived as apprentice musical practitioners. All music students . . . ought to be viewed and taught in the same basic way: as reflective musical practitioners engaged in the kind of cognitive apprenticeship we call music education" (1995, 105). What is being described above is the basic model of the private music lesson, applied to all of music education. Elliott does not address how it would be applied in ensembles or classrooms.

In fairness, we feel Elliott would agree that learning to listen through performance is a difficult process that requires focused teacher intervention. His book was not intended as a method book, so specific teaching strategies are not expected. Still, we feel he has neither explored nor articulated the difficulties and potential problems—problems unique to music listening—with applying an activity-based learning paradigm implied by praxial philosophy to music education. Our fear is that in the absence of a clear articulation of how listening can and should be included, a simple making-music paradigm will be substituted.

Consider that Elliott repeatedly cautions against listening to recordings in music education contexts. "Students have the rest of their lives to listen to recordings of musical performances after schooling is over," he writes. "The best preparation for listening to musical performances is full participation in music making in the present" (1995, 104). And again, "Listening to recording excludes (or anesthetizes) part of the self, performing partakes of the self as a whole" (103). Although we know of no general listening-only music programs, Elliott is particularly concerned that "general music programs geared to recorded music do not provide the proper conditions for developing the several kinds of knowledge required for intelligent listening because recordings place the student-as-listener outside the artistic decision-making process. . . . In contrast, music making places the student-as-listener inside the musical works and practices he or she is endeavoring to learn" (99). He further implies that the usefulness of listening to recordings for developing listening skills is, at best, limited. "When artistic music making (which includes artistic music listening) is at the center of the music curriculum, then listening is properly contextualized. As a supplement to music making, listening to recordings provides students with additional opportunities to develop supervisory knowledge" (101).

We believe his case is overstated to the point that music listening becomes negatively associated with listening to recordings in any music education context. Listening to recordings is not the problem; how students listen and how they learn to listen, whether from any of the insider or outsider perspectives articulated earlier in this essay, is the crux of the matter. If listening is truly a matter of thinking-in-action, then how students are challenged to think in the act of listening, either to live or recorded music, is the critical issue. We contend, for example, that the teacher directive "listen for the melody" is equally ineffective (from our point of view) whether uttered in reference to music students who are making music or in reference to recordings to which they are listening. In order to help students develop increasingly sophisticated levels of listening expertise, teachers (both in ensembles and classrooms) must have sufficient ability as listeners themselves to find points of access for focused listening and then skillfully question and guide students as they think in the act of listening.

We return to these points, then: listening as thinking-in-action or thinking in the act of listening, whether to live or recorded music, *can* be enhanced by making music, but music making does not guarantee the advancement of listening skills, nor is the development of listening skills past the novice level dependent on music making. Elliott has devoted considerable effort to convincing the reader of the validity of his praxial theory with respect to listening. But in so doing, he may have led educators to assume that listening skills are being developed through performance-based experiences alone (whether in ensemble or classroom settings) and done an injustice to the challenges that the educator will encounter when actually attempting to develop listening ability.

Therefore, we propose the following questions: What are the challenges unique to music education of implementing music instruction based on a praxial philosophy as it concerns the development of listening skills? What are the underlying issues of these challenges? In what ways is the reflective-practice model adaptable to music learning? What degree of teacher intervention is necessary to achieve enhanced listening skills, both when listening while making music and when listening to live or recorded music that one is not making oneself? How is the model of music instruction being proposed different from the private music lesson model already in place, and how does it work for music listening?

Listening

One of the challenges in reading Elliott's work with respect to listening is that procedural knowledge is not the equivalent of music making. Procedural knowing (which implies action) includes the "thinking-in-action" that Elliott describes as characteristic of both music listening and music making. Still, Elliott's discussion centers on listening within the context of music making, even in the listening chapters. His ideas about the kinds of thinking-in-action that occur when one is listening only are less well developed and obscured by the repeated emphasis on music making.

Furthermore, throughout *Music Matters* Elliott places music making in the lead position. He emphasizes that music making is the essential means of knowing about music, critical to acquiring most types of musical knowledge, and fundamental to listening skills past the novice level. But musicers are able to make music precisely because they have heard, often since infancy, the sounds of music around them. The musical practices individuals come to know through enculturation alone are the very practices in which they first engage as young children. Musicing does not happen apart from enculturated knowledge of music acquired by listening first.

Listeners—no matter who they are, what they listen to or for, or what their experiences as musicers may be—have lived experiences from which they construct their own meanings about what it is to be a listener, what it is to listen, and what it is to be in a community of like-minded listeners. We have no doubt that making music does indeed contribute to understanding in ways that only performing, improvising, composing, arranging, and conducting can. However, when it comes to listening, we cannot afford to privilege the musicer's perspective because we cannot claim to know what the listener knows. Apart from a significant body of work on preference and perception, we know very little about how people listen, particularly with regard to listeners in popular-music cultures. As researchers and educators, we rarely listen to the listeners, and when we do, we are not always willing to accept their answers unless they match our own understandings. In short, if listeners do not hear what musicers think they should, or if they fail to describe what they hear in ways that musicers understand, then listeners' perspectives may be discounted. It may be that individuals who are only listeners possess a kind of musical understanding that musicers can never hope to attain.

While praxial theory offers insights about the end point of expert listening for music makers, it seems less clear for other listeners, other types of listening, and other listening experiences. If one accepts that music listening expertise can be attained only through music making, then it can be argued that expert listening is actually the exception, not the rule, in most Western societies. Music education (at least in the United States) is intended and designed to teach the masses, not the select few who may achieve the level of expert listener in a performance setting. While one would hope that the attainment of this level of listening skill might be a goal of music education, we must acknowledge that this is unlikely given present-day realities. Music education must deal also with developing listening skills that are more in keeping with what one sees in society as a whole.

In this regard, praxial philosophy has a few gaps. The importance—to the listener and to the development of music listening—of culture, emotion, repeated listening, and movement needs to be accounted for in a philosophy of music education that will be useful to the profession as it exists today. At present, key issues involved with nurturing listening skills are unresolved or unaddressed in praxial theory. Conversely, the theory, as presented, seems to be robust enough to allow for expansion to incorporate other ideas. We believe there may be answers to the questions we pose in the research, writing, and conversations that will be part of our collective future.

References

American Symphony Orchestra League. 2001. *ASOL facts online*. http://www.americanorchestras. org/knowledge_center/quick_orchestra_facts_2000-2001_.html.

Cheek, Y. 1979. *The effects of psychomotor experiences on the perception of selected musical elements and the formation of self-concept in fourth grade*. Ph.D. diss., University of Michigan.

Country Music Association. 2000. *MRI country music listener analysis.* www.cmaworld.com/ marketing/Default.asp.

Csikszentmihalyi, M. 1990. *Flow: The psychology of optimal experience.* New York: Harper and Row.

Damasio, A. R. 1994. *Descartes' error: Emotion, reason, and the human brain.* New York: Avon Books.

———. 1999. *The feeling of what happens: Body and emotion in the making of consciousness.* New York: Harcourt Brace.

Elliott, D. J. 1995. *Music matters: A new philosophy of music education.* New York: Oxford University Press.

Finnäs, L. 1989. How can musical preferences by modified? A research review. *Bulletin of the Council for Research in Music Education* 102:1–58.

Frederickson, W. E. 1999. Effect of musical performance on perception of tension in Gustav Holst's First Suite in E-flat. *Journal of Research in Music Education* 47:44–52.

Hedden, S. K. 1981. Music listening skills and music listening preferences. *Bulletin of the Council for Research in Music Education* 65:16–26.

Kepner, C. 1986. *The effect of performance familiarity, listening condition and type of performance effort on correctness of performance error detection by 50 high school instrumentalists as explained through a sensory blocking theory.* Ph.D. diss., Kent State University.

Lewis, B. E. 1989. The research literature in movement-based instruction with children: Implications for music education. *Update* 7:13–17.

Mark, M. L., and C. L. Gary. 1992. *A history of American music education.* New York: Schirmer Books.

Masson, G. 2000, April 29. World sales remain stagnant. *Billboard,* 10ff.

Moore, J. S. L. 1984. *Rhythm and movement: An objective analysis of their association with music aptitude.* Ph.D. diss., University of North Carolina at Greensboro.

O'Hagin, I. B. 1997. *Effects of a discovery approach to movement instruction on children's responses to musical stimuli.* Ph.D. diss., University of Arizona.

Recording Industry Association of America. 2000. *2000 consumer profile.* www.riaa.com.

Tour attractions promise $1 billion take in 2000. 2000, March 11. *Billboard,* 1ff.

8

Why Musical Performance?

Views Praxial to Performative

WAYNE D. BOWMAN

Why should we learn ourselves instead of enjoying the performances of others?

—Aristotle, *Politics*

States arise out of like activities. It makes no small difference, then, whether we form habits of one kind or another from our very youth; *it makes a very great difference, or rather all the difference.* [Italics added]

—Aristotle, *Nichomachean Ethics*

The gist of Aristotle's answer to the question in the first of these two epigrams is that although the actual practice of music can and does make a difference in human character (since music's objects, more than those of any other art, resemble moral qualities), the nature of that "difference" is largely negative if performance skill is developed to any real degree of proficiency. Pursued to advanced levels, musical performance is a vulgar, degrading affair; the kind of thing properly dignified people would only do in jest or in states of intoxication. Children should play, perform, and sing, then, but only to the point at which they can take pleasure in noble melodies and rhythms—in other words, as appreciative listeners to others' performances. This suspicion toward performance has had an exceptionally long life. Indeed, and quite ironically, given the pivotal role performance plays in most North American music programs, vestiges of this notion can be found even in views espoused by some contemporary music educators. Clearly, then, the question Aristotle asks is a crucial one for the music education profession, for without a cogent answer, there is little assurance of congruence between our advocacy arguments and our actual instructional practices. To argue that music education is important on grounds that are primarily perceptual and receptive in nature while our instruction is predominantly performance based puts us in a very precarious situation. And that is precisely what North American music education has done for decades.

Among the most conspicuous contrasts between David Elliott's (1995) praxial philosophy of music education and the version of aesthetic education best known to North American music educators is the role each envisions for musical performance. For many (if not most) adherents to the aesthetic rationale, musical perception and response as manifest in listening are educationally paramount. Performing or making music, then, are but ways of attaining the goal of enhanced "aesthetic sensitivity." Moreover, performance skills are presumed to be rooted in something like talent—innate executive capacities possessed by relatively few and amenable to development only with inordinate amounts of work.

Implicit in Elliott's arguments, on the other hand, is an assumption that musical practices draw upon dispositions and executive abilities that are relatively widely distributed in societies and that performance is not a rare capacity or an undertaking accessible only to exceptional individuals highly endowed with "talent." Thus, the development of musicianship through active engagement in various kinds of musical production is both educationally practical and well suited to most people's interests and abilities.

His arguments take a further, normative step, however: insisting that musicing—active practical experience in productive musical engagements—is crucial to any instructional program that is truly musical or musically educational. And this, apparently, is because people who engage in music as practitioners or performers (more broadly, "musicers") have, in virtue of their musicianship or artistry, a kind of privileged access to what musical actions and practices entail. The performer's cognitive processes are more fully and properly musical than those of people whose musical experience excludes such artistic, productive components, in particular people whose sole or primary mode of musical engagement is receptive instead of productive: in other words, listeners. And finally, for these reasons, performance-based music education is inherently superior to listening-based music education. Making and doing music are far preferable to listening to recordings (a "doing" that does not entail making or, whose making, if it be such, is largely covert and extensively subjective), because such actions (or knowings-in-action) assure the development of a musicianship more fully attuned to the multiple dimensions that constitute a given musical practice. In short, Elliott's philosophy maintains, on purportedly praxial grounds, that performing music, engaging in it as a practitioner, is the best way to teach and learn it.

This position has been greeted enthusiastically by those into whose instruction performance figures centrally. At the same time, it has encountered predictable animosity in those with commitments to reception-centered curricular arrangements, most notably advocates of aesthetic sensitivity who regard listening as musically fundamental and have invested heavily in instructional approaches where it is central. Elliott's most vocal detractors contend that performance-centered music education is exclusive or elitist because performing is a mode of musical engagement suited to the few rather than the many. Listening constitutes a valid musical praxis and an instructional method different from and, indeed, superior to performance. Perhaps, it has even been suggested, performance is becoming a thing of the past, a mode of musical involvement and an instructional strategy rooted in musical practices whose currency is waning.

The fervidness of Elliott's renunciation of listening as instructional method can be traced, I believe, to certain historical shortcomings in music education philosophy: its willingness to reduce musical experience to listening and equate it to aesthetic response, to treat listening as the primary or exclusive instructional method for developing such responsiveness, and to regard listening as the preeminent way of "being musical." Despite a pivotal role for listening in Elliott's accounts of musicianship and its development, then, he is generally reluctant to endorse it except as an adjunct to performing, improvising, arranging, composing, or in short, "musicing." Listening, he seems to argue, is necessary but not sufficient to musicianship. Artistry, as contrasted with aesthetic responsiveness or sensitivity, entails engagement, action, and productivity. Thus, Elliott's negative thesis, that listening is neither the only nor the best way of relating to music, arises from essentially positive convictions: in order to listen, one must have something to listen to; and the generation of such "listenables" is no dumb feat of execution, but a rich, wonderful way of knowing and being, a phenomenally unique state with tremendous pedagogical and motivational potency, and one of the best ways to grasp fully what is distinctive and moving about a given musical practice.

Elliott often uses the word "performing" to designate the active engagement he advocates. But what performing means specifically, and why it should be instructionally paramount, are matters that warrant fuller treatment than Elliott gives them. Moreover, "performing" seems at times to serve as a kind of shorthand for productive engagement in general (musicing), leaving open important questions as to the nature and significance of performance proper as opposed, for instance, to things such as composing and arranging. Most people bring abundant conceptual baggage to terms such as "artistry" and "performing," which makes for highly divergent, idiosyncratic understandings of their significance and how they might best be developed. There is, hence, a need to define better and to conceptualize more clearly what "musical performance" means and how it may relate to other modes of musical engagement. An important preliminary concern of this essay will thus be to examine what performing entails, and what appears to be distinctive about this particular mode of "musicing."

Among the more important perspectives from which musical performance begs consideration are performance as action, as contrasted to contemplative perception; performance as creation or production, as opposed to reception; performance as participation, as opposed to alienation or individuation; performance as play; performance as distinctively processual, or temporal; performance as a uniquely bodily experience; and performance as the articulation of identity, both individual and collective.

This essay will attempt only a cursory, preliminary examination of these issues. But it will take only a brief overview, I think, to render problematic many of the ways we have been taught to conceive of "music," "performing," "listening," and the like.

Since it is one of my main points here, I want to be clear that I do not think a commitment to performance necessarily follows from music's praxial nature. That is, I am not persuaded that either performing or listening is logically implicated as an instructional method by the fact of music's praxial nature; nor is either performing or listening necessarily and unconditionally "good." As such, I propose to examine listening and performing, pro and con, and speculate about the kind of case that might be made in favor of and against each. To anticipate one of my argument's conclusions, I do not think we can substantiate the claim that musical performance is the most musical of all possible musical involvements, in comparison to which all others must be found wanting, inauthentic, or deficient.

However, the fact that performance is not implicated by music's praxial nature does not mean a strong case cannot be made for it on other grounds. One of the ends to which I hope this essay may contribute is the identification of such grounds. Praxial arguments represent an important step forward in music philosophy, but they do not give us directly, in themselves, the kind of justification of musical performance the profession requires. What is needed are specifically performative arguments, arguments that speak directly to the constitutive features of performing that make it an exceptionally potent means of music education. But such arguments will need to be made from a sufficient critical distance for us to see that the potency of musical performance (including attributes such as "flow") can serve both desirable and undesirable ends, and that the most important reasons for engaging in musical performance are not so much ontological as they are pedagogical, psychological, social, and political. Among the things I hope we may learn along the way is that musical performance need not beat all contenders to have considerable merit as a way of learning and growing musically.

Performance: Pro

Let us begin with an examination of what performing means: a short inventory of the more persuasive claims that may be advanced on its behalf. First, we need to recognize that using "performance" as the generic label for productive musical engagement can lead to confusion. "Performing" is convenient, familiar, and less awkward and artificial-sounding than terms such as "musicing": it is probably most people's verb for music making, and indeed, for most people who teach music or write about teaching it, performing is the most familiar and gratifying mode of musical engagement. But when we engage in philosophical discourse, we need to be clear whether we mean performing as such, or music making more broadly. In *Music Matters* Elliott uses "performance" both ways, making it difficult at times to know whether, in advocating performance as the preferred means of musical instruction, he is advocating performance per se or music making more inclusively. In general, he appears to have in mind the latter, for his discussions show that he would prefer we include composing, arranging, improvising, and all the various ways of authentic music making, not just performing. What *Music Matters* seems to advocate explicitly is musicing, not performing per se.

Yet, it is hard to miss Elliott's implicit conviction that performing in the narrower, less inclusive sense of hands-on, productive engagement with actual sonorous musical materials is paramount. There is a strong implicit message that performing is a very distinctive way of being musical, one with special links and even a kind of privileged access to "musicianship." I propose here to set aside the modes of musicing that do not directly involve the generation of musical sound and ask what kind of argument we might actually make on behalf of performing itself—"performing" in the narrower sense—the kind of musical activity that figures centrally in the vast majority of music education ("aesthetic" rhetoric notwithstanding).

Despite a long history of misrepresentation and misunderstanding in which performance has been treated as mere technical skill or a means to ends more easily attained in other ways, it is obvious that a great many people continue to engage in musical performance and to take deep satisfaction in it. One of the things we might reasonably hope to accomplish here is an understanding of why people seem so compellingly drawn to such behavior; perhaps then we can better explain whether or why the musically educated need to engage in it.

Before we proceed, let us see if we can dispense with some of the unnecessary baggage that often attends the word "perform": connotations that tend to prejudice the uninformed against it. We need to resist tendencies to attribute to all musical "performance" those attributes that are practice specific. For instance, performance is not invariably the creation and execution of polished sonic events for the edification of attentive, receptive audiences, even if that is what the term brings to mind for many. Performing often involves public presentations, enactments, or demonstrations of skill to an appreciative audience, but not always or necessarily. Let us agree to use the word in a broader sense, one that encompasses, say, rehearsals, jam sessions, improvisations, sessions with or without audiences, formal and informal, professional and amateur—all manner of hands-on engagements with sonorous musical materials. Let us also distinguish musical from theatrical performance, even though the two sometimes coincide. Musical performance is not necessarily a matter of obediently following a script, of creating a representation, copy, or imitation of an "original." Again, it may at times be so, but not necessarily or always. In short, musical performances need not be ostentatious spectacles; nor are they necessarily concerned with complex technical execution or showy displays of virtuosity; nor are they necessarily replications or re-creations of something preexistent.

We need to distinguish musical performance's occasional attributes from its more pervasive ones, resisting conventional stereotypes and taking a broader, more inclusive view of what performers of music are experiencing and doing when they engage in musically generative activity. Viewed experientially, from the inside, performing music is a highly distinctive kind of processual human agency: a direct, productive, meaningful engagement with sound. It is not exclusive or elitist (although, like any human endeavor, some will develop exceptionally high levels of expertise), nor is it a showy exhibition (although some may pursue this end, and it may at times be appropriate), but a natural and broadly accessible way of being musical, which is richly rewarding in its own right. What can we say in defense of the experiential uniqueness and instructional validity of these kinds of musical makings and doings?

One of the first points we should make has already been alluded to: performing music is an act of giving form, in the moment, to a temporally fleeting phenomenon that exists nowhere outside that moment. It is a here-and-now manner of being that reclaims the present moment from the mundane worlds of might-be, was, and might-have-been in which we live most of our lives. At its most potent, it is an experience of centeredness, of oneness, of wholeness that transcends and dissolves obnoxious dualisms like subject and object, feeling and knowing, body and mind, inner and outer. And because of this processual/productive nature, performing music puts everything on the line, so to speak. The act of making music is a fragile, risky affair, in which there are no second chances and there is no turning back. Performing music is living in the moment, the present time.

"Performing" is sometimes misconstrued as a translative activity in which a performer functions as a kind of conduit for the composer or the work. This, again, is the view from outside. From the inside, musical performance is constructive, and as Eleanor Stubley (1995) puts it, "transactional": it is not just a matter of mechanically retrieving a given "work," nor is it simply a matter of giving shape to "the music." Performing is a living in and through music. It is a unique event, an experientially concrete way of being where the remarkable sense captured in T. S. Eliot's (1988) memorable phrase "you are the music while the music lasts" is neither metaphorical nor occasional, but physically actual and always the rule.

So, music making is at once distinctively temporal and somatic, facts Elliott's phrase "knowing-in-action" conveys somewhat obliquely. That musicianship amounts to a special kind of knowledge is a fact we need only note in passing here, thanks to Elliott's persuasive arguments. But it is important to note that in performing music, the agent of this knowing is distinctively embodied. Performing music is at once a making and a doing, and as such is always and fundamentally a corporeal fact. As I have argued elsewhere, it is a "somatic semantic." Or as Keil (Keil and Feld 1994) puts it in his ever-unaffected way, performing consists in "an apprehensible reality that is in your hands, fingers, feet, butt, hips, gut, and unified mind-body."

Not only does performing involve living through a vivid, embodied present, but this vivid presence is also and always something musical performers experience together, as "we." Alfred Schutz (cited in Keil and Feld 1994) states succinctly that "living through a vivid present in common constitutes" the mutual tuning-in relationship, the experience of "we." So, performing music is not just about generating pleasing patterns of sound, it is a distinctive way, as Stubley (1998) puts it, of being in the body and in the sound; and this processual voyage is not typically undertaken alone, but with others. Musical performance is not just physical, then, and not just psychological, but social as well. It is not just about sounds and selves and "flow," but also about people and relatedness. On this particular point it is important to be very clear: the social is not simply the context in which music making occurs, it is a fundamental component both of the making and what is made. Viewed this way, performing music is always also a way of being together, and what is performed is never "just the music," never "music alone." Music making is an assertion and a ritual enactment of identity, both individual and collective. Music making is not just about the skillful execution and manipulation of sound, nor is it just about self-growth and self-knowledge: it is about the creation, through enactment, of self, and the creation, through enactment, of social relations. Musical performance gives us constructive knowledge of self, yes, but also of self in relation to others: of "I" and of "we." Neither "I" nor "we" is pre-existent, foundational, or essential. Rather, personal and social identities are themselves performative—doings that constitute beings—and musical performance is among our most potent vehicles for their enactment, articulation, or creation. We are what we do. And in performing music, we make musical selves and musical relations with others. Performing music, as Stubley (1998) so movingly relates, is about self and music dialectically engaged in a dialectical process of mutual formulation and reformulation: an exquisite and vivid sense of, as she puts it, "identity in the making." That identity, I would add, consists not just in a dyadic relation to a musical other, but also in a rich and often complex web of relations with sounds and musically sounding others.

Although I will not explore it at length here, please note that broadening the scope of musical performance to recognize its implication in matters personal and social brings into the sphere of "matters musical" moral, ethical, and political concerns. This moves musical performance decisively out of the seemingly innocuous realm of mere entertainment, pretense, and executive skill, establishing for it crucial relevance to real-life human concerns. This cuts both ways, a fact on which I will expand later. For the present, it only remains to assert that these aspects of music making are not occasional characteristics, "optional dimensions," ways musical performance may sometimes be: a performative understanding of music making will not permit that. All musical events are social events and all participants are performers—audiences included.

One of the most distinctive features of performing is that it is always, in a crucial sense, a making action. Musical performance is productive and constructive rather than receptive or consumptive. The lived-through character is paramount in music making, not the pieces, works, recordings, or commodities that are its residue. As Christopher Small (1977) puts it, "It is the process of exploration, not its product, that is precious" (199). In performance, music's "use value" is preeminent. And in a capitalist and materialist age, where consumption is so easily mistaken as the quintessentially human activity and the primary purpose of human life, actions such as music making constitute crucial reminders of what it means to be fully alive to the world—to be a productive agent rather than a spectator, receiver, or consumer. Surely this is part of the reason music making is so often called "playing."

Although each of these dimensions or characteristics is significant in itself, what is truly remarkable and unique to musical performance is the way it brings them all together at once: temporal fluidity, vivid presence, mental alertness, centeredness, embodiment, sociality, productive agency, and sound. Performing music is an immensely potent synthetic experience that blends, balances, and fuses together elusive and fleeting aspects of human existence as nothing else does. It is fully mindful, yet an utterly unique mode of consciousness. Of the many valiant attempts to characterize this ineffable state of being, I particularly like Keil's. What he calls "participatory consciousness" is the opposite of alienation from body, from nature, from others, from the fruits of our labor. It is, he urges, a revolutionary state of being, a way of being in the world and in the body and in society that is radically unlike any other. But its existence is imperiled by commodification, and by the passivity and receptivity to which such commodification leads. Music making, Keil urges, is "our last and best source of participatory consciousness" (Keil and Feld 1994, 20), a potent weapon in the battle to reclaim the live moment, the present time, a unique way of being that should be sought, savored, and treasured.

Now, let us remind ourselves of Elliott's arguments favoring music making. Musicing, he insists, gives us a distinctive kind of knowing, a knowing-in-action. And musicianship amounts to a kind of know-how that can be developed only by engaging in the kind of actions engaged in by musicers in a given tradition, because musicianship is a multidimensional kind of procedural knowledge. The only way to develop such musical know-how is to immerse oneself in the practice. Musicianship, as a productive kind of knowledge, many of whose dimensions are tacit, is situated: it cannot be adequately and authentically grasped in all its richness unless one has engaged in the actual practice as its practitioners do. Keil (Keil and Feld 1994) puts it this way: "In order to understand what any musician is doing, you have to have done some of it yourself. I used to think you could do it just through listening, but that alone won't let you connect to the music or to other people. Unless you physically do it, it's not really apprehensible, and you're not hearing all there is to hear in the music" (29). So the crux of the matter is, to return to Elliott's (1995) terminology, that music consists of practices, things people do, modes of human action, "shared traditions and standards of effort" (42). Music's praxial nature necessitates that to make music education true to what music really is—to make it "authentic"—music teaching and learning must involve learners in the kinds of actions and judgments characteristic of those whose music is being learned. And among the more significant implications that Elliott believes follow from this is that listening-based instruction fails this test of praxial authenticity: for listening alone cannot develop musicianship or enable people to hear in music all that is there to be heard. Listeners whose musical experience is limited to receptivity and "aesthetic responsiveness" do not know music as it really or essentially is. Let us call this the ontological argument for musical performance.

Performance: Con

The claims I have been advancing for musical performance have a highly inspirational ring about them, as if performing were good unconditionally and inevitably. But as I suggested in my introductory remarks, that is not necessarily the case. In fact, there is a very long history of skepticism about the worth and about the "critical informedness" of musical performing, not all of it unjustified. In this section let us consider the grounds for, and the potential validity of, criticism of musical performance.

Earlier, we considered several common misconceptions about musical performance—that it is invariably a kind of staged presentation for the edification of an appreciative audience, for instance, and that "to perform" means to mount some kind of masquerade. But there are other misconceptions that need to be dispelled as well. First, and most obviously, critics of performance often seem to conceive of it as requiring innate skills and abilities that are inaccessible to ordinary people or extraordinarily and excessively difficult to develop. Since Elliott has argued persuasively against these particular fallacies, we need not pursue them here. So, too, the groundless notion that musical performances are mindless feats of digital celerity, or displays of technical skills that are more motor than cognitive and hence not really "knowledgeable" in any important sense. Again, Elliott has described effectively the mindful nature of music making, its status as a kind of procedural knowledge. Thus, we can set aside the baseless beliefs that performing involves technical feats beyond most people's abilities and that it is not really a mindful undertaking.

Another variant of these critical themes has been advanced by people who, while they may be prepared to grant the mindfulness of performing and similarly inclined to grant that it is a widely shared human capacity, are not quite prepared to concede the necessity of such experience, or to commit to formal instruction for its development. Desirable though performance skills may be, the argument goes, their refinement takes copious, even inordinate amounts of time and resources. On the (unexamined) assumption that performance is a means to some further end ("aesthetic sensitivity," for instance), it is alleged that there are other, more efficient ways of getting the job done. Harry Broudy (1991), for instance, suggests that developing the "skills of expression" (as he calls performing skills) is not the most efficient or most direct way of developing the "skills of impression." Note, however, the subtle implication that music-making skills are means to other ends rather than valid or valuable ends in themselves: the assumption is that the time and resources required to nurture performance skills are expendable only if they are regarded as optional means to ends effectively attainable by other means. But this is something advocates of musical performance need not concede.

This gets us directly to the heart of a matter I will explore in more detail later. Those who advocate listening-based music education sometimes do so on grounds that the aim of music education for the general public is to develop sensitivity, or appreciation, or responsiveness, and not to develop musicianship. On this view, one need not engage in music making at any level of proficiency in order to derive deep musical meaning and pleasure from listening. But even if we grant for the sake of argument that deriving meaning and pleasure from music is among the primary reasons for becoming musically educated, the question remains whether making music is more meaningful, or its pleasures richer and deeper, than those that attend listening alone. Or if, alternatively, we grant that potential listening pleasure is among the primary outcomes of a musical education, the issue is whether the listening pleasure of one who has engaged in performing is potentially greater than one who has not. A significant part of the musical pleasure to be derived from listening, one might well argue, comes from appreciation of the skill, imagination, and ingenuity (in a word, the artistry) with which music is performed; and performing experience is the surest, most direct way of developing such awareness. Let us set this matter aside with a promise to return after we have finished our critical examination of performance.

I doubt that many of us need to be strenuously persuaded that music making is not the inherently mindless activity its more ardent detractors seem to believe. However, it may be and sometimes is the case that performers fail to transfer or apply their musicianship to their listening, and that their making is not so reflectively informed as one might expect of the educated. Criticism of performing as uninformed, unreflective practice, or as virtuosity for its own sake, can be traced back nearly 2,500 years to the writings of Plato and Aristoxenus. Of course, the observation that some performance is unreflective hardly establishes that all of it is. But the point is well taken that the possession of practical musical skills is no guarantee that they will inform one's listening or be exercised reflectively. We all know skilled performers whose attention is technically oriented to the detriment of broader musical understanding and communication. There is a tendency for practitioners to become so obsessed with the doing of music (and its attendant pleasures) that they fail to reflect on what they do. Formal knowledge is, as Elliott reminds us, an indispensable dimension of musicianship. True though that may be, the extent to which it informs practice and the emphasis it receives in performance-oriented instruction varies quite widely. It is more common than we might care to admit that performing and practical musical instruction emphasize technique and executive concerns at the expense of the bigger musical picture. At its most extreme this can manifest itself in a kind of impatience with reflective thought and theory, an anti-intellectualism as utterly unbecoming of a musician as it is of any educated person. Performing, claims Roberta Lamb provocatively, is "untheorized practice" (1995, 111). Clearly, that is not necessarily or invariably the case; but a careful examination of instructional practices in performance does show that musical doings are not always extensively supported or informed by reflection. Too often, teaching and learning resemble training (or even indoctrination) more than education. The do-it-this-way mode of instruction, in which modeling rightly figures centrally, can, if not carefully monitored, foster critical compliance and nurture dependence rather than the independence and empowerment that are hallmarks of true education. Performance may not be untheorized practice, then, but it is decidedly under-theorized.

Given the nature of performance skills and the immersion by which they are arguably best taught and learned, significant potential exists for practice to become unreflective, a problem that is probably exacerbated by music education's disciplinary separation from performance studies in formal postsecondary education. These are serious concerns, or at least they should be. For if they are not explicitly and strategically addressed, it may be that in becoming proficient performers, our students are not necessarily becoming the kind of people they or we might wish. In such circumstances, performing music is hardly the wonderfully liberating thing we might like to believe it is. Rather than being an unconditional "good," then, performing may actually harm people, a danger made all the more serious by the seductiveness of musical "flow" experience and the like.

The wonderfully distinctive bodily basis of musical performance likewise has its potential down side, for bad habits and the excessive repetition of certain musical actions can lead to physical discomfort and even debilitating injury. Fortunately, professional musicians have become much more sensitive to this potential problem; yet, in their enthusiasm for performing, music educators sometimes forget that physical harm is among the potential outcomes of performance-based music education. Nor is performing music always and necessarily emotionally healthy. Psychological stress in pursuit of what Keil (Keil and Feld 1994) calls the "perfect performance ideal" is a very real possibility, and excessive competition and stress are likewise very real concerns about which educators need to remain vigilant. Clearly, music making is not an inherent, inevitable, or unconditional good: it all depends.

I must add parenthetically that this contingency—this capacity for musical performance to do both good and harm—is the unavoidable consequence of granting its power and influence. For when we establish music's relevance and potency, we automatically open the door to potential neglect and abuse. And that awareness, I submit, is one of the things that should distinguish praxial convictions from idealistic alternatives: the necessity for ongoing monitoring and self-critical awareness, to assure music's power serves desirable ends rather than undesirable ones.

I have urged that musical performance is a fundamentally social thing, and that sociality is part of what the music is, not merely a context within which music proper occurs. Conceding the social significance of performing brings to light quite a num-

ber of discomforting questions and issues heretofore (under dubious doctrines of aesthetic insularity and musical autonomy) dismissed as extramusical. If musical practices are social, if they are ways of being together, it behooves us to ask precisely how
various performance practices put us together, and what, besides "the music," is being
performed, taught, and learned? I think, for instance, of R. Murray Schafer's (1976)
memorable characterization of bands as purveyors of "herdesque happiness" (235),
of choral singing as a "perfect example of communism" (223), and Keil's (Keil and
Feld 1994) characterization of the "urge to merge" as potentially fascistic. The ways
we come together, or perform togetherness musically, are, arguably, important parts
of what we teach as music educators. It is therefore important to ask ourselves what
kind of social relationships we enact in our musical performances. Indeed, audiences
are performers as well, as Susanne Cusick (1994) observes, so that all performances
are "ensemble" affairs. Certain performance practices are ritual enactments of hierarchical power, where musicians subordinate their wills to a conductor who, in turn,
subordinates her or his will to the composer's. Similarly, formal concert attire is often
designed in part to efface individuality and enhance an image or spectacle of unifor-
mity. Is it possible, as Cusick suggests, to view some performance practices as acts
of subjugating one's self, as self-abnegation or self-suppression, or as enactments of
submission to authority? Is it conceivable that among the things school administrators find so impressive about large performing ensembles is the reassuring images of
conformity, obedience, and submission to authority they present? How do the social
models inherent in a jazz combo differ from those in an orchestra? Provocative questions like these are the unavoidable outgrowth of a performative understanding of
music and present intriguing contrasts to Elliott's noncontingent claims to self-growth
and self-knowledge. Keil's "urge to merge" is doubtless one of the human needs met
in musical performance (or participation). Because of the distinctive way we experience sound, and because of music's extraordinary capacity to center us psychologically and situate us socially, we need to recognize musical performance as an important place where people are, in Feld's words, "working out the politics and poetics of
identity" (Keil and Feld 1994, 297). If performing is "identity in the making," as
Stubley (1998) rightly suggests, then I believe the question "what kind of identity?"
cannot go unasked or unexplored. Not only does this question beg our critical scrutiny,
but a performative view of musical practice raises it to the level of an ethical obligation.

It is fundamentally important for music educators to confront these questions vis-
à-vis their particular instructional strategies as well, since the power typically vested
in the performance teacher interacts in extraordinarily potent ways with the beauty
and intensity of the performing experience to make undesirable identities or roles appear natural, inevitable, and pleasant when they are not. These contradictions—the
potency of the "urge to merge" and the unparalleled centeredness of the experience
of making music, versus the hurt or harm they may cause—are fundamental facts of
musical performance. And enactments of self-effacement and subordination should
be of particular concern in light of what we now know about the way gender in-
equities are created and perpetuated in societies. Not only is unreflective musical
practice musically undesirable, it is socially, morally, and politically so. Here again
we see the profound implications of deconstructing the notion of an inherently or in-

trinsically musical domain, and the potential significance of a socially informed, performative understanding of music making.

There remains one further claim to consider in this inventory of what we might call the case against performing, one that will serve as a convenient segue to my discussion of listening: the allegation that live music is a thing of the past, an historical relic destined for elimination by technology. Clearly, this is a matter that should be of utmost concern to music educators, for it implies that what I have described as some of musical performance's fundamental values—its bodily and social dimensions, for instance—may not be as central to music making as I have suggested. As well, it advances as desirable the idea of a music without people, a music without musicians. It may well be that technological developments are reaching the point where another praxis, and an alternative way of making and enjoying music, is fast evolving. From a praxial perspective, however, this is not necessarily cause for alarm, because evolution, fluidity, diversity, and variability are precisely what praxial views bring to our understanding of music. But, for the responsible music educator, the story does not end with the existence and validity of alternative musical performance practices (or praxes). The bigger question remains one of choice: Which practice? Which music? Whose music? Why? With these questions in mind, let us turn our attention to music listening.

Listening: Con

Since many of the potential arguments against listening-based music education are at the same time arguments favoring performance-based music education, let us begin our examination of listening there. First, we will want to distinguish between two kinds of listeners and, perhaps, two kinds of listening. On the one hand, presumably, there is the kind of listeners engaged in by performing musicians: let us call it "musicianly." On the other, there is what Thomas Regelski (personal communication 1998) calls "just listening": listening uninformed by experience as a musical performer or producer, which may range from the unfocused and naive to the highly refined listening of the musical connoisseur. In this section I explore claims that "just listening" is necessarily inferior to musicianly listening, and that, moreover, listening may be a less fundamentally musical behavior than performing.

Keil's remarks in the previous section are representative of the arguments typically advanced against the efficacy of listening as a primary means of musical engagement and musical instruction. Listening alone, or "just listening," fails on two counts according to Keil: first, it fails to make connections to other people; second, it fails to make apprehensible everything that is really there, in the music. Although we appear to have two kinds of failings here, one social and one that is musical and perceptual, or ontological, I doubt Keil would want to concede that they are separable, and I know I would not. But before submitting these points to closer scrutiny, let us make the case against listening a little more boldly and emphatically. "Just listening," Keil and some others seem to believe, is simply not as musically full or rich or as vitally participative an experience as musical doing. It is an act of appreciative consumption: what amateurs and audiences do, not musicians. Though not invariably or inevitably passive, "just listening" is a predominantly receptive or contemplative act, and the attitude or orientation typically assumed toward the music is deferential and submissive: to impose or inject too much of oneself into the music is not good listening form. A good listener, as Cusick (1994) puts it, should be "all ears" and little else, which is to say that appropriately disciplined listening is expected to restrict itself to what meets the ear. Moreover, although it is an action, it is, as Elliott (1995) says, covert. As such, it may be difficult to monitor it, and to assess when it is appropriately engaged.

Listening-based musical instruction is also troublesome because it seems to suggest that listening is the most natural, or perhaps the only realistic musical activity of which the average person is capable. The implicit message is that the quintessential musical attitude is receptive in nature, and what is to be received are the spectacular, almost superhuman musical achievements of performers, the "true" musicians. In other words, listening-based music instruction seems to concede the division of the population into haves and have-nots, actives and passives, makers and appreciators. It is not that the advocate of performance is elitist, then—it is that the advocate of listening seriously underestimates the ubiquity of human musicality. A blunt statement by Keil, taken slightly out of context, makes the point especially forcefully: "every single person on the planet has this emergent, expressive self, and depriving them of the opportunity to experience it amounts to nothing less than a conspiracy to shut them up, to pacify them and leave them in a corner appreciating the 'true talents'" (Keil and Feld 1994, 172).

I have exaggerated to make the point, and I have also run together quite a number of distinct notions or claims. But the basic point is clear: compared to performing, listening is a kind of emaciated, derivative experience. And from that conviction, several different kinds of argument might be advanced: first, people without performing experience do not hear music as performers do; second, the act of making music is experientially richer than listening, even among performers; and third, the way performers hear music, the kind of "musicianly" listening in which performers engage, is musically superior to "just listening." The first two claims are probably valid, but not the third. The first claim needs little support: indeed, it would be extraordinary if performers, for all their hours of intense, listening-guided practice, heard music no differently than people without such experience. To experts in any field, little differences make all the difference; and since performers are, of necessity, expert listeners, it is not unreasonable to expect their listening to be better attuned to certain musical features that elude nonperformers. I advance the second claim on the strength of personal conviction and experience: listening is experientially very different from performing, and although both are sources of unique pleasure, performing requires modes of musical engagement that are, in listening, implicit, covert, or tacit.

The third claim, that "musicianly" listening is superior to "just listening," cannot, I think, be sustained. Although it seems clear and uncontroversial that performers listen differently, their listening is not self-evidently superior. Indeed, "just listening" is a musical practice in which humans can indeed be found to engage, a widespread form of musical behavior with traditions and acknowledged standards of rightness and wrongness—which is to say, "just listening" is a praxis in its own right. It is only natural that the performer's listening should be privileged in important respects, that the performer should hear music differently than a nonperformer. Perhaps performers even hear different music in what might appear to be the same sonic material. But different does not mean superior. That the nonperforming listener's musical experience would differ in important ways from that of a performer-musician only makes logical sense; but to establish its inferiority, we would have to somehow identify one definitive ontological way that the music "really" is. And an important part of what praxial convictions do, I think, is to deny such definitive ontological ground. There is no one way music is, only various musical practices and various ways of constructing and construing it. When it comes to music education, that eliminates "inherent musicality" as a basis for choosing between things such as listening- and performance-based instruction; but again, this neither absolves the responsible music educator of choosing, nor does it establish that valid criteria do not exist or cannot be found somewhere else.

Since we cannot dismiss listening-based instruction on grounds of the necessary inadequacy of amateur listening, let us return to the various interrelated strands of the case against listening-based music education and explore them one by one. One of the strongest arguments is that listening is inherently a receptive or contemplative act, a matter of consumption rather than production. The original state of music, it is apparently assumed, is ritualistic and collective productive engagement. "Just listening," then, is an alienated, artificial, or inauthentic way of relating to music. Music's fundamental way of being is in collective social agency, not listening. When the listening gets separated from the music making, music atrophies, becoming a kind of shadow of its true nature. It petrifies, becomes a product rather than a process, a commodity rather than a state of being and way of behaving. This commodification is an act of reification, wherein music's use value as action is suppressed and eventually replaced by its exchange value as commodity. Musical events degenerate into musical works or pieces, whose raison d'être has less to do with human social agency than with appreciative consumption. But the vast majority of musical practices in the world do not exist primarily for the edification of nonparticipant listeners. They are undertaken, rather, for the active gratification of those involved in the generation of the musical event itself. From this perspective, the act of "just listening" amounts to a kind of voyeurism of looking in from the outside (and in certain Western traditions, carried out in darkened halls). Put differently, "just listening" is a kind of musical false consciousness that transforms processes into products: for consumption, for exchange, and ultimately, for sale.

Another thread of the argument against "just listening" is closely related to the one just considered, but focuses more on the experiential than the ontological nature of music: on how music is experienced, instead of what it is. From this point of view, listening and its attendant tendency to commodification gives us what we might well describe as "all works and no play." There is a phenomenologically unique character to music making, an intensely serious playfulness, which listening alone is incapable of capturing, especially if it is not informed by music making. The exquisite sense of oneness with the music, of embodied wholeness, and of existing entirely in the present moment, here and now—these are things listening is hard pressed to deliver in the sustained, intense ways performing does. These phenomenal features may be elusive in the listening experience even of those whose background includes performance. Yet, there comes of performing, one might argue, a fuller sense of what a musical performance entails and conveys, a deeper sense of empathy with what the performer is doing, and how and why. This may manifest itself in a deeper awareness of the physical and executive origins of such musically expressive achievements as phrasing, or a heightened sensitivity to the timbral differences when a violinist plays a passage in one position rather than another, or the physical impetus represented in a particular musical gesture. Listening without benefit of performance experience is predominantly an aural (all-ears) experience, it might be argued, whereas performance-informed listening is a profoundly corporeal experience in a highly inclusive and broadly distributed sense. Performers hear with their fingers, their arms, their entire bodies; they can scarcely resist breathing along with the phrase or moving with the line or gesture.

From this, it may follow that "just listening" fails to engage or raise to the level of conscious experience important dimensions that are arguably there in the music. This may have been part of what Edmund Gurney (1966) had in mind in distinguishing between what he called definite and indefinite hearing. The musical dimensions missing from "just listening" are not just the bodily, to which we have just alluded, but moral, ethical, and identity issues as well. As observed earlier, listening, even at its most active, is receptive, submissive, attentive—an act in which self is suppressed and the heard is paramount. If musical performance is a kind of self-expression or self-assertion, musical listening (particularly if it is without benefit of performing experience) might be characterized as an act of self-suppression. (Lest we underestimate the true complexity and contradictoriness of our subject, however, recall that listening is not the only self-suppressive performance.) There is danger, then, that "just listening" may yield a kind of superficial acquaintance with music, in contrast to the immersion that is constitutive of performance. To the extent that it approaches music from the outside, listening may mistake the limits of the hearable for the limits of the musical, thereby seriously neglecting the range of authentically musical variables in a given practice. "Just listening" overestimates its portability, its generalizability, the suitability of its interpretive schemata to disparate styles and musical practices—practices in which, for instance, "just listening" is neither a typical mode of engagement nor "the point" of the music.

We have spoken so far as if "just listening" were of one cloth. It is not: and this is arguably among the more important issues with which music education must come to grips in its deliberations over instructional method. The relationship of audience or listener to live performance is radically different from that between listener and recording, where sounds are split from the people who produce them. Musical mediation, as Jacques Attali (1985) has shown vividly, is a profound rupture and a radical transformation of the relationship both between listener and music, and between performer and performance. The capacity to mass-reproduce and disseminate performances not only devalues live performances vis-à-vis their commodified reproduction in recordings (such that the recording becomes the criterion by which live performance is judged), but the fissure between action and consumption opens into an immense chasm. Listening to recordings neglects a great deal of what is individuating and unique about different musical practices, and of what is unique and distinctive to the experience of making music. As Keil observes, "What happens in recording studios [is] a classicizing, perfecting, dream-world thing, and that takes [music] away from the dancers, which takes it away from public space, the streets, clubs. All recordings are inherently Apollonian just as all performances tend toward the Dionysian" (Keil and Feld 1994, 214). On this view, listening to recordings differs profoundly from listening to live music. Fundamental to the condition of contemporary musical life is a kind of dialectical tension between activity and passivity, agency and consumption, making and receiving, participating and observing. Mediation, Keil worries, "is taking over jazz, taking over rock, taking over anything . . . revolutionary, critical, or consciousness changing. The revolutionary spirit got stuck in scores in Beethoven's day, and now it gets commodified over and over again" (21).

The arguments against listening-based music education follow, as we have seen, from convictions that listening is a kind of second- or thirdhand, derivative way of relating to music or being musical. Music making is richer and more meaningful, it is assumed, than listening; and musicianly listening is more fully musical than listening that is uninformed by performance experience. As Keil asserts, one has to have done and made some of what musicians do and make in order to "get" all that is potentially there, in their musical doings and makings. Among the dimensions that distinguish performing from listening and musicianly listening from "just listening" are a bodily or executive involvement, direct social engagement, and a fuller awareness of what is being done, and how, and why. Listening lies on the passive and receptive side of a praxial divide and is complicit in the commodification process that replaces agency with consumption and reduces processes to products. More disturbing yet, if all musical experience is performative, we need to ask exactly what is performed in acts of listening—one potential answer to which is self-negation. And finally, "just listening" to mediated music or a recording is musical engagement at its most profoundly alienated, music purged of people.

Our investigation into listening appears to have uncovered three different issues: first, how listening relates to performing; second, how musicianly listening relates to "just listening"; and third, the kind of "performance" listening may be. The case against listening seems to be made in two different, though related, ways: one is ontological, attributing to performance a privileged access to the way the music "really is"; and the other is performative, having to do with the ways performers and listeners act. Both these arguments appear to partake of a common implicit assumption: that while performing is at once a making and a doing, listening is a doing that is not a making. I think we must concede that, at the least, listening and performing are radically different ways of being musical or, to say the same thing rather differently, they are very different kinds of performances. It is likely, then, that musicians listen very differently from listeners who listen without benefit of performing experience. But the advocate of performance-based music education might well point to our discussions of the relative merits of musicianly and "just" listening as persuasive evidence that the greatest disadvantage of listening-based instruction is its implicit message that listening is the most authentic way of being musical: one does not engage in musical performance primarily to become a better listener, or because performing helps one hear the "real" music more fully, but because performing is a valuable way of being and becoming in its own right. That would appear to be one insight listening experience alone could not provide.

Listening: Pro

The power of mediation and the prevalence of commodification are clearly significant challenges with which listening-based music instruction must contend. The potential for passivity in a covert process such as listening is indeed a significant issue. But the undeniable existence of problems and challenges is no more cause for rejecting listening as an instructional practice than it would be for performance, which, we have seen, is not unconditionally good either. Having acknowledged some of the problems that potentially attend listening as a predominant mode of musical instruction, let us now ask what can be said in its favor.

First, if self-evidently, listening is of the utmost importance to music, whether performed or appreciated. Whatever else it may be, music involves aural perception, understanding, and the construction of meaning from experience with musical others and with sound. Better to engage listening directly, it might be argued, than simply to perform and trust listening to follow. In fact, although listening and performing doubtless share a great deal, musicianship is neither wholly synonymous with listenership, nor does proficiency as a performer guarantee sophistication as a listener. Elliott claims that the kinds of knowing required for performing are the same as those required for listening, and they may be in some degree: but the fact that they share some dimensions (formal, informal, supervisory, etc.) clearly does not make them coextensive. Whatever their commonalties, performing and listening remain distinct in important ways.

Music listening is a distinctive mode of musical engagement, one that can be improved with instruction and practice, and those, too, may be important reasons to teach it. With this claim, Elliott would agree. At issue for him is whether listening should be taught in and of itself, or in conjunction with performing, and only there a normative stance follows from the view of music as praxis. I am not persuaded that praxial convictions undermine the case for listening-based music instruction, because it seems clear that "just listening" constitutes a valid and widely pervasive praxis in its own right. I do not think we can effectively use the idea of musical praxis to argue against listening-based curricula; but that is not to say persuasive arguments do not exist or cannot be mounted. What this means in the present context, simply, is that praxial orientations need not preclude musical instruction centered on listening, since listening is a valid praxis with standards of practice that are relatively objective and noncontroversial, and since listening is the kind of endeavor that is amenable to improvement with instruction and practice. I see no reason, then, why praxial convictions cannot be mustered in support of listening-based music instruction.

We can argue in listening's defense that it is a natural activity, rooted in innate human capacities, and one that is easily accessible to musical amateurs who exist in significant numbers and who can benefit from instruction. Note that "amateur" need not imply novice status, and the amateur may in fact be highly skilled: amateurs are simply nonprofessionals. By resisting the temptation to equate expertise with professional status we can avoid wrongly attributing listening sophistication exclusively to people with high levels of musicianship. Producers, performers, and music makers do not have a monopoly on musical listening; or, to put it differently, listening the way musicians do is not the only valid way of listening. As in sports, where avid appreciation is both a widespread and a legitimate mode of engagement, an undertaking in which considerable expertise may be developed without benefit of extensive hands-on experience, so too for musical perception, response, and appreciation. Listening to music is a natural mode of musical engagement in its own right, and one that, while it may certainly benefit from musical performing experience in certain ways, does not require the kind of musicianship acquired via performing. Moreover, appreciative listening is a practice whose fundamental purposes differ from those of performance. Since people's reasons for listening differ from people's reasons for performing; listening excellence cannot be gauged by the same standards as performing excellence.

The fact that listening can and often does occur without executive or productive engagement may actually be to its advantage as a means of musical instruction. Since, in listening, one's attention need not be wholly occupied with the productive or executive concerns so crucial to performance, more of that attention is arguably available for such things as critical or reflective awareness—the listening equivalents, perhaps, of the performer's "supervisory knowledge" (Elliott 1995). If this is so, it seems entirely reasonable to suggest that instruction be designed and executed in ways that assure the enrichment and cultivation of such capacities. And especially if, as we have implied, such capacities are not coextensive with musicianship, there would seem to be defensible grounds for maintaining that nonperforming amateur and proficient performer alike might benefit from such instruction.

The claim that listening is predominantly receptive and passive clearly is one that requires careful attention because of what I have had to say about the kind of performance listening sometimes is, and because of the potential for listening to become soporific and superficial. Listening is receptive, yes, but not wholly so, and receptivity need not be passive: it may be resistant, and it is unavoidably constructive. It may, in fact, be highly imaginative, a point implicit in the fact that listening linked to performance is on a somewhat shorter tether than "just listening." Perhaps, then, I was too hasty in granting that, in contrast to performing, which involves both making and doing, listening involves doing, only. For listening is in many crucial respects a making: each of us, in listening, creates musical meaning from sonic materials that are in themselves utterly devoid of meaning. And if listening is imaginative construction, instructional interventions may well influence the kind of constructions we attempt and achieve. Arguably, then, passivity is precisely the kind of propensity that listening-based music instruction exists to counter.

Among the distinctive advantages we attributed to performing was its physical or bodily dimension—the profound sense of wholeness and oneness with the music that attends direct involvement in its production. So, where performing engages mind, ear, and body, listening is executed by mind and ear alone. But this, too, is too hasty a conclusion, because musical listening is a fundamentally and profoundly corporeal feat. I have argued elsewhere (Bowman 2000) that music is a bodily or corporeal acquisition, and that perception of such fundamental musical features as movement, tempo,

gesture, tension and release, tonality, and the like are fundamentally bodily achievements. It follows from this, I think, that all of us ("just listeners" included) have the
basic hardware necessary for musically valid listening experience. The body, I believe, gives each of us embodied humans the means for a direct, natural route to musical responsiveness and understanding. Performing proficiency may extend or aug-
ment the possible points of corporeal access and perhaps their kind as well, but such
proficiency is not a fundamental prerequisite for valid musical experience.

There are at least two important reasons we can claim that one need not be a performer to hear all there is to hear in music. The first is, as I have just argued, that all
human beings are hardwired for listening: all the necessary equipment is in place. The
second is that music is not the kind of thing of which there is an "all," a "wholly and
purely musical" dimension that some "get" while it eludes others.

In short, since active, appreciative listening is a musical practice in its own right,
we cannot claim it is musically inauthentic, or musically inferior to performance. As
one of the world's most pervasive musical practices, and one becoming ever more predominant as media and technology transform that world, refining people's musical
listening abilities by means of formal instruction seems not just feasible but, particularly if we grant that music and identity are intertwined in important ways, obligatory.

Conclusion

Let us now see what can be done to draw together the various strands of the arguments I have been developing here. First, although it hardly seems earthshaking, we
have shown that neither performing nor listening is an unconditional good. As human
practices, they both take many forms, have many dimensions, and many potential values, good and bad. This recognition is made possible by the "praxial turn," a refusal
to equate music with "the notes" or restrict it to patterns of sound, and an awareness
that musics are human practices whose uses, meanings, and values are situated, diverse, and practice specific. At the same time, I have suggested that different practices, even musical practices as different from each other as performing and listening,
are not closed books, hermetic undertakings whose "true" meanings are revealed only
to experts after lifelong immersion in them. In a way, practices are like conversations,
where participants alternately understand and misunderstand each other, yet somehow generally manage to grasp each other's intended meanings at least well enough
to muddle through, though often much better. The meanings that arise from them are
dialectical affairs, constrained by and emergent from the particulars of the conversation at hand and the way it unfolds. Yet even when we speak different languages, to
strain the metaphor, things such as facial expressions, speech modulation, and body
language still enable us to gauge, within certain tolerances, what is going on. Rarely
do we encounter situations in which we are left completely without a clue as to what
is meant, or what is going on.

The praxial turn situates musical meaning and value in human practices, which is
to say, social matrices, which are fluid, diverse, historically emergent, spontaneously
mutating, and constantly evolving, as opposed to those abstract, timeless absolutes,
universals, and "essences" that are philosophical idealism's legacy. Praxial convic-

tions direct us to replace the concept "music" with multiple musics and ways of being musical, and to look for their natures and values in what people do with them or use them for. Music has no essential core, no way it always must be for all people and all times.

As such, while praxial insights represent an important advance for music education philosophy, I do not think praxial convictions can yield (on praxial grounds alone) a comprehensive view of all music or music education. What praxial orientations tell us is not so much that music is "a diverse human practice" as that the term "music" (MUSIC, in Elliott's lexicon) is really a kind of convenient fiction, shorthand for what actually amounts to a diverse and vast (perhaps even potentially infinite) array of human practices that are themselves constantly evolving, mutating, and generating new hybrids. Musical practices (praxes) include kinds of actions or ways of being musical (performing, improvising, arranging, singing, composing, and listening), and types of musical doings or categories into which these actions can be seen to fall (organum, bebop, raga, march, symphony, and rap). There is, Regelski (1998) declares, "a bottomless supply of separate praxes, both in the sense of actions and types, each of which has its own phronesis and thus its own requirements." Regelski goes on to argue that claims to hierarchical superiority for one praxis over another are a kind of "category mistake," taking differences in kind for differences in quality or value.

I have argued that praxial convictions neutralize the ontological argument for performance-based musical instruction, because performing is not, on praxial views, more inherently musical than other modes of musical being or doing. And although the same must be said for listening, we need to acknowledge that its status as a praxis with its own traditions, standards, priorities, and values also means we cannot declare it, on ontological grounds, inferior. Simply put, practices are not those kinds of things. Performing and listening (or composing, or improvising, etc.) are not superior or inferior to one another in virtue of bringing us closer to the absolute or essential condition of music, because music does not have an absolute or essential condition.

This does not negate the possibility or, indeed, the professional necessity of choosing. It simply means we must choose on some basis other than music's praxial nature (and here I submit that many of Elliott's claims for music seem to derive more from performative than from praxial assumptions). In the past, advocates of aesthetic education wrongly construed musical sensitivity, receptivity, and feeling as the most inherently musical ways of being and gravitated toward listening-based instruction as a result. To suggest that performing lies closer to the essential condition of music is to commit the same error in reverse. I believe we must acknowledge the musical validity of both, and the contingency of any claims we might wish to make on behalf of either, and then choose on the basis of our own local needs, beliefs, and aspirations. Perhaps what matters is not so much which we choose, but why we choose and how we implement that choice in light of the potential outcomes, both positive and negative, associated with it. To the question "What is the best way to teach music?" the best response is probably "That depends on what you want to achieve."

But I do not think this is quite right, yet. For it almost sounds as if it makes no difference what choice we make, which it is not the case at all. As my second epigram asserts, the kinds of habits we choose to nurture make all the difference. I believe it matters which we choose, and that performing music is extraordinarily important for quite a number of reasons even though the praxial turn does not in itself establish what these are (or negate the potential validity of other musical engagements and instructional endeavors). If what is wanted is a philosophical basis for musical performance, let us attempt to articulate an explicitly performative one: one that speaks directly and forcefully to the possibilities and concerns that attend musical performance as instructional method. A performative understanding of music suggests that we acknowledge the situatedness and constructedness of musical meanings and at the same time their performative nature—corporeal, social, and processual. On this view, musical activities are creations, articulations, and enactments of identity. Human identity is no more an ahistorical, noncontingent matter than music is. We are, then, as Aristotle suggests, what we do repeatedly. And from this realization, I think it is possible to advance a strong argument favoring musical performance (construed inclusively, as productive engagement, as making) for reasons pedagogical, curricular, psychological, motivational, social, and political, if not "praxial" per se.

There is no need to reiterate in detail what has already been said about the positive values of performing. But let us remind ourselves briefly. Music performance is, as Keil insists, a tremendously rich and potent source of vital, participatory consciousness—of living processually, here and now, embodied and in the present moment. It affords an experience of centeredness, wholeness, and oneness that is fleeting, evanescent, and evasive elsewhere in life. It offers a powerful antidote to the hegemony of the visual in human affairs, and to the distance and aloofness that is phenomenally characteristic of visual experience and of intellection in general. It is a mode of action—of direct, bodily engagement in production of musical sound that offers a powerful and much-needed alternative to the pervasive consumer-orientation of most educational practice. It is an enactment of self- (or selves-)expression or self- (or selves-)assertion, a valuable alternative to the self-suppression typical of most educational practice. Because of its unique phenomenal characteristics, it can be highly motivating and rewarding, and its overt, productive nature makes it amenable to evaluation. It gives firsthand insight into how musical makers and doers (and makers and doers more broadly) behave, how decisions-in-action are made, and how "right action" is gauged in given musical practices. Since its fragile, in-the-moment character requires exceptional mental alertness and constant vigilance to everything that is being done, it can be an exceptionally potent way to learn what given musical practices entail. More broadly, musical performance develops character by helping fix standards by which the worth of other experience is measured: like all genuinely educational experience, it creates impatience with the pedestrian and the mundane, demanding that other experience rise to its level and quality.

As we have seen, each of these claims is contingent: none follows inevitably from musical performance. Since performing is not good in and of itself, whether it helps or harms depends upon how we engage in it and upon what we perform. But that is not a sign of deficiency: it is, rather, a natural consequence of its power and import. The outcomes of musical performance are not "just musical"; they are personal, social, and political, involving important moral and ethical considerations—and not tangentially, but centrally. We need to be critically vigilant not only about the musical quality of what we perform, but of everything we are performing musically.

We are what we do. People's identities and character, both individual and collective, are neither essential nor absolute: they are constructed, elaborated, modified, and reconstructed, enacted, performed. And musical doings carry out that work and play in ways that can be, because of the special way we experience sound and the special ways music making brings people together, exceptionally potent, enriching, and vital. In performing music, we are always performing more than just "the music." And although, as I have said, even listening is a kind of performance, it is important to maintain places of prominence in music education for performances that affirm identity and agency rather than effacing them. Performing music is a valuable way of being and becoming—and in its own right, not in service to some further end. There are, then, compelling, even urgent reasons for keeping it at the forefront of music education. If these reasons are more performative than praxial, they are no less urgent and compelling for that, and possibly a good bit more.

As we have seen, sound reasons may be found both for listening-based and performance-based musical instruction. It would be a tragedy if people's musical educations were limited to practices and traditions for which time and resources required extensive engagement as performers. On the other hand, it would be profoundly irresponsible for us to proceed as if the unique experience of firsthand engagement in the process of music making were somehow inessential to, or expendable in, the process of becoming musically educated—as may appear to be the case for people not themselves musicians. We are professionally obligated, as musician-educators, to strike and maintain an appropriate balance between performing and listening (two different kinds of musical performance), the productive and the receptive, activity and critical reflection, and to resist strenuously the kind of thinking that suggests highly desirable instructional options must mutually exclude each other. Again, since the best way to teach and learn music can be determined only in light of our local goals and objectives, it is crucial that our instructional methods—the musical experiences we provide as educators—be congruent with our desired educational outcomes. To that end, it is imperative that we develop educationally and philosophically rigorous accounts of why and how we do what we do. It is no less a professional obligation, I believe, that a central and fundamental part of what we do as music educators and students of music is make music together.

References

Attali, J. 1985. *Noise: The political economy of music*. Trans. B. Massumi. Minneapolis: University of Minnesota Press.

Bowman, W. 2000. A somatic, "here and now" semantic: Music, body, and self. *Bulletin of the Council for Research in Music Education* 144:45–60.

Broudy, H. 1991. A realistic philosophy of music education. In R. J. Colwell, ed., *Basic concepts of music education*, 2:7–93. Niwot: University Press of Colorado.

Cusick, S. 1994. Gender and the cultural work of a classical music performance. *Repercussions* 3 (1):77–110.

Eliot, T. S. 1988. Dry salvages. In *Four quartets*, 117–149. New York: Harcourt, Brace, Jovanovich.

Elliott, D. J. 1995. *Music matters: A new philosophy of music education.* New York: Oxford University Press.

Gurney, E. 1966. *The power of sound.* New York: Basic Books.

Keil, C., and S. Feld. 1994. *Music grooves.* Chicago: University of Chicago Press.

Lamb, R. 1995. Tone deaf/symphonies singing: Sketches for a musicale. In J. Gaskell and J. Willinsky, eds., *Gender in/forms curriculum: From enrichment to transformation.* New York: Teachers College Press.

Schafer, R. M. 1976. *Creative music education: A handbook for the modern music educator.* New York: Schirmer Books.

Small, C. 1977. *Music, education, society.* New York: Schirmer Books.

Stubley, E. 1995. The performer, the score, the work: Musical performance and transactional reading. *Journal of Aesthetic Education* 29 (4):55–71.

———. 1998. Being in the body, being in the sound: A tale of modulating identities and lost potential. *Journal of Aesthetic Education* 32 (4):93–105.

9

Composing and Improvising

JEFFREY MARTIN

In this chapter I focus on Elliott's praxial conceptions of composition and improvisation in relation to two central themes: composing and improvising as intentional activities capable of engaging students in reflective musical thinking; and the processes and products of composing and improvising as inseparable from the contexts in which they are situated. My objective is to examine these themes against current conceptions of composing and improvising. In doing so, I invoke my own research on student composing, my experiences as a working improviser and composer, and my experiences as a teacher in both domains.

Composition and Improvisation as Reflection

In *Music Matters*, Elliott presents "music" as a form of intelligent action and knowledge. Thus, to make music is "to act thoughtfully and knowingly." Although Elliott's conception of music (and the other arts) as modes of thinking and knowing is not new, his perspective reflects recent and important developments. Earlier attempts to liberate knowledge from its confinement to analytic and empirical propositions focused on the *content* of "artworks" at the expense of the knowledge involved in the actions of art *making*. As Elliott rightly notes, this old emphasis, which was epitomized by Langer's distinction between "discursive" and "presentational" symbols (1953; 1957), led to the unfortunate characterization of music as comprising affective knowledge that, in an educational context, would complement the conceptual knowledge afforded by more traditional subjects (Ross 1984; Witkin 1974). In this "aesthetic education" view, composing and improvising were merely subjective, "right-brain" processes, void of any critical reflection or discourse.

Best (1992) observes that this old position fails to justify the inclusion of the arts in the curriculum; rather, it eliminates the possibility of learning them, since there can be no criterion for evaluation. Nor is the polar separation of feeling and conceptualization defensible:

> The object of the emotion cannot be characterized independently of the individual's understanding of the phenomenon to which he is responding. The object, in this sense, is a central criterion of the feeling and it is identified by one's understanding. For instance, I could not be afraid of ghosts if I had no concept of a ghost. (104)

The more promising conception of music in *Music Matters* is grounded in an awareness of the importance of critical reflection in (not merely about) human action (Scheffler 1965, 1988; Schön 1983, 1987). Elliott conceives music making (which, he insists, *always involves listening*) as unfolding "thoughtfully and knowingly" through the intentional actions of "selecting, deploying, directing, adjusting, and judging" (1995, 50).

This perspective has implications for studies of composing and improvising directed at informing teaching and learning in these domains. For example, in my protocol analysis of tertiary music students' beginning compositions (Martin 2000), I observed the workings of both reflection-in-action and reflection-on-action, albeit in varying degrees of ability. Throughout the protocol transcripts there were numerous verbalized evaluations of ideas and procedures, justifications for decisions taken or not taken, and moments for critical considerations of the productive processes. In addition to this explicit reflection-*on*, there was also evidence of subjects' reflection-*in*-composing, which was implicit in students' ways of working. In Schön's conception, this latter form of reflective thinking involves such patterns as reformulating problems, conducting experiments, and activating past experiences.

Regarding the first of these, each subject in my study attempted to develop a unique conception of materials and structures, as well as the procedures he or she used in her work. For example, one assignment required students to compose a piece for piano using four pitch classes. The ill-defined nature of this task led the students to formulate a variety of approaches, from using the set as both a motive and a source, to conceiving a "contrasting" set, to deriving tonal material from the "atonal" set. Unique goals for overall structure were considered both prior to and during the process.

Also, subjects conducted experiments with their material, mainly through the use of keyboard exploration, in which prospective ideas were tested and previously generated ideas were developed through exploratory improvisations. Even in the seemingly random exercises of free play on the piano, there was evidence of conscious effort and interactions between the material produced and the students' intentions. There appeared to be a reciprocal relationship between planning and execution in which ideas were both proposed and discovered in the situation, an observation corroborated by others (Smith and Smith 1994; Snowden 1993).

For Schön (1983), experimentation involves a "transaction" or "conversation" with the situation in which practitioners attempt changes to phenomena while accepting that the phenomena may indicate otherwise (150). In either case, the experimenter is intentionally involved rather than detached from the situation: "The inquirer's relation to this situation is transactional. He shapes the situation, but in conversation with it, so that his own models and appreciations are also shaped by the situation. The phenomena he seeks to understand are partly of his own making; he is in the situation that he seeks to understand" (Schön 1983, 150–151).

Finally, the ways my subjects deployed their past experiences, comprising mainly piano performance (at least grade 7 of the Associated Boards of the Royal Schools of Music, and more or less the equivalent level in theory) was particularly interesting. While they transferred both their propositional and performance-based knowledge to the composing task, my subjects' verbalizations also revealed difficulty, and sometimes overt errors, in describing musical concepts; their tendency toward awkward descriptions and sometimes misnaming (of tonal functions, for instance) seems to indicate a deficit in their propositional grasp of music. Yet, this proved to be no impediment in their successful completion of compositions, many of which were graded highly by the instructor.

Here, it seems, vaguely known elements of the subject's musical experience are being transformed into components of an active musical discourse during the composing process. Thus, their musical understanding is demonstrated in the "procedural" decision making rather than in the verbal, declarative statements. This observation concurs with the conception Elliott describes in *Music Matters*:

> Verbal information (or formal knowledge) about music is no substitute for the ultra-specific nonverbal conception of musical works that a student exhibits when he or she performs (improvises, composes, arranges, or conducts) intelligently. Having a concept of something is not limited to the ability to match a word with a phenomenon. Knowing musical concepts is something a student evidences practically in the consistency and quality of her musical thinking-in-action. (1995, 75)

So, it is *reflective* or *intelligent* engagement in music that seems to facilitate the increase in understanding. The success of these students is apparently the result of an active effort of generating, experimenting with, and evaluating musical ideas (as Elliott also states in these same words). Moreover, it is apparent that my students acquired the tacit musical knowledge they used and developed in the composing task through performing. Indeed, the impact of performing on composing is not restricted to those with extensive performing experience; studies of children's composing have also identified patterns derived from previous performance experiences (Burnard 1999; Folkestad 1998; Swanwick and Franca 1999). Thus, while studies of harmony, counterpoint, and analysis are often considered mandatory preparation for composition, performing experience (even at a beginning level) is arguably a more basic and practical starting point for composing (as Elliott also argues), because performing gives students a firsthand, practical experience of the materials and the procedures of musical discourse in specific musical-cultural practices.

Still, there are unique aspects of compositional thinking that need attention during instruction. For example, since events can be modeled outside of real time, there are, according to Austin and Clark (1989), three possibilities: "temporal modeling," analogous to performance time; "spatial modeling," visualizing the material and structural elements in advance; and "narrative modeling," plotting an intended sequence of musical events. Part of what composing involves is an interaction among these three modeling procedures (Austin and Clark 1989, 19). Also, while interpretive performance allows for active decision making and judgment, composing and improvising also include the discovery of problems and the origination of musical ideas out of performing and listening experiences. Presented as an ill-defined task, composing a work involves selections within a wider range, potentially including choice of instrumentation, structure, working time, idiomatic tendencies, and other self-imposed constraints.

Because unique features such as these characterize composing, I cannot agree with Elliott's decision to include composing alongside performing and improvising only "as time permits" (1995, 172–173). Composing offers its own particular challenges in the development of musicianship that take the learner beyond that which is possible within the limits of the performed piece and "the different conceptions of that work held by the performers involved in the performance" (Stubley 1992, 12). At the same time, however, I do agree with Elliott (also on the basis of the above observations) that performing provides an effective foundation for the development of students' composing.

This summary of my own research is intended to demonstrate an accord between my results and Schön's concept of reflective practice and, thus, with the views Elliott offers in *Music Matters*. However, because these observations concern music students engaging in composing for the first time, I need to say more about the advanced composer. The popular conception is that composing rests on the inspiration of rare genius, rather than deliberate, reflective decision making. Can composing be viewed as reflective practice?

If we accept Paul Hindemith's (1952) views as evidence, a perspective not unlike popular opinion emerges. For Hindemith, musical inspiration is "the most characteristic quality of the composing mind" (55), and if composers "cannot, in the flash of a single moment, see a composition in its absolute entirety, with every pertinent detail in its proper place, [they] are not genuine creators" (71). But given that artists do not always give a true report of their work (Perkins 1981), views of other notable composers reveal a conception closer to the reflective model. For example, Roger Sessions rejects the view "that the capacity for significant achievement in the arts is somehow sui generis, and that it involves modes of thought and action which are inaccessible and inconceivable to those of lesser talents" (Sessions 1970, 82).

Although Sessions (1939) accepts inspiration as a first step, leading to an overall conception, he emphasizes "execution," which involves "listening inwardly to the music as it shapes itself" and "allowing the music to grow" (22). Parallel to the reciprocal nature of planning and executing in my subjects' work, Sessions notes that in the composing process "conception and execution are inseparable and in the last analysis identical" (25). In this view, then, inspiration is absorbed into the procedural working-out of the piece. Notice also, that Sessions considers the composer to be "a *practical* musician" (italics in the original), and therefore that "both some training and some experience as a performer are vitally important for a composer" (1970, 73).

Stravinsky (1947) also places the emphasis on the thoughtful, attentive act of composing, but he holds a more radical view. For him, inspiration is not even a first step but rather a "chronologically secondary" emotional response, a sense of satisfaction following a chain of discoveries, which itself results from "grappling" with an "unknown entity" (50). In stark contrast to the popular romantic view, composing for Stravinsky is not the confident, passive reception of ideas, but the conscious process of search and discovery in which the composer "improvises aimlessly the way an animal grubs about" driven by a need for satisfaction (55).

To the extent to which accounts by Sessions and Stravinsky can be considered evidence (Sloboda 1985), compositions seem to emerge out of the active, thoughtful interaction between composer and material within the context of a particular situation. Notice the way cognition is "distributed" (Solomon 1993) in the process, comprising aural feedback and bodily kinesthetic experience along with the composer's goals and conceptions. Clearly, reflection-in-action involves not merely mental activity, but a variety of modalities relevant to the composer's conversation with the composing environment.

Interestingly, Bowman (2000) critiques Elliott for an insufficient emphasis on corporeal modality in *Music Matters*. Bowman's concern is that, while the distributed nature of reflective practice is implied, recurrent reference to concepts of "thinking" and "knowing," isolated from their somatic origins, effectively undermines Elliott's nondualistic perspective, such that reflection becomes a "disembodied and abstract" other (46). I disagree. I fail to see an emergent idealism. Yes, I agree that *Music Matters* focuses more on establishing that "our musical thinking and knowing are in our musical doing and making" (56) and less on how reflection is distributed in the conversation or transaction with the situation. But as I noted earlier, my students' compositional thinking was shaped and constrained by their performance backgrounds. And here, bodily movement patterns (which Elliott refers to continuously as *procedural* thinking and knowing) interact with the subject's capacity for "selecting" and "judging" in his or her musical "thinking" process (which, for Elliott, is always a multi-dimensional form of thinking that includes action-bodily-somatic doing-thinking). Both sides of the interaction between the composer and the composing environment are needed in a complete account of compositional thinking.

This point carefully noted, recurrent emphasis on thinking and knowing is, however, understandable in a discussion of the educational value of music making. The opinion that action is thought-less is still too prevalent. Stravinsky (1947) was well aware of the traditional tendency to view composers' "intelligence" as simply their capacity to reflect-on: "if it is true that we are *intellectuals*, we are called upon not to cogitate but to perform" (52).

The effort to establish composing as a reflective practice is even more difficult with improvisation because popular opinion places spontaneity over and against "thought." On the basis of both the preceding discussion and Elliott's view of performing, improvising certainly involves reflection-in-action, but this process is often considered inaccessible to the ordinary performer. However, as Elliott rightly observes, the apparent spontaneity of improvisers and improvising is actually the result of extensive work and experience in acquiring the musical vocabulary of an improvising style community and, gradually and painstakingly, developing ways to extend that vocabulary in personal ways.

Berliner's (1994) ethnographic study of how (traditional) jazz musicians learn improvisation elaborates this view. In his account, the path of the emerging jazz improviser includes, among other aspects, memorizing passages and tunes from recordings or demonstrations; embellishing learned material; studying tonal harmony; acquiring usable melodic patterns; and absorbing stylistic features of various improvisers and transforming and personalizing them. This process eventually leads to the capacity to produce original solos, which is itself a combination of "precomposed" and novel ideas conceived within the learned structural and stylistic constraints.

Once again, jazz improvisers are not "thoughtful" merely in the sense of planning every event in the moment. As in composing, "thinking" involves an interaction between premeditated ideas and patterns generated by muscle memory in the course of an improvisation. According to Berliner, improvised melodic lines are initially guided by preconceptions he calls the "singing mind" (1994, 180) that at times give way to bodily actions, "such as articulating a well-worn vocabulary pattern" (190), while conscious thinking attends to the next idea. Improvisers also engage in reflection-on-action. All of this supports Elliott's contextual and reflective-practice themes, as well as his concept of creativity as a critical contextualized endeavor.

Berliner opposes the common view that composition (with notation) is less constrained in extended development, considering its capacity for review and revision outside performance. Rather,

> the imaginative field of improvisers is far richer, and their processing capabilities far greater (both in terms of developing their own ideas and in responding to those of other artists within the group), than scholars have allowed. During practice routines, jazz musicians routinely subject their ideas to procedures comparable to those of written composition without the use of musical scores. Furthermore, with respect to revision in particular, they may revise ideas from one improvisation to another, as well as over the duration of a single performance. (Berliner 1994, 795n4)

Given that rehearsal time permits the development and revision of ideas, and that improvising ability emerges from the imitation and gradual transformation of musical ideas, I cannot see why student improvisers necessarily require "the more deliberate and forgiving tempo of compositional-notational time," as Elliott suggests (1995, 170). Although composition is involved in improvisation, it does not follow that it can or need be effectively separated from this context for learning purposes. In Berliner's account, student improvisers learn to compose in real time by gradually assimilating and transforming models, both composed pieces and improvisations, absorbed by aural imitation. The acquired vocabulary for real-time composition includes not only characteristic patterns and motifs but also the exemplar ways they can be realized. Thus, "performing" cannot be abstracted from context, since here it is not mere performing, but *performing improvisations* that is crucial to its development. Also, real-time composing can be attempted and developed outside "the rapid passing of real time" during rehearsals.

Another weakness in Elliott's account of improvisation is that his focus is exclusively on the solo improviser. Besides the interaction between muscle memory and conscious input, improvisational thinking also involves reacting to the ideas of other group members. Berliner (1994) devotes the third part of his book to collective jazz improvisation, the interactive feature of which is the subject of a book by Monson (1996).

Sawyer (1999) views improvisation in general as "fundamentally a *group* activity" that, when taught in this way, promotes the learning of "collaboration, group problem-solving, and collective creativity" (193, italics in original).

A central feature of reflection-in-action in group improvisation is the capacity to respond appropriately to another's impulse in order to maintain musical coherence and continuity. This also requires time and effort to develop; it is not simply a matter of "follow the leader" or "question and answer." It is a dynamic process in which musical roles constantly switch among members according to the needs of the moment. Nunn (1998) discusses the "relational functions" involved in group "free improvisation," some of which are: *solo*, where a single voice directs the improvising, but only momentarily; *support*, the active accompaniment to the dominant voice(s); *ground*, a more or less static accompaniment, such as a drone or ostinato; *dialogue*, involving imitation, call-and-response, and overlap with two or more members; and, *catalyst*, in which a particular gesture causes a change in the perceived direction of the music (48–50). None of these functions alone guarantees a successful improvisation; again, their effective use will be the result of experience in group collaboration.

In summary, the evidence appears sufficient to suggest that composing and improvising can be regarded as forms of reflective practice, as explained in *Music Matters*. Moreover, while I have not yet emphasized the social and cultural aspects, I hope it is clear from my account, above, that the teaching of composition and improvisation cannot be reduced to what Jorgensen (1997) wrongly calls "training" wherein teacher-directed procedures stand in opposition to "reflection" and "speculation" (12). Rather, self and environment (and, in group improvisation, other selves), on the one hand, and procedural and propositional knowledge, on the other, interact in a complex process of exploration and discovery.

Composing and Improvising in Context

Composition and improvisation are examined in chapter 7 of *Music Matters*. A major focus here is the context-embedded nature of music making. "Context" here is not only the sociohistorical background surrounding a musical action or work; rather, Elliott follows Brown, Collins, and Duguid (1989) in proposing that musical actions and products are inseparable from situations that produce them. I have already addressed this theme and emphasized that compositional and improvisational efforts are not limited to mental processes; instead, these are distributed among situational aspects such as instruments and other people. Beyond the immediate context of the activity itself is the structure of the environment, including the meanings and purposes of the activity. For example, in my research on student composers, the individual work of my subjects had to be conceived in relation to its being an assignment in an introductory composition course, and an elective part of their requirements for the bachelor of arts program at the National Institute of Education in Singapore. Also important was the fact that that their instructor was the British composer and educator

John Howard, then division head, whose nonprescriptive, learner-centered approach encouraged students to view composing as a personal endeavor.

Also, in my previous discussion of improvisation above, I argued that the apparent original and spontaneous actions of jazz improvisers are in fact the result of music makers learning and absorbing the features, actions, and values of an established musical tradition of improvisation. This is true of all musical *practices* (in Elliott's sense of musical communities) in which fixed "points of departure" for improvising are established by the musical culture (Nettl 1998, 13). Also, the term "free improvisation," in the sense of works lacking a specified point of departure, is a misnomer: no improvisation is "free" because the materials and structural tendencies involved derive from the musical experience and influences of the players. As Alperson (1984) observes, "Even the freest improviser, far from creating *ex nihilo*, improvises against some sort of musical context" (22).

Elliott argues, correctly, that even composers who are motivated by entirely personal, "nonutilitarian" purposes include "social and practical realities" in their work (1995, 163). Elliott observes (citing Wolterstorff) that composers, even while often working alone, "do not lock themselves in with sounds," rather "social practices are embodied in their works . . . [at times] being constitutive of the identity of those works" (Wolterstorff 1987, 125). The social and practical features that permeate composing range from personal and professional relationships, to musical traditions and audiences, to the constraints of instrumental practices and materials. With the exception of the found sounds of musique concrète, even the organizations of musical tones are seen as "the result of generations of theoretical and practical development," as Elliott puts it (1995, 163).

In fact, Elliott could go further than this, for even the recorded found sounds in an electroacoustic work are theory laden. Pierre Schaeffer (1966), who originated the concept of musique concrète, worked from the perspective of recorded material as sound objects (*objets sonores*) which, owing to his inherited aesthetic paradigm, were intended to be perceived on their own, completely abstracted from the context of their sources. The social climate of today's electroacoustic composers has produced a different paradigm for some. For example, Claude Schryer (1998) takes an "ecological" view of composing with recorded sounds and views the perception of their contexts as essential to his works.

I find it curious, however, that Elliott's discussion stops where it does, when the unraveling of contextual layers could continue to even more profound levels. Indeed, as O'Toole suggests (see chapter 16), the realization that musical practices and institutions are dependent on the multiple meanings and identities people construct leads to a major critique of past assumptions about music and music making. In other words, commonsense notions about music are so ingrained that one easily forgets Geertz's (1983) observation that they are also socially situated.

So, the concepts of "composer" and "composing" are also questionable. In the case of *Music Matters*, the performance and design dimensions of musical works are separated for the purpose of discussion (1995, 92). While Elliott's presentation could be adjusted to apply to various contexts (especially since "improvised design" is included), it ultimately derives from a Western conception of the composer (e.g., one who provides designs for realization and interpretation by a performer through whom the composer's decisions are "completed," 166). This view may account for the subordination of composing to performing and improvising in their educational application (173). Thus, part of Elliott's discussion of composing (161–163) is bound to a perspective in which composers, using performance-based knowledge, produce "blueprints" in the service of performers who provide the music.

In fairness though, alternatives to this concept of composing are found in other places throughout *Music Matters*. For example, in the section on improvising (168–170), Elliott rightly claims that performing often occurs "before, after, or in" the act of composing (169). In fact, my discussion of the composing process noted that my subjects used keyboard explorations throughout the development of their pieces. In such a case, argues Alperson, "the process of composing a piece of music explicitly involves the process of performing it" (1984, 19). So, composition, from this perspective, is an activity concerned with making "designs" and making music in the process.

Other variations on this idea include acts of composition outside the paradigm of Western "concert music" (for lack of a better term). Rock music offers a paradigm in which the composer (individual or group) performs and records music during the process of conceiving a piece. Recording allows feedback for critical reflections on the process, the gradual construction of the piece through multiple tracks, and the eventual realization of the completed piece. Note, also, that the recorded product need not be final: there is always the possibility of a new mix.

Musical practices developed from oral traditions provide more perspectives. In such instances (again, solo or group), a composer may or may not be identifiable. An example of the former is found in Nettl's (1974) description of song creation by the peoples of the North American plains. Here, an individual constructs a song in response to a vision, which, while presumably improvised, is eventually fixed and taught to other tribe members, who remember the song and the name of its composer (5). Nettl offers other examples demonstrating that in practices where composers perform, and performers compose, it is difficult to determine whether a musical work is an improvisation or composition.

However, it is not only non-Western and popular musicians that render the composer-performer dichotomy problematic. The twentieth century saw major changes to the accepted paradigm in concert music because of recording technology. Composers' uses of the electroacoustic medium to create and store pieces resulted in a radical change: the performance dimension was apparently reduced to the function of loudspeakers. However, and despite what it seems, performance has not been eliminated. Besides the ritual associations in public performances of electroacoustic works (particularly in Montreal's Rien à Voir festival, where the hall is a former chapel), composers have the opportunity to conceive their works from start to finish in a performing mode. It is this capacity to work directly with musical sound that attracts composers such as Hildegard Westerkamp to the medium: "The sound studio allows for immediate interaction with sound, an intimacy, a conversation, like a slow motion improv. In a sound studio one can be a [performer] and composer at the same time" (Westerkamp 1995, quoted in Schryer 1998, 25).

In summary, the arguments advanced in *Music Matters*—that composing and improvising are socially, historically, and practically situated, as opposed to being autonomous forms of human activity — have important consequences for pedagogy and for revising old assumptions toward more accurate ideas about the interdependencies among all forms of music making, another point Elliott emphasizes in his tome.

Conclusion

Apart from the few reservations I've noted throughout this discussion, I generally endorse the conceptions of composing and improvising, implicit and explicit, in *Music Matters*. Elliott's praxial view of composition and improvisation as reflective practices is consistent with the demonstrated reports of practitioners and with the views of such psychologists as Perkins (1981) and Weisberg (1986), for whom creative processes comprise ordinary procedures, not special talents.

This praxial perspective enables all music students to engage profitably in composing and improvising. It should also encourage teachers to become composers and improvisers and learn how to teach their students to do the same in some selected musical styles.

Also, Elliott's premise that composing and improvising are "situated," meaning that they should be taught in context, underscores the need for effective alternatives to abstract (acontextual, aesthetic) notions of "creativity," which many teachers accept uncritically. Today, "creativity" is more often considered to be the outcome of doing, learning, and making in particular contexts of effort (e.g., musical styles), as Margaret Barrett also explains in the next chapter of this book. Thus, there is no substitute for engaging in style-related projects of composing and improvising. Doing so *matters*, not merely as occasional diversions from performing, but as related processes that, in their interactions with performing, contribute to the development of musicianship-listenership and, therefore, to each student's achievement of musical enjoyment and musical self expression.

References

Alperson, P. 1984. On musical improvisation. *Journal of Aesthetics and Art Criticism* 43 (1):17–29.

Austin, L., and T. Clark. 1989. *Learning to compose*. Dubuque, IA: Wm C. Brown.

Berliner, P. 1994. *Thinking in jazz: The infinite art of improvisation*. Chicago: University of Chicago Press.

Best, D. 1992. *The rationality of feeling: Understanding the arts in education*. London: Falmer.

Bowman, W. 2000. A somatic, "here and now" semantic: Music, body, and self. *Bulletin of the Council for Research in Music Education* 144:45–60.

Brown, J. S., A. Collins, and P. Duguid. 1989. Situated cognition and the culture of learning. *Educational Researcher* 18 (1):32–42.

Burnard, P. 1999. Bodily intention in children's improvisation and composition. *Psychology of Music* 27:159–174.

Elliott, D. J. 1995. *Music matters: A new philosophy of music education*. New York: Oxford University Press.

Folkestad, G. 1998. Musical learning as cultural practice as exemplified in computer-based creative music-making. In B. Sundin, G. E. McPherson, and G. Folkestad, eds., *Children composing*, 97–134. Sweden: Lund University.

Geertz, C. 1983. *Local knowledge*. New York: Basic Books.

Hindemith, P. 1952. A *composer's world: Horizons and limitations*. Cambridge, MA: Harvard University Press.

Jorgensen, E. 1997. *In search of music education*. Urbana: University of Illinois Press.

Langer, S. K. 1953. *Feeling and form*. New York: Charles Scribner's Sons.

———. 1957. *Philosophy in a new key: A study in the symbolism of reason, rite, and art*. Cambridge, MA: Harvard University Press.

Martin, J. 2000. *Developing musical thinking: A study of the composing process of tertiary level students*. Ph.D. diss., National Institute of Education, Nanyang Technological University, Singapore.

Monson, I. 1996. *Saying something: Jazz improvisation and interaction*. Chicago: University of Chicago Press.

Nettl, B. 1974. Thoughts on improvisation: A comparative approach. *Musical Quarterly* 60 (1):1–19.

———. 1998. An art neglected in scholarship. In B. Nettl and M. Russell, eds., *In the course of performance: Studies in the world of musical improvisation*. Chicago: University of Chicago Press.

Nunn, T. 1998. *Wisdom of the impulse: On the nature of musical free improvisation*. Self-published.

O'Toole, P. 2000. Music matters: Why I don't feel included in these musics or matters. *Bulletin of the Council for Research in Music Education* 144:28–39.

Perkins, D. N. 1981. *The mind's best work*. Cambridge, MA: Harvard University Press.

Ross, M. 1984. *The aesthetic impulse*. Oxford: Pergamon.

Ryle, G. 1949. *The concept of mind*. London: Hutchinson.

Sawyer, R. K. 1999. Improvised conversations: Music, collaboration, and development. *Psychology of Music* 27:192–205.

Schaeffer, P. 1966. *Traité des objets musicaux*. Paris: Éditions du Seuil.

Scheffler, I. 1965. *Conditions of knowledge*. Chicago: Scott, Foresman.

———. 1988. Making and understanding. In B. Arnstine and D. Arnstine, eds., *Proceedings of the Forty-third Annual Meeting of the Philosophy of Education Society*, 65–78. Normal: Illinois State University Press.

Schön, D. 1983. *The reflective practitioner: How professionals think in action*. New York: Basic Books.

———. 1987. *Educating the reflective practitioner: Toward a new design for teaching and learning in the professions*. San Francisco: Jossey-Bass.

Schryer, C. 1998. Searching for the Sharawadji effect: Electroacoustics and ecology. *Musicworks* 70:22–29.

Sessions, R. 1939. The composer and his message. Reprinted in E. T. Cone, ed., 1979, *Roger Sessions on music: Collected essays*. Princeton, NJ: Princeton University Press.

———. 1970. *Questions about music*. Cambridge, MA: Harvard University Press.

Sloboda, J. 1985. *The musical mind*. New York: Oxford University Press.

Smith, B., and W. Smith. 1994. Uncovering cognitive process in music composition: Educational and computational approaches. In M. Smith, A. Smaill, and G. Wiggins, eds.,

Music education: An artificial intelligence approach, 56–73. New York: Springer-Verlag.

Snowden, S. 1993. *Creativity and composition: Contextual facilitators and inhibitors in the lives of eight composers*. Ph.D. diss., University of Rochester. *Dissertation Abstracts International*, 54/05-A, 1718.

Solomon, G., ed. 1993. *Distributed cognitions*. New York: Cambridge University Press.

Stravinsky, I. 1947. *The poetics of music*. Cambridge, MA: Harvard University Press.

Stubley, E. 1992. Philosophical foundations. In R. Colwell, ed., *Handbook of research in music teaching and learning*, 3–20. New York: Shirmer.

Swanwick, K., and C. Franca. 1999. Composing, performing and audience-listening as indicators of musical understanding. *British Journal of Music Education* 16 (1):5–19.

Weisberg, R. 1986. *Creativity, genius, and other myths*. New York: Freeman.

Westerkamp, H. 1995. Sounding out genders: Women sound artists/composers talk about gender and technology. Paper presented at the 1995 Inter-society for the Electronic Arts, Montreal.

Witkin, R. 1974. *The intelligence of feeling*. London: Heinemann Educational Books.

Wolterstorff, N. 1987. The work of making a work of music. In P. Alperson, ed., *What is music? An introduction to the philosophy of music*. New York: Haven.

10

A Systems View of
Musical Creativity

MARGARET BARRETT

Drawing from recent studies of creativity (e.g., Csikszentmihalyi 1988; Gardner 1993), Elliott argues for a multidimensional and contextual view of musical creativity. He proposes a dialectical process between the standards and traditions of a musical style *domain* (however old or recent), the music makers and listeners who make up the domain's human *field*, and *individual* music makers as performers, improvisers, composers, arrangers, and conductors. Elliott emphasizes that "creative" music making is both reflexively thoughtful and contextually embedded.

Elliott's view of creativity (1995, 215–238) is more robust than previous efforts in music education. It moves our profession beyond the excesses of the progressive child-centered movement where an "anything goes" kind of "self-expression" was the guiding principle for teaching the arts (Abbs 1987, 38–46). For Elliott, creative musical achievements can only arise in a context in which issues of domain and field (e.g., knowledge in a field) are considered in *conjunction* with individual makers. Also, Elliott's concept of creativity goes far beyond traditional notions of creativity-as-composing to include *all* forms of music making: arranging, composing, conducting, improvising, and performing. And, when he discusses composition as musical creativity, Elliott (161–163) does not see it as a "stand-alone" activity. Rather, he sees each kind of composing (defined by its context of traditions, standards, and style elements) as embedded in a web of social-historical-musical thinking-in-action.

Elliott's position echoes British educator John Paynter (1982,1992) whose efforts during the last three decades in the United Kingdom have made compositional experiences central to children's musical development. For Paynter and Elliott, musical creativity is not and should not be conceived as an isolated activity within a music curriculum, or "creative experience" for its own sake. Paynter views music composition as a primary means of constructing musical understanding. He asserts that "composing is not an optional extra; in effect it underpins the whole curriculum, and it is the surest way for pupils to develop musical judgment and to come to understand the notion of 'thinking' in music" (1997, 18). Writing of creative experience in general, Paynter (1992) comments that creative experience in music education "is especially important" as "a way of coming to know through independent, innovative responses to ideas and to the means of expression" (10).

Elliott (1995) agrees with Paynter on most points, but he disagrees about music composition being the "primary" or the "surest way" to develop musical understanding. For Elliott, composing is a "major" but secondary means of developing musicianship suggesting: "unless or until students come to know the essential nature of musical works as performances, composing should not be the primary way of developing musicianship" (173).

These contrasting views suggest a schism in the ways in which music educators view compositional and creative experience in the music curriculum. A number of factors may account for this. For example, these contrasting views may arise from the conflation of the terms "creativity" and "composition" within music education writings. As Elliott and others have pointed out, although musical ideas may be generated, sequenced, and classified loosely as "composition," this does not mean that the products of such activity are necessarily creative, as judged by experts (including music teachers) in a particular musical style domain.

Alternatively, these differences may be accounted for by examining the arguments offered for the inclusion of compositional experiences in the music curriculum (see Barrett 1998). Whilst the tangible products of compositional experiences may not be of sufficient merit to be considered for inclusion in the context or practice of music education, these may be secondary considerations in an educational setting where the primary focus is not the generation of cultural capital, but student learning outcomes.

In developing a praxial view of creativity in music education, Elliott draws on the literature of creativity in general. This literature has tended to focus on the factors that contribute to the development of creative products and achievements in the world of the adult artist. It is interesting to note that Elliott has not drawn on the corresponding and extensive research that has attempted to examine the creative processes, products, and achievements of school-aged children. In this chapter I expand on the issues highlighted above and provide a critical examination of the relationship between Elliott's philosophical view of creative experience in music education and the findings of a range of current research studies investigating children's creative processes, products, and achievements.

Studying Creativity

Interest in creativity as a topic of research is a relatively recent phenomenon. Many identify Guilford's presidential address to the American Psychological Association (1950) as the catalyst that renewed interest in what was, until that time, a relatively neglected field. However, in the broader sweep of history, creativity has been a topic of philosophical debate in Western intellectual life since the time of Plato and Aristotle. Consequently, the philosophical literature in the arts and the sciences provides many views on the nature and definition of creativity. For example, Plato viewed creativity as some form of divine mental "infection" in which rational thought played no part. In the dialogue *Ion*, the creative process of the poet is described as one in which "there is no invention in him until he has been inspired and is out of his senses, and reason is no longer in him" (534/b, in Tillman and Cahn 1969, 7). This view of the artist as possessed is also reflected in the romantic conception of the creative artist as one set apart, an outsider from cultural and social norms.

Since Guilford's address, the study of creativity has witnessed a diversity of approaches, including psychometric (Torrance 1974), psychodynamic (Storr 1972/1992) cognitive (Finke, Ward, and Smith 1992; Weisberg 1993), and sociopersonal approaches (Amabile 1983; Eysenck 1993). In brief, psychometric approaches focus on the examination and measurement of individual differences in creativity. Psychodynamic approaches view creativity as the result of unconscious drives. Cognitive approaches concentrate on the mental processes and structures that underlie creative thought and action. Sociopersonal approaches focus on the examination of personality and motivational variables and the effects of the sociocultural environment on the individual's creative output.[1] What is common to the above approaches is a tendency to view creativity as a unidimensional concept—as a function of a single component such as cognitive style, psychological make-up, or personality.

More recently, researchers have adopted "systemic" or "confluence" approaches to the study of creativity in which creativity is seen to occur when a number of components converge (e.g., Amabile 1996; Csikszentmihalyi 1988, 1996; Gardner 1993; Sternberg and Lubart 1999). Amabile describes a "componential model of creativity" in which domain-relevant skills, creativity-relevant skills, and task motivations are all viewed as necessary components of creative performance (1996, 243). Recent research by Amabile and colleagues lends support to the model. Summarizing a substantial body of research in the areas of motivation and creativity, Ruscio, Whitney, and Amabile (1998) suggest that intrinsically motivated individuals demonstrate deeper levels of engagement in creative problem solving than do their less intrinsically motivated peers. These researchers further suggest that such engagement is linked to interest in the problem; enjoyment in the search for a solution; greater risk-taking; pursuit of unorthodox solutions and exploratory behaviors; and more sustained and persistent efforts—all of which results in more creative solutions than those produced by less intrinsically motivated peers (Ruscio, Whitney, and Amabile 1998, 244). In summary, it may be that intrinsic motivation in conjunction with domain-relevant skills and creativity-relevant processes (personality and individual difference variables, including cognitive style) yield highly creative products (257).

Sternberg and Lubart (1995) propose an "investment theory of creativity" that draws on economic theory to suggest that creative people are those who are able to "buy low and sell high." That is, creative individuals pursue an initially unpopular idea until it is recognized and adopted. These authors maintain that investment theory requires "a confluence of six distinct but interrelated resources: intellectual abilities, knowledge, styles of thinking, personality, motivation, and environment" (Sternberg and Lubart 1999, 11).

There is some overlap between Sternberg and Lubart's investment theory and Amabile's componential model of creativity, specifically the need for domain-relevant skills and knowledge and creativity-relevant processes (e.g., intellectual abilities, styles of thinking, personality, and motivation). However, Sternberg and Lubart also emphasize the role of environmental factors in leading to creative endeavor, noting that "one needs an environment that is supportive and rewarding of creative ideas" (1999, 11).

Csikszentmihalyi proposes a systems model of creativity. He moves beyond a focus on intrapsychic processes (such as thought processes and motivations) to include the influences of what he terms the "domain" and the "field." Csikszentmihalyi describes the systems view of creativity as one in which "a set of rules and practices must be transmitted from the domain to the individual. The individual must then produce a novel variation in the content of the domain, and the variation must then be selected by the field for inclusion in the domain" (1999, 315). Whilst the above description emphasizes the sociocultural factors of domain and field, Csikszentmihalyi does not ignore the contribution of the individual's personality and psychological processes to the creative enterprise. In earlier writing, Csikszentmihalyi suggests that the "creative individual" has an "autotelic" personality (Csikszentmihalyi and Rich 1997, 125) and is characterized by ten "dimensions of complexity" (Csikszentmihalyi 1996, 58–73). Specifically, he observes that creative individuals:

1. exhibit both physical energy and the capacity to be quiet, at rest;
2. tend to be both smart and naive;
3. are both playful and disciplined;
4. alternate between imagination and fantasy and a sense of reality;
5. are both extroverts and introverts;
6. are simultaneously humble and proud;
7. are psychologically androgynous;
8. are traditional and conservative, as well as rebellious and iconoclastic;
9. are both passionate and objective; and
10. alternate between periods of suffering and pain, and periods of great joy.

For Csikszentmihalyi, creativity is not an intrinsic quality that can be detected in objects and events, and subsequently judged on a scale of relative merit. Rather, creativity is "a phenomenon that is constructed through an interaction between producer and audience. Creativity is not the product of single individuals, but of *social* systems making judgments about individuals' products" (1999, 314). In summary, Csikszentmihalyi views creativity to be the outcome of a convergence of *individual* factors (including genetic endowment, environmental influences, cognitive processes, and personality traits), *domain* discipline (including age of introduction to the domain; depth, breadth, and complexity of involvement in the domain), and *field* (including those who make judgments concerning what constitutes an original contribution to the domain).

Csikszentmihalyi's model has attracted increasing attention, and it underpins Gardner's (1993) definition of a creative individual as "a person who regularly solves problems, fashions products, or defines new questions in a domain in a way that is initially considered novel but that ultimately becomes accepted in a particular cultural setting" (35). Gardner suggests also that "it takes about ten years for an individual to gain mastery of a domain," a suggestion that is supported by others (Hayes 1989; Simonton 1994). Gardner's work reinforces the systems perspective as presented by Csikszentmihalyi and positions creative endeavor as being (in part) dependent upon a thorough, disciplined, and intensive engagement with a domain over a protracted period of time.

Summary of the Praxial View of Creativity

I have devoted considerable space to a summary of Csikszentmihalyi's systems model of creativity because his view informs the view of creativity in music education presented by Elliott. Specifically, Elliott argues that creative achievement in music occurs when an individual creator with considerable skills and knowledge in a musical practice makes a tangible contribution to that practice as judged by members of the field (1995, 219). Elliott's emphasis on "tangible products or achievements that people deem valuable, useful, or exceptional in some regard" (216) effectively dismisses notions that creativity is a trait of particular individuals, a specific set of abilities, an innate capacity, or a feature of an environment. Further, his emphases admit the musical processes of arranging, composing, conducting, improvising, and performing as potential vehicles for musical creativity. However, Elliott argues (220–221) that, by itself, listening to music is not "creative" because listening produces no tangible musical product or achievement. (Elliott points out that music criticism, for example, combines music listening and writing and manifests itself as a literary product. As such, it can be evaluated as creative, or not, as a specific form of writing).

For Elliott, there are a number of educational implications that arise from this particular view of creativity and creating. In this view, creative achievement is indeed a potential outcome of music programs in which students learn competent or proficient musicianship; operate in a supportive environment that promotes risk-taking, constructive feedback and appraisal, and independent problem finding and problem solving; devote sustained periods of time to creative endeavors; and are allowed, taught, and motivated to participate in a reasonable range of musical style-practices. For Elliott, music educators develop students' music making and listening abilities (musicianship) *concurrently* through listening, performing, improvising, composing, arranging, and conducting in realistic musical style contexts. Praxial teaching-learning strategies for developing musical creativity include teachers and students taking on roles as coaches, guides, models, constructive listeners, and advisers (1995, 224–227, 234). Creative development depends on students' building sufficient musical skills and understandings to be competent music listeners and makers. For Elliott, the key to creativity lies in developing musicianship and creative strategies *concurrently* (not consecutively), beginning at the earliest stages of instruction. In an important point, Elliott asserts that no form of music making is inherently more creative than any other because all judgments of creativity must be viewed in terms of originality and significance.

Discussion of the "Systems View"

The systems view of creativity adopted by Elliott is a significant departure from earlier views of creativity because it recognizes the influences of historical and sociocultural dimensions of creativity, it emphasizes the development of individual skills and understandings from novice to competent and proficient levels of music listening and making (1995, 70–71; 227), and it views the processes through which the individual works in contexts of real musical practices.

However, in taking into account the sociocultural dimensions of creativity, the complexity of these dimensions must also be admitted, including the notion that social, cultural, and historical contexts are subject to multiple interpretations, definitions, and perspectives. Sawyer (1998) draws our attention to the perception that much creativity research is viewed as "elitist and Eurocentric, focusing as it has on those forms of creativity most highly valued in European cultures—scientific innovation and the privileged 'high arts'" (17). Sawyer also suggests that systems approaches to creativity are equally Eurocentric, as the notion of differentiated systems exists primarily in modern industrial societies (17).

Whilst the notion of a "field" that judges creative achievement may sit well with primarily Western, high-art views of creativity, the identification and accessing of the field that decides what is an original and significant contribution is not so easily achieved in non-Western settings. Crucially, it may not be so easily achieved in classroom settings, or when examining children's creativity as it occurs in non-school settings. In later writings that build on the systems model, Csikszentmihalyi and Rich (1997) broaden the notion of the "field." They note that in the "domain" of creativity research "the *field* usually consists of teachers or graduate students who judge the products of children or other students. It is they who decide which test responses, mosaics, or portfolios are to be considered creative" (47). In this description, not only is the notion of the field modified, but also the nature of the contributions to the domain (i.e., test responses, mosaics, or portfolios). This suggests that in the domain of creativity research in education children's responses to targeted tasks may be judged as creative against other contributions of a similar nature made by their peers. The implication for the judgment of creative achievement in music education settings is that children's responses to creative tasks in music should be judged by "teachers or graduate students" who judge the responses against peer responses to those tasks.

Elliott (1995) argues for the context dependency of all musical practices, insisting that musicianship is a matter of induction into musical practices; that is, students must enter and become part of the contexts of the musical practices (or music cultures) they intend to learn: "The musicianship underlying any practice of music making and listening has its roots in specific communities of practitioners who share and advance a specific tradition of musical thinking" (67).

To some extent, this view places music educators on the horns of a dilemma. Given Csikszentmihalyi's apparent rethinking of the nature of the "field" and "domain" aspects of creativity research in education, perhaps we should ask: "What constitutes the community of practitioners in the music classroom?" Is it the larger community of practitioners to whom Elliott refers—that is, the musical community beyond the classroom and school setting where the "practitioners who originate, maintain, and refine established ways and means of musicing" (1995, 67) dwell? Is it that micro-community of practitioners who operate in specific schools and classrooms encompassing all the social and cultural features of these settings? Alternatively, is it the community of practitioners who originate, maintain, and refine established ways and means of musicing in the domain of music education? In learning a musical practice, says Elliott, interactions with significant others, including teachers and the wider community of practitioners, whether in person or on recordings (161), is essential. However, should students' creative endeavors be judged against those of the wider musical community or (as Csikszentmihalyi and Rich now seem to suggest) in comparison to the micro-communities of the school and the domain of music education? Crucially, what about the musical practices of children engaged in music practices beyond the school setting?

In considering non-Western settings for creativity, it should be noted that notions of individual and collective creativity differ significantly in different cultural settings, further problematizing the task of identifying and accessing the field (see Colligan 1983; Gaines and Price-Williams 1990). Significantly, what constitutes a tangible product of creativity may also be disputed. Elliott suggests that listening, by itself, is not a creative activity because there is no tangible musical outcome from such activity. However, Racy (1998) writes extensively on the notion of "creative listening" by audience members when participating in a performance or improvisation in Arab music. Racy notes that the listener is considered a primary player in the creative *tara* process and carries considerable responsibility for the overall effectiveness of a performance (101). Active performer-listener communication is viewed as an essential component in the social construction of a creative performance in these contexts. Such communication rests in the audience's "knowledge about music and about how musicians function, what their needs are, how they feel, and the circumstances under which they perform and excel" (102). Tellingly, Racy observes that "musicians often summarize the lack of creativity in their performances by referring to the overall atmosphere of the performance" (102).

In the context of the Arab tradition described by Racy, the tangible musical product is the result of a collaborative interaction between the performer and a receptive and informed audience. The notion of receptivity to the music-listening experience, and knowledge of and about music as "creative listening," may have some application in the music education context. For example, the development of an original musical insight may be the tangible musical product or achievement of a listening experience. When working with children, this may be poorly expressed owing to the lack of a formal musical vocabulary and require some interpretation from adult co-listeners. However, it is the insight, not the expression of that insight, regardless of how well or poorly achieved, that is the focus. As Elliott suggests, "Knowing how to do something intelligently and knowing how to watch or listen to someone do something well are two sides of the same conscious coin" (1995, 56).

Through the efforts of scholars (e.g., Kristeller 1970) to establish a "modern system of art," it has been a relatively easy task to identify the domains in which creative endeavors in the arts occur in Western contexts.[2] However, this task is not so easily performed in cultures where distinctions between domains are more blurred and movement between them is more fluid. In some cultural contexts, creative activity may be restricted or prohibited in certain domains of practice, which suggests that the "level of creativity permitted on a topic is often inversely related to the topic's role in the maintenance of deep cultural patterns" (Lubart 1999, 342).

Additionally, whilst Western notions of creativity hinge on the identification of a tangible product or achievement judged to be a novel and significant contribution to a domain of practice, Lubart suggests that Eastern conceptions of creativity, for example, are less focused on innovative products and more concerned with "the re-interpretation of traditional ideas" (1999, 340). The dual emphasis on the features of novelty and "usefulness" as defining characteristics of creative endeavors in Western conceptions of creativity is not necessarily a promising way of defining creativity in the arts. For example, in what terms might we call a musical work "useful"? Although an abundance of uses may be attributed to the musical sounds that constitute a nation's national anthem, it is difficult to find a similar set of uses for the majority of musical works. Similarly, problems are encountered when the feature of novelty is examined in the context of creative endeavor in the arts.

Elliott (1995) draws our attention to the criteria of musical "originality and [domain-style] significance," emphasizing that judgments of musical originality and significance are made *in relation to similar* musical achievements; they are judged against an historical backdrop or context of ongoing practice (215–219).

However, we can speculate that within some oral cultures the establishment of an historical context of practice may be problematic due to the absence of musical preservation techniques (e.g., a system of notation) so that differing values placed on current achievements necessarily builds on and extends what is "recollected" from the past.

Conceptions of creativity are inevitably culturally based and reflect the *weltung-schauung* of that culture, including the valuing of individual versus collective action, the valuing of innovation versus conformity, and the establishment of domains of practice within which creative endeavors may be identified and practiced. The adoption of Csikszentmihalyi's systems model of creativity as the framework for conceptualizing musical creativity in music education settings has a range of implications. I discuss these in the following section with specific attention to children's creative musical processes, products, and achievements.

Children's Musical Creativity

Much of the study of children's creativity in music education has reflected researchers' interest in the ways children acquire the creative behaviors modeled by the dominant culture (i.e., those of the music classroom, and by implication, of the adult and primarily Western musical world). Consequently, creativity research has tended to examine children's musical products[3] and processes[4] as they occur in classroom (or related laboratory) settings and in the accepted musical conventions of composition and improvisation. Compositional and improvisational tasks completed by children in these studies have included strict parameters (e.g., instrumentation, musical structures, and materials) and more independent tasks where decisions were entirely the concern of the children. This interest in the ways in which children create music may be linked to a number of factors. These include the desire of progressive educationists in the latter half of the last century "to provide creative experience for all students," the view that experience in composition introduces children to the materials and techniques of contemporary music, the view that composition underpins the development of musical thinking and understanding, and the desire to teach composition more effectively as a musical process.[5]

Music curricula tend to reflect the musical worlds beyond school and beliefs concerning the ways in which learning in a domain is most effectively achieved. One of Elliott's premises is that "the nature of music education depends on the nature of music" (1995, 12). He advocates building music curricula to "induct" students into a reasonable range of musical practices in the world beyond school. For Elliott, this is achieved through the development of active and "realistic" musical "practicums" that situate the teaching and learning of musicianship. For Elliott, musicianship (the ability to listen to and make music) develops through "progressive musical problem solving" in teaching-learning environments designed as close likenesses of real music cultures (260) of the adult musical world. In an important observation, Elliott stresses that "musical creativity and musicianship are mutually interdependent and interactive" (227) and that a competent or proficient level of musicianship is a prerequisite for creative endeavor. This view suggests that children are incapable of creative endeavor in music until they have attained sufficient levels of musicianship in real music cultures.

I am not suggesting that this is not a worthy aim of music education. Rather, I suggest that in pursuing this aim strictly we may ignore (to our detriment) the musicianship that children bring to the music education enterprise, with a concomitant potential loss of musical richness and diversity in their, and our, lives. Through an exclusive focus on the communities of practice evidenced in the adult musical world, we may lose the opportunity to learn more about and from the communities of practice of the child's musical world.

A number of researchers have examined the ways children create when not constrained by the exigencies of the classroom or laboratory setting. In studies of children's musical play, as it occurs beyond the institutional boundaries of the music classroom, researchers have identified a range of ways in which children engage in creative processes. These studies have investigated the variation and transmission processes employed by children engaged in musical play (such as singing and clapping games) in order to provide an alternative perspective on our understanding of children's creativity.

Addo (1997) suggests that children's singing games are a "secular art form" and that "while it may not be possible to attribute a singing game to one composer, it is nonetheless the creative undertaking of children" (30). Whilst his comment is made with specific reference to West African singing games, this view is relevant to the creative undertaking of children in a number of cultures. Working in Australia, Marsh suggests that children's playground singing games provide a rich context for creative experience and, potentially, the development of compositional skills (Marsh 1995a, 1995b, 1997, 1999). Marsh observed children's musical play, specifically singing and clapping games, in a Sydney inner-city school playground with a particular emphasis on the variation and transmission processes employed by children. Marsh (1995b) noted that children drew on an established repertoire of familiar games and songs and adapted these through the employment of a "battery of innovative techniques" including reorganization of formulae, elaboration through addition of new material or expansion of known material, condensation through omission or contraction of formulae, and recasting of material (4). Marsh (1995a) defines this activity as compositional in nature rather than improvisatory, commenting that children move through an ongoing cycle of composition and performance (185), or "composition in performance" (Lord 1995).[6] It is important that the activity is one of co-construction, involving group processes of collaborative interaction.

Social processes similar to those described by Marsh are evident in the song-writing processes of young rock musicians. Shehan-Campbell (1995) describes the processes of collective composition employed by adolescent rock musicians working in a noninstitutional setting. "As in the acquisition of a new song, other players watched and listened, and then began to play along. At no time did the songwriter dictate what parts group members would play. Instead, it was left to players to experiment with and to refine their parts over the course of repeated playings" (18–19).

In a study of the improvisation practices of African American girls participating in singing games, Harwood identifies a range of social constraints that act upon the transmission and variation processes that occur in this particular community of practice. Harwood (1998a) defines improvisation as an activity that occurs in a group setting with standard repertoire as the basic material. Specifically:

> Improvisation includes musical, gestural, or textural elements spontaneously generated without apparent premeditation or composition—the improvised elements conform to stylistic conventions accepted by the community. They are not random, arbitrary or unduly idiosyncratic in nature, nor are they simply the result of mistakes in performance. (124)

Harwood identifies four elements that are characteristic of the ways in which African American girls vary and improvise with the standard repertoire that is transmitted orally in their musical play: special dispensation, improvisation as transition, routines, and mandatory improvisations.

Harwood (1998a) suggests that the process of improvising in the game is not open to all, but, rather, is the domain of a few "acknowledged masters" and "game leaders" who have "special dispensation" to vary the musical tradition. In her account, Harwood notes that on the periphery of an activity, or in the transitions between activities, one would see the "spontaneous eruption of physical gesture and vocal back-up extending into short dance, one or two players moving, clapping, and vocalizing" (116). Older girls would develop improvised routines to a range of texts, including rap and pop songs. Harwood observes that these routines drew on the moves developed through musical play experiences and those observed in the media (e.g., MTV). They were the property of individual girls who controlled the transmission of such moves beyond a designated group. Mandatory improvisations are described as those that occur in circumscribed spaces within song and game forms that require individual variation. Such improvisations may be novel or may consist of stock phrases and responses (117–118).

As Harwood describes it, these girls are being initiated into a community of practice and, in the reflexive way of such communities, contributing to the continuing evolution of that community through their observations of rule systems and the accommodation of individual variations within these. In particular, Harwood notes that the improvisational activity in the contexts she describes is supported and nurtured by the group, with apparent links between the more stylized movements of the standard repertoire the girls draw on and their subsequent, more spontaneous improvised dancing (1998a, 122). Significantly, the repertoire the girls work with makes allowances for a range of levels of competence. For Harwood, "the community of fellow players is essential for musical and social support" (123).

Of particular interest in Harwood's study are her observations concerning children's musical competence. She notes that children who appear quite competent musically in one context may appear incompetent to perform the same musical tasks in another context. For example, children who easily execute mixed meter patterns in hand-clapping games (singing in duple while clapping in triple groupings is quite common) would likely be unable to perform the abstract task of clapping two against three. Individuals who are keen to improvise vocally or verbally in call-and-response games with a circle of appreciative co-participants are not necessarily able to summon the same level of improvisatory prowess in the less supportive atmosphere of a classroom or testing situation (1998b, 58).

Similarly, we may speculate that given varying contexts, children's capacity to demonstrate creativity may be similarly affected.

The emphasis on the social context as an essential component of the creative process in the context of children's informal music making is further reinforced in Riddell's powerful description (1990) of the ways children produce variations on existing hand-clapping games. Two children who are hand clapping are involved in a more intense situation than learning a song from the music teacher at school. They are touching one another and watching each other intently for cues and responses that are difficult to describe in terms of musical concepts. They are creating something that is fresh, something that contains surprises; the players can't predict the outcome because it depends upon another person. It is never boring. It can't be done casually; full concentration is always required. Often, its seriousness is punctuated by silliness and laughter (Riddell 1990, 391).

This description of the ways in which hand-clapping games are transmitted in informal learning contexts has rich parallels with the characteristics of "performance creativity" as described by Sawyer (1998). Sawyer distinguishes between performance and product creativity, suggesting that the former is characterized by the concurrent development of the process and the product, whilst in the latter the relationship between these two factors is sequential (11). Sawyer emphasizes the role of context, cultural, and social features of performance creativity. He suggests that the study of performance creativity may provide access to a "more common, more accessible form of creativity than privileged domains such as the arts and sciences. In many non-Western cultures, performance is a daily, central aspect of the construction of meaning and identity" (12). Drawing on the work of Csikszentmihalyi (1996), Gardner (1993), Simonton (1988), and Sternberg and Lubart (1995), Sawyer emphasizes the role of social factors in creative performance, suggesting that these factors may be equally important as motivational, cognitive, or developmental factors. Sawyer identifies these social factors as unpredictability and collaboration, use of motifs and scripts, and collaborative emergence/end product (Sawyer 1999b). In an earlier elaboration, Sawyer includes individual agency and a teasing out of the collaborative aspects identified here into nonreducibility and intersubjectivity, with a specific focus on complex communication within a system (Sawyer 1999a).

Performance creativity as presented by Sawyer has strong parallels with "improvisation," a term that may be viewed as both equally contested and as subject to conflation as "creativity" and "composition." However, Sawyer does not exclude the possibility that performance creativity is also possible in contexts where an established, "scripted" musical work is interpreted and communicated through the medium of performance. In such contexts, collective group processes play an important part in the realization of a work, because a realization can vary significantly from performance to performance. Further, in individual "scored" performance, the collaborative relationship with the audience and the performer's reading of his or her audience (and his or her subsequent response to it) may be described as part of a continuum of collaborative emergence. Indeed, Sawyer suggests that all performances fall on a spectrum from relatively improvised to relatively constrained. However, in his view, there are elements of improvisational process (and emergence) in any social, collective performance.[7]

In recent work, Csikszentmihalyi and Rich (1997) extend the systems model to argue that the same personal, social, and cultural factors that apply to creativity where a tangible product is evidenced also apply in instances of "performance creativity" (63). They suggest that in a performance situation (e.g., musical improvisation), "what we call creativity is a phenomenon that is constructed through an interaction between producer and audience" (46).

Nettl (1998) provides an illuminating cultural analysis of the role of improvisation in the conception of music in the Western musical world. Working from the premise that (in the musicological world) improvisation is often regarded as the "music of the improvident" (6), Nettl presents a view of improvisation as occupying one of the lowest rungs in the Western musical world. He comments that "the musical establishment to which the profession of musicology belongs connects improvisation as a musical practice, but even more as a concept, with a kind of third world of music. Jazz, the music of non-Western cultures, folk music, and all music in oral tradition are somehow included here" (6–7). Nettl suggests that it is a common conception that improvisation is characterized by absence of precise planning and discipline, resulting in a view that correlates art music "with discipline, art for art's sake, reliability, and unpredictability, while the opposites of these characterizations apply in the case of jazz" (7). Nettl concludes: "Improvisation as the music of people who don't plan ahead and don't have elementary musical technology: can this be the white musical world's way of expressing a racist ideology?" (7).

Nettl's identification of musics that arise from oral traditions as candidates for classification as "third world" resonates with the ways children's musical play is viewed in the music education research world. Since the work of Moorehead and Pond (1941/1978), researchers have recognized the role of improvisatory activity in the music making of children. However, the ways in which such activity is valued vary immensely. In some views, improvisation in children's music making is a kind of "musical doodling," a form of play that precedes and is inherently inferior to any compositional activity. Blum (1998) suggests that the perception of freedom embodied in such views of improvisation evolve from an "ignorance of the pertinent constraints" (28) that operates in various contexts. Researchers who have investigated the oral traditions of children's musical play have alerted us to the range and depth of "the pertinent constraints" that operate in the context of children's musical play, and they have provided the music education community with rich insights into the musical complexity and rigor of this world.

A Systems View of Children's Creativity

A systems view of creativity, as presented by Csikszentmihalyi, focuses on the relationships that hold between the elements of the domain, the field, and the individual creator. In this view, the creative process is described as one that "involves a person's ability to innovate while interacting mentally with the rules or practices of a domain, and while keeping in mind the judgments and practices of the field" (Csikszentmihalyi and Rich 1997, 48). When we speak about children's creativity as it occurs in settings where children are the "controllers" of the "musical community of practice," these elements of the domain and field must be defined as part of and within the parameters of that "community of practice." Consequently, the field is made up of experts in that domain, that is, other children. This is powerfully illustrated in Harwood's description of the ways in which African American girls monitor the varying of their musical tradition, specifically through the identification of acknowledged masters and game leaders and the observance of rule systems and individual variations of these in the musical practices of singing and hand-clapping games in the domain of children's musical play. Children are the experts in the domain of children's musical play, and individuals evidence their creativity in the ways in which they innovate, whilst interacting with the rules and practices of the domain and keeping in mind the judgments and practices of the field. Within the communities of practice that constitute children's musical worlds, they not only learn and acquire the social and cultural processes and practices of group membership. As Gee and Green (1998) remind us, "Members have agency and thus take up, resist, transform, and reconstruct the social and cultural practices afforded them in and through the events of everyday life" (148).

Implications for Children's Creativity

Sociocultural perspectives in the field of learning suggest that knowledge is generated from within a culture, that "human mental functioning is inherently situated in social interactional, cultural, institutional and historical context" (Wertsch 1991, 81). Rogoff et al. (1993, 1) take the perspective that "children's development occurs through active participation in cultural systems of practice." Analyses of the studies of children's musical play cited earlier suggest that these children possess considerable musicianship within their community of practice and are able to engage in creative musical endeavor within that community of practice. There are a number of educational implications in this view.

Many children bring to school considerable musicianship within a particular community of practice. Too often a deficit view of children's musical ability pervades music teaching-learning interactions in school settings, as educators measure children's musical ability solely against the communities of musical practice extant in the adult musical world. I suggest that a greater understanding of children's musical cultures, and the ways in which musical meanings are negotiated within these cultures, would contribute to a more positive view of children's musical ability and more informed educational practices.

Like Elliott, Sawyer (1997) notes that "most performance genres socialize new members through a highly participatory form of apprenticeship, not by identifying a body of explicit knowledge and attempting to 'transfer' it to the student" (4). The study of children's musical performance genres outside the institutional setting supports this observation. In fostering children's musicianship and creative capacities, a balance is needed between the imparting of a body of explicit knowledge and initiation into specific communities of musical practice, as Elliott also emphasizes. It is important to note that the recognition and promotion of children's agency in their own music making is needed to tap the musicianship that children bring to the school setting.

The identification of the social dimension of creativity in specific communities of musical practice is of importance to music educators. Sawyer (1999a) writes of "collaborative emergence" as a description of the ways in which a performance is the result of the interactions of a number of individuals. He asserts that the creative products or phenomena that emerge cannot be understood by analyzing the group members individually (449) because, in a creative interaction, the intention of a statement (verbal or musical) is not finally realized until it has been responded to. Consequently, "individual intention may be and will be subverted to some extent by the responses of the other agents in the group" (455). This suggests that models of creativity that characterize the creative process as individual problem-solving activity ignore the social dimension of all activity, unless that problem solving is seen to occur in a community of practice and interaction. Writing of solo improvisation, Sawyer (1997) observes (as does Elliott): "Despite the seeming autonomy and even solitude of improvisational musicians, their performances are always collaborative products. The player internalizes not only a musical tradition, but inevitably also absorbs the tastes and preferences of his or her reference group—respected predecessors, peers, audiences, and critics" (63).

Conclusion

Cropley (1997) advocates the fostering of creativity in the classroom on the grounds that the development of creative potential contributes to the common good. He suggests that creative experience in the classroom results in better learning, improved mental health, and benefits society in preparing all young people for the "richest and most productive life possible" (84). Elliott argues that "the desire to achieve creative results is one with the human drive to differentiate and integrate consciousness by seeking more and more complex challenges" (229). Both writers argue that educating for creativity is very possible and very desirable on a range of grounds.

In presenting a systems view of creativity in music education, Elliott has provided the music education community with a powerful model for the development of children's creative musical capacities, products, and achievements. Elliott's model connects the creative enterprise of children to musical worlds beyond schools and affirms the centrality of music listening and music making (of all kinds) as basic components of any creative musical enterprise.

In this chapter I have attempted to highlight a range of issues that arise when a systems view of creativity in music education is adopted. To recognize the socio-cultural aspects of creative endeavors (especially the domain and field dimensions) strengthens the position of creative activity in the music curriculum and raises a number of questions. Through recognition of the influences of the domain and field, we gain a more robust view of creative activity, with a concomitant deepening of curricula emphasis on issues such as the development of competent music-listening and music-making abilities (or what Elliott calls "musicianship," for short). However, our recognition of the sociocultural dimensions of creativity also requires that we acknowledge the complexity of these dimensions and the diversity of ways in which children participate in musical communities of practice within and without the school setting. It is important to note that it requires that we recognize the musicianship that children bring to music education encounters, seek ways to help children build on their musical foundations, and further their musical aspirations.

Notes

1. For a more comprehensive analysis and critique of these approaches see Sternberg and Lubart 1999, 3–15.

2. Kristeller comments that the "modern system" is not a fixed entity, pointing to examples of art forms that have enjoyed varying positions of status over time. He cites the domains of gardening and film as particular examples of this phenomenon.

3. See Auh 1997; Barrett 1996; Davies 1992, 1994; Green 1990; Salaman 1988; Swanwick 1988, 1994; Swanwick and Tillman 1986; Tillman 1989.

4. Bunting 1987, 1988; Burnard 1995; Carlin 1997; DeLorenzo 1989; Folkestad et al. 1998; Kennedy 1999; Kratus 1989, 1991, 1994; van Ernst 1993; Wiggins 1994; Younker and Smith 1996.

5. For a more comprehensive analysis of these factors see Barrett 1998.

6. Edwards and Sienkowicz describe the notion of composition-in-performance as a type of re-creation where a performance is created by drawing on the traditions of the genre rather than relying on rote memorization. Through the use of "structural props" such as the formulae, special language, music, and meter (1990, 13), performers simultaneously create and perform.

7. Personal communication, March 2000.

References

Abbs, P. 1987. *Living powers: The arts in education*. London: Falmer Press.

Addo, A. O. 1997. Children's idiomatic expressions of cultural knowledge. *International Journal of Music Education* 30:15–25.

Amabile, T. M. 1983. *The social psychology of creativity*. New York: Springer-Verlag.

———. 1996. *Creativity in context: Update to the social psychology of creativity*. Boulder, CO: Westview.

Auh, M. S. 1997. Prediction of musical creativity in composition among selected variables for upper elementary students. *Bulletin of the Council for Research in Music Education* 133:1–8.

Barrett, M. 1996. Children's aesthetic decision-making: An analysis of children's musical discourse as composers. *International Journal of Music Education* 28:37–61.

———. 1998. Researching children's compositional processes and products: Connections to music education practice? In B. Sundin, G. E. McPherson, and G. Folkestad, eds., *Children composing*, 10–34. Lund University: Malmo.

Blum, S. 1998. Recognizing improvisation. In B. Nettl and M. Russell, eds., *In the course of performance: Studies in the world of musical improvisation*, 27–45. Chicago: University of Chicago Press.

Bunting, R. 1987. Composing music: Case studies in the teaching and learning process. *British Journal of Music Education* 4 (1):25–52.

———. 1988. Composing music: Case studies in the teaching and learning process. *British Journal of Music Education* 5 (3):269–310.

Burnard, P. 1995. Task design and experience in composition. *Research Studies in Music Education* 5:32–46.

Carlin, J. 1997. Musical preferences for compositions by selected students aged 9–15 years. *Bulletin of the Council for Research in Music Education* 133:9–13.

Colligan, J. 1983. Musical creativity and social rules in four cultures. *Creative Child and Adult Quarterly* 8 (1):39–47.

Cropley, A. J. 1997. Fostering creativity in the classroom: General principles. In M. A. Runco, ed., *Handbook of creativity research*, 1:83–114. Cresskill, NJ: Hampton Press.

Csikszentmihalyi, M. 1988. Society, culture and person: A systems view of creativity. In R. J. Sternberg, ed., *The nature of creativity*. New York: Cambridge University Press.

———. 1996. *Creativity: Flow and the psychology of discovery and invention.* New York: HarperCollins.

———. 1999. Implications of a systems perspective for the study of creativity. In R. J. Sternberg, ed., *Handbook of creativity*, 313–335. Cambridge: Cambridge University Press.

Csikszentmihalyi, M., and G. J. Rich. 1997. Music improvisation: A systems approach. In R. K. Sawyer, ed., *Creativity in performance*, 43–66. Greenwich, CT: Ablex.

Davies, C. 1992. Listen to my song: A study of songs invented by children aged 5–7 years. *British Journal of Music Education* 9 (1):19–48.

———. 1994. The listening teacher: An approach to the collection and study of invented songs of children aged 5–7. In H. Lees, ed., *Musical connections: Tradition and change*, Proceedings of the Twenty-first World Conference of the International Society for Music Education, Tampa, Florida, 120–128. Auckland, NZ: Uniprint, University of Auckland.

Delorenzo, L. C. 1989. A field study of sixth-grade students' creative music problem-solving processes. *Journal of Research in Music Education* 37 (3):188–200.

Edwards, V., and T. J. Sienkowicz. 1990. *Oral cultures past and present: Rappin' and Homer.* Oxford: Basil Blackwell.

Elliott, D. J. 1995. *Music matters: A new philosophy of music education.* New York: Oxford University Press.

———. 1996. Consciousness, culture, and curriculum. *International Journal of Music Education* 28:1–15.

Eysenck, H. J. 1993. Creativity and personality: A theoretical perspective. *Psychological Inquiry* 4:147–178.

Finke, R. A., T. B. Ward, and S. M. Smith. 1992. *Creative cognition: Theory, research and applications*. Cambridge, MA: MIT Press.

Folkestad, G., D. J. Hargreaves, and B. Lindstrom. 1998. Compositional strategies in computer-based music-making. *British Journal of Music Education* 15 (1):83–97.

Gaines, R., and D. Price-Williams. 1990. Dreams and imaginative processes in American and Balinese artists. *Psychiatric Journal of the University of Ottawa* 15 (2):107–110.

Gardner, H. 1991. *The unschooled mind: How children think and how schools should teach.* New York: Basic Books.

———. 1993. *Creating minds.* New York: Basic Books.

Gee, J. P., and J. L. Green. 1998. Discourse analysis, learning, and social practice: A methodological study. In P. D. Pearson and A. Iran-Nejad, eds., *Review of research in education*, No. 23, 119–170. Washington, DC: American Educational Research Association.

Green, L. 1990. Assessment of composition. *British Journal of Music Education* 7 (3):191–196.

Gruber, H. 1980. The evolving systems approach to creativity. In S. Modgil and C. Modgil, eds., *Towards a theory of psychological development*. Windsor, UK: National Foundation for Educational Research.

———. 1981. *Darwin on man.* Chicago: Chicago University Press.

Gruber, H., and D. B. Wallace. 1999. Understanding unique creative people at work. In R. J. Sternberg, ed., *Handbook of creativity*, 93–115. Cambridge: Cambridge University Press.

Guilford, J. P. 1950. Creativity. *American Psychologist* 5:444–454.

Harwood, E. 1998a. Go on girl! Improvisation in African-American girls' singing games. In B. Nettl and M. Russell, eds., *In the course of performance: Studies in the world of musical improvisation*, 113–126. Chicago: University of Chicago Press.

———. 1998b. Music learning in context: A playground tale. *Research Studies in Music Education* 11:52–60.

Hayes, J. R. 1989. Cognitive processes in creativity. In J. A. Glover, R. R. Ronning, and C. R. Reynolds, eds., *Handbook of creativity*, 135–146. New York: Plenum Press.

Kennedy, M. A. 1999. Where does the music come from? A comparison case-study of the compositional processes of a high school and a collegiate composer. *British Journal of Music Education* 16 (2):157–177.

King, N. R. 1987. Elementary school play: Theory and research. In J. H. Block and N. R. King, eds., *School play: A source book*, 143–166. New York: Garland.

Kratus, J. 1989. A time analysis of the compositional processes used by children ages 7–11. *Journal of Research in Music Education* 37:5–20.

———. 1991. Characterisation of compositional strategies used by children to a melody. *Canadian Music Educator* [Special ISME Research Edition] 33:95–103.

———. 1994. The ways children compose. In H. Lees, ed., *Musical connections: Tradition and change*. Proceedings of the 21st World Conference of the International Society for Music Education, Tampa, Florida, 128–141. Auckland, NZ: Uniprint, The University of Auckland.

Kristeller, P. O. 1970. The modern system of arts. In M. Weitz, ed., *Problems of aesthetics.* London: Macmillan.

Loane, B. 1984. Thinking about children's compositions. *British Journal of Music Education* 1 (3):205–231.

Lord, A. B. 1995. *The singer resumes the tale.* Ithaca, NY: Cornell University Press.

Lubart, T. I. 1999. Creativity across cultures. In R. J. Sternberg, ed., *Handbook of creativity*, 339–350. Cambridge: Cambridge University Press.

Marsh, K. 1995a. Creative processes in children's musical play: the playground and the classroom. In H. Lee and M. Barrett, eds., *Honing the craft: Improving the quality of music education*. Proceedings of the Australian Society for Music Education, 10th National Conference, 184–191. Hobart, AUS: Artemis Press.

———. 1995b. Children's singing games: Composition in the playground? *Research Studies in Music Education* 4:2–11.

———. 1997. *Lessons from the playground: Teaching and learning singing games in a multi-cultural society*. Paper presented at the Australian Society for Music Education 11th National Conference, Brisbane, July 1997.

———. 1999. Mediated orality: The role of popular music in the changing tradition of children's musical play. *Research Studies in Music Education* 13:2–12.

Moorehead, G. E., and D. Pond. 1941/1978. *Music of young children*. 5th ed. Santa Barbara, CA: Pillsbury Foundation for Advancement of Music Education.

Nettl, B. 1998. Introduction. In B. Nettl and M. Russell, eds., *In the course of performance: Studies in the world of musical improvisation*, 1–23. Chicago: University of Chicago Press.

Paynter, J. 1982. *Music in the secondary school curriculum*. Cambridge: Cambridge University Press.

———. 1992. *Sound and structure*. Cambridge: Cambridge University Press.

———. 1997. The form of finality: A context for musical education. *British Journal of Music Education* 14 (1):5–22.

Racy, A. J. 1998. Improvisation, ecstasy, and performance dynamics in Arabic music. In B. Nettl and M. Russell, eds., *In the course of performance: Studies in the world of musical improvisation*, 95–112. Chicago: University of Chicago Press.

Riddell, C. 1990. *Traditional singing games of elementary school children in Los Angeles*. Ph.D. diss., University of California at Los Angeles.

Rogoff, B., J. Mistry, A. Goncu, and C. Mosier. 1993. Guided participation in cultural activity by toddlers and caregivers. *Monographs of the Society for Research in Child Development* 58 (8): Serial No. 236.

Ruscio, J., D. M. Whitney, and T. M. Amabile. 1998. Looking inside the fish bowl of creativity: Verbal and behavioural predictors of creative performance. *Creativity Research Journal* 11 (3):243–263.

Salaman, W. 1988. Objectives and the teaching of composition. *British Journal of Music Education* 5 (1):3–20.

Sawyer, R. K., ed. 1997. *Creativity in performance*, Greenwich, CT: Ablex.

———. 1998. The interdisciplinary study of creativity in performance. *Creativity Research Journal* 11 (1):11–19.

———. 1999a. The emergence of creativity. *Philosophical Psychology* 12 (4):447–469.

———. 1999b. Improvised conversations: Music, collaboration, and development. *Psychology of Music* 27:192–205.

Shehan-Campbell, P. 1995. Of garage bands and song-getting: The musical development of young rock musicians. *Research Studies in Music Education* 4:12–22.

Simonton, D. K. 1988. *Scientific genius: A psychology of science*. New York: Cambridge University Press.

———. 1994. *Greatness: Who makes history and why?* New York: Guilford Press.

Sternberg, R. J., and T. I. Lubart. 1995. *Defying the crowd: Cultivating creativity in a culture of conformity*. New York: Free Press.

———. 1999. The concept of creativity: Prospects and paradigms. In R. J. Sternberg, ed., *Handbook of creativity*, 3–15. Cambridge: Cambridge University Press.

Storr, A. 1972/1992. *The dynamics of creation*. London: Penguin Books.

Swanwick, K. 1988. *Music, mind, and education*. London: Routledge.

———. 1994. *Musical knowledge: Intuition, analysis, and music education*. London: Routledge.

Swanwick, K., and J. Tillman. 1986. The sequence of musical development: A study of children's composition. *British Journal of Music Education* 3 (3):305–339.

Tillman, F. A., and S. M. Cahn, eds. 1969. *Philosophy of art and aesthetics: From Plato to Wittgenstein*. New York: Harper and Row.

Tillman, J. 1989. Towards a model of development of children's musical creativity. *Canadian Music Educator* 30 (2):169–174.

Torrance, E. P. 1974. *Torrance tests of creative thinking*. Lexington, MA: Personnel Press.

van Ernst, B. 1993. A study of the learning and teaching processes of non-naive music students engaged in composition. *Research Studies in Music Education* 1:22–39.

Wallace, M., and Gruber, D. 1989. *Creative people at work*. New York: Oxford University Press.

Weisberg, R. W. 1993. *Creativity beyond the myth of genius*. New York: Freeman.

Wertsch, J. V. 1991. A sociocultural approach to socially shared cognition. In L. B. Resnick, J. M. Devine, and S. D. Teasley, eds., *Perspectives on socially shared cognition*. Washington, DC: American Psychological Association.

Wiggins, J. H. 1994. Children's strategies for solving compositional problems with peers. *Journal of Research in Music Education* 42 (3):232–252.

Younker, B. A., and W. H. Smith. 1996. Comparing and modelling musical thought processes of expert and novice composers. *Bulletin of the Council for Research in Music Education* 128:25–36.

11

Praxial Foundations of Multicultural Music Education

C. K. SZEGO

> Recalling the African who could claim to understand a certain piece of music by knowing the dance that goes with it, we might begin to perceive a dancer's feet, to which in fact there might often be rattles attached, as a part of the music: if a dancer with rattles tied onto his feet made a mistake, we would hear it. In African music, it is the listener or dancer who has to supply the beat: the listener must be *actively engaged* in making sense of the music; the music itself does not become the concentrated focus of an event, as at a concert. It is for this fundamental reason that African music should not be studied out of its context or as "music": the African orchestra is not complete without a participant on the other side.
>
> —John Chernoff, *African Rhythm and African Sensibility* (1979), 55

In the excerpt above, ethnomusicologist John Chernoff refers to the dense textures created in West African performance traditions by polyrhythmic layering: drummers, hand-clapping bystanders, and dancers "play" cyclic rhythmic patterns in response to and in opposition to each other. The music they generate is not organized metrically and has no constant, audible pulse to keep everyone in synchrony;[1] thus, "it is the listener or dancer who has to supply the beat."

Readers of *Music Matters* will be familiar with the work of Chernoff, whose observations on the nature of music making and musical understanding in West Africa regularly punctuate David J. Elliott's writings. This particular description of musical apprehension serves as a productive starting point because it accents a number of themes that resonate with Elliott's theoretical remodeling of music education. In addition to invoking a specific model of listening and musicing, Chernoff touches on the embodied nature of music making, the role of performance or active participation in musical understanding, and the folly of treating sound phenomena as independent, decontextualized aesthetic objects. He forcefully reminds us of the culturally contingent nature of musical experience and meaning making, and even the definition of "music" itself. These themes will serve as the foundation of my response to Elliott's vision of multicultural music education and the constellation of ideas surrounding it.

If, at a practical level, only one portion of the penultimate chapter of *Music Matters* is devoted directly to a discussion of multiculturalism in music education, at a theoretical level (where Elliott's thinking is mostly aimed) *Music Matters* is devoted to the topic entirely: the claim that "MUSIC is inherently multicultural" (1995, 207) is woven throughout the book. As such, it is cause for celebration among advocates of culturally expanded curricula and ethnomusicologists alike. Though there have been several passionate and articulate advocates of world music in education over the last two decades (e.g., Lundquist 1991), Elliott's distinguished achievement has been to synthesize elements of a post-positivist epistemology emerging in education, cognitive studies, aesthetics, and musicology with the musical and cultural inclusiveness of ethnomusicology. A philosophical project of this magnitude and ambition has to be regarded as a work in progress; it thus invites calibrated responses from those invested in its theoretical refinement and practical applications. In this essay I elaborate and particularize some core concepts and definitions and present a number of counterexamples and arguments to soften Elliott's position on performance and listening. In addition, I attempt to problematize notions of authenticity and multiculturalism in order to avert simplistic models in the actual delivery of music education. All suggestions are tendered with a general endorsement of Elliott's manifesto; one can only hope that this appreciation is sustained through even the most critical moments of the essay.

Because *Music Matters* is largely a theoretical work, before considering the practical, pedagogical applications of Elliott's praxial philosophy, I would like to spend some time examining its conceptual foundations, beginning with a definition of the term "music."

MUSIC, Music, music

One of the central premises of *Music Matters*—that "MUSIC is inherently multicultural"—is founded on a triad of definitions centered on the word "music":

> MUSIC is a diverse human practice consisting in many different musical practices or Musics. Each and every musical practice (or Music) involves the two corresponding and mutually reinforcing activities of music making and music listening. . . . The word music (lowercase) refers to the audible sound events, works, or listenables that eventuate from the efforts of musical practitioners in the contexts of particular practices. (Elliott 1995, 44–45)

The concept to be affirmed here, at least from an ethnomusicological perspective, is *practice*. Each definition in the nested triad of MUSIC/Music/music engages human beings as doers, as active agents working in particular sociomusical spheres; MUSIC/Music/music is more than a sonic event. Elliott's view is that MUSIC engages people as producers/makers and consumers/listeners principally, though I would add that the myriad other ways in which people are engaged with music, for example as movers and meaning makers, are equally important.

The overarching and comprehensive definition that Elliott provides is by necessity frequently abbreviated; its most common form is the statement that "MUSIC is inherently multicultural." And, argues Elliott, if "MUSIC is inherently multicultural, then music education ought to be multicultural in essence" (1995, 207). For those who reject the notion that some styles of music are inherently more valuable than others and therefore more worthy of study in North American classrooms,[2] this is a most welcome move.

Recognizing the inadequacy of a single term to capture so many culturally distinct phenomena, Elliott is careful to add that "MUSIC is an open concept" (1995, 128). Elaborating this idea, whenever we deal with an apparently cross-cultural phenomenon, we need to question whether, in fact, it *is* the same phenomenon we are examining. Regarding the universality of the term "music," Nettl (1977) argues that all people seem to have something that can be recognized as music—at least by people for whom "music" is a meaningful category—though the phenomenon may not necessarily be understood as music by its practitioners. This kind of semantic snarl arises, as Wachsmann (1971) points out, when "phenomena for which we can find no meaningful summary as to the property which unites them, resemble each other more closely than do anything else in the Universe" (384).

Indeed, finding a common property or cluster of properties seems unlikely. Consider, for example, the challenges to standard conceptualizations of music presented by twentieth-century Western avant-garde composers: Where does speech end and song begin? What threshold of denotative tolerance does noise cross? And what if sounds are not generated by human beings? Given these variables, Boilés (1984) has argued that applying the term "music" universally is misleading at best; one can only say what is intentionally musi*cal*. Boilés's definition of "musical" is an "organized set of particulars [that] produces patterns in time and space . . . [and is] perceived through [the] senses as having unique duration or qualities of duration" (51). Stated in this fashion, what Boilés describes may be aural, perhaps even visual (e.g., dance), and thus includes an amazing array of phenomena, including speech. In addition to the adjectival hedge (i.e., the use of "musical"), the solution of most ethnomusicologists who face this cross-cultural dilemma is to render the boundaries of the sonic phenomena they describe with utmost clarity.

I elaborate the nonuniversality of music not as a critique of Elliott, whose oblique recognition of the problem and whose considered use of the phrase "musical practice" is especially commendable, but for the sake of music educators faced with the practical task of working with this conceptual conundrum. If the issue of definition seems somewhat arcane, it will become less so when teachers encounter the instructional challenge of conveying the musical concepts of other cultural groups to students. Several examples come to mind.

Musiqa is an Arabic term borrowed from the Greek language around the eighth to tenth centuries; in Persian the same word is *musiqi*. Though they share a common origin with the English word, the meanings of these related lexemes diverge in interesting ways. According to Ibsen al Faruqi (1985), *musiqa* applies only to certain secular genres in Islamic cultures, though in fact there is a broad spectrum of genres in the Islamic world, sacred and secular, that most Euro-Canadians (for example) would consider music*al*. Ibsen al Faruqi presents this spectrum as a hierarchy of sound-art expression, or *handasah al sawt*; the hierarchy distinguishes between *musiqa* and non-*musiqa*, between genres that are illegitimate or at best controversial and those that are legitimate. The most valued genre, the one that receives "full and unequivocal acceptance" (9) by both Muslim clerics and society at large, is Qur'anic recitation. A form of pitched, unaccompanied, improvisational chant, Qur'anic recitation is not considered *musiqa* and has none of *musiqa*'s questionable associations, despite the fact that in competitions among Qur'anic chanters, judges evaluate music*al* aspects of their performances (Ibsen al Faruqi 1987). Within the category called *musiqa*, there are also fine distinctions: the closer a genre is to Qur'anic recitation in terms of its sonic qualities, function, and moral associations, the more approval it is likely to garner within the Islamic world. Islam's exclusive definition clearly leaves out much of what Euro-Canadians might be willing to identify as music. However, ethnomusicologists who study all categories of sound-art expression imply, through their study of them, that they have some relationship to music as Westerners generally conceive it (Gourlay 1984, 28).

To provide further illustration of the nonuniversality of the word "music," I summon the example of the Kaluli people of the Southern Highlands province in Papua New Guinea. Just as there is no African language with a term that corresponds to music, so the Kaluli have no equivalent term (Feld 1980). In contrast to the Islamic model, Kaluli make judgments and engage in the production of sound phenomena that many North Americans might not consider music, but that they might recognize the "musicness" of (e.g., the sounds of birds, insects, and waterfalls, the chopping of wood, and stylized weeping). However, while the Kaluli have several named categories of sonic production, including *gisalo* (meaning "song," "melody," or "ceremony"), there is no collective term that gathers all named categories under the same taxonomic heading.[3]

The final example of the nonuniversality of "music" comes from India. The Sanskrit word *sangita* (Hindi, *sangit*), most commonly translated as "music," denotes phenomena not ordinarily subsumed even by many liberal Western definitions. Significantly, *sangita* includes performing arts associated with music, namely dance, and thus indicates a "broader affective channel" of communication (Gourlay 1984, 35). It is not that there is no distinction between music and dance in India, but that they form a duality; they are both manifestations of the same fundamental phenomenon.

Having gone down this terminological path, it should be reiterated that Elliott's MUSIC, characterized as a collection of music*al* practices, accommodates the ideas put forth here rather proficiently, though its attribution to human beings alone might be at odds with some culture-specific formulations. Therefore, any uneasiness I feel is not conceptual, but a matter of communicating within the limits of our shared linguistic conventions. By virtue of its focus on doing, Elliott's initial definition is inclusive and flexible: music is more than a sonic event or a set of sonic properties; it is something humanly achieved—something crafted, performed, perceived, and interpreted. This sense, however, cannot be carried through in subsequent abbreviated statements such as "MUSIC is inherently multicultural," which tend to reify or thingify; nor can such statements adequately communicate the nonuniversality of "music."

The Embodied Nature of Music Making: Mind and Body

The denotative field we have just traversed opens up an extraordinarily broad set of musical practices. The view that "to dance is to music," as is the case in West Africa, or that dance helps constitute a core musical concept, as in India, has to be reckoned with by music educators. Because this notion is so fundamental in so many societies, and because it implicates the body in so direct a manner, in this section I consider elements of Elliott's praxial philosophy that bring the *body* into play. I expand on some points of distant and more recent Western intellectual history Elliott raises, for the sake of clarifying the theories that underpin his praxial philosophy.

Music Matters does not avoid the thorny epistemological and ontological questions that customarily accompany philosophical treatments of a subject. To justify his position on the centrality of music making in music education, for example, Elliott tackles a number of fundamental questions, including the nature of human consciousness. Profiling a number of traditional and more current theories, Elliott rejects notions of consciousness that posit a clean split between mind and body, between "pure" mental consciousness and physical matter. Since Elliott does not trace the historically deep roots of this divide in Western intellectual history, a thumbnail sketch of the development of mind-body dualism and its effects on Western arts scholarship is in order.

Though mind-body dualism is apparent in classical Greek thinking, the French Enlightenment philosopher René Descartes is most often credited with transforming what was only a conceptual fissure at the beginning of the seventeenth century into a deep chasm. Descartes's famous aphorism *cogito ergo sum* ("I think, therefore I am") located human be-ing in cognition and in thought specifically; and though he recognized the ways in which the mind could affect the body, mind and body were still conceptualized as discrete entities. This view denies any reciprocal influence between mind and body that are put forward, for example, by theories of psychosomatic pathology.

The problem with dualism is not only theoretical or philosophical; its real and practical legacy lies in the kind of attitudes toward the body that it has fostered. Descartes came to doubt the existence of his own body because he was aware of the ways in which human beings could be deceived by their sensory experience of the external world. While suspicion of the senses originating in the body cannot be attributed to Descartes alone, he gave added impetus and theoretical valency to a particular way of thinking about be-ing in the world. As Elliott explains, one of the outcomes of a dualistic approach to consciousness is an unexamined assumption that "action is physical and therefore dumb" (1995, 51). Physical prowess of various kinds has thus often been regarded as admirable and even valuable for the diversion it provides but dismissed as subordinate to mental prowess. Consider expressions such as "dumb jock" or "bonehead musician"—common idioms that recognize sportspersons' and musicians' ability to finely manipulate their physical apparatus but fail to acknowledge what they do as evidence of "intelligence," in either the conventional sense or Gardner's (1983) more recent use of that word.

Elliott calls on more contemporary theories to demonstrate the ways in which mind and body are connected for the purpose of shoring up his position on music performance in education. He cites materialist theory that reunites mind and body, as well as Johnson's (1987) work on English idiomatic expressions. Through a close analysis of metaphor, Johnson shows how "our bodily orientations and interactions in and with our environment" permeate our consciousness and are revealed in our language use. Where physicality was once believed to be exclusive of rationality, Johnson concludes that the "mind is in the body" and the "body is in the mind": "Our embodiment is essential to who we are, to what meaning is, and to our ability to draw rational inferences and to be creative" (xxxviii).

Despite the reunion of mind and body in disciplines such as contemporary philosophy, cognitive science, and medicine, the legacy of dualism is still with us. Most notable for our purposes is the fact that there are still very few departments of dance in universities and colleges throughout North America and Europe and very few schools or departments of music where dance is the subject of sustained scholarly focus. In addition to its historically mistaken separation from human intellection, dance has traditionally been marginalized in academic study not because it is located in the body (all human endeavor is), but because it brings attention to the body in ways that have been slow to find sanction in Western academic culture. But as some dance ethnographers and anthropologists have shown, it yields to the same kinds of analyses as music and other visual and plastic arts. Human movement is not arbitrary; even those from the old school of "aesthetic education" can be satisfied that it has identifiable form and structure that coalesces into particular styles. And dance is something that is humanly achieved—that mediates people's experience of the world, and that people attach meaning to and interpret symbolically.

I raise these points on the heels of an examination of definitions of music because so many definitions implicate dance in some fashion or another. And while Elliott uses theories about the embodied nature of human experience to justify his emphasis on vocal and instrumental performance, as we soon shall see, he does not use them in explicit support of dance instruction. This might seem like an unreasonable expectation, given that Elliott's is a philosophy of music education, but if his call to include all human musical endeavors in education is genuine, then it must also come to terms with dance. The praxial philosophy, which rejects mind-body dualism and which acknowledges the diversity of music*al* practice, certainly paves the way for such an undertaking.

Multicultural Music Education as Performance

To reiterate, Elliott raises the question of consciousness and mind-body dualism to set up his assertion that music be viewed as "something that people do," as something embodied. This provides the philosophical foundation for Elliott's proposal that performance be the baseline for a musical education. While his proposal is heartening, his absolute insistence on it poses some problems.

First, the insistence on performance is based on an assumption of universal musical competence: that all individuals *can* perform musically. This assumption is historically rooted in the work of Blacking (1967, 1971, 1973), an ethnomusicologist whose work among the South African Venda suggested to him that fundamental music skills were distributed equally among the populace. If basic musical competence was not universal among the Venda, then it was very close: "*Most* Venda children are competent musicians: they can sing and dance to traditional melodies, and many can play at least one musical instrument" (Blacking 1967, 29; emphasis added). Though Blacking's qualification remains unexplained, he later adds that "music and dancing permeate every social activity from youth to old age, and no one is excluded from performances" (32), even (and especially) those who are physically challenged. In time, Blacking extended his observations on the musical capabilities of the Venda to the species as a whole, borrowing from linguistic theory to suggest that all human beings are biologically predisposed (or hardwired) for music making. The notion of a universally shared musical competence has, in the decades since Blacking's original formulation, found broad acceptance and has been recast as an "intelligence" in Gardner's (1983) theory of multiple intelligences.

Although using these assumptions about human musical capability as the foundation of a philosophy of music education is a bold and refreshing move, there are some practical difficulties with a praxialist position that puts performance at the unqualified center of multicultural music education. Drawing on personal experience, whenever I read the excerpt from Chernoff's exposition on West African music making that opens this essay, I feel a pang of guilt: guilt that I am not yet to the point where I can provide my students with the rich, socially textured musical transactions that characterize the musicing he talks about. Without a tradition bearer in our midst and with no West African music training of my own, our classroom enactments have been limited and feeble at best. Instead, we opt to read Chernoff and listen to lots of music with the hope that his exegesis will sharpen our aural and conceptual antennae. And, I rationalize, there are other music and dance traditions I am much more familiar with where performance is a realistic possibility. The very issue of teachers not being conversant in the performance tradition to which they would like to expose their students will be the greatest stumbling block for those who pursue a performance-oriented multicultural music education. This is true even within the confines of a relatively narrow cross-cultural social milieu (e.g., Western European classical, and European American jazz, popular, and folk musics).

Though I hesitate to raise more instances where performance may not be realized, for fear that these might be taken as excuses for perpetuating a culture of passive, armchair musicianship, not performing may be justified in particular circumstances, sometimes by virtue of the culturally specific meanings attached to "music" discussed in the first section of this essay. A case in point is Kushner's (1991) work among schoolchildren in Britain. Kushner reveals a situation in which Muslim children have to negotiate conflicting messages from home and school cultures about the merit of making music. At home, students are taught that singing and playing instruments is morally suspect, while their non-Muslim teachers naturally encourage musical participation and creation. Active interpreters and managers of their instructional world, the children act this conflict out among themselves, but are adept at concealing it from their unwitting teachers. Again, this should not be construed as an excuse to eliminate performance whenever Muslim students share the classroom. What Kushner's case does recommend is that music educators know their students well, that cultural sensitivity be recognized as part of their required professional knowledge, and that they be willing to negotiate the conditions of instruction. Although some Muslim students (or their parents) may wish to refrain from performance entirely, more liberal members of that religious group might happily engage a broader range of musical behavior. For example, members of Muslim society have been known, historically, to indulge their fondness for music and have circumvented restrictions placed on music making by treating it as an intellectual exercise (Nettl 2001, 53).[4]

So far, I have presented fairly safe arguments for circumventing performance. There are other arguments for learning music conceptually, and only conceptually, that are also worthy of consideration. Besides a lack of materials or instructor expertise, and barring the ideological conflicts presented by religious affiliation, students' musical performance may also be delimited by the values that particular musical practices represent or by their status as cultural property.

Performance and Representation

All performance involves some element of representation, either of a group's or an individual's music. Representation, however, is rarely benign, especially when it involves public display and, even more, when it involves some other group's or individual's music. By virtue of bringing artistic practice into a public space, performance privileges the sound or image being (re)presented over other potential sounds or images and makes the chosen sounds or images available for consumption and interpretation.

Both the representation and the act of representation are contingent on a number of variables, including the status of the performers and the context in which the performance takes place. These factors can either enable or constrain performance. For example, in both European and North American society, a great deal of repertoire that originated in the context of Christian worship has gradually moved from church to concert stage. As a non-Christian who appreciates the music of Monteverdi, I have been glad for opportunities to learn and perform his *Vespers* in venues outside the church. Naturally, not all changes of context provide the same level of comfort for all people, and current debates in North America surrounding school-sponsored performance of Christian music during seasonal celebrations are testimony to this. But the issues are not always ideologically centered. A Euro-American colleague of mine who was raised in Birmingham, Alabama, in the 1960s and witnessed the brutal treatment of African Americans during the initial stages of school integration still cannot bring himself to use spirituals in the repertoire of the youth choir he conducts, though he is deeply moved by them. While spirituals represent different things to different people, including different African Americans, to him they express a profundity of feeling that he believes he can neither comfortably represent nor his young choristers adequately communicate. One might argue that he has put an unreasonable burden on himself by expecting the group to sing spirituals "authentically" (i.e., with the same conviction and depth of emotion that gave rise to such expressions in the first place). Indeed, most of us do not question the religious convictions of those who might choose to perform Monteverdi's *Vespers*. But when given the choice of representing the music of a (still) persecuted people, he declines. This should not be construed, by any means, as an admonition against performing spirituals. What it should suggest is the capacity of music to represent oneself and others, and the highly personal conditions under which the performance of even so popular a genre might be untenable.

Music educators may also legitimately choose to study but not perform music that promotes unsociability or compromises the dignity of human lives. Of course, they will be unable to obtain universal agreement on matters of such delicacy and will therefore have to think deeply and choose judiciously in order to live by their decisions. To offer a rather superficial example from my own pedagogical experience, I recall assigning a classic essay by Glassie (1970) that documents the construction of a folksong over a three-year period. Words to the song "Take That Night Train to Selma" were composed and performed by Dorrance Weir, a good-humored but politically conservative white laborer from upper New York state. Begun in 1965 as a satiric song to taunt a fellow worker, Weir gradually extended the lyrics, revealing his reaction to events of the civil rights movement and the death of Martin Luther King in 1968. The song's message seems to have been ameliorated by the medium, for despite its racist overtones it gained acceptance even among more progressive and liberal whites within the region. In the university folklore course where Glassie's essay was used, students regularly performed the songs they read about; in fact, performance had a way of bringing us to an altered understanding of the songs we had studied. However, by the time we finished with "Take That Night Train to Selma," none of us had any appetite for singing the song, and very few had even a desire to hear a recorded version of Weir's creative work. Performing the song felt like a legitimization of Weir's racist attitudes; and some, like myself, may have feared the allure of a catchy melody or rhyme and the possibility of betraying our own revulsion.

Cultural Property

The choice to waive performance may be motivated by other, less personal reasons. Optimally, music educators will have the benefit of working with tradition bearers as pedagogical consultants or as in-service providers. Where optimal conditions do not exist, educators are left with the responsibility of finding performance materials to appropriately represent the musical tradition they are working in. Klinger (1996) has shown this to be fraught with hazards. Documenting the constraints on teachers interested in transmitting the music of cultures other than their own, Klinger's case study of an American elementary school music teacher's attempts to teach "authentic" African musical materials to her students highlights the obstacles to that cause: even when notated and recorded materials were available, the teacher had little knowledge of their source or how original materials had been adapted for perceived classroom needs, and explanatory or contextualizing documentation was almost completely lacking.

More fundamental than the notion of authentic reproduction is reproduction itself, which must honor originators' rights, fulfill expected societal and personal obligations, and comply with the laws of the nation(s). These matters have become particularly prominent in the last decade, signaled in part by the 1993 United Nations Draft Declaration on the Rights of Indigenous Peoples. Unfortunately, there is still much uncharted territory in the realm of rights, obligations, and laws, and even many ethnomusicologists are not sufficiently versed in their applications. Seeger (1992) discusses the specific case of the Suyá of Amazonian Brazil, for whom ownership and control of songs are finely articulated but completely incongruent with Western notions of the same or with American copyright law. On seeking permission to record songs, which he successfully received, Seeger later wondered: "Whom should I have asked? The animal who originated the song? The person who transmitted it? The person who was dead who had sung it [and to whom it first belonged]? The person who was singing it [now]?" (Seeger 1992, 350). If this seems remote to the music educator, the next stage, in which Seeger produced a commercial recording for public distribution, should not be. He says: "Tacape Records and I may indicate our control of the use of the master tape on which [a] particular version of 'Big Turtle Song' is recorded, but if someone else wants to use its musical ideas, there isn't much that I, the record company, or the Suyá can do about it" (353).

With good reason, music educators who have read Seeger's exemplary work on the Suyá (Seeger 1987) might well consider moving their students to an understanding of Suyá song genres by having them sing a song. And with good reason, one might choose the "Big Turtle Song" as presented on the Tacape label because it helps fulfill a particular pedagogical need. But music educators would have to resist the temptation to lift recorded sound material which is not in the public domain and for which they have not obtained performance rights. Ethical constraints on performance, personal or otherwise, may not be everyday issues for the average music educator, but they are not so rare either. Despite his insistence on performance, the care that Elliott has taken to include the sociocultural dimension in his view of musical works already suggests a willingness to accommodate the types of scenarios that have been outlined here.

Authenticity

Hovering in the background of the previous discussion was the idea of authenticity, a concept that Elliott invokes but does not elucidate. His use of the qualifier "authentic" is frequent and seems to have a number of denotata. First, authenticity is a call to performance: making music is the most genuine musical endeavor as well as the source of all musical experience. Second, musicianship and listenership are authentic to the extent that they are grounded in authentic performance of styles and genres. Achieving authenticity can therefore necessitate a set of mutually dependent conditions. Third, one can assess the authenticity of a performance on the basis of how true to style the performers sing or play, as well as the context in which the music is sung or played. And finally, there are some styles and genres of music that are inherently authentic, while others, such as school music, which have been contrived for pedagogical or other purposes, are not. Of these four points, issues centering on the accuracy of style and representation have concerned ethnomusicologists most, though all have generated some degree of interest and commentary. The remainder of this essay will serve as a response to some of the positions Elliott has taken with respect to authenticity, as well as a more general discussion of issues underlying the goal of authenticity in a multicultural vision of music education.

In his critique of music programs that deny students a sustained program of performance and banish them to the role of listener, Elliott draws on the writings of the formalist aesthetician Peter Kivy. Putting musical apprehension in a category separate from all other forms of artistic apprehension, Kivy and Elliott contend that "to love, appreciate, and enjoy musical performances, one needs to know MUSIC as performing art" (Elliott 1995, 102). Elliott is only willing to concede that

> perhaps students can learn to experience music in the passive sense of becoming distanced and impersonal consumers without learning how to make music well. But achieving *an* experience of the special kind of event-performance we call a musical work requires an understanding of musical performing; it requires that students learn how to perform and improvise competently themselves, as well as to compose, arrange, and conduct. (102)

It is important at this juncture to once again affirm the general value of performance in music education. Providing students with practica in music allows them to know the challenges, physical and mental, of bringing coherent streams of sound into existence; and producing the patterns they might otherwise only hear gives them another hook to hang their cognitive apparatus on. While there is no doubt that performance can modify understanding of music and that music education should provide the means for exercising that capacity in students, the argument that listening without benefit of performance is something flat and "impersonal" or that nonperforming listeners' perspectives are "moot in the most essential regard" (Elliott 1995, 57) does not hold—either in terms of reported experience or in terms of phenomenological theory, which conceives of human beings as irrepressible meaning makers.[5] It is argument by fiat.

An alternative way of thinking about musical apprehension, founded on principles of phenomenology,[6] is outlined by the ethnomusicologist Steven Feld (1984).[7] In concordance with Elliott, Feld acknowledges that even the most untutored listeners attend to musical structure in a general way; that is, by discerning patterns of repetition, variation, contrast, and development. What is more important from Feld's perspective is that listeners "attend to [musical structure] from a vantage point of familiarity or strangeness, features which are socially constituted through [their] experiences" (7). Indeed, listeners rarely engage a sonic object without performing what Feld calls "interpretive moves." Interpretive moves are "social processing conventions" that link sounds to listeners' prior musical and social experiences,[8] thus generating meaning. They are, furthermore, informed by listeners' preferences and expressive values, their identities, and their ability to perceive coherences—that is, to intuit homologous relationships between sound and the social domain. These "frames," as Feld calls them, help to shape meanings without determining them. The frames that listeners bring to a musical encounter may change with accumulated life experience (including performance) and may even be altered by the listening process itself.

Research on contemporary Native Hawaiians' listening practices (Szego 1999) serves as illustration of interpretive moves and frames. One of the findings of a study that asked Native Hawaiian high school students to listen to music and record their moment-by-moment responses was that many listeners imputed personal attributes to singers on the basis of vocal timbre. This interpretive strategy reveals a cultural sensitivity to vocal nuance and at the same time reflects contemporary Hawaiians' social concerns. Specifically, their social interpretation of vocal timbre seems to reflect the centrality of harmonious and lasting interpersonal relations in Hawaiian culture. Hawaiians' investment in affiliation requires them to develop strategies for determining others' trustworthiness, and they "have discovered that . . . focusing on expressive cues is the surest path to reliable knowledge" (Howard 1974, 31).

Implementing this sensitivity to expressive nuance, Hawaiian listeners often treated the musical performances they listened to as if they were social encounters. They imputed personal attributes and intentions to singers on the basis of their perceived vocal qualities. A voice whose raspiness and creakiness reminded listeners of aging people could inspire profound feelings of trust, evoking the affection they felt for their elders, though the same voice could elicit criticism if it did not blend sufficiently in a choral setting. Because of the Hawaiian emphasis on interpersonal harmoniousness, listeners also interpreted well-blended voices as an indication of cohesive social relationships among singers.

Returning to Feld's theory, none of the richness of meaning constructed by these or any other listeners is predicated on their ability to perform musically, though the kinds of meaning attributed to sounds may certainly be affected by such ability and experience.[9] Nor is there a requirement that listeners employ specific kinds of knowledge in the process of listening. The difficulty with Elliott's prescription for what listeners need to do in order to be considered expert, as opposed to Feld's description of what listeners can do, is that it discredits those kinds of listening that do not fulfill the prescription. Elliott says that "the kinds of musical knowing required to listen competently, proficiently, or expertly for the works of a given musical practice are the same kinds of knowing required to *make* the music of that practice: procedural, formal, informal, impressionistic, and supervisory musical knowledge" (1995, 96). If this is true, then there is little likelihood that even the West African listeners described by Chernoff—those who "supply the beat"—fit Elliott's profile of proficient and expert listeners. If they lack formal knowledge (as I suspect many of them do), or if Native Hawaiian youth lack procedural knowledge (as many of them do), they cannot live up to his model of expert listenership.[10] Furthermore, by virtue of its emphasis on "listening *for*," Elliott's model does not validate listeners as perceptual agents. I am thinking here of their ability to achieve or generate aural and even visual perceptions as they listen—perceptions that cannot easily be reduced to or accounted for by reference to the standards and traditions of a musical practice they have acquired. Examples abound: moving to a melody in imagined space, or catching a lyric and replaying it in the foreground of their consciousness as words to the song move on, creating a virtual polytextual motet (see Szego 1999).

Although Elliott has been rightly critical of the Western elitist position that restricts musical participation to a select few, there is a danger of creating a reverse inequity by imposing a standard model that diminishes the listenership of those who do not possess or make use of formal, declarative knowledge, or who have not pressed fingers or lips to a musical instrument, either by choice or by circumstance. And, as we have already seen, matters of choice and circumstance are particularly salient when viewed in global perspective. In many societies there is a clear division of musical labor between performers and listeners.[11] Elliott admirably attempts to tear down performer-listener boundaries as they exist in Western music culture, but it would be inadvisable to impose that ethic upon other performing and listening traditions.

Uncomfortable as I am with a position that fails to fully value (nonperforming) listeners' meaning-making propensities and capabilities, one of the most important and defensible claims of Elliott's philosophy is that "there is no one way to listen for all musical works everywhere" (1995, 155). In the same way that human beings cultivate different styles of music, so do they cultivate different ways of perceiving and interpreting sonic events. Apprehending West African polyrhythms may require listeners to "supply the beat," but this is not necessary for apprehending Mozart symphonies or disco.[12] Elliott's recognition of the ways that cultures structure sound and provide pathways for the apprehension of it is a necessary move for anyone advocating the study and performance of any of the world's musics. In this sense, his approach to music listenership represents a significant advancement on the aesthetic position in that it acknowledges the socially variable nature of musical interpretation. Proponents of the aesthetic education position act as though by accounting for the formal structure of music they have accounted for how people apprehend it as well—as though there were an isomorphic relationship between a sonic event and the perception of it.

Finally, in presenting his case for the role of performance in producing competent, proficient, and expert listeners, Elliott recalls Johnson's phrase that the "body is in the mind." His reading and application of the literature on mind-body relationships, especially Johnson, is a matter for further comment. To be clear, the issue for Elliott is not the sonic object toward which listening is intended. It is that listening is never enough; human beings must also engage the body, in the most literal sense, by making music. Statements like Johnson's assert and recognize, however, that all forms of cognition—thinking metaphorically, reasoning, and imagining, as well as listening—are just as much bodily acts as kicking a ball or playing an instrument. This is because our physical orientation to the world leaks into everything we do, even at the most abstract and metaphysical level. Indeed, the point of most contemporary "body philosophy" is that all human practices are embodied; by extension, whether one makes music or not, bodily practice will inform musical perception or listening. However, because the relationship between body and mind is not linear, a specific bodily "input" such as making music does not guarantee the nature of a mental outcome such as musical perception. Thinking in linear, behavioral terms reduces mind to body, eliding the dialectics between the two. Again, this is not to deny the value of performance in music education. This discussion only serves the point that principles like "the body is in the mind" cannot be used to support a specific mandate for performance;

nor can they be used to support judgments that value performers' apprehension of music over that of nonperformers, or that define them as expert.[13]

Authenticity and Context

Chernoff's recommendation quoted at the beginning of this essay—that "music . . . not be studied out of its context"—is echoed throughout *Music Matters* and is an implicit call for authenticity. Among ethnomusicologists who have weighed in on the issue of context and authenticity, Blacking represents the most hard-line view. Speaking of the South African Venda, he freely admits that "the surface of sounds in Venda polyrhythms can also be produced in a 'non-African' way." "But," he says, "in an alien environment, and without the tension of the original performance context, they cannot have the same significance for performers and audience. They lose their artistic force, in much the same way as a string quartet performed on a piano" (Blacking 1985, 5). Lest music educators be too discouraged by Blacking's statement, it is helpful to remember that a great deal if not most performances in the modern age separate sound from their original context—think of Monteverdi's *Vespers* sung at Carnegie Hall. Even in the best of all possible worlds, it is unlikely that music educators will be able to live up to the most stringent demands for recreating performance context. This observation has been made by Palmer (1992), who perhaps understates the situation when he says that "transferring music from its original cultural context to the classroom increases the chances that authenticity will be in jeopardy" (33).

In addition to its meaning as performance, space, occasion, and/or function, "context" is commonly used as a catchall referring to "any and all factors that may be shown to impinge directly upon the production of musical sound" (Waterman 1990, 214) or its meanings. Elliott's opposition to and critique of aesthetic education is that it does not pay sufficient attention to what is human about music making. He argues that except for biographical details about "great" composers and references to the zeitgeist in which particular works of art were produced, "understanding music" (in the view of aesthetic educators) has largely been a matter of discovering through "objective," analytic methods the principles that account for the internal logic of a piece of music or work; thus, it says too little about the ways that "music means" to people.

The purpose of an anthropologically grounded ethnomusicology, on the other hand, has been to get at participants' understandings of their own musical practices. Sounds taken by themselves, and especially those representing cultures other than one's own, do not simply speak for themselves. To make any sense of them requires a commitment to teasing out the principles that guide social life (economics, politics, kinship, and religion) and their behavioral manifestations (modes of interaction, forms of expressive culture, and so on). In the type of holism that characterizes anthropology, every cultural phenomenon serves as context for every other cultural phenomenon.

Given Elliott's obvious attachment to anthropological perspectives and his rejection of mind-body dualism, his repudiation of integrated arts education is most surprising. His rationale for segregating the arts, except in the case of non-Western musics, seems to stem from a particular set of sociopolitical and institutional realities. Elliott argues that multi-arts education in schools has weakened the position of music because it has been treated as just another piece of the artistic pie. His abdication of integrated arts education is curious because stubborn social realities have not stopped Elliott's advocacy in other areas. For example, most people in North American society still believe that musicality is a special quality, often genetically determined, that few individuals possess in any large degree. Yet Elliott is willing to stand up to this belief and the ways it has been institutionalized.

Because Chernoff and other ethnomusicologists quoted in *Music Matters* link music to other arts so unequivocally, Elliott is willing to make an exception to his position on artistic segregation for non-Western musical practices. But within the Western world, the division between music and dance remains clear: "the development of musicianship depends on inducting children into musical practices and on targeting their conscious powers on progressively more subtle aspects and dimensions of musical works. Neither condition is present when the attention of learners is being directed to nonmusical matters such as balance and focus in painting or gesture in dance" (Elliott 1995, 249). It is true that the Western classical concert experience has attempted in the last century to stifle the bodily participation of its audience members. However, if one looks closely, it is difficult to draw a line between movement and musicality at any point in the history of Western culture, whether we consider the works of Rameau at the court of Fontainebleau (see Isherwood 1973; Rice 1989), Stravinsky's compositions for the Ballets Russes, or twentieth-century musicals.[14] Instead, the separation of music from other arts and dance in particular only entrenches historical attempts to decouple mind and body.

To quote Elliott further,

> each performing and nonperforming art is a specific kind of human practice that rests upon an independent form of situated thinking and knowing. Hence, each kind of artistic knowing needs to be taught and learned in its own context through active involvement in artistic making. Musicianship, for example, involves an entirely different kind of cognition than the knowing required to understand visual art, dance, or poetry. (Elliott 1995, 249)

While the last claim about human psychology may be true, it is not definitively so. Furthermore, and more important, it is very much at odds with actual human musical practice, except, perhaps, as it occurs in North American classrooms. Consider this description of singing among the Kalapalo in the Upper Xingu region of the Amazon:

> A tune cannot be easily sung without the movement of the body, especially the legs (in nonperformative contexts, a person might swing in his or her hammock or merely tap a hand on a nearby house post to represent this bodily motion), nor is the song complete without the rhythmic accompaniment of the dancers' feet. The movements of Kalapalo dance also help to mark changes in the direction of the melody. . . . Kalapalo musical pieces typically consist of a pair of melodic lines of complex rhythm that are repeatedly exchanged, and with each change the dancers reverse their movements; sometimes this exchange is between a pair of singers. Dance motions also emphasize changes from one of these repeated pairs to the start of a new melody and set of rhythms. Finally, Kalapalo dance brings out the spatial side of the musical symbol by uniting discrete places, dissolving the differences between autonomous houses, and uniting the residents into an undifferentiated whole. From a musical point of

view, space is used as an important compositional resource, as important as are
the tones themselves. . . . Hence the salience of rhythm and space as devices for
structuring a ritual event would seem especially important for developing the
aesthetic of patterned repetition. (Basso 1985, 250)

Here, movement, both stylized and unstylized, is matched to sonic design and to
the act of singing. In practice they cannot be pulled apart; the evidence suggests that
as cognitive operations they are highly integrated.

Not only do the other arts serve as "context" for music, but also intimacy with
dance and poetry are often integral to its sympathetic appreciation and understanding. This principle becomes more cogent when we recognize how musicians manipulate sound, movement, and poetry to sometimes reflect, sometimes model, and sometimes symbolically invert the stuff of their sociocultural existence.

There are a number of examples from the ethnomusicological and anthropological
literature one could further cite, but I shall limit myself to only one. Kaeppler (1978)
hypothesizes that there is a three-part structure underlying Tongan sociopolitical organization that gives rise to the tripartite structure—leading part, drone, and decoration—found in music, dance, and even bark-cloth design. One can surmise from her
arguments that while Tongans have much (and probably the most) to learn about
music by performing it, musicianship and kinesthetic intelligence are not easily dis-
entangled, and profound understanding can only be achieved through engagement
with the full panorama of Tongan cultural life. Singing, dancing, and painting bark
cloth may or may not require independent, discrete cognitive operations, but understanding is surely more than the firing of synapses in any one of these cognitive domains. In summary, one cannot argue for multicultural music education—using "musical practice" as a baseline definition of music—*and* segregated arts too. The two
concepts are simply anathema to each another.

Authenticity and Representation

Elliott's consistent appeals for authentic performance seem to be motivated by a genuine respect for diverse musical practices and the people who generate them. The desire for authenticity is also a needed corrective to colonial and postcolonial modes of
education that disregarded and even denigrated ways of music making by cultural
others.

Recalling my earlier discussion of representation, performance invokes power
relations as a matter of course, especially when it takes place in a public forum. Again,
the word "power" is used here not in the sense of one person or group coercing
another to do something, but in the sense of individuals' and groups' access to and
control over cultural objects and images. Masterful or compelling performances also
bestow an element of social power or authority upon its producers. Speaking of verbal performance, Bauman (1977) maintains that

through his performance, the performer elicits the participative attention and
energy of his audience, and to the extent that they value his performance, they
will allow themselves to be caught up in it. When this happens, the performer
gains a measure of prestige and control over the audience—prestige because

of the demonstrated competence he has displayed, control because the determination of the flow of the interaction is in his hands. (43–44)

The same principles are at work in musical performance: the ability to manipulate and control a sense of what is valuable to an audience empowers performers and creates an asymmetrical relationship between representer and represented. Being able to "determine the flow of . . . interaction" also gives performers a kind of social authority that one can only hope is warranted. Elliott's petition for authenticity, for fidelity to some authoritative source (slippery though that concept may be), recognizes the delicacy of this position and the responsibilities incumbent upon performers.

Fidelity to Style

The most salient meaning of authenticity in reference to musical practice is fidelity to style. Palmer (1992) lists the many possible violations to absolute authenticity that can be committed through school-based performance. Most notable are the use of inadequate translations; "new and inappropriate textual underlays"; "simplified versions and other didactic adjustments" of original material, such as the removal of ornaments from highly embellished melodic lines; modifications to tuning systems; added harmonizations; and general "arrangement." It is difficult to say, however, how any or all of these modifications would be regarded by tradition bearers themselves. Some might disapprove and others approve.

While the objective of absolute authenticity will necessarily be compromised in some fashion, steps that music educators can take in the pursuit of the more attainable goal of respectful representation are to consult with tradition bearers and experts; to read widely in the scholarly literature; and to inform students and audiences of what is happening. To illustrate, one of the most common kinds of material that music educators have at their disposal are arrangements of folksongs, some recent and some dating back over more than a century. In folk-music scholarship, early publications of songs often misrepresented the musical and acoustic data that had been collected.

> Because notation was undertaken by those who had been trained in the conventions and values of Western European classical music, the melodies were frequently altered to make them more congruent with the aesthetics of that tradition. [Subsequent] settings of songs for piano and voice . . . allowed them to be performed more widely, but did not necessarily lead to a high valuation of traditional performance practices or of the tradition-bearers. (Lundquist et al. 1998, 113)

Though I would be careful not to encourage overuse of the practice, it is entirely possible that circumstances might move a teacher to use a highly Westernized arrangement of a non-Western song. If that is all the teacher does (i.e., use the arrangement and let the performance stand for itself), then he or she runs a very high risk of misrepresentation and thus of reinforcing a power differential. But if the teacher chooses to use the arrangement with a critical pedagogy—asking students to identify what has changed in the process of transformation and how meaning may have been altered—and convey that to audiences too, then an ostensibly inauthentic perform- ance will have some compelling and value-creating force behind it. The harm lies not in performances that only approximate "the real thing," but in the conviction that we are somehow doing "the real thing."

Again, because performances have rhetorical power, it is easy to give a false, shal- low, or uninformed representation of unwarranted authority, especially in the case of performances that are appealing or demonstrate a high level of skill or mastery. Sometimes only a small gesture given in the absence of substance—like putting a sombrero on the recorder player who toots "Guantanamera"—has the capacity to fix a stereotypical image in students' or audience members' consciousness.

Recognizing the Variability of Human Practice

When talking about authenticity, it is also important to recognize that within any given culture there are probably no single authoritative musical representations of the group. Even in the most homogeneous societies or music cultures, one is likely to en- counter many different genres and multiple stylistic approaches to each genre (e.g., Glenn Gould's vs. Wanda Landowska's approach to baroque keyboard music). Some stylistic approaches or genres might be characterized by influence from another cul- ture and will thus be eschewed by cultural purists while embraced by others. Even performances that demonstrate a reasonable degree of fidelity to musical style can- not, therefore, be said to represent the musical values or preferences of an entire cul- tural collectivity. Music educators must be prepared to negotiate these heterogenei- ties and to communicate them effectively to students and their audiences. Failing to do so again runs the risk of misrepresentation and glosses over the complexity and multidimensionality of music making as a human and social endeavor.

As the presumption of homogeneity within cultural groups or subgroups becomes less and less secure, so do definitions and models of multiculturalism that treat each group as a discrete entity.

> As we move into an age in which cultural space becomes unfixed, unsettled, porous, and hybrid, it becomes increasingly difficult either to defend notions of singular identity or to deny that different groups, communities, and people are increasingly bound to each other in a myriad of complex relationships. Modes of representation that legitimated a world of strict cultural separation, collec- tive identities, and rigid boundaries seem hopelessly outdated as the urban land- scape is being rewritten within new and shifting borders of identity, race, and ethnicity. (Giroux 1994, 40)

The sociocultural scenario Giroux describes is not unique to the contemporary urban landscape. It is impossible, for example, to discuss the music of First Nations in Canada without acknowledging centuries of cultural commerce between indige- nous and foreign peoples:

> Interaction between Native and European music in [Labrador and Quebec] has a long history. Fiddle music and Christian hymns, for example, have been ac- tively adapted to create syncretic styles, and newly created pieces have been

composed within the Native communities since the late 16th and early 17th
centuries; hence, these repertoires are regarded as "traditional" music in many
communities. Among the earliest Christian converts, many Naskapi and Mon-
tagnais people have large repertoires of hymns and cantiques in their own languages. (Diamond, Cronk, and von Rosen 1994, 191)

Hybrid and syncretic genres that mix the music of one culture with another are no
less authentic than those that have ostensibly been fixed through time. Our pedagogy,
if it is to move students to the self-growth that Elliott advocates, needs to recognize
the realities of multiculturalism—that is, both the fluidity and impermeability of cultural borders, as well as the tensions that may be inherent in that social model.

Thus, while "authenticity" is a very valuable guiding principle, it is a rather elusive objective, complicated by the crossing of historical, cultural, and even genera-
tional boundaries. The essential point to be drawn from recognizing the variability of
cultural practice and the hybridization of cultures is not that anything goes—it is still
possible to misrepresent others. The responsibilities of cultural representation require
near-constant vigilance to look beyond surface appearances and to avoid catego-
rizing people and their music too neatly. Our goal as music educators with a multicultural mandate is to be cognizant of what we are doing by teaching the music of
cultures other than our own, of who and what is being represented, and how these representations might be interpreted.

Conclusions

Music Matters is a watershed in the history of philosophizing about music education
for two reasons: it approaches music not just as sound but as practice—something
that people actively achieve—and it holds the musical practices of all cultures in
equal regard. Treating music as something actively achieved is important because it
moves the focus from sonic objects to living beings. Elliott considers not only the
cognitive operations of musical agents, but also the ways that their musicing is informed by specific social and cultural conditions.

At the core of the praxial philosophy are a number of theories. One of the most
important addresses human consciousness and the relationship between body and
mind. Elliott contends that because body and mind have historically been treated as
discrete entities and mental function as more essential and valuable than physical action, performance has been grossly misunderstood and oversimplified (as "physical
dexterity" or "skills" alone) in music education. My argument has been that dance has
been treated in much the same fashion, for many of the same reasons, and that it deserves inclusion in music curricula because so many non-Western definitions of musical practice include stylized movement.

Elliott's enthusiasm for putting performance in the foreground of the educational
experience is almost completely supportable. Assuming that all human beings possess the capability to make music, it is hard not to advocate a performance-rich curriculum, especially for general music students who have traditionally been denied the
experience. Although keeping performance at the center of music education is a valu-

able objective, I maintain that effective and meaningful listenership is not dependent on it. While music listening can be deeply informed by the act of music making, privileging of some kinds of listenership over others cannot be sustained by certain mind-body arguments.

Performance is as important to the project of multicultural music education as it is to music education generally. However, since performance involves some element of representation, it is never innocent, and there are a number of special considerations that attend the learning of music of cultures other than one's own. Ethical and ideological convictions can justify nonperformance in particular instances, but when performance is carried out, especially in the public domain, representation should be thoughtful and respectful. Pursuing "authentic" representation often reveals a number of cultural tensions. In some cases it is a tension between tradition and modernity; in others, between romantic idealizations of cultural purity and hybrid musical realities created by cultures that have bumped up against each other. But multicultural music educators, if they are to be true to their mandate, cannot back off from an engagement with the compelling and sometimes sensitive questions surrounding musics of the world's cultures and their performance. Full intellectual engagement with issues of representation and cultural variability, as well as full engagement with the array of arts that constitute musical practice, will enrich and animate their own students' musical practices.

Notes

1. I use the expression "metrically organized" in the strictest sense. Metric refers to the organization of beats or pulses into regular groups with assigned patterns of accent.

2. The book seems to be implicitly directed toward readers in Canada and the United States, though its principles probably have much broader applicability.

3. Some of the most important expressions used by Kaluli vis-à-vis "music" are used to describe style. "Lift-up-over-sounding," for example, is a spatioacoustic metaphor that describes for the Kaluli, who think of themselves as "voices in the forest," an aesthetic ideal (Feld 1988). Like tumbling waterfalls, the sounds of drums or axes arch up and out over the dense acoustical strata of their rain forest environment. Kaluli sing with birds and cicadas, lift-up-over-sounding against the overlapping sounds that their rain forest environment provides to them. And when they sing, they emulate, both texturally and melodically, their sonic environment.

4. Naturally, the issue of class participation would arise if students were asked to dance. If multicultural music education is to include dance, as I am about to suggest, music educators should be aware of the kinds of tensions that might ensue. I have found that even at the university level it is advisable to let students know that they have choices, especially where religious doctrine or health prevents students from participating.

5. The phrase "moot in the most essential regard" is actually a reference to nonplaying sports enthusiasts, who are offered as an analogy to nonperforming listeners.

6. The fundamental goal of phenomenology, as elucidated by the philosopher Edmund Husserl, is description—not of things, but of the human experience of things or phenomena (Hammond, Howarth, and Keat 1991, 1). Musical phenomenology concerns itself, therefore, with how music is present to human subjects. Experience is regarded as intentional, which is to say that it is intended or directed toward some object. As such, experience "always refers to

something beyond itself and therefore cannot be characterized independently of this" (2–3). In its attempt to describe experiences of things, phenomenology stands in opposition to the logical-positivist position: it shifts emphasis from questions about the reality of the world to questions about the contents of consciousness, i.e., that which appears to consciousness.

7. With apologies to Feld, the ensuing summary greatly simplifies his model of listening.

8. Acknowledging that there may well be others, Feld identifies five interpretive moves or social processing conventions: locational, categorical, associational, reflective, and evaluative. As examples, a locational move is one in which a listener relates the sonic event to a range of like and unlike items or events. A reflective move consists of relating the sonic event to personal and social conditions, experiences, or attitudes. An associative move relates sound to particular visual, musical, or verbal images held by the listener.

9. Since the author uses several sports analogies, I will offer one too, drawing on my experience of football. I love football; I appreciate and enjoy it. There's a social dimension of watching the game that I no longer participate in: I haven't been to a Grey Cup party in years, and it's been even longer since I sat on a hard bleacher on an autumn afternoon, the smell of leaves, greasy French fries, and musty leather wine flasks commingling in the brittle air. Time and private television viewing have displaced my loose community of high school game boosters. Still, I marvel at many things: the strategic planning and execution of plays, the elegance of a ball thrown (at the last possible moment by an embattled quarterback) with a high arching trajectory into the stratospheric void and then caught in a twisting, gravity-defying arabesque. My appreciation of the game is certainly touched by a remembrance of things past and is also informed by a vague cognizance of the structure and rules of the game: second down, third quarter, last time-out, offside, one-point conversion. But my love, appreciation, and enjoyment are not dependent on an ability to play. They are dependent on my experience of being embodied; I can imagine, and often do, physically reaching for that ball in midair. There's no doubt that my understanding of football would be greatly revised by my donning a helmet and shoulder pads, that I could become a more expert watcher, but expert in what way, to what degree, and to what end?

10. On the subject of listening, Blacking says: "'My' society claims that only a limited number of people are musical, and yet it behaves as if all people possess the basic capacity without which no musical tradition can exist—the capacity to listen to and distinguish patterns of sound. The makers of most films and television serials hope to appeal to large and varied audiences; and so, when they add incidental music to the dialogue and action, they implicitly assume that audiences can discern its patterns and respond to its emotional appeal, and that they will hear and understand it in the ways that its composer intended. They assume that music is a form of communication. . . . The film makers may not be aware of the grounds for their assumptions; but we can be sure that, if experience had proved them wrong, they would have rejected all incidental and mood music as unnecessary. Instead, they seem to have shown increasing confidence in their audiences' musicality by abandoning continual background music in favor of more selective heightening of the drama. This may be only a response to the pressures of musicians' unions; but, even if this were so, film makers continue to commission composers of music, at considerable extra expense" (Blacking 1973, 8). Elliott recognizes this kind of listening but regards it as facile.

11. The social roles of performer and listener are sometimes assigned on the basis of gender. In other instances, they are drawn along ideological lines. Speaking of Islamic societies, Nettl (2001) notes that in an attempt to reconcile ambivalence toward music with a desire to

hear it, "a great deal of musical activity has been turned over to members of non-Muslim minorities, particularly Jews and to a smaller extent Christians. While there have certainly been many Muslim musicians [including members of the Sufi sect, which embraces music], there has always been a disproportionate number of Jewish musicians" (53).

12. To be expert listeners, however, they would still require the five kinds of knowledge, as specified by Elliott.

13. I am grateful to Harris M. Berger for helping me think through these issues and for suggesting some language in which to couch these ideas.

14. Indeed, silencing the bodies of the audience is very likely a project of the early twentieth century, when patrons and leaders of the arts attempted, with great success, to turn the concert into highbrow entertainment (see Levine 1988).

References

Basso, E. B. 1985. *A musical view of the universe: Kalapalo myth and ritual performances.* Philadelphia: University of Pennsylvania Press.

Bauman, R. 1977. *Verbal art as performance.* Rowley, MA: Newbury House.

Blacking, J. 1967. *Venda children's songs: A study in ethnomusicological analysis.* Johannesburg: Witwatersrand University Press.

———. 1971. Towards a theory of musical competence. In E. J. de Jager, ed., *Man: Anthropological essays presented to O. F. Raum,* 19–34. Cape Town, South Africa: C. Struik.

———. 1973. *How musical is man?* Seattle: University of Washington Press.

———. 1985. A false trail for the arts? "Multicultural" music education and the denial of individual creativity. In M. Ross, ed., *The Aesthetic in Education,* 1–27. Oxford: Pergamon Press.

Boilés, C. 1984. Universals of musical behaviour: A taxonomic approach. *World of Music* 26 (2):50–64.

Chernoff, J. 1979. *African rhythm and African sensibility: Aesthetics and social action in African musical idioms.*

Diamond, B., M. S. Cronk, and F. von Rosen. 1994. *Visions of sound: Musical instruments of First Nations communities in Northeastern America.* Waterloo, Ontario: Wilfrid Laurier University Press.

Elliott, D. J. 1995. *Music matters; A new philosophy of music education.* New York: Oxford.

Feld, S. 1980. *Sound and sentiment: Birds, weeping, poetics, and song in Kaluli expression.* Philadelphia: University of Pennsylvania Press.

———. 1984. Communication, music, and speech about music. *Yearbook for Traditional Music* 16:1–18.

———. 1988. Aesthetics as iconicity of style, or "lift-up-over-sounding": Getting into the Kaluli groove. *Yearbook for Traditional Music* 20:74–113.

Gardner, H. S. 1983. *Frames of mind: The theory of multiple intelligences.* New York: Basic Books.

Giroux, H. A. 1994. Living dangerously: Identity politics and the new cultural racism. In H. A. Giroux and P. McLaren, eds., *Between borders: Pedagogy and the politics of cultural studies,* 29–55. London: Routledge.

Glassie, H. 1970. "Take that night train to Selma." In *Folksongs and their makers,* 3–68. Bowling Green, OH: Bowling Green University Popular Press.

Gourlay, K. 1984. The non-universality of music and the universality of non-music. *World of Music* 26 (2):25–36.

Hammond, M., J. Howarth, and R. Keat. 1991. *Understanding phenomenology*. Cambridge, MA: Basil Blackwell.

Howard, A. 1974. *Ain't no big thing: Coping strategies in a Hawaiian-American community*. Honolulu: University of Hawai'i Press.

Ibsen al Faruqi, L. 1985. Music, musicians and Muslim law. *Asian Music* 17 (1):3–36.

———. 1987. Qur'an reciters in competition in Kuala Lumpur. *Ethnomusicology* 31 (2): 221–228.

Isherwood, R. 1973. *Music in the service of the king: France in the seventeenth century*. Ithaca: Cornell University Press.

Johnson, M. 1987. *The body in the mind: The bodily basis of meaning, imagination, and reason*. Chicago: University of Chicago Press.

Kaeppler, A. 1978. Melody, drone and decoration: Underlying structures and surface manifestations in Tongan art and society. In M. Greenhalgh and V. Megaw, eds., *Art in society*, 261–274. London: Duckworth.

Klinger, R. 1996. From glockenspiel to mbira: An ethnography of multicultural practice in music education. *Bulletin of the Council for Research in Music Education* 129:29–36.

Kushner, S. 1991. Musicians go to school: A case of knowledge, control, and cross-professional action. *American Educational Research Journal* 28 (2):275–296.

Levine, L. W. 1988. *Highbrow, lowbrow: The emergence of cultural hierarchy in America*. Cambridge: Harvard University Press.

Lundquist, B. R. 1991. Doctoral education of multiethnic-multicultural music teacher educators. *Design for Arts in Education* 92 (5):21–38.

Lundquist, B. R., B. Nettl, R. Santos, E. Solbin, and C. K. Szego. 1998. *Musics of the World's Cultures: A Source Book for Music Educators*. Perth: ISME/CIRCME.

Nettl, B. 1977. On the question of universals. *World of Music* 17 (1–2):2–7.

———. 2001. Music of the Middle East. In *Excursions in world music*, 46–73. Upper Saddle River, NJ: Prentice-Hall.

Palmer, A. J. 1992. World musics in music education: The matter of authenticity. *International Journal of Music Education* 19:32–40.

Rice, P. F. 1989. *The performing arts at Fontainebleau from Louis XIV to Louis XVI*. Ann Arbor: UMI Research Press.

Seeger, A. 1987. *Why Suyá sing: A musical anthropology of an Amazonian people*. Cambridge: Cambridge University Press.

———. 1992. Ethnomusicology and music law. *Ethnomusicology* 36 (3):345–359.

———. 1991. Singing other peoples' songs. *Cultural Survival Quarterly* 15 (3):36–39.

Szego, C. 1999. *Musical meaning-making in an intercultural environment: The case of Kamehameha Schools*. Ph.D. diss., University of Washington.

Wachsmann, K. P. 1971. Universal perspectives in music. *Ethnomusicology* 15:381–384.

Waterman, C. A. 1990. *Jùjú: A social history and ethnography of an African popular music*. Chicago: University of Chicago Press.

12

Curriculum

Implications of Aesthetic versus Praxial Philosophies

THOMAS A. REGELSKI

"Critical" consideration of curriculum theory is missing from the preparation of most music teachers today.[1] Instead, "methods and materials" courses typically stress the "how-to" delivery of prepackaged, teacher-proof teaching materials such as basal song series and instrumental methods books; or, under the auspices of what I have called "methodolatry" (Regelski 2002), the assumption reigns that a systematic teaching method itself is the curriculum,[2] or that a history of concerts—the so-called ensemble program—amounts to effective curriculum for ensemble students. Furthermore, the teaching of the national standards has recently become a panacea in music education, and the standards are rapidly becoming the de facto curriculum of content and skills to which teachers are widely expected to devote their efforts.[3]

Such curriculum traditions and practices and their underlying assumptions are the rule, not the exception, in music education. Among the first analyses of the moribund status of traditional curricular thinking in music education is David Elliott's innovative *Music Matters* (1995). Elliott offers a comprehensive challenge to traditional aesthetic philosophies of music education and an in-depth analysis of curriculum theory. His critique of the abstract, atomistic content and isolated skills of the conventional objectives-oriented and structure-of-the discipline approaches to music curriculum drew upon and thus reflected the most recent trends in curriculum theory in the early 1990s. He also advanced a provocative and incisive theory of curriculum-as-practicum, designed and organized "to engage learners in musical actions, transactions, and interactions that closely parallel real music cultures" and making, in consequence, "the music classroom . . . a reflective musical practicum, a close representation of viable music-practice situations, or music cultures" (206).

However, Elliott did not undertake to analyze the overall philosophical assumptions and postures at stake in conventional approaches to music curriculum. The present essay surveys and critiques the three dominant philosophical traditions that have had direct consequences for both general education and music education—and, in particular, for the current obsession of both with standards and for what in North America, at least, has been dubbed "music education as aesthetic education" (or MEAE). Following my summary and analysis of these traditions and passing mention of certain aspects of them that may have subtle echoes in Elliott's praxial theory, alternative philosophies of more recent vintage are considered that collectively contribute to my own approach to music curriculum and teaching as and for praxis in which certain differences, or divergence of understanding, of focus arise in comparison to Elliott's praxial theory.

Curriculum and Philosophy

At its heart, curriculum is a matter of values. The most basic curricular thinking involves the question: Of all that can be taught, what is most worth learning? There is always more to teach than time and resources permit, and decisions concerning what to teach and for what ends involve important questions about the value of music and, hence, of music education. The clarification of value has always been a major undertaking of philosophy.[4]

Most teachers may not think of themselves as involved in daily matters of philosophizing and are typically unaware of the practical implications of the philosophical choices they do make.[5] Therefore most teachers entirely fail to appreciate that the question "What is music?" (e.g., Alperson 1994; Erskine 1944) is inescapably philosophical to begin with. Consequently, music teachers who are philosophically uninformed about what music is leave themselves open to creating and suffering all sorts of problems.

One of the most consequential problems facing music teachers, then, involves the question of whether music's meaning and value is cerebral, abstract, autonomous, intrinsic, universal, timeless, and immanent to the sounds of musical works; or whether musical meaning is personally, socially, and culturally constituted to the degree that individual works are not the autonomous sources of but, rather, particular instances of broader, situated processes and varied meanings that are not entirely "in" the score or sounds of the moment. Philosophies of music advancing the former, modernist premise see music as aesthetic, while the latter premises result in newer postmodern and critical philosophies that understand music as praxis.

As Elliott (1995) and this writer (Regelski 1997, 1998a, 1998b, 1999) have shown, the practical consequences of this philosophical distinction for curriculum are decisive. Different philosophical schools of thought have produced somewhat different aesthetic premises and conclusions. Music education has traditionally been justified in schools as making a contribution to being generally well educated. However, because of the scholastic or academic environment of schools, curriculum for music education has been influenced by philosophical and curricular ideas that are simply unsuited to its nature and to its important role in human life. This influence deserves to be interrogated in light of the perpetual challenges to the relevance of music education in schools.

Traditional Philosophy, Curriculum Theory, and Music Education as Aesthetic Education

Traditional philosophies fall into three broad schools: idealism, realism, and neo-scholasticism.[6] For idealism, as originally modeled by Plato, reality and truth take the form of a priori and thus disembodied or "pure" ideas that have logical and internal consistency. Knowledge, then, is not gained through experience, and therefore knowledge of values involves ideas of goodness and beauty that are absolute and eternal. Art and music, then, objectify various ideas that transcend mere sensory perception and the human body in favor of reflecting ideal or universal ideas, essences, or forms that are contemplated intellectually.

Not surprisingly, intellectual learning is most important to idealist conceptions of schooling, since idealists see knowledge as governed by the mind. Teachers' minds, then, are more highly informed, and they thus pass on knowledge of reality, truth, and beauty to students. The curriculum is predicated largely on abstract ideas—mainly verbal concepts, propositional knowledge, and symbolic thinking; instruction, in turn, is dominated by techniques for transferring information from the teacher to students. For idealists, it is not necessary that knowledge be useful to be valuable. Thus, schooling typically remains "merely academic." Such knowledge and ideas—as defined by experts, authorities, and inherited "wisdom" from the past—are therefore "good for their own sake"; schools protect and pass on such knowledge rather than effect change.

Idealism has been the predominant aesthetic philosophy of music (Bowman 1998). It has resulted in a bewildering and often conflicting variety of aesthetic theories that stress the intellectual, cerebral, cognitive, and symbolic values of music—values that, despite certain key distinctions, overlap realist and neoscholastic aesthetic theories at superficial levels of comparison. An aesthetic ideology or orthodoxy dominated by idealist strains has thereby arisen and dominated music education at all levels. According to this orthodoxy, "good music" is the art music of High Culture, and aesthetic meaning and value are contained within music's sounds (alone) as governed by the scores of particular works. Such music exists for its own sake, and thus an aesthetic distance is maintained that separates musical contemplation from any social functions (such as worship or celebration) or personal uses (such as recreation and entertainment). Instead, aesthetic meaning is said to transcend any particular time, place, or person in favor of universal meanings of a metaphysical and cognitive kind.

While the aesthetic orthodoxy allows popular, folk, improvisatory, and similar kinds of lay, indigenous, and functional musics to be called "music," a strict hierarchy is maintained, with the Eurocentric art music canon at the very top and other musics variously arrayed on a descending continuum beneath. In the idealist view, all music has a single essence or fundamental nature; the very idea of a pluralism of musics, each unique on its own terms, violates the idealist aesthetic assumption of rational universality. Aesthetic experience is held to be cerebral, intellectual, and abstract and takes the form of disembodied ideas of various kinds. Powerful bodily based feelings, somatic residuals, and other embodied experiences are, as a result, treated by idealist traditions with deep suspicion, or their value and role is actively denied as merely satisfying base, bodily appetites or as providing only superficial entertainment (i.e., as "ear candy"). Real and thus embodied feelings (as opposed to cerebralized and abstracted ideas or symbols of feelings) are ultimately seen as distractions from the real meaning of music, which is said to involve cognitive and intellectual ideation. Thus, so-called expression is known or symbolized but not directly felt as real feelings, and therefore idealist aesthetic philosophies of music separate the mind (ideas) from the body (sentience) and give precedence to the former while denying or depreciating the value of the latter.[7]

The body is also denied or discredited in important ways by a certain downplaying of the physical aspects of performance. Listening and composing are accorded the highest priority—the latter because the composer's creativity is said to encode the purely aesthetic ideas into notes on the page that the performer then only instantiates, and the former because contemplation of music for its own sake is the ultimate value. Performance is thus accorded a certain secondary status as mainly (or merely) artisanship, and recorded performances can be the aesthetic equivalent of live performances (Reimer 1989b).

Music education as aesthetic education has been, for all practical purposes, the prevailing philosophy supporting music education.[8] This has been the case despite the fact that, traditionally, ensemble directors have focused almost exclusively on large group performance ensembles to the almost total exclusion of musical contemplation (or, for that matter, composition studies, England being a notable exception). General music teachers, on the other hand, do attempt to teach concepts as the cognitive and ideational bases for exactly the kind of musical contemplation described by idealist supporters of MEAE (e.g., Reimer 1989a, 1989b; Schwadron 1967)—even though social psychology shows that it is precisely the use-value of music that most attracts young people (Zillmann and Gan 1997). Keep in mind that such use-value is viewed by idealist and other aesthetic traditions as detrimental to the fullness or authenticity of aesthetic responding. Such research also identifies "taste publics" and "taste cultures" (Russell 1997) that reflect exactly those social variables and values denied by aesthetic theories but confirmed and advanced by praxial accounts of music and musical value. In other words, ordinary people of varying educational backgrounds find a host of values in and from musics the value of which are denied or downplayed by the idealist-dominated aesthetic orthodoxy and by MEAE, with its penchant for abstract ideas and musical purity.[9]

Realism does emphasize the senses; and thus for realists such as Aristotle matter is independent of mind.[10] Accordingly, the physical world and its natural laws, not the mind, are the source of truth and knowledge. Realism has thus served as the source of modern empirical science. Along with idealists, realists see values as absolute and eternal, but because they are based on natural law. "Good art," then, is expected to reflect or "re-present" the orderliness and rationality of the natural world. Thus, realist aesthetics are sometimes called naturalistic aesthetics.

For realists, schooling exists to convey an understanding of the logic and order of the universe. Mathematics and the social and natural sciences receive the most emphasis. Primary importance is given to transmitting data, facts, and information—what some people call "the basics"—without indicating what such knowledge is supposedly basic to. Thus, knowledge, truth, and beauty (as with idealism, but again for different reasons) exist outside the learner's experience; they are merely passed on and passively received, despite teaching methods by realists that favor the senses, such as demonstrations, experiments, and the like.

Realist aesthetics of music present several problems. First is the fact that while musical sounds have physical properties, it is not auditory brain mechanisms that mechanically convert sound into music but the situated and embodied mind that constitutes music as and in terms of a social praxis.[11] Secondly, with the exception of trite imitation, music does not refer directly to or imitate the things of the world. Thus, even program music—music inspired by stories and visual images—depends on titles and other hints to the listener who otherwise would have no idea about any realism that might have inspired a composition.

Although realism moves thinking from the purities of formalist aesthetic theories (i.e., music as pure form, or as balance, proportion, and symmetry, or as a pure architecture of sound) to expressionist aesthetic theories, the feelings, ideas, and emotions contained in and expressed by music are not real. Such expression is neither the composer's nor the listener's but is aesthetically universalized and encoded in the score. As Harry Broudy (a leading MEAE proponent of aesthetic realism) writes: "That is why, emotion felt in listening to music has been called aesthetic emotion, intellectual emotion. . . . It is not the real thing somehow" (Broudy 1991, 81). Thus, while music is processed in part by the brain, in the realist's view musical experience as such does not call attention to or take the sentient form of bodily experience, of felt emotions. And thus, not unlike idealist aesthetic theory, realist aesthetics results in disembodied products of perception that are appreciated based upon claimed intellectual, symbolic, or metaphorical association with lived experience.

Along with idealism, realism strongly emphasizes a connoisseurship of listening as the intelligent basis for music appreciation.[12] Music deemed to be good by those Broudy describes as the "experts of successive ages" is therefore imposed on students in the belief that it will "enhance the pupil's enjoyment of music and life" (Broudy 1991, 91, 92). Whatever useful contributions music other than the Eurocentric canon might make to practical, religious, or social occasions is not to be confused with aesthetic values; these, not the value of music and in for personal and social praxis, should be the sole focus of formal music education (77). The emphasis, again like idealism, is largely on contemplative and "cultivated" or "refined" listening to "classy" music. Again, performance is relegated to a secondary realm; Broudy hardly mentions performance in relation to music education. Instead, meaning resides objectively in the score, the work, and is only apprehended in a detached and thus basically cerebral form of enlightened cherishing.

The comprehension and discrimination needed to develop such "good taste" and "aesthetic appreciation" are supposedly developed educationally, largely through listening, because young performers lack the technical skills to properly realize the aesthetic value of "good music" through performance. For similar reasons, however, all manner of amateur recreational, lay, naïve, and indigenous kinds of music and music making are all but ignored. Instead, according to Broudy, "musical training affords the learner a basis for objective and informed judgments about certain aspects of musical quality" (Broudy 1991, 86).[13] This idea of music education as discipline or training for connoisseurship is similar in certain respects to neoscholastic philosophy.

Scholasticism is a theory that developed at the same time and in interaction with the beginning of formal schooling in the Middle Ages. "Schooling" gets its name from the wandering scholars of that age; "scholar" and "scholarship," in turn, stem from Greek words for leisure devoted to learning for its own sake. This merely academic concept of learning and its value has been, it seems, inextricably wed to some of the most basic paradigms of schools and schooling.[14] Neoscholasticism is a contemporary philosophy rooted in renewing the old-time emphasis on rational knowledge and approaches to learning. It has so much in common with realism that it is sometimes called "scholastic realism" or "classical realism."[15]

Underlying scholasticism is a conception of mankind as a rational animal; the ability to think rationally is considered the most noble and valued human capacity. For rationalists, the mind can seize upon truth logically in the form of self-evident ("analytic") truths or in connection with certain kinds of scientific or empirical (i.e., "synthetic") truths that depend on experience for confirmation. This tension between rationalism and empiricism (abstract reason and sensory experience), usually antithetical beliefs, results in considerable overlap of neoscholasticism with idealist and realist theories (and thus with their aesthetic theories). However, of the two, rational knowledge is seen by neoscholastics as being of a higher order than sensory knowledge. Values, then, ultimately depend on rationality, and a good life is lived in agreement with reason. Therefore, base (i.e., bodily) desires and emotions are to be controlled by the rational intellect. However, concerning art, intellect sometimes reaches beyond reason to certain kinds of insights or revelations that are subsequently contemplated and enjoyed rationally.

Through studying the leading disciplines of knowledge and their internal logic (i.e., the structure-of-the-disciplines curriculum), neoscholastics hold that schooling develops the disciplined habits of thinking that can most properly inform and guide a good life. Systematic subjects such as mathematics and foreign languages, and especially the "great ideas" and "great works" of the past, are particularly favored in the belief that they carry and promote rational thinking and an intellectual understanding of the world. The watchword for neoscholasticism is the mental and personal *discipline* that results from enforced training. Thus, students are regularly exposed to and expected to study and master subject matter in which they often have no interest precisely because no important practical or personal use can be demonstrated.

Because of its heritage in the Middle Ages, when art and music were entirely praxial, serving church, royalty, and folk culture, neoscholasticism has no clear aesthetic philosophy. Therefore, it tends to share an often contradictory mix of idealism and realism that focuses sometimes on rational ideas and sometimes on intuitions of cognitively experienced feeling. Neoscholasticism, however, does make its distinct mark on elementary and secondary music curricula in two regards.[16] First, the movement known as discipline-based music education, as predicated on an earlier development in art education called discipline-based art education, presents and teaches music as a formal discipline of study. In such programs, hands-on production or performances are downplayed in deference to a theoretical (and, thus, a strictly cognitive) approach to musical perception that focuses on connoisseurship, conceived largely as a form of music criticism and good taste.

Secondly, neoscholasticism is a severely conservative movement that finds expression in the educational theory of perennialism. Perennialism arose early in this century as a reaction against progressivism, the child-centered theory that portrayed each learner's interests as central to the why and how of teaching and learning. In progressive schools, individual interest, a sense of personal relevance, and other unique and situated needs enable children to be active constructors of their own learning and meaning, not just passive repositories of received knowledge. The progressive teacher is authoritative in facilitating and guiding learning, not authoritarian in force-feeding it, as is the wont of neoscholastics (and idealists and realists). Progressivism also stresses the practical value of learning for life use and social renewal and transformation; thus, problem-solving and cooperative forms of learning are stressed over rote memorization of inert facts and information.

Against such claims, perennialists argue that schooling should be uniform since human nature is uniform in being, at its best, rational. Therefore, rather than addressing students' individual needs or interests, or their evolving personal and social needs, perennialists believe that uniform and prescribed subject matter should be the focus of the curriculum. With such a standardized curriculum and its emphasis on the disciplining of standardized results, neoscholasticism readily fosters the present obsession for national standards, accountability, and other objectives-oriented curricula. Furthermore, perennialist instruction is not just teacher-directed, as is the case with progressivism; it is teacher-dominated. Hence, the teacher is decidedly more active than students: in other words, a subject is studied because the teacher and the school say it should be, and they also dictate how and why it is studied. As a result, students need to be disciplined to study content and skills that often hold no intrinsic interest, no practical use, and no personal relevance for them. Given the neoscholastic emphasis on developing discipline (and disciplines), inevitable student resistance to this process is euphemistically called "discipline problems."

As regards music, in line with perennialist faith in "great ideas," the "great works" of the past in music and the other arts are seen as containing values that have stood the test of time (see Adler 1994). Thus, a steady diet of the classics is featured as eternally relevant. School, in the perennialist view, should not preview or model real life. Rather, academics, at most, prepare the mind and disposition only with the abstractions neoscholastics claim are needed to deal with life rationally. The very fact of their seeming irrelevance to students is a measure of their importance in developing personal discipline and rationally controlled behavior in mastering the disciplines as bodies of knowledge studied for their own sake.

In general, idealism, realism, and neoscholasticism all share this abstract, largely academic and impersonal approach to schooling, as well as other traits all too familiar as "school culture." For all three, knowledge, truth, and beauty are eternal and unchanging facts that exist independently of, and thus prior to, the experience of particular individuals. For all, a good life is a life of contemplation lived in accordance with reason. Conventional aesthetic theories accord well with this general paradigm, resulting in a focus on listening, good or refined taste, "great works," and the fine arts. The abstractness of facts and the inertness of information for students is, in part, a direct result of the metaphysical and contemplative claims of all three traditions. But it is also a consequence of the inability of teachers to model or otherwise demonstrate the actual (or even potential) relevance of such studies for life outside of school. The direct instruction required to teach such abstractions (namely, the lecture method) is likewise a liability. Knowledge, then, is only abstractly received from outside the personal subjectivities, life-worlds, and needs of individual students. Thus, for typical students, it is largely inert in terms of any foreseeable consequence of its actual use in life.

Music curricula predicated on any one or any synthesis of these traditional philosophies falls prey to similar problems, particularly in general music and other classroom instruction, such as music theory. And performance-based instruction is, as we
have seen, largely ignored or downplayed. But whether in classes or ensembles, the
metaphysical claims of the various versions of MEAE concerning what music is and
is good for convey a picture of musical meaning that is timeless, placeless, and face-
less. This accounts for the abstractness and inertness of such learning and its irrelevance in the eyes of most students.

There is, then, a mounting realization in philosophical circles that conventional
aesthetic theory, in its claim to be the best or only philosophy of music, is increasingly irrelevant to the actual practices and pleasures of music, and that it confuses
more than enlightens thinking about the real world of musicing. The philosopher
Michael Proudfoot begins his introductory overview of aesthetic theory this way:

> It would be hard to think of a subject more neurotically self-doubting than aes-
> thetics. Claims that the subject is dreary, irrelevant, muddled and misunder-
> stood have been a persistent theme, not only of recent, that is to say, post-war
> writers, but from the very start of the subject. Alas, these claims have all too
> frequently been justified. (1988, 831)

Nonetheless, while admitting to the existence of this confusion, irrelevance, and
muddle of aesthetic theories, Reimer (1989a, xi) has claimed that aesthetics serve as
the "bedrock" of the profession.[17] However, the befuddled and befuddling largess of
competing and conflicting aesthetic theories cannot serve as an effective basis for the
practical choices and actions called for by the needs of curriculum by music educators.

To begin with, Proudfoot also points out that "aesthetics has so often lagged behind other areas in philosophy" (1988, 852), in part because it has ignored the influence of Ludwig Wittgenstein, whose *Lectures on Aesthetics* begins, "The subject
(Aesthetics) is very big and entirely misunderstood as far as I can see" (Wittgenstein
1966, 1). In his *Philosophical Investigations*, Wittgenstein warned that the meaning
of words—such as "music"—do not take a single, essentialist form. Instead, meaning
takes the form of "language games" that are conditioned by how words are actually
used in practice. The meaning of a word such as "music," then, is always multiple or
pluralistic, often circular and even contradictory, all as dictated by the circumstances
and situatedness of its use. Thus, as Wittgenstein points out in his *Lectures on Aesthetics*, "it is not only difficult to describe what [aesthetic] appreciation consists in,
but impossible. To describe what it consists in we would have to describe the whole
environment" (7). The actual environments in which music and the arts are appreciated are, Wittgenstein points out, so "enormously complicated" that words referring
to aesthetic ideas and criteria have negligible importance in typical circumstances
(2; see also 11). "We don't," he cautions, "start from certain words" describing aesthetic qualities or criteria, "but from certain occasions or activities" (3)—in other
words, from music as praxis!

This need to get back to the unique requirements of active music making as they
exist in particular conditions of situatedness is, in fact, a defining trait of any praxial
theory of music and therefore of a praxial orientation to curriculum for music education. As Proudfoot puts it:

> Aesthetic theory often seems false to our experience of art. . . . Recently, such inadequacy to our experience of art has been evident; a result, I believe, partly of aestheticians' preoccupation with what it is to treat something "aesthetically," and partly from *a concentration on works of art in isolation from the circumstances in which they are actually created or appreciated*. (1988, 850; italics added)

Praxial theory directly engages; indeed, it depends on just such "circumstances in which [music is] actually created or appreciated" as primary ingredients concerning what music is and why it is valued. Thus, it rejects the misrepresentation and falsification of musical experience by various aesthetic theories as being autonomous and isolated from the important contexts of its use.

Music as Praxis

Music Matters boldly critiques the aesthetic misrepresentation and falsification of musical experience and just as daringly proposes to root music, and thus music education, in actual circumstances of musical praxis. But while the idea of praxis is central to Elliott's project, there really is relatively little direct mention of the term or idea, for a book that has come to be so singularly identified with praxial philosophy. Elliott's view of praxis is based on a few references to Aristotle. However, the contemporary idea of praxis has evolved into a much richer and more varied account than can be found in Aristotle's foundations. For example, Elliott's interpretation that Aristotle's "right action" refers to "active engagement in productive music making" (1995, 175) has some merit, but it is an incomplete interpretation and is thus limiting as far as both music and curriculum are concerned. Similarly, expanded notions of praxis from Marxism, neo-Marxism (critical theory), other social theory, sociology, and postmodernism that offer a richer and more comprehensive concept of musical praxis are either overlooked or fail to receive central attention.[18] Contributions from pragmatism and existentialism are likewise not directly mined for their support, though some implicit themes can be gleaned.[19]

In addition to Aristotle (see Regelski 1998b), then, the broader account of music as praxis I want to sketch here draws, among its many sources, from the contemporary philosophies of existentialism, phenomenology, and pragmatism—and, more recently, from "practice theory" in both philosophy and social theory (Schatzki et al. 2001). From the former two it gains an emphasis on the primacy of the individual and the important role played by each person's consciousness of inner life and experience. In practice, existentialism and phenomenology are more concerned with the subjectivity, introspectiveness, and immediacy of lived experience than simply with the rational intellect or detached, speculative metaphysics. Meaning is thus not received ready-made but is uniquely apprehended or constructed by each individual.[20] Self-actualization is, in fact, a matter of self-creation; and self-actualization is an agency that both reveals one's values and proposes them as models for others to explore. Learning, valuing, and meaning, then, are all highly unique products of personal agency.

Schools that force-feed values to students and repress their individuality (despite giving predictable lip service to individualism) are seen by existentialists as outright harmful. On one hand, such force-feeding prevents students from self-actualizing and thereby realizing self-created meaning in action. On the other hand, students are quickly taught that learning is something schools and teachers do *to* you, not something in which you participate for your own sake. But if the musicianship skills that support any musical praxis are also approached in this way, as a preexisting body of knowledge, the results for students are as inauthentic and disempowering as those of any of the other disciplines students are obliged to study.

Though progressivism is a direct reflection of pragmatic theories of education, many aspects of teaching influenced by existentialism—particularly the influences from so-called humanistic psychology, which is a correlate of existential psychotherapy and philosophy—are similar to or overlap the descriptions given earlier of progressivism. Thus, teachers facilitate rather than dominate; they help students explore problems rather than memorize and recall learning that is force-fed because of its inertness and consequent inability to move students' interests. This aspect fits well with the idea of curriculum as an apprenticeship. Music education also fits especially well into a philosophy that focuses on the central importance of self-creation and re-creation through such actions as making and listening to music (Regelski 1973). Elliott's emphasis on flow and "self," "self-growth," "self-identity," and "self-knowledge" thus reflects premises that are at least similar to those of existentialism and humanistic psychology—though, as has already been noted, the embodied emphasis contributed by phenomenology and second-generation cognitive science (Lakoff and Johnson 1999) seems to be missing.

Pragmatism shares or overlaps many but not all existential traits, giving each, however, its own spin and adding some qualities of its own. Pragmatism shares with realism a respect for concrete experience but otherwise has little in common with classical, metaphysical realism. Pragmatism's thoroughgoing naturalism argues that there is simply no way of confirming the metaphysical claims concerning "ultimate" reality, truth and beauty. All people can (and do) know and value, according to pragmatism, is their own experience.[21] Thus, pragmatism involves a type of "experiential realism" (Lakoff and Johnson 1999) where knowledge is fully embodied and results from the experience of mindfully confronting and dealing with the multiplicity of problems that daily life involves. This body-based experiential knowledge is actively created and personalized (Polanyi 1962) through interacting with the environment, not passively received as inert fact at one time or place in life, such as in school.

Values, including those in music, are situated and temporally conditioned and thus relative to and personalized by individuals—responding to the range and specific conditions and affordances for action of the situations they experience.[22] Different values can coexist because the experience of life (or music) and what it affords is not everywhere uniform, and thus values are pluralistic (see Bowman 1991). Pluralistic meanings and values are not, however, necessarily wildly subjective or merely personal (Bowman 1996). Rather, they are confirmed, demonstrated, warranted by the pragmatics of the objective conditions occasioning any experience in the first place.

The pragmatic criterion holds, then, that the worth of any "thing"—a method, event, action, object, institution, praxis, and so on—is seen in the tangible and practical consequences that come about from its use. Thus, good results are a matter of the worth of the thing in relation to the problem, needs, or use in question. Importantly, then, a musical (or any other) praxis is defined in large part in terms of what the practice is "good for"—that is, in terms of the use-function that brought it into being in the past and, as important, that instantiates it in the present moment. It bears an aside here that Elliott addresses (or at least assumes) certain past situatedness in repeatedly stressing the musicianship traditions and routines associated with a customary musical praxis, but the constituting conditions that occasion a present instance of praxis—and the possibility that affordances for such a present instance may vary from previous meanings, even over time for the same person—do not receive their due focus.[23]

This is one instance where pragmatism and "practice theory" (Schatzki et al. 2001) can clarify praxial theory in music and music education, because the criteria of value in art and music, too, are rightfully subject to the pragmatic criterion—rather, that is, than taking the form of metaphysical pronouncements by aestheticians, revelation by teachers and other supposed experts, or even rule-based praxis claims[24] concerning received traditions treated as antecedent, ultimate, or essentialist values. In this regard, then, questions of goodness, worth, or value take two—usually interacting and pragmatic—forms. First, as Robert Dixon, a critic of aesthetic theory, puts it, "art is good which is good of its kind" (Dixon 1995, 53). Thus music is good relative to the type of praxis—for example, jazz, or the classics, or rap, rock, or reggae, but also church music, amateur performing, and music for aerobics. Questions of quality, therefore, are not judged along a single dimension of musical quality where the "art music" classics are at the top (or similar hierarchies assumed for any other praxis). Rather, as Dixon also points out, the so-called fine art of the classical Eurocentric canon "is not a quality of, but a kind of art" (6; see also 44) and thus represents only one "highly peculiar 'taste'" (57). This, of course, is true of any praxis, as well.

Secondly, as I have argued elsewhere, considered pragmatically, music can be judged good only in relation to what it is good for (Regelski 1997, 1998a, 1998b, 2002–2003).[2] Thus, the goodness or value of any music is in part—but importantly—determined by the conditions of particular use to which it is put, which is to say, *in relation to the human praxis that occasions its use (traditionally, or for the moment) in the first place*. Again, this aspect of praxis seems to be underserved or submerged in Elliott's theory. His idea of praxis appears to stress existing types of music more than, or in preference to, the social groundedness of music. If this is the case, it fails to sufficiently acknowledge that different types of music (jazz, rock, art music, etc.) have evolved according to certain use-functions (needs, intentions, interests, benefits, "goods," etc.) and continue to serve various functions in the present—though not always in the ways connected with the originating conditions.[25] To understand this second condition more fully, it is instructive to turn briefly to the root meaning of the term pragmatism in Aristotle's original idea of praxis (for full details, see Regelski 1998c).

In his writings on ethics and politics, Aristotle distinguished between three types of knowledge: theoria, techne, and praxis. Theoria involved knowledge developed and contemplated for its own sake—what students today call the "merely academic" or "theoretical" learning of schools. In general, then, theoria describes perfectly well much of the rationalist agenda for schooling advanced by idealists, realists, and neoscholastics. Concerning music, it especially encompasses the kinds of meanings and values advanced by the aesthetic theories of those three schools of philosophy, theories that underlie various versions of the MEAE orthodoxy described earlier. Thus, for all three, music is rationally contemplated in metaphysical and intellectual terms for its own sake, and a sharp distinction is made between an aesthetic attitude and the sociality of music as praxis.

Techne referred to the kind of know-how used to produce predictable and taken-for-granted results. It is concerned with what the Greeks called *poeisis*, the making of products or things. As such, it involves technical competence learned through apprenticeship and hands-on doing. Pragmatists often refer to "instrumental knowledge" in such terms as the kind of knowledge that is instrumental in bringing about certain desirable results. But techne has two further qualifications that must be understood in distinguishing it from praxis, which is another kind of instrumental knowledge.

First, for techne, the nature of the techniques and craft in question is largely impersonal. There is little contribution to the existential self of the craftsperson whose results are not unlike those of another competent individual—for example, section players in ensembles. Secondly, with techne, mistakes are simply discarded, and the practitioner simply begins again, with no harm done. Thus, the competent potter discards a poor result and starts over without learning anything new about the process. In music, as Elliott points out (1995, 70), techne does include technique, not just of performance, but the various procedural techniques of musicianship and other supporting skills. While mentioning that praxis is distinguished from techne on the basis of "other *forms of knowing* linked to specific goals, ideas, and values of musical doing and making" (70), these other variables are not detailed despite the fact that they are crucial in distinguishing techne from praxis.[26]

One important governing trait of praxis that takes it beyond mere "making" to a much more complex act of doing is its governing ethic of *phronesis*, the need for prudence or care-fullness that focuses on the need to bring about "right" or "good" results for, and in terms of, the requirements of human situations, which are always unique and thus require discerning diagnosis. This ethical dimension of praxis arises from the responsibility to the needs of people, not simply to produce things or to perpetuate practices in isolation from the "goods" they exist to serve.[27] Things may well be involved—for example, the house designed by an architect. But praxis requires that such results (including non-things such as musical results and benefits) clearly serve the needs of the present situations for which they have been produced. Secondly, both the doing of praxis and the knowledge that results for the practitioner are extremely personal and amount to a unique personal style. In music, this goes well beyond mere technique (techne). For experts and professionals, it amounts to what some call artistry; and for amateurs, and everyday musics and music making, it invokes a host of highly situated variables, criteria, and standards of personal satisfaction (e.g., in recreational performing) or practical success (e.g., dance music).

Furthermore, the satisfactions involved in such doings, such as composing, performing, or listening to music, are not just unique to the individual; in praxis they are self-actualizing in the sense associated with existentialism, as well as with Csikszentmihalyi's idea of flow (Csikszentmihalyi 1990), which Elliott has drawn upon. Thus, the self is rewarded and defined in key and unique ways by the nature and fullness of the engagement with or in praxis. However, unlike mistakes of techne and given the condition of *phronesis*, the "doings" of unsuccessful praxis become part of the new situation, the new problem faced by the doer, the practitioner. Thus, a doctor's misdiagnosis or the teacher's failed lesson becomes a factor that has certain inescapable human consequences that must be contended with if a new attempt is to reach the intended right results. Such experiences do result, then, in new praxial knowledge for the practitioners' future use. This process, in general, reveals the pragmatic spirit behind all praxis or, put another way, reveals the praxial conditions behind pragmatic knowledge, truth, and value.

In sum, praxis depends on technical kinds of instrumental knowledge and also engages various kinds of practical consequences of theoretical knowledge. In its applied form, such theoria is no longer to be contemplated for its own sake; its value results from being put into practice. Praxis, then, is a functional synthesis of all three types of knowledge, as Elliott makes extensively clear in his own terms. Theoria and techne are thus undertaken not for their own sake but according to the situated needs for right results that bring about the occasion for praxis in the first place.

The impression remains, nonetheless, that the situated needs and conditions Elliott has in mind concerning a praxis are those of certain established musical traditions, types, and genres, and that the artistic values and musicianship processes involved—which Elliott takes to be more stable and singular than seems to be the case, given the frequent disagreements on musical quality between equally competent experts[28]—have somehow floated free from their practical, personal, social, political, and cultural roots. Attention to *phronesis*, however, reminds us that the values and qualities of any praxis are not intrinsic, purely or essentially aesthetic *or* artistic, fixed forever, or for their own sake.

That the regulating (i.e., musicianship and other supporting) processes of any music praxis exist at all, and in the ways they do, is governed by the constituting conditions (i.e., originating use-function) of the praxis; and many common though important musical practices exist that do not engage or depend on highly developed artistry or specialized knowledge. It is in this sense, then, that a praxial philosophy, as originally proposed by Alperson (1991), must account for all musics, including the many musics served by regulating criteria that are less dependent on the kinds of highly developed expertise and musicianship Elliott at least stresses.[29] Any implication of a hierarchy of musics based on presumed levels of musical expertise (virtuosity, artistry, musicianship, and the like) fails to understand the complex relationship between *phronesis*, the infinitely varied human, social, and cultural roles music everywhere serves, and the quality (i.e., pragmatic success) that can be judged only in connection with those differing practices.[30]

Bringing pragmatism to the support of praxial theory reinforces the connection between music and experience, between music and everyday life. Thus, on one hand, pragmatism rejects metaphysical accounts of aesthetic essences (whether of the idealist, realist, or neoscholastic kind) and similar metaphysical claims treating questions of beauty, meaning, and value in music in absolute terms as eternal and universal, including those tracing their heritage to Aristotle.[31] In particular, the idea that musical works are autonomous is vigorously denied; but Dewey also argues throughout *Art as Experience* (1934/1980) against the idea that art has an autonomous essence accessible only to a cultivated few, stressing instead the varying affordances of music and the other arts for the everyday life of ordinary people.

The distinction aesthetic philosophers make between autonomous and stable intrinsic qualities, meanings, essences, and values as opposed to extrinsic qualities, meanings, values, uses, and other such conditions is actively denied by pragmatism. Such extrinsic qualities, those that I have observed appear at times submerged or insufficiently addressed by Elliott, are specifically dignified by pragmatists such as Dewey. In a pragmatically reinforced praxial theory (and in the view, generally, of ethnomusicology and sociological analyses of music—see, e.g., Shepherd and Wicke 1997; Small 1998), musical meaning does not inhere in the sounds, artistry, traditions, or techniques, nor can it be analyzed in or from the score.

Music's affordances are appropriated and actualized in an infinite variety of ways according to the often conflicting, even changing intentions, needs, meanings, and values of users—on an occasion between users and over time for the same agent. Musical meaning, relevance, and value, then, are always underdetermined by the score, the sounds of the moment or even the traditions of musical praxis informing and regulating the moment. In addition to such objective features,[32] the highly unique and situated particulars of use—what the music is judged to be good for by an individual or group under particular constituting and governing conditions—actualize the particular musical affordances in certain ways as against others (DeNora 2000). Seen in this way, praxis involves hermeneutic processes (Grundy 1987, 59–68) that, for schooling, also need to extend to curriculum (69–78 and passim). In this regard, music's semiotic function is somewhat parallel to that of spoken language, where meaning is seen interpreted in use, not in the dictionary sense of words.

First of all, in neither music nor language do sounds inherently signify immanent or fixed meanings. There is nothing about the sound of the word "pain" that is homologous with the experience of pain. Similarly meanings associated with the sounds of music depend on a variety of social and cultural structures and are ultimately governed by the way and the situations in which they are used and thus evolve over time. For instance, a Bach chorale as part of a church service has a significantly different meaning and value than that same score performed on the secular concert stage.[33] In fact, in the same manner, a secular love song used in a wedding ceremony takes on a religious, ceremonial, and highly personal meaning, and gospel song easily became soul music when the words were secularized. So, too, in 1999 the Vatican sanctioned the use of hula music and dance for the Catholic liturgy in Hawai'i.

Just as the meanings of words and expressions evolve and change according to usage, as is chronicled in good etymological dictionaries, so too do the meanings afforded by music respond to ever-new sensibilities and interpretations, new life situations and experiences, even new technology. Furthermore, any praxis quickly adopts considerably different meanings when its affordances are put to unusual use, such as a jazz or folk mass. Sometimes these meanings are so at variance with the original conditions of praxis as to constitute a basically new practice, as when recorded classics of any genre are used in film or advertising. A praxial theory of music by definition should account for all such practices, and a praxial theory of curriculum needs to at least consider these wider implications, applications, and examples of praxis.

Musical sociality, in this expanded account of praxis, conditions a range of possible meanings without providing the kind of uniform or built-in meaning implied by the aesthetic orthodoxy. It also suggests that intelligent musical meaning (or music making) is similarly not an orthodoxy that depends simply on performance expertise within the praxis. Were this the case, concert halls would be all but empty, and recorded music would serve only incredibly small in-groups of individuals having a background of performance expertise in the music at stake.[34] While not just any meaning can be invested in or derived from particular musical affordances, individual circumstances do condition results. Thus, for example, amateur performers tend to listen more often to music for their own instrument or ensemble. As with professionals, they often will also listen with more attention and interest to and appreciation of technique than will a listener who has never performed.[35] Yet amateur performers as audience listeners may also appropriate or interpret certain other affordances in ways that are just different from what concerns and interests experts. And the many music lovers who regularly attend concerts or faithfully participate in other musical pursuits despite a lack of expertise are certainly experiencing qualities the value of which cannot and should not be denied or denigrated. As DeNora (2001) demonstrates, many variables arise due to personal history—influences, learning, and other traits that have little or sometimes nothing to do with a personal history of performance.[36]

In a very real and important sense, any praxis—musical or otherwise—is not simply some thing that is out there, like a library or museum. Institutional theory and thinking tend to reify institutional dynamics into a thinglike facticity. However, by its very nature, a praxis, even a highly institutionalized one, is altogether more like a collection of mutual "doings" that, though afforded by the praxis, result in richly diverse meanings, values, and benefits. This is no less true of, say, the practice of religion (or of a given religion) or of those in attendance at a museum than of any musical praxis. Thus, a particular musical practice is more like a living organism that, while affording certain opportunities in common, is defined in effect by the intentionality brought to such occasions by different agents. The museum concept of music against which Dewey argued (1934), and the possibility that any musical praxis can become so reified or deified as to take on more importance than those it serves, are always a danger—even for praxial theories. Music as praxis affords much more than what musicians usually understand as music. Furthermore, the world of music, which is to say, the range of musical practices in the world, is far wider and richer than this or that musical type, style, genre, tradition, and so on.

The praxial theory I advance includes, then, in addition to the kinds of traditional musical practices Elliott seems to focus on, all manner of down-to-earth and everyday musical "doings" that bring about "right results" of all kinds for all kinds of people, whether or not educated musically in performance. First of all, in accordance with the twofold account of pragmatic value explained earlier, the very existence of an inconceivable variety of kinds, types, styles, and genres of music is in itself dramatic evidence that music is as varied as human sociality. Secondly, my theory of praxis points to the fact all the various kinds, types, and genres of music, are good for an equally unimaginable diversity of good results. All kinds of pragmatic (praxial) uses of music, then, properly fall within the aegis of a praxial theory that takes into account the kinds of considerations I have argued for here and elsewhere. What the singer Ani DiFranco describes as "the indigenous, unhomogenized, uncalculated sound of a culture becoming itself in the streets, bars, gyms, churches and back porches of the real world" (DiFranco, quoted in Farley 1999)—in other words, the overwhelming preponderance of music in the world—is clearly made for a bewildering variety of life uses.

In this connection, the autonomy claimed by aesthetic theory and the psychic distance required of aesthetic experience denies or deprecates the aesthetic value of such "everyday music" (DeNora 2001); or it attempts to tear such music from its natural and necessary context in order to exhibit it for contemplation alone as though it was or could become, by such evisceration, purely or essentially aesthetic despite its origins in situated sociality and as praxis. Such attempts by aesthetic theorists to apply aesthetic criteria to, for example, world and multicultural musics of various kinds result, then, in a colonialism and exploitation by Eurocentric aesthetic theory that misappropriates and misrepresents the music in question and devalues the kinds of authentic musical meanings engaged in situ by its creators.

Praxial theory, as I view it, must not lose sight of the connections of music to the constituting conditions that are outside of the sounds of the moment themselves. If the "good for" of a musical praxis is lost sight of—in the conduct of the praxis itself or in the schooling of any praxis—it takes on an autonomous nature that approximates the same kind of museum culture from which most art music has suffered.[37] In fact, the antidote to such a museum culture of any praxis, as I see it, is regrounding music—any music—in its constituting praxial conditions. The "goodness" of music can be advanced, thus, by repeatedly stressing what, in life, music is good for and by undertaking to enable students to partake, at least at beginning levels, of such "goods."

In sum, then, my theory of praxis accounts for all kinds and uses of music and finds musical value not in disembodied, metaphysical hypotheses concerning aesthetic meaning, but in the constitutive sociality of music and the functional importance of music for the human processes that govern social and thus individual consciousness.[38] It addresses concert music (of all kinds) that is presented for "just listening" as equally shot through with sociality and as a discrete praxis of its own that is no more or less important than other kinds of musical "doing." This kind of praxial theory redresses the imbalance the aesthetic orthodoxy has promulgated on behalf of listening and particularly reasserts the importance of musical agency through various kinds of amateur performance. Furthermore, in regard to "just listening" in concert situations or to recordings at home, my praxial theory accounts for and points to the "good time" that results, regardless of how the music's affordances are appropriated and interpreted. In general, whether via listening or performing, music "makes special" (Dissanayake 1990, 1992) time in a way that creates "good time"—time that is deemed as "worthwhile" in relation to both its sociality and its individuating benefits and other meanings, benefits, and uses. Thus, as opposed to time we kill, simply pass, waste, or spend at other pursuits (such as work), the "good time" resulting from musical praxis engages a variety of socially structured meanings in which the individual participates in a way that is nonetheless self-defining and self-enhancing (on "good time," see Regelski 1997).

In particular, then, my praxial theory provides support for all kinds of amateur and recreational uses of music (Regelski 1998a)—practices that in no stretch of the imagination are accounted for as aesthetically valid or valuable by the aesthetic orthodoxy at the root of MEAE. Whether such uses entail playing jazz as an amateur, country fiddling, banjo picking, washboard playing, garage bands of aspiring rock musicians, or folk guitarists and lay or naive music making of all kinds, such as community ensembles, church choirs, Christmas caroling, singalongs, and the like, each, as I see it, has a proper place and personal, social, and thus musical value in a praxial account of music. Each is its own valid and valuable praxis, and in general these kinds of praxis need to be regarded and valued as such, including in decisions concerning curriculum.

Furthermore, "just listening" does not only take the form of the cerebral pleasures of concert music; it expands in my praxial account to include forms of listening where music is fully integrated in such social practices as religious ceremonies, weddings, ceremonies, and the like. In these cases, music does not just accompany such occasions; it is intrinsic to and defining of their very nature and value-structure at the same time that the sociality entailed is intrinsic to and defining of the music and its meaning and value. The role of music in these examples is a type of listening praxis of its own, regardless of the types of music employed (e.g., jazz mass, folk wedding).

In my praxial account, then, music is not only for experts or an elite few connoisseurs; it is also of and for the down-to-earth conditions of everyday life and life well lived in terms of the "good time" thus created. It is not above life in some intellectually or cerebrally abstract, disembodied, otherworldly aesthetic realm of metaphysical ideals, expressions, or understandings that exist for their own sake. Rather, in this praxial account, music's meaning and value are in and for personal agency, and such personal agency constructs an infinite variety of meanings from the same musical affordances according to personal and other situated conditions. Consequently, music is altogether more engaged with everyday people and everyday life than is allowed by the aesthetic orthodoxy and, thus, by music education as aesthetic education. A praxial theory that includes all such musicing is altogether more down to earth as a foundation for the decisions guiding curriculum for music education.

Curriculum for and as Praxis

Aside from the philosophical problems pointed out by Elliott and others summarized here, conventional aesthetic theory has distinct practical liabilities in connection with schooling. For example, in MEAE isolated concepts tend to be taught as ready-made abstractions for presumed application to future aesthetic experience rather than developed as action skills from engaging students in holistic praxis at appropriate developmental levels. Secondly, because aesthetic experience is, by definition, not directly observable, neither teaching nor learning can be adequately assessed. Finally, it is abundantly clear to most teachers that it is the "doing" of music that is its prime attraction for most learners (and, for that matter, for most adults)—especially for most adolescents everywhere. Thus, attempts by well-meaning teachers to aesthetically convert students typically fall on deaf ears, whether in classes or ensembles.

Because music as praxis is rooted in the doing of music, the planning, executing, and evaluating of instruction and learning are all benefited instead by abundantly observable results that, as praxial benefits, also further motivate students. Such a curriculum, as I view it, properly begins with a written curriculum guide—a document that serves music teachers as a blueprint serves carpenters. The curriculum guide originates in the attempt by the teacher (or group) to describe the general kind(s) of musical praxis to which instruction will be directed.

These real-life kinds of praxis are considered action ideals—not "ideal" in the sense of being idealistic or utopian, but in the sense that there can be no single instance or any ultimate state of perfection that could ever be reached. In this regard, action ideals guide or regulate teaching in certain desirable but general praxial directions that can take no single or ultimate form and can always take improved or other form; for example, a good marriage and good health are action ideals.[39] Each ideal is accompanied by a description of the musicianship knowledge and skills necessary for students to be able to take part in the praxis in question. Because such knowledge is understood in holistic terms, these descriptions are not so detailed (as in the objectives of behaviorist-style curricula) as to become atomistic or piecemeal or technicist (i.e., techne for its own sake), conditions that (like the currently ballyhooed national standards) lose sight of the final functionality in praxis of the product envisaged. They are, however, stipulated in action terms as "doings" of the ideal praxis (or practices) in question, not simply as abstract knowings or understandings.[40] Finally, in recognition of the potential for harm or good of the "hidden curriculum" (Bennett and LeCompte 1990) and the importance of inspiring students for life with the benefits and joys of the play of music, each praxis is described in terms of the affective and "good time" conditions instruction needs to model if students are to want to and, ultimately, to choose to continue to be involved in the musical praxis in question. This ensures that the practices in question model the personal (and social) benefits and relevance for life at the time of instruction.

In its use of such a formal guiding document, the praxial curriculum organizes and delivers instruction according to something approaching an apprenticeship model; that is, the action ideals in question are approached in the manner of a practicum (Elliott 1995)—the holistic immersion of students in the "learning by authentic doing"— of praxis, not mere techne. The required authenticity refers to real-life models of musical praxis, and authentic evaluation of teaching and learning employs holistic assessment of the actual praxis adjusted for students' developmental and age levels. Such a praxial curriculum invokes a developmental spiral or progression of musicianship refinement resulting from encounters with ever more realistic examples and practical challenges of the ultimate kinds of praxial consequences pointed to by the action ideals at stake.

Given the limiting conditions of scheduling and resources and of the youthfulness of the learners in relation to any mature praxis, school instruction in music cannot become too specialized too early. Thus, musicianship is most pragmatic that amounts to general musicianship—that is, basic yet flexible or adaptable skills and concepts that can be further honed by the unique requirements of a specific praxis. However, such general musicianship must also be functional—that is, sufficient to taking part in a practice at all and thereby beginning the process of acquiring any further specialized abilities.[41] Elliott allows (1995, 54) that the "kinds of knowledge that make up musicianship likely hold across most (if not all) musical practices," but that the "precise contents of [such] knowledge categories are context-dependent." I maintain that the nature of schools and schooling necessitates focusing more on the former shared, common, or general musicianship abilities that at functional entry levels will, for most students, become more precise as they are employed and developed in context-dependent situations.[42]

I argue that most of the kinds of praxis Elliott seems to have in mind—types of music that have traditional literature (notated or not) and routinized procedures—are not easily or effectively addressed in most schools, particularly in the early years, when the authentic ingredients are simply beyond the understanding of students.[43] The problem also arises concerning which of such highly specific practices are to be included in the curriculum and why. Certainly not all can be included, and, at least by pragmatic and utilitarian criteria, it might be expected that emphasis would be given to those standing the best chance for incorporation in the lives of students outside of and after graduation from school.

This only takes us back to the question posed earlier: "Of all of what can be taught, what is most worth teaching?" And to answer "music as praxis" still leaves the value aspects, judgments, and diagnoses of curricular decision making insufficiently guided. It also once again points, then, to the desirability of approaching general music classes (including classroom studies at the high school level) and ensembles as musicianship laboratories where certain general musicianship traits and skills can be promoted that are eventually transferable (at least at beginning levels) to similar and common musical practices and that can be further focused more particularly in action by engagement in and study of a highly specialized practice. Some of the latter can begin in the secondary schools on elective bases (e.g., jazz ensembles, string quartets, barbershop singing, etc.), but the practical limitations of school schedules, resources, and so on typically militate against most of the kinds of specialized practicums Elliott seems to have in mind.

Furthermore, other realities of schooling—particularly the wide variety of ages, abilities, interests, intentions, and socioeconomic and ethnic backgrounds of students—suggest that more of the everyday kinds of musical praxis at large in society be addressed by instruction, at least or perhaps particularly in general music classes. It is unclear whether Elliott means to acknowledge such use-practices as musically valid or valuable. I have argued that they are every bit as important—to individuals, society, and culture—as the kinds of specialized types that Elliott seems to address. Thus I would urge that music educators everywhere be attentive to the many instances of what music is good for in life, as evidenced by the practices of nonmusician adults,[44] particularly those that are uniquely evident in given communities and that represent the socioeconomic and cultural diversity in those communities, and that the most common or promising of these be addressed by curriculum wherever and to whatever degree possible. The action ideal is twofold: to encourage and enable more people to choose to make such everyday musicing a part of their "good life" and to expand the resources of agents who avail themselves of such practices to participate more fully than current agents are able to do. In this regard, though, models from the community are important if school-age students are to set for themselves the action ideal of such adult opportunities for lifelong musicing.

When instruction is focused (and at developmentally appropriate student levels) on musicianship in connection with various kinds of musical praxis, the holism that results ensures that the knowledge and skills addressed by instruction are actually useful—a factor contributing not only to the efficiency of instruction but also to evaluating the effectiveness of learning as well. And a considerable consequence of this holistic approach is the fact that at each level, the joys, interests, and benefits of the praxis in question are experienced and thus modeled for the future, at the same time ever-new heights of praxial functioning are clearly often naturally evident.

Furthermore, despite competent amateurs' failure to reach expert status, the insights they gain from praxis lead to greater interest and unique discernments as listeners. People who perform listen more often to the type of music they play and listen with different interests and insight. On the other hand, I understand audience listening to be its own praxis: it has its own conditions, criteria, and "goods" and therefore profits from its own apprenticeship. This means, among other things, that audience listening ought to be one of the key action ideals in curricula for performance instruction and thus deserves a dedicated and direct apprenticeship of its own in addition to cultivating performance expertise.

General music instruction, in particular, also needs its own practicum for listening. But this needs to include performing and compositional praxes of various kinds and degrees that inform listening in productive ways. But instead of having "just listening" as the sole intended consequence of the general music curriculum, as is typically the case with MEAE, a praxial approach to general music class will also focus on developing an interest in and nurturing the skills for various kinds and levels of performing and creating music for recreational purposes. The bottom line in general music class, like elsewhere in the praxial view of curriculum, is a pragmatic concern with the kinds of holistic, real-life musical praxis students can do at all or better as a result of instruction.

Critical Matters

I have throughout this essay identified what appear to me to be certain critical matters in relation to *Music Matters*. These have been offered in the spirit of expanding the still developing theory of praxis in connection with music and music education. Now I will attempt to summarize briefly some of my reservations and suggestions.

First, there are many philosophical forces, aesthetic and otherwise, impacting on music curriculum today, and all these need to be critically addressed by any curriculum and/or curriculum theory. Time and attention devoted to such matters in the larger context of schooling will have more lasting impact than arguing against the Reimer-Langer theory, which, at best, figures in the teaching of most music teachers no more centrally than do the inspirational posters about music that often adorn the walls of their music classrooms. For praxial theory, in any case, theorizing should be focused on the value added—namely, the progressive and tangible differences a praxial approach to music, curriculum, and instruction make over aesthetic and other conservative traditions (e.g., discipline-based music education).

Secondly, *Music Matters* is clearly a pathbreaking work. But in the foregoing analysis I have had occasion to question whether the path thus cleared is sometimes narrow and (not surprisingly, in any innovative work) whether echoes of older thinking and influences and other obstacles to clarity still appear now and then. And, as concerns curriculum, the kinds of destinations, that is, the kinds of praxis Elliott has in mind will profit from greater detail. I have here and elsewhere argued that "the idea of praxis must be broadened beyond a concern only with musical traditions to include the most common 'goods' music serves in the life well lived, many of which are amateur, recreational, lay, and naïve in nature and purpose" (Regelski 2000, 87). It is unclear whether Elliott means to exclude or include such "goods" as praxis or as among the kinds of praxis worth addressing in school. However, since the idea of praxis is inherently inclusive—that is, by definition it must account for all musics and musicing—grounds for excluding this or that praxis or kind of praxis would need to be argued and, doubtless, defended.

Thirdly, some of the questions raised here (and by others) will benefit from being either clarified or reconsidered in light of suggestions and other or more recent scholarship. Among these matters have been observations about the mind-entrapped orientation that overlooks important embodied aspects of musical experience and value; concerns about treating musical practices as somehow singular, stable, or autonomous traditions; and the lack of explicit attention to everyday and nontraditional musical practices.[45]

My main bête noire is the contention that intelligent music listening is dependent on performance expertise. I have advanced (here and Regelski 2000), instead, the proposal that music listening is its own praxis. Just as performing and composing practices exhibit infinite varieties of types, so too does listening realize different "goods" and meanings according to the intentions constituting the agency of the moment, and these are of different kinds, not different qualities, degrees, or levels. The kind of listening (intentions, pleasures, meanings, values) that is informed by "learning how to make music well" is but one way in which musical affordances can be appropriated.

Elliott never really says how well one must perform in order to listen intelligently, but one conclusion seems to be that listeners who presumably enjoy listening without benefit of any performance experience or expertise are somehow unintelligently experiencing music—are somehow missing musical meaning that is divined only by insights gained via performance. If this is the conclusion to be drawn, it is not just unfortunate for its denial of several basic premises of the praxial theory I have delineated regarding the constituting conditions of praxis; it also has unfortunate echoes of the kind of essentialism and autonomous meaning and value that characterize analytic aesthetic theories in the idealist and realist traditions.

Moreover, the implication may linger between the lines that musical meaning is somehow "strictly" musical or, at least, that it can somehow be cut loose from its socially constituted bases as praxis.[46] And a certain kind of perennialism may linger in particular assumptions about the qualities of musicianship and expertise assumed to be the traditional or historical content of the apprenticeship that is the practicum for a particular practice. Except for students who have already become turned on (by schooling or some other influence) to a praxis, the danger exists that a practicum that assumes the perennial value of such musicianship can become merely academic in the minds of students for whom the practice (or models of it in real life) are still remote and abstract. A general music class that, say, addresses a particular drumming tradition in some depth can fail to convert students for the same reasons that force-fed diets of the usual aesthetic fare fail to contribute to students' musical choices and lives.[47]

Furthermore, in this regard, taken too literally, the idea of a practicum or apprenticeship for any praxis typically entails encountering certain realities (variables and inconsistencies, problems and problematics, challenges and impediments that characterize the uniqueness of any instantiation of any praxis) that cannot be fully approximated in schools. At best, then, the idea of a school curriculum as practicum points to certain general "doings" that progressively develop a beginning but functional competence that, for most at least, promotes only entrance to a praxis. Thus, like the golf, tennis, rock and wall climbing, and aerobics of the new physical education curriculum, general students (as opposed to those on teams or who compete as individuals) are introduced to the practices in question not only at a level and in a manner that, hopefully, both allows and inclines them to develop their interest and expertise further, but also at eventual levels that suit their personal needs and images of a "good life."

In sum, praxial theory (in and outside of music) profits from a rich account of social and contextual variables, influences, and implications. In particular, I submit that praxial theory is more fruitful and productive when it draws from both philosophy (old and new) and various social sciences, thus situating praxis at the interstices of multiple disciplines and benefiting our understanding of it from multiple perspectives. Elliott set out to write a philosophy; however, the idea of praxis has since rapidly expanded to a social theory.[48] When various musicological scholarship (e.g., semiotics of certain kinds), ethnomusicological findings, and cognitive studies are also added to the philosophical and sociological parameters of praxis, the theory that emerges is already considerably wider than Elliott's starting point just a few years ago. The expanded account of praxis that emerges is very powerful against the immateriality and peripheral nature of aesthetic theory and the various traditions of neoscholasticism that linger in curricular thinking concerning music.

Despite these critical issues, *Music Matters* has indeed provided a needed and important jump-start in the thinking of many musicians, educators, and theorists. This has been entirely to the good. The idea of offering it for critical commentary will hopefully prevent the kind of gospel status that has surrounded other theories of music education, aesthetic and otherwise. Praxial theory in music and music education holds forth much promise, but this promise is not yet adequately realized in the work of any thinker. It is in a dynamic, growing state that can only benefit from collegial dialogue and debate over differences, and according to the new and rich resources that can and should be brought to bear on it from multiple disciplines.

Notes

1. Following Grundy (1987, 104), I shall use "critical" in the sense of "discerning"—meaning discriminating, astute, judicious, perceptive and constructive, as in the critique that constitutes a music lesson.

2. See, e.g., L. Choksy, R. Abramson, A. Gillespie, D. Woods, and F. A. York, *Teaching Music in the Twenty-first Century* (Englewood Cliffs, NJ: Prentice-Hall, 2001), where the authors conflate "curriculum" and "method" when they write: "The music student entering teaching today is faced with a plethora of *curriculum* choices" and, among these, "the *method*s being considered in this book" (1; emphasis added) are seen to have "emerged" (24) as successful cur-

riculum options from the various discussions and models that arose in the second half of the previous century (the book was originally published in 1986 under the title *Teaching Music in the Twentieth Century*).

3. The *Performance Standards for Music, Grades PreK–12* (MENC 1996) are claimed to "offer a vision for a new curriculum in music" (v) and are said to "provide a common foundation for music curriculum throughout the nation" (1). However, the standards, or what some call "the national curriculum" are mired in the tradition of Tyler (1949), despite the new-sounding jargon. Elliott has effectively critiqued the Tylerian rationale and curricular process, as has virtually every text and monograph on curriculum theory in the last fifty-plus years.

4. As seen by the sociology of education, on the other hand, the criteria that make up the problematic of teaching vary considerably and are often at cross-purposes. They involve social, political, and economic values, as well as important philosophical criteria concerning the nature of knowledge, its value and use for individuals and society, and, in the case of music and the other arts, competing visions and versions describing the value added by the arts to schooling and to life.

5. This is not to blame individuals; it is music teacher education programs that ignore the contributions philosophy (and curriculum theory) can make to teaching as reflective praxis— i.e., to teachers as professionals (Regelski 2002).

6. There are as many variants of each of these "isms" as there have been philosophers arguing for a particular school of thought. Here, the main contentions of each are summarized irrespective of such variants and subtleties.

7. Paraphrasing Bowman (2000), music somehow becomes mind entrapped; "knowing" becomes the measure of its worth; and music is valuable to the extent it functions cognitively (47). One possible reason for this, to be discussed here later, is that Elliott's account of musical practices stresses artistic (instead of aesthetic) criteria of music in a way that can often seem disconnected from the social and embodied practices that have given rise to a type of "musicing" (1995, 49) in the first place. As a result, his picture of praxis often seems confined to what Bowman (2000) dubs "music's insides" (48) and downplays what music is "good for" to begin with, considerations that go well beyond treating musical practices like distinct or autonomous genres or types.

8. At least in North America. But in certain parts of Europe, Germany, and Scandinavia, "aesthetic education" often refers to "doing music" in various praxial ways as an antidote to overly intellectualized traditions of musical appreciation as intellectualized contemplation.

9. I have already commented (Regelski 2000) that Elliott, in arguing that only those musicianship skills developed through performing are the proper bases for "intelligent music listening" (1995, 174), also either tends to overlook or actively deny musical validity or intelligence to the experiences of "ordinary listeners" who understand and enjoy music in a variety of ways and for a variety of reasons not particularly rooted in specialized musicianship. More on this follows.

10. Here I treat traditional metaphysical realism, and not the experiential realism or naturalistic realism of, say, pragmatists such as John Dewey.

11. This is a "social mind," even if highly personal or individuated, since the individual does not typically exist in a social vacuum. Even the sounds available, for example, are influenced by social and cultural variables. On the socially constituted or assigned "status function" of music, see Regelski (2002–2003).

12. This connoisseurship-via-history-and-theory background to intelligent listening is in

distinction to what sometimes seems to be a connoisseurship-through-performance-based-musicianship that Elliott argues is necessary to a fully (and properly) *musical* appreciation of music (1995, 174). More on this follows.

13. If such training is approached through performing rather than, as Broudy means, through listening, then Broudy's "proper" listening (1995, 86) seems remarkably similar to Elliott's criteria for "intelligent" listening (174). In both cases "quality" seems to be assumed as a priori and uncontestable: for Broudy in the score, learned and realized via listening; for Elliott in or as a musicianship tradition learned first through performance and only then realized in audience listening.

14. Here the arch-idealist Plato and the arch-realist Aristotle come together. The Academy in which Plato taught was named after the war hero Academus, and Aristotle studied there. Though Plato and Aristotle differed widely in their philosophies of what ideas are and how they arise and work, the a priori nature of knowledge, truth, and beauty contributes to the association of academics as dealing merely with abstract ideas that are thus disconnected from life.

15. Scholasticism arose under the influence of St. Thomas Aquinas, who was the leading interpreter of Aristotle for the age. Some authors thus refer to "Thomism" (and "neo-Thomism").

16. In higher education, scholasticism is often *the* major basis of the training musicians get in music theory and history, both of which are thus taught for their own sake as disciplines, and not *as*, *through*, or *directly for* their relevance to praxis.

17. Reimer further confuses the term "aesthetics" by mixing the aesthetic philosophy of Langer (which is in the Kantian idealist metaphysical tradition) with that of Dewey (which is naturalist, pragmatist, and thus antimetaphysical and anti-Kantian). Regardless of this additional level of confusion, music educators who are unsophisticated in such matters flocked to Reimer's philosophy because it made a nice, noble, and profound-sounding rationale for their efforts. Its emphasis on intellectualized contemplation of presentational symbols of feeling and its structure-of-the-discipline approach both comported well with the overall neoscholasticism of the school—particularly in the general music classroom, to which Reimer also contributed a basal song series predicated on his theory. Given that aesthetic ideas are abstract and thus neutral with regard to artistic medium, Reimer's song series also advanced a version of aesthetic education that drew on related arts.

18. Some of these themes are mentioned in the discussion of curriculum—however, even there, not in a direct or comprehensive way.

19. Dewey is mentioned, though mostly in connection with curriculum theory rather than in terms of the broader contributions Dewey can bring to praxial theory as a leader in applying pragmatism to schooling and as an alternative to Kantian aesthetics.

20. And for the phenomenologist Merleau-Ponty, it is thoroughly embodied in key ways, thus overcoming the mind-body dualism of Kantian and most analytic aesthetic theory, which disembodies the musical experience to a purely rational realm of ideas. The constructivism of contemporary cognitive psychology also supports basic tenets of praxialism in music that have to do with the "affordances" of music, mentioned below.

21. Which, for pragmatists, always involves a social mind, because experience is always socially situated, amplified and laden with sociality. In contrast, the existential view of experience denies or, perhaps more accurately, resists or rejects the givenness of social meaning in favor of emphasizing the individual mind and individualizing aspects of experience—sometimes, alas, at the expense of other(s), a theme of some existential novelists.

22. An "affordance," as discussed by DeNora (2001) in connection with music, is a fea-

ture of a thing that can be appropriated and used in different ways according to different needs, intentions, and values of an individual. A nonmusical example is a tennis ball that is intended for tennis, but also "good for" playing with dogs and in other games, and even, cut in half, as a doorstop. The features of music that afford different (sometimes even contradictory) uses and meanings are infinitely more complex yet no less central to the meanings and values resulting from varied appropriations and interpretations of those features. One can, for example, actually choose to dance to jazz, and thus not to listen for virtues and values that are missed on account of the physical activity.

23. Given the particulars of an instantiation, musicianship may require adaptation, even innovation. Many common musical practices, including those here called ubiquitous and "everyday," do not have routine conditions and thus lack set regulating rules (routine musicianship or other governing variables, etc.). See DeNora (2001) for some examples.

24. For the pros and (mainly) cons of defining praxis as a kind of rule following, see Schatzki et al. (2001, 9, 26, 50, 53, 95, 122 [and a variety of entries in the index concerned with "rules"]). Differences between practice theorists on this account can have a specific bearing on music praxis to the degree that, for instance, musicianship is regarded as "rule following." Such rule following can appear not only as, for example, rules of voice leading in Bach, but to the degree that, say, a backbeat or intonation is claimed to have rule-governed criteria.

25. If "music is good relative to the type of praxis," then the purposes for which a "type" of praxis exists to begin with determine the criteria for the "goodness" of the music. Thus, for example, various amateur, naive, everyday, recreational, and social musical practices—all of which use-functions I accord the full status of praxis, not reserving the term solely for established or "high" musical traditions or musical types of any sort—have their own criteria of goodness and their own unique musical value. For his part, Elliott seems to understand praxis as encompassing certain traditional types, genres, and styles of music. The result is, first of all, to distance the music from the important constituting use-conditions that originally brought the type of praxis into being (historically and for the moment) and to instead focus too singly on the subsequent regulating conditions (musicianship) that sustain it as a type—though even those evolve, are less stable, or vary more according to the instantiation than Elliott may prefer to allow (see Regelski 2002–2003 for the distinction between constituting and regulating conditions and on the status or use-functions behind socially created practices such as music). Secondly, by focusing on such musical traditions or types of music, the wider and more abundant musical practices of everyday personal, social, and cultural life—music as worship, ceremony, celebration, "a good time" (recreation), therapy, entertainment, "making special" (Dissanayake 1990, 1992), and the like—can end up being ignored or seen as somehow musically deficient or unworthy, and thus not particularly worth addressing via curriculum. The status of and regard for such musical praxis is at least unclear in *Music Matters*. That such musics are ubiquitous among large portions of a population could point to the need to expand their importance or resources via schooling, not to address instead the more inaccessible musics of certain narrow or small taste publics.

26. And to making sure that curriculum-as-apprenticeship is not merely a practicum in techne. Entire books (e.g., Dunne 1993; Grundy 1987) have been devoted to the distinction; it is that important. It is not realistic to expect that Elliott would or could delve very deeply into the subject, but his few discussions of praxis (and, particularly, the brief attempts at distinguishing techne from praxis; 1995, 69–70) miss or underrepresent the complexities and subtleties that need to be addressed to some effective degree in consideration of curriculum predi-

cated on praxis. For a précis of these distinctions—just in Aristotelian terms—and their importance for curriculum, see Grundy 1987, chapter 10—a work Elliott otherwise cites as opposing the kind of "technical rationality" that comes in curricular thinking from insufficient attention to the differences between techne and praxis.

27. In institutionalizing certain practices, over several generations institutions become more and more remote from the conditions and problems they originally served. The practices themselves (including musical ones), then, come to be seen as the raison d'être for the institution and are preserved and protected even when, because conditions have changed, the practices no longer serve the original problems or meet the original needs. This conservative stasis is seen conspicuously in many practices institutionalized as part of primary and secondary level schooling and not a few aspects of music pedagogy at tertiary levels of music education.

28. Or considering the widely diverse instances that, say, the blues can take, not even considering truly innovative changes within an established praxis.

29. Many ubiquitous kinds of musical praxis are served by quite basic musical abilities, a truism that trained musicians often overlook. Thus the church choir may in fact favor the intelligibility of the chorale text and plenty of fermatas over the artistic tone quality and well-shaped line favored by concert choir directors. Such musicians may regard such supposedly low-level musical expertise as reason to ignore or devalue such practices as musically unworthy or as musics to avoid (or as annoyance, such as the professional musician enduring a church choir's tone). An extreme example of the assumption that even a ubiquitous practice requires high-level skills came recently when a new mother, a conservatory-trained violinist, admitted to me that she refused to sing to her newborn child because she had poor vocal tone and technique!

30. The musicianship must serve the needs of the praxis; this is often a matter of kind, not degree or level.

31. In comparison to either techne or praxis, Aristotle saw theoria as the decidedly superior route to the "good life." Reliance on Aristotle alone for an understanding of praxis must also eventually run afoul of his metaphysics and other impediments. Thus, subsequent thinkers who have expanded on Aristotle's original distinction in their own ways give a still evolving substance and importance to the idea of praxis. They need to be consulted to gain the fullest understanding of the conditions and significance of praxis, musical and otherwise, in human life. A considerable part of this literature exists in social theory rooted at least in part in sociology and social psychology. Pragmatists such as James and Dewey actually form a bridge between philosophy and such social theory and create a hybrid social philosophy that, for example, in George Herbert Mead (1938), stresses social aspects of mind and action that have been ignored or denied by mainstream and analytic philosophers with their roots in Descartes and the traditions sketched earlier in this essay.

32. While it is useful to speak of musical affordances as objective or physical features of musical reality, their existence, too, is highly interpretative and variable—e.g., the existence, location, and significance of a modulation.

33. At stake here, too, are the semiotics of space. Spaces are created with certain meanings and values in mind. A Gothic cathedral, then, is a space the symbolic meanings of which have a bearing on what takes place in that space. Even a concert (of sacred or secular) music in a church setting can be significantly influenced by the spatial semiotic. A contrasting semiotic of space is at work in the typical concert hall (see Small 1998). Jazz heard from a proscenium stage or in a church can sometimes suffer from, or at least needs to overcome, the semiotics of such spaces in comparison to spaces in which it is most typically heard. In a thoroughly

secular space, then, sacred texts no longer serve their liturgical functions and secular texts in a church service thereby gain liturgical affordances.

34. When praxis is regarded as a type or genre of music, the further issue is raised concerning styles within a genre. Thus, can a jazzer whose expertise is in, say, only hard bop, listen intelligently to, say, free jazz or Dixieland? And, in the art music traditions, can those whose expertise ranges only from the baroque to late romanticism listen to, say, late-twentieth-century or pre-Renaissance musics? And what of the musicianship (not just technical) variables that obtain between various instruments? Is, say, an orchestral percussionist in a position to intelligently listen to, say, saxophone literature, or can a trombonist ascertain the esoterics of musicianship involved in the standard art song literature? And is, say, a person who took piano lessons in the classics thereby automatically enabled to listen intelligently to orchestral music, opera, chamber literature of all kinds, etc.? How "practice-specific (or 'situated')" (Elliott 1995, 54) must musicianship be in order for musicing to be "intelligent"? When the Canadian Brass plays arrangements, is this a new praxis of its own requiring its own expertise (because such performances often fall outside many of the typical musicianship and artistry expectations of the original literature)?

35. To the argument that details of technique are essential to the music's being properly or intelligently music, I offer that praxial theory, as I have understood and explained it, with its constituting conditions and defining connections to other important affordances of importance to musical meaning and value, in fact is evidence against either technicist or essentialist claims. Technique is but one affordance offered by any music. While it is true that a deficiency of technique (or musicianship) relative to the regulating needs of a certain praxis negatively affects the values involved, I submit again that expertise, broadly understood, is relative to the requirements of a praxis, and that the use-function of any praxis for a particular individual or circumstance is often satisfied by criteria of expertise that are situation specific. Thus my playing of jazz or Mozart can be fully satisfying *to me* (the sole beneficiary of such praxis) regardless of any negative comparisons to professional standards. And the ordinary listener in concert audiences often brings all kinds of variables to bear on listening—many developed as learning from repeated listening—that would be decried by, say, the intellectual interests of trained musicians in the same audience. For more on this, see Regelski 2000.

36. And a listener who grew up in a home of, say, a pianist who played jazz or a family of opera lovers will informally hone listening skills despite a personal lack of performance skills.

37. Professional musicians (i.e., those earning a living by performing) in various genres sometimes assume that the audience exists in order to give them the opportunity of making a living, as opposed to the musical profession's existing to serve the people. Section players in some fine ensembles sometimes give such evidence of having lost the raison d'être of their musical expertise, and the star system of virtuosi (in all genres) also has its critics for this same reason (e.g., Lebrecht 1997).

38. Nor, again, in musical praxis that is disembodied from the social and personal instantiations by which the musical affordances at stake are given particular meaning and power.

39. Compare "musicianship," then, to "marriageship" or "doctorship," where results are highly variable according to the individuals affected by the praxis.

40. Thus treating concepts not as formal abstractions or ideas, but as cognitive skills.

41. No matter how simple a musical praxis might appear to be at first glance, some degree of further honing of particular kinds of musicianship is almost always desirable or possible. That musical practices are commonplace does not mean, on the other hand, that they cannot

profit from expansion, advancement, and development of various kinds—e.g.; the guitar player who learns to play in a new key, or who learns a new chord or new strums. A conceivable exception is amateur involvement seen by the agent as rewarding under present conditions of expertise—somewhat like the "duffers" in golf who are happy to shoot the same high score time after time because they enjoy the overall activity, of which the score (expertise) is only one affordance of meaning and value.

42. On how general knowledge and situated praxis interact, see Lave and Wagner 1991, 33–34.

43. Suzuki students are a notable exception, and something like the Suzuki method may be what Elliott might has in mind. Yet, even with that in mind, it is simply not practicable to approach each school student's music education in this way from such an early age, especially given the wide range of type of music praxis from which there is to choose. Thus, in Japan at least, the Suzuki method is typically taught outside the schools. Given typical school situations, in which there are twenty to thirty children in a class, an apprenticeship-practicum of the type created by Suzuki is just not workable. And, in any case, the Suzuki method also demonstrates the problems of treating a praxis as an autonomous collection of skills that, to be fully effective in praxis, needs to be inculcated from a very early age.

44. I typically argue that anyone who engages in musicing of any kind, at any level of expertise, is properly a "musician" (just as people will say "I'm a golfer" without implying any claim to expertise). Here, however, I'll lapse and use "nonmusician" to refer to people who either have not engaged in performance or composition to any significant degree—for example, those who listen to and enjoy avidly music in church and concert hall—or whose performance expertise is comparable to, say, the duffer in golf or the hunter who rarely succeeds with the hunt yet pursues the activity with zeal and pleasure.

45. As Grundy observes (1987, 185–189), traditions treated as autonomous do not necessarily represent "the good" required by *phronesis* for present situatedness and also necessitate other considerations if praxis is to be fully effective.

46. For an account of situated learning as an apprenticeship that centrally includes immersion in the social practice per se, see Lave and Wagner 1991, 49–52. These authors also make important clarifications of the idea and ideal of apprenticeship as a mode of learning (29–43).

47. How much depth in a tradition is enough to constitute the kind of enabling musicianship Elliott defends is arguable; findings from both cognitive psychology and ethnomusicology suggest that to experience musicing as a native would require a depth of musicianship that, if not entirely out of reach of most outsiders, certainly is not achievable in typical school circumstances.

48. It may be that the "critical matters" I observe are differences of emphasis: My own approach increasingly sees praxis as a social theory that has a central philosophical component, while Elliott seems to have concentrated more on strictly developing a philosophical theory. Nonetheless, given the social nature of music, I would contend that such a philosophical theory will profit from a more explicit detailing of social ingredients and implications, especially if it is to serve schooling, which is quintessentially a social institution.

References

Adler, M. J. 1994. *Art, the arts, and the great ideas*. New York: Macmillan.

Alperson, P. 1991. What should one expect from a philosophy of music education? *Journal of Aesthetic Education* 25 (3):215–229.

————. 1994. Music as philosophy. In P. Alperson, ed., *What is music? An introduction to the philosophy of music*. University Park: Pennsylvania State University Press.

Bennett, K. P., and M. D. LeCompte. 1990. *The ways schools work*. New York: Longman.

Bowman, W. 1991. A plea for pluralism: Variations on a theme by George McKay. In R. Colwell, ed., *Basic concepts in music education*, vol. 2. Niwot: University Press of Colorado.

————. 1996. Music without universals: Relativism reconsidered. In L. R. Bartel and D. J. Elliott, eds., *Critical reflections on music education*. Toronto: University of Toronto and Canadian Music Education Research Center.

————. 1998. *Philosophical perspectives on music*. New York: Oxford University Press

————. 2000. A somatic, "here and now" semantic: Music, body, and self. *Bulletin of the Council for Research in Music Education* 144:45–60.

Broudy, H. S. 1991. A realistic philosophy of music education. In R. Colwell, ed., *Basic concepts in music education*, vol. 2. Niwot: University Press of Colorado.

Csikszentmihalyi, M. 1990. *Flow: The psychology of optimal experience*. New York: Harper and Row.

DeNora, T. 2000. *Music in everyday life*. New York: Cambridge University Press.

Dewey, J. 1934/1980. *Art as experience*. New York: Perigee/Putnam's Sons.

Dissanayake, E. 1990. *What is art for?* Seattle: University of Washington Press.

————. 1992. *Homo aestheticus: Where art comes from and why*. New York: Free Press/ Macmillan.

Dixon, R. 1995. *The Baumgarten corruption: From sense to nonsense in art and philosophy*. East Haven, CT: Pluto Press.

Dunne, J. 1993. *Back to the rough ground: Phronesis and techne in modern philosophy and Aristotle*. Notre Dame: Notre Dame University Press.

Elliott, D. J. 1995. *Music matters: A new philosophy of music education*. New York: Oxford University Press.

Erskine, J. 1944. *What is music?* New York: J. B. Lippincott.

Farley, C. J. 1999. "Sounding the Waters." *Time*, 11 January, 95.

Grundy, S. 1987. *Curriculum: Product or praxis*. Philadelphia: Falmer Press.

Lakoff, G., and M. Johnson. 1999. *Philosophy in the flesh: The embodied mind and its challenge to Western thought*. New York: Basic Books.

Lave, J. and E. Wagner. 1991. *Situated learning: Legitimate peripheral participation*. Cambridge: Cambridge University Press.

Lebrecht, N. 1997. *Who killed classical music?* Secaucus, NJ: Birch Lane Press/Carol Communications.

Mead, G. H. 1938. *The philosophy of the act*. Chicago: University of Chicago Press

Polanyi, M. 1962. *Personal knowledge: Towards a post-critical philosophy*. Chicago: University of Chicago Press.

Proudfoot, M. 1988. Aesthetics. In G. H. R. Parkinson, ed., *The handbook of Western philosophy*. New York: Macmillan.

Regelski, T. A. 1973. Self-actualization in creating and responding to art. *Journal of Humanistic Psychology* 13 (4):57–68.

————. 1996. Taking the "art" of music for granted: A critical sociology of the aesthetic philosophy of music. In L. R. Bartel and D. J. Elliott, eds., *Critical reflections on music education*. Toronto: University of Toronto /Canadian Music Education Research Center.

————. 1997. A prolegomenon to a praxial theory of music and music education. *Canadian Music Educator* 38 (3):43–51.

————. 1998a. Schooling for musical praxis. *Canadian Music Educator* 40 (1):32–43.

————. 1998b. Action learning: Curriculum and instruction as and for praxis. In M. McCarthy, ed., *Proceedings of the Charles Fowler conference on arts education.* College Park: University of Maryland Press.

————. 1998c. The Aristotelian bases of praxis for music and music education. *Philosophy of Music Education Review* 6 (1):22–59.

————. 1999. Action learning: Curriculum and instruction as and for praxis. In M. McCarthy, ed., Music education as praxis, 97–120. College Park: University of Maryland Press.

————. 2000. Accounting for all praxis: An essay critique of David Elliott's *Music Matters. Bulletin of the Council for Research in Music Education* 144:61–88.

————. 2002. On "methodolatry" and music teaching as "critical" and reflective praxis. *Philosophy of Music Education Review,* 10 (2):102–124.

————. 2002. Musical values and the value of music education. *Philosophy of Music Education Review* 10(1): 49–55.

Reimer, B. 1989a. *A philosophy of music education.* Englewood Cliffs, NJ: Prentice-Hall.

————. 1989b. "Music education as aesthetic education." *Music Educators Journal* (in 2 parts) 75 (6):22–28; 75 (7):26–32.

Russell, P. A. 1997. Musical tastes and society. In D. J. Hargreaves and A. C. North, eds., *The social psychology of music.* New York: Oxford University Press.

Schatzki, T. R., K. K. Cetina, and E. V. Savigny. 2001. *The practice turn in contemporary theory.* London: Routledge.

Schwadron, A. 1967. *Aesthetics: Dimensions for music education.* Washington, DC: Music Educators National Conference.

Shepherd, J. 1991. *Music as social text.* Cambridge: Polity Press.

Shepherd, J., and P. Wicke. 1997. *Music and cultural theory.* Cambridge: Polity Press.

Small, C. 1998. *Musicking: The meanings of performing and listening.* Hanover, NH: Wesleyan University Press.

Tyler, R. 1949. *Basic principles of curriculum and construction.* Chicago: University of Chicago Press.

Wittgenstein, L. 1966. *Lectures and conversations on aesthetics, psychology and religious belief.* Ed. C. Barrett. Los Angeles: University of California Press.

Zillmann, D., and S. Gan. 1997. Musical taste in adolescence. In D. J. Hargreaves and A. C. North, eds., *The social psychology of music.* New York: Oxford University Press.

13

Critical Matters in Early Childhood Music Education

SHEILA C. WOODWARD

Children are not simply musical embryos waiting to become musical adults but have a musical culture of their own, with its own musical and social rules, and with functions such as integration of person and expression of ethnicity.

—Bruno Nettl, foreword to Patricia Shehan Campbell,
Songs in Their Heads (1998)

Musicality is an inherited biological predisposition that is unique to the human species (Blacking 1973; Papoušek 1996). The psychobiological source of music—musicality in human motives—is "a talent inherent in the unique way human beings move, and hence experience their world, their bodies and one another" (Trevarthen 1999, 155). The robustness of the evolved human capacity to perceive pitch, duration, intensity, and temporal or spatial patterning of sounds at birth, and even earlier, is well documented. In a few decades, the music education literature has progressed from proclaiming that neonates are unable to perceive rhythm (Moog 1976) to an undeniable acknowledgement that musical experience begins with the first perceptions of sound in the womb (Woodward 1992a, 1992b).

The critical matters I wish to address in this chapter are that music learning (whether structured or informal) happens very early, and long before we used to believe, and that it takes place as a result of children's innate propensity for learning. Indeed, young children are natural music makers. All children possess musical intelligence and the capacity for developing musicianship, not just as consumers, but also as performers and creators of music. Furthermore, children's spontaneous music making, from the first mother-infant musical interactions to playground rhymes and jeers, is the springboard of music learning. However, the contexts in which early musical experiences occur are critical, and adult interventions require balancing challenge and skill to achieve musical focus and self-growth in young children, as Elliott suggests teachers should do at all ages.

Musical Understanding, Memory, and Spontaneity

"Inside a young child are many songs."

—Barbara Andress, *Music for Young Children* (1998)

Today, the nature of children's musicality is being acutely observed, from the earliest neurophysiological and cognitive responses at the fetal stage, to the first vocalizations of the neonate, to more advanced stages of listening, performing, and composing in the later stages of early childhood. Investigations of musical competence in very young children reveal that children display musical understandings and abilities far beyond what previous scholars expected or recognized. For example, early infant vocalizations evidence many musical features (Dissanayake 2000). Trevarthen's (1999) research with infants elucidates the rhythmic and prosodic foundations of sympathetic engagement in expressive exchanges. Pitch matching, auditory recognition, and musical anticipation are all present in infants' sound making (Minami and Nito 1996).

Relinquishing the instructor mode, today's researchers are stepping back to observe young children's musical explorations in their natural free play (Campbell 1998; Custodero 1998; Littleton 1991; Moorhead and Pond 1978; Tarnowski 1996). Some children younger than three have a reliable feeling for the beat of music, sing with pitch accuracy, and can imitate or pick out a simple tune on an instrument (McLaughlin 1994; Suzuki 1969). A computerized rhythm performance test showed that more than half of three-year-old children tested in the United States, South Africa, and Australia could tap a steady beat (Flohr, Woodward, and Suthers 1998).

Thus, as our bank of information on young children's musical abilities expands, we become increasingly aware of how little we know about children's musical capacities. However, what we do see is that children spontaneously make music in free play both alone and in groups; they communicate and express their thoughts and feelings through music; they create and imitate melodies and rhythms; they chant, beat, tap, stamp, dance, or clap, using whole songs, short fragments, individual words, nonsense syllables, games, calls, jeers, rhymes, exclamations, and stories (Campbell 1998; Custodero 2000; Omi 1992). They make music on and with their heads, fingers, hands, limbs, or whole bodies, incorporating musical and/or nonmusical objects into their music making. Some children's spontaneous music making uses melodies and rhythms that have been passed on through generations; others are more recent; some are spur-of-the-moment improvisations.

Although we know that children are musically responsive and active from their earliest days, we are still largely speculating about their early cognitive experiences and understandings of music. As a result, we may underestimate the musical learning capacity of young children. (Consider that a child may carry out an instruction to fetch a ball before he or she can say the words or describe what he or she is doing.) Thus, the literature supports Elliott's explanations that, through "procedural" and "impressionistic" knowledge, a child can sense what musical decisions to make without necessarily being able to explain why ("formal" knowledge). Similarly, Wendy Sims (1995) has documented that musical understanding may occur long before a child's capacity for production. Furthermore, Sims observed that children were often able to demonstrate understanding and discrimination through imitation before verbalization. Indeed, young children sometimes show difficulty verbally expressing themselves about music (Flowers 1993; McMahon 1986; Sims 1990). However, this does not detract from their ability to be deeply moved by it, nor does it limit their awareness of variations in melody, rhythm, tone color, and so forth.

Anecdotal evidence of children's musical understandings implores us to investigate rigorously the early musical learning of young children. An Australian mother told me that whenever she played the piano to her baby son she had the habit of saying the name of the relevant composer as she started each performance. His obvious pleasure in listening to the works caused her to repeat the repertoire during his first years. When he was eighteen months of age, the mother did not need to say the composers' names. The boy would spontaneously respond to the first few notes of those same pieces by identifying the appropriate name of the composer. My own eighteen-month-old son, Dayne, heard Scottish bagpipes being played on a beach in South Africa. I told him, "Those are bagpipes." We did not hear or speak of bagpipes again until two weeks later when bagpipes sounded on the radio. Dayne leapt up spontaneously saying, "Bagpipes! Bagpipes!" In neither of these situations was it the intention to teach the child to verbally respond to the music. However, their spontaneous verbal responses are clear indications of an early infant ability to cognize and recognize components of music, such as tone color, melody, and rhythm.

A South African mother told me how her four-year-old daughter reacted strongly to a particular style of religious music. The previous time this music had been played in her home was during a time of tragedy in her life, when the child was only six months old. The mother would hold the baby in her arms and grieve while listening to recordings of that religious music. Now, hearing this style of music at four years of age, the child told her, "Don't play that music, Mommy, it makes you cry!"

Now consider this question about musical quality: what musical mode is an infant learning when he or she is daily exposed to a wind-up toy that is out of tune? Some think it is acceptable to give children's institutions old pianos that are beyond their prime and out of tune on the assumption that "they won't know the difference." A music professor at the University of South Florida, Tom Brantley, recounted how his two-year-old son spontaneously ran to the television in response to a particular jazz rendition of superior quality. The diversion of the child's attention from his previous activity (during which other music had been playing), and his lengthy engrossment in this particular piece, was dramatic, leading Brantley to speculate about his child's musical understanding.

Most people lose any conscious memory of sounds. However, anecdotal evidence of prenatal music memory does exist. As described earlier in this chapter, auditory memory is evident even from before birth. For example, Hepper (1988) showed that neonates exposed to the music of a television soap opera that their mothers had listened to daily during pregnancy displayed behavioral responses remarkably distinct from those of babies whose mothers had not watched the program. Then, again, a South African mother explained to me how her two-year-old ran up to her in response to hearing a radio broadcast of a particular opera. The mother believed that the last time the child could have heard this music was when she was pregnant and performing the opera nightly. The child's excited words were: "That's my music! That's my music!" Similarly, Thomas Verny (1981) tells us that the conductor Boris Brott recounted to his mother that, when conducting certain scores for the first time, he would know the flow of the piece before turning the page. He found an explanation: these were the same pieces that his mother had been playing while pregnant with him. These glimpses into the early musical perception and memory provide a strong impetus for further investigation.

Whether experimenting, improvising, or imitating, young children demonstrate frequent use of repetition, extension, variation, and representation to construct their understandings (Custodero 1998; Gromko 1994, 1996). Some sounds are intentionally used to creatively represent people, objects, situations, or emotions. Most often, musical play is intricately interwoven with movement—whole-body twisting, turning, and dancing, all the way down to tiny finger movements or head bouncing. Sometimes children's musical play accompanies other activities such as role-play acting, drawing, playing games, playing with toys, and using playground equipment. Through their music making, they express their values and intimate thoughts. We see their opinions, prejudices, judgments, hurt, anger, and delight expressed in vocal chants and rhythmic motifs. Children's emotional experiences in music making and listening are generally very evident in their behavior. We see how music soothes or stimulates them in myriad ways. We watch them express emotions, images, and stories in music making (Campbell 1998; Omi 1992). At times they incorporate elements of music they have been taught by adults and peers, including nursery rhymes and playground chants. Some children approximate styles and motifs from commercial recordings that form part of their day-to-day life. They twist and turn the material in novel and unusual ways.

Early Childhood Music Education and Praxialism

> Children are "incipient musicians all, awaiting the intervention and stimulation of strong instructional programs."
>
> —Patricia Shehan Campbell, *Songs in Their Heads* (1998)

The key factor to consider in any discussion on early childhood music education is that music learning takes place from before birth, whether adults play an active role in the process or not. Through a natural process of enculturation, young children learn the musical culture of their environment (Sloboda 1985). More and more research appears to be corroborating Elliott's proposal that, worldwide, children begin to make sense of their culture's musical sounds early, without formal education. He explains that young children learn to distinguish the sounds of their music from other sounds;

to separate their culture's music from other Musics; to identify and remember familiar musical patterns; and to tell when their music is beginning, ending, or repeating.

However, parents, families, teachers, and the community play a significant role in early music learning by influencing the musical environment available to the young child, whether informally or formally. Scott-Kassner (1992) proposes that parents provide from a child's earliest days a structured yet flexible music education that takes place naturally in everyday life. They should balance a lifestyle that includes spontaneously occurring musical activities with others that are predetermined and designed specifically to meet the current musical and motivational level of the child in order to develop his or her music-listening and music-making abilities.

The essence of early childhood music education matches the core of the praxial philosophy. Elliott defines music as a diverse human practice of music listening and music making; he insists that music education must, by its nature, be practice based. This concept is naturally suited to the needs of young children. Just as listening and speaking are essential to speech acquisition, listening and music making are essential for the development of musicianship (Gruhn 1999). The foundational principles of many internationally recognized approaches to early childhood music education (e.g., Orff, Kodály, Suzuki, and Dalcroze) concur with Elliott's theory that the most significant music learning for a young child is not formal knowledge about music, but the practical experience of it. Effective early instruction features teachers who demonstrate rather than explain and children who imitate and create rather than sit silently (Campbell 1991). Furthermore, like praxialism, these venerated approaches are designed for all children in the belief that all normal children possess musical intelligence and the capacity for musicianship. Also, these approaches dovetail with Elliott's belief that children's musicianship is developed through the combination of listening and making music and accompanying processes: reflecting on the sounds created and how actions alter those sounds; determining goals for sound production; and solving and seeking musical problems. Orff, Kodály, Dalcroze, and Suzuki also recognized that children's practical experience of musical concepts can internalize learning without direct verbal knowledge thereof.

Furthermore, as Elliott posits, it is widely accepted that evaluations of young children's music learning are more appropriately achieved through observations of children's musical performing, composing, and improvising than through verbal responses, and those observations have been shown to be more accurate (Sims 1995). (Elliott describes performance as the ultimate nonverbal description of a work. The level of musical understanding is conveyed in the quality of musical interpretation.)

Early music education models commonly reflect Elliott's proposal that the role of adult intervention lies in the selection and presentation of musical challenges that confront children with "real" situations that contain "problems" to solve in context. They concur with Elliott's tenet that these challenges are designed to take children beyond slavish memorization and repetition, engaging their attention on musical problem targeting and solving. Further investigative research might illuminate other related issues: descriptions of optimal musical experiences for young children at each stage from before birth; whether these experiences meet children's emotional, physical, and cognitive readiness and needs; the kinds of contexts in which these experiences should occur; and the long-term musical and nonmusical benefits thereof.

Context Issues

All musical experiences are culture-specific and take place in very particular contexts. For example, even before birth, the fetus's heart rate adjusts as a result of the
emotional response of the mother when she listens to music (Zimmer et al. 1982).
Also, since infants express their listening responses in nonverbal or verbal ways, Elliott's interpretation of listening as thinking-in-action and knowing-in-action seems
entirely plausible. Indeed, we see this in the fetus who remembers, discriminates between different sounds, and analyzes the significance of sounds in context (Leader et
al. 1982). We observe the neonate remembering of sounds, turning toward sounds,
giving attention to them, and showing distinct modifications in behavior to activate
familiar sounds (De Casper and Fifer 1980). Infants may be quietly mesmerized when
listening to one piece of music and bob up and down to another. Young children's verbal and nonverbal interpretations and representations of music appear context-based,
as expressed by their original characterizations of musical works as "tall," "fizzy,"
"bearlike," or "sleepy." Elliott explains that the very young typically display responses that appear to be subjective, strongly influenced by context, and potentially
conditioned by adult responses. Elliott specifically warns against music teachers' assigning their own emotional and representational descriptions to music on behalf of
children. Doing so may minimize the essence and intricacies of the music and apply
a very individual "teacher's" response that would limit the child's musical thinking
and understanding. We see the negative effects of this, for example, if young children
automatically categorize all music in a minor mode as "sad."

Furthermore, much music, including certain children's music, is designed to be
representational or depict specific emotion. For example, when children elect to hop
like a rabbit or swim like a turtle in response to different styles of music, they may be
able to display their musical thinking and understanding better then they would in
verbal descriptions. Of course, one needs to be aware of the possibility of misinter-
preting children's nonverbal actions and judging their responses according to our own
contextual interpretations. As they advance, children develop more intricate ways of
expressing their musical understandings that increasingly reflect their cultural and
contextual experience of music.

Much of the early childhood music literature correlates with Elliott's theory that
children develop their musicianship in culture-based and practice-centered ways of
musical thinking. Through formal and informal music education, children are inducted into music cultures that surround them. The interpretations, performances, improvisations, and compositions of young children are situated and social, drawing on
their past and present musical environments. Adults play an important role in contextualizing formal musical knowledge, allowing children to understand the practical
meanings and values of that knowledge in varieties of settings.

Custodero (1998) describes the context of music learning in early childhood as
crucial and complex. Tarnowski and Leclerc (1994) investigated different teaching
personalities, such as the "entertainer," the "director," and the "responder," as well as
the effect of having no teacher interaction at all. She determined that most children's
vocal explorations and singing behaviors occur when the teacher observes only. This
is consistent with Custodero's finding (1998) that noninstructional periods elicited

more self-initiated musical activity than adult-guided portions of preschoolers' music classes. Consider, too, that EEG activity differences are noted in children during exposure to music, influenced by contextual experiences of music training (Flohr et al. 1996). Barrett (1990) suggests that a context in which learning experiences are reflective of the natural learning model, and in which children are encouraged to make original statements in the medium of music, is the most effective for music learning to occur.

So, early childhood musical experiences should occur in a context of acceptance, and of playful, positive exploration in which appropriate adult intervention involves guiding children rather than training them. There must also be tolerance for the young child's time needs "to adapt, integrate, participate and learn" (Poch de Grätzer 1999, 52). Indeed, young children sometimes struggle to achieve coordination between what their minds intend doing and what their bodies achieve. When facilitating musical experiences for the very young, respect for their choice of activity is imperative. Adult intervention should aim to coach rather than to push or force. A context in which children experience musical actions as intrinsically meaningful will impact children's learning (Barrett 1992).

Children's early music making absorbs the characteristics of their musical cultures and environments. From the first vocal pitch matching observed in infants, imitation is an active manifestation of learning through enculturation. With increasing movement of population groups globally, teachers in many parts of the world are working with groups of children who come from a wide diversity of cultures. By giving status to children's own musical cultures in the formal music education environment, and by using their spontaneous music making as a springboard for adult-directed learning programs, we can provide contexts that offer children security and respect.

"Flow" in Early Childhood Musical Experiences

Elliott's praxial philosophy of music education promotes not only the appreciation of musical works, but also a depth of learning and understanding that constitutes an achievement of self-growth. Maslow's (1970) early constructs describe a hierarchy of human needs (physical, emotional, and intellectual) in which each layer of the pyramid is essential in achieving self-realization in the individual.

Elliott offers that music is less a human need than a tendency, in which musicers and listeners find many values in acts of making and listening to music. He argues that the primary values underlying the purposes of musical practices are musical enjoyment, self-knowledge, and self-growth. The dynamic nature of most musical practices provides the conditions for the ongoing development of self-esteem. Elliott refers to the "flow" experience described by Csikszentmihalyi (1990, 1996, 1997) as a state in which challenge and capacity are entwined, creating an internal balance that facilitates self-growth. A mismatch in the level of challenge or skill will hinder flow, causing feelings of apathy, boredom, or anxiety. Elliott describes "flow" as a lack of obstruction, a focused purposefulness, and an ease of action. Furthermore, he proposes that achieving self-growth and flow leads to higher levels of self-esteem.

Lori Custodero (1997) has operationalized the idea of flow in early childhood music education. She demonstrates that flow is observable both in young children's free musical play and in structured learning environments with adult intervention. When children are engrossed in making music, they are not just using a tool to create something outside of themselves, they become the music. That is, their attention is diverted away from their physical and psychological selves to their musical activities. The doer becomes one with his or her chosen pursuit. This merging of the self with the intent of the self is particularly apparent as children create spontaneous representations in music; they appear not only musically to act the part of the represented character, but to become the character.

When adults help children record their improvisations using original schemes of notation, or words or stories that name and describe their works, or audio and video recordings, the children can exhibit a heightened awareness of ownership of their musical creations. Custodero (2000) points out that children have a need for a sense of agency; she reminds us that to be in flow, the individual must have sense of control over the activity, a feeling that what he or she does matters. In order to sustain flow, strategies must be spontaneously adjusted to balance challenge and skill. Custodero has found that children have the motivation and ability to do this for themselves. She believes that children's views of what counts as a challenge in an activity is evidenced in their conscious attempts at self-correction (problem solving) and self–assignment (problem finding). In young children, focus on a musical task is seen to be consistent with deliberateness of gesture (Custodero 2000). This deliberateness can be seen in children's careful execution of sounds with particular characters — soft or loud, long or short, E or E-flat. Thus, teaching strategies must ensure that young children are sure of the goals for the task, have opportunities for meaningful action, and possess the necessary skills to sustain a level of flow.

Children display distinct enjoyment in musical activities. Optimal musical flow experience presents itself in young children as their total immersion in the music (however short-lived): a total focus and a loss of self-awareness. Young children are capable of relatively long attention spans, not the few seconds or minutes sometimes accredited to them (Littleton 1991). Custodero (1998) demonstrates that, by the age of four, children "need longer blocks of time to discover, self-correct, expand, and extend their musical experience." Observing children in weekly music sessions, Custodero discovered that the introduction of new material resulted in less flow than interactions with more familiar material. This may be due to the attention required to define goals for the new activity. Musical flow was experienced within two to four weeks after introduction of a new activity. Thereafter, it appeared appropriate for adults to intervene to offer further complexities and novelties.

However, adult intervention has the potential to restrict children's flow experiences by diverting their focused music making. There is a strong distinction between what Custodero calls "invited" and "uninvited" intervention in children's music making. Indeed, it is important for teachers to know when to intervene and when to allow children the extra time they need for self-discovery. A child's self-consciousness can be triggered by a teacher's verbal announcements, including instructions and praise that distract children from their concentrated listening. Teacher's talk can divert a child's attention from the music to the self. This may be avoided, however, by guiding children's music making with recognizable nonverbal signals, or by reserving comments for periods of time before and after children's musical engagements.

On several occasions, I have witnessed adults interrupting and obstructing young children's focused music listening or making. On one occasion, four- and five-year-old children attending a children's theatrical music production in Athlone, South Africa, could not contain their joy in the music. They spontaneously clapped the beat to the songs, moving and jiving in their seats. The producer stopped the show. He walked to the front of the stage and told the children in a stern manner that they were not to clap along, as they would not hear the words of the songs. Thereafter, the subdued children's joy in the music evaporated. Clearly, the producer was unaware that community participation in music making is a natural phenomenon in many African cultures. But, in fact, I have witnessed events where children responded in a similar fashion in many parts of the world.

On another occasion, a teacher in an elementary classroom in the United States facilitated a magical experience of Halloween, where eight-year-olds acted as witches and ghosts, accompanied by eerie musical sounds they created. One child, who was showing more enthusiasm for musical expression than any other, was told to remove himself and sit at the side of the room because his movements were overexuberant. His spirit was visibly crushed, along with his enjoyment of the music. Here is another complexity in music education: teachers face serious difficulties when they must balance the control requirements of formal education settings with the need to nurture children's freedom of musical expression.

Besides the intrinsic motivation in musical activity, Custodero (2000) demonstrates that young children sometimes show a need for external motivation: for example, seeking approval, permission, or camaraderie in their musical activities from facilitators, parents, and peers. She observes that the "afterglow" of being in musical flow often leads to an awareness of success, which manifests itself in children's desires to share their joyful experiences with a significant other. Custodero suggests that "the social context of learning and flow experience is crucial and complex" (24).

Elliott's designation of flow as one primary value of music education matches current early childhood practices and research. The core process of early music learning involves the emergence of children's innate musicality through active musical experiences. This active process of learning through constructivist enculturation can be enhanced or obstructed by adult intervention; it requires a delicate balancing of challenge and skill. Custodero's model advocates children as agents of their own learning. Adults can complement children's spontaneous music making and self-initiated learning with guidance and demonstrations that foster listening, performance, and improvisatory skills, thereby facilitating the quality of children's musical experiences.

Practical Applications: Multiculturalism

Elliott's strong arguments (1989, 1990, 1995) for providing a multicultural curriculum are widely operationalized in early childhood music education (Andress 1998; Campbell and Scott-Kassner 1995; Van Rysselberghe 1992). Early music education programs should promote and protect the rights of all children to practice their musical cultures, to love their cultures, to realize their cultural aspirations, and to achieve cultural reconciliation with one another. As Elliott suggests, to begin with, every child should be immersed in the music of his or her own culture. A child's music is his or her identity, his or her natural musical home.

It is through the indigenous musics of their cultures that children receive the stories of their people, those that ancestors pass down from generation to generation, and others that are contemporary and reflect new customs. Folk music is the treasure trove of children's values, beliefs, cultures, knowledge, games, and stories. The music of children's own cultures must be given respect and status in the classroom, indirectly giving children a sense of their own values and status. Receptivity toward the music of other cultures can be developed from this point of reference, thereby fostering cultural awareness, tolerance, and respect.

Ensuring early exposure to many musical cultures may play a key role in leading children to a position in later life where ethnocentrism may be diluted. The tendency "to view from one's own culture, to attribute superiority to one's own and to evaluate others in reference to one's own" may be less rigid when children grow up in a multicultural musical environment (Abeles et al. 1984; Sumner 1960). Children have the capability of being musically multicultural—learning several musical cultures simultaneously. It is widely recognized that young children who are well exposed to two or more spoken languages learn those languages with an accuracy of intonation and grammatical construction that is generally acquired with far less ease at a later age.

Whenever possible, age-appropriate music should be presented within its cultural context, giving children a good sense of the original social setting of the music, its meaning, and its associations. In respecting the music of different cultures, it is essential that the quality of the music of each culture be maintained with accurate representation. Perhaps one of teachers' greatest disservices to young children is their arbitrary translation of other culture's musical texts. Chen (1994) illustrates how putting Chinese words to Western folk tunes makes nonsense of the original texts. This is because the Chinese language is a tonal language and the melodies in any Chinese folksong match the natural pitch of the words.

It may seem obvious to state that the choice of music in a multicultural curriculum must be appropriate for young children. However, Manins (1996) points out his discovery of an elementary school textbook in New Zealand that included a Maori song. His investigation led to the translation: "The young man is a virile, energetic young man of great force, repeatedly thrusting!" Besides considering the appropriateness of lyrics, Manins stresses the need, where relevant, to ask leaders of indigenous cultures for their permission to use particular songs in early childhood music education. The reason is that only certain persons may intend particular songs for performance on specific occasions. To use music outside of its context would be dishonorable to the culture involved.

By building the multicultural musical experiences of the young, we are nurturing the familiar cultures of the children and facilitating their musical development within and across cultures. The musical experiences the children have now are those from which they create the music of their future.

Children's spontaneous and imitative music improvisations reflect their thinking, their criticisms, their values, and their aspirations. They represent transformations in their own evolving musical cultures. The global blending of musical cultures is manifest in the rich diversity emerging in contemporary musical cultures across the world. Young children who are subject to world influences are not only absorbing their own cultures; they are also in the process of creating what their dynamic musical cultures will become.

Early Music Making

Teachers use demonstration and imitation to lead children to explore new possibilities of musical experience. That children from as young as two years of age can acquire outstanding musical achievement through imitation (the same way they learn to speak the mother tongue) has been clearly demonstrated (Suzuki 1969).

From before birth, children learn the music of their environment through enculturation. Parents play a significant role in determining the quality of their children's early musical experiences. Thus, they might consider avoiding some of what is commercially labeled "children's music," which too often involves out-of-tune wind-up musical toys, recordings of poorly sung nursery rhymes, and inferior, electronically digitized music.

In free play situations, deferred imitations signal that children are remembering previous experiences. In their play centers, we hear children imitating parents, teachers, and siblings, rehearsing words and actions they have witnessed, and expanding on those words and actions as they improvise in dramatic form. Children often create improvisatory representations of previous experiences and reflect real-life experiences in their drawing, talking, and spontaneous singing. Custodero (1998) found that, when improvising, young children imitate each other more than their teachers and imitate their peers to adjust their flow experience—either to give them confidence in the right way to do things, or to give them ideas about how to make the activity more challenging. Thus, children should be immersed in an environment of rich musical experiences (Barrett 1990). Barrett regards real-life demonstrations of musical skills as an essential component of this environment, leading to children's active engagements.

Research suggests strongly that three- and four-year-olds are capable of responding to symbolic representation (Adachi 1992; Gromko and Poorman 1998a; Hetland 2000; Tommis and Fazey 1996). But for notations or symbols to be meaningful to a child, the child must see the connection between his or her experience and the symbol. If the symbol represents musical sound, the symbol must embody and convey what the child has felt and heard in ways that are sensible and meaningful to the child. When children invent their own notations or symbols for musical sounds, we find that what they draw reveals what they know. Children who show good perception of rhythms and melodies—through singing in tune and playing melodies accurately—reflect these musical abilities in the symbols they create (Gromko 1994). Furthermore, music instruction that includes having children read notations that are developmentally appropriate may significantly enhance children's memory for music's spatial-temporal sequence (Hetland 2000).

Because children must experience sounds before they can find symbolic notation meaningful, researchers have sought the conditions under which children's experiences of sound can be rich and engaging. They have devised nonverbal techniques involving imitation in an attempt to overcome children's difficulties in expressing themselves verbally (Sims 1986). Researchers have also designed choreographed dances that follow the rhythms and the contours of the music; results show that dances deepen children's engagement with musical sounds (Gromko and Poorman 1998b). In a recent study with elementary children as young as seven years, Fung and Gromko (2001) found children's experiences of sounds were significantly enhanced when children engaged in spontaneous kinesthetic actions while listening to whole compositions of world musics. Through interactive music experiences, children seem to liberate their capacity for anticipating, extending, and expanding musical materials (Custodero 1998).

Children do not learn to speak through reading their mother tongue. Their language acquisition is achieved aurally, and reading follows later. The importance of developing early aural skills is emphasized by informal observations of university students who, having been trained from early childhood to acquire performance skills through reading notation, have extreme difficulty learning to play by ear in early adulthood. It is as though a new language must be learned. Conversely, young adults who play by ear seem to struggle in learning music reading, indicating that early music learning should be facilitated in both areas. However, I would stress that children should experience a sound before any demonstration of its symbolic notation (see Tommis and Fazey 1996). Similarly, Barrett (1990) proposes that literacy should arise naturally from notating children's improvisatory compositions in various ways: indeed, use of standard Western notational procedures should be preceded by the development of children's own notational systems.

In a number of programs throughout the world, young infants are participating in formal music programs, imitating, understanding symbolic representation, improvising, and performing. Even eighteen-month-olds have demonstrated dispositions toward participating in adult-directed music-related activities (Metz 1989). Scott-Kassner (1992) recommends that we investigate whether implementing these formal programs for children under three years of age constitutes optimal musical experiences for long-term emotional and musical benefit.

Music Listening

According to Abeles, Hoffer, and Klotman (1984), the predominance of popular music in the child's environment has resulted in listening expectations peculiar to that medium. Abeles concludes that children's listening skills are being conditioned to accommodate high decibel levels, short time frames, and limited thematic development. Thus, children are less able to cope with the contrasting and evolving features that occur in art music.

In the commercial world, the manipulative powers of music are relentlessly thrust at children, in cinema, video, and radio broadcasts. The lucrative value of the "wallpaper music" found in shopping malls, restaurants, and entertainment venues involves the exploitation of children for financial gain.

Accordingly, developing children's ability to attend to recorded music is an important and valuable aspect of the curriculum (Sims 1986). Sims observes the benefits of maintaining eye contact with children during listening activities and involving children in movement activities that are directly responsive to prominent characteristics in the music. Compared to sitting passively, she finds that children engaged in relevant movement activities attend longer. Sim's research leads her to question old theories that small children have short listening spans.

Working with groups, we face the problem of accommodating the different listening stances of different children. Unfortunately, some teachers attempt to solve this by gearing the length of listening to those with the shortest listening spans, ignoring the listening needs of those with longer spans. Sims recommends we provide young children with regular opportunities to listen to music individually, for as long as they like (e.g., provide access to a classroom listening center with playback equipment and headphones).

Elliott's focus in this area lies more with the listening that takes place in performing, improvising, and composing. Practice-based methodologies in early childhood music education inherently incorporate Elliott's idea that children learn to listen primarily by listening for their own efforts to make music well and make artistic musical choices, assessing the outcomes of their choices and generating alternatives (with teachers' guidance, of course). Elliott points out that children's decisions are the result not only of formal education, but also of informal learning and of the children's intuitions that one musical action sounds better than another. He explains that music making places the child-as-listener inside the musical works and practices they are experiencing.

Creativity

Musical creativity appears to be a natural proclivity in young children. However, many teachers observe a decline in improvisatory music making as children begin formal schooling. We need to investigate whether our traditional teaching methods are responsible for this phenomenon, particularly those that are notation centered and technique based and neglect the development of composition and improvisation skills. Formal music education for young children should cherish and nurture their individual needs for expression, spontaneity, and originality. It should avoid viewing children as absorbing and regurgitating entities; instead, programs should facilitate flow through spontaneous improvisatory music making. In alignment with Elliott's concept of educating children's musicianship through meaningful music making, Andress (1998, 1) promotes programs that provide "exploratory and participatory music play experiences that nurture children's natural propensity for music."

Elliott proposes that adult intervention in children's creative musical activity needs to be seen in terms of providing an emotionally safe, affirming environment that is receptive to creativity, encourages risks, encourages children to create and to formulate multiple approaches to musical problems in improvisation and composition, and provides helpful feedback. Indeed, by observing children's creative musical works, we gain insights into their musical development that enable us to construct appropriate models for music instructional programs. Barrett (1996) claims that, by examining children's musical discourse as composers, we have direct access to their musical thinking and decision-making. Through examining their compositions, Barrett observes that children are engaged in processes of describing, analyzing, interpreting, and evaluating sound combinations—actions that are difficult for them to express verbally. As described earlier, young children's verbal expressions of music learning are less accurate than nonverbal expressions. Thus, finding alternative means of assessment is critical for our field.

The pursuit of musical creativity in early childhood gives children the freedom to express themselves—an essential means of exploring, protesting, reinforcing, celebrating, and offering alternative visions. Their compositions and spontaneous improvisations provide a window to their thoughts, feelings, and musical understandings. The music that children create is the narrative of their culture (Loots 1997). However, these musical expressions not only reflect the traditions of their cultures but are a powerful force for change. Through creating music, children craft and construct their evolving cultures, intricately weaving together all the hereditary and environmental influences that combine to make their culture unique.

Conclusions

The early childhood music education literature is constantly refining specific knowledge, deriving new meanings, finding new implications, making new connections, and synthesizing arguments. Many critical questions still remain unanswered. We are witnessing an upsurge of relevant investigations and systematic reviews. Further integrations of science, philosophy, and artistry promise to help parents and educators to identify and diagnose children's educational needs and make informed decisions about providing quality music education for the young child.

Although many aspects of children's musical development seem to be replicated in all cultures, some researchers notice differences (Flohr, Woodward, and Suthers 1998; Littleton 1994). Although all education is value driven, individuals need to adapt guidelines for use within their own contexts. Our goal is to optimize children's musical experiences from before birth, empowering them musically, culturally, psychologically, politically, and economically. Children's natural and spontaneous music making emerges from their innate musical abilities and grows when they are immersed in rich musical environments. Our human capacity for early musical learning makes issues of adult intervention critical. The roles of parents and caregivers in creating musically rich environments for young children from before birth cannot be overemphasized. Assessments and evaluation of early music learning need to be relevant and appropriate, seeking evidence of musicianship rather than knowledge about music. Furthermore, we need to ensure that children's natural propensities for music making are not stifled by inappropriate formal programs or by the elimination of music education from school curricula. Early childhood arts education (informal and formal) is the umbilical cord of the community's culture.

Elliott's praxial philosophy pushes us to probe our assumptions; develop and express our differences; scrutinize our strategies and methodologies; develop musicianship through curricula that are well anchored, selected, planned, and organized; and identify our strengths and ways of maintaining them. In developing models for adult intervention in early music experience, we need to balance the relationship between the instinctive and the acquired, the innate and cultural (Bannan 2000). Through observing and facilitating children's natural music explorations and expressions, we can develop programs that have music practice at their core and are developmentally appropriate for children's emotional and musical needs. Early music education is not only about music; it is a process wherein children explore life (Small 1977). By achieving flow in young children's participative musical experiences, we can nurture their innate musical capabilities, guide them to extend their musical horizons, and lead them to self-growth.

References

Abeles, H. F., C. R. Hoffer, and R. H. Klotman. 1984. *Foundations of music education*. New York: Schirmer Books.

Adachi, M. 1992. Development of young children's music reading via instruction. In W. Sims, ed., *Proceedings of the fifth international seminar of the Early Childhood Commission of the International Society for Music Education*. Tokyo: International Society for Music Education.

Andress, B. 1998. *Music for young children*. Fort Worth, TX: Harcourt Brace College.

Bannan, N. 2000. Instinctive singing: Lifelong development of the child within. *British Journal of Music Education* 17 (3):295–301.

Barrett, M. 1990. Graphic notation in music education. In J. P. B. Dobbs, ed., *Music education: Facing the future; Proceedings of the nineteenth world conference of the International Society for Music Education*, 147–153. Christchurch, New Zealand: University of Canterbury.

———. 1992. Music education and the natural learning model. *International Journal of Music Education* 20:27–34.

———. 1996. Children's aesthetic decision-making: An analysis of children's musical discourse as composers. *International Journal of Music Education* 28:37–61.

Blacking, J. 1973. *How musical is man?* Seattle: University of Washington Press.

Campbell, P. S. 1991. *Lessons from the world. A cross-cultural guide to music teaching and learning*. New York: Schirmer Books.

———. 1998. *Songs in their heads: Music and its meaning in children's lives*. New York: Oxford University Press.

Campbell, P. S., and C. Scott-Kassner. 1995. *Music in childhood*. New York: Schirmer Books.

Chen, L. 1994. Effect of pitch relationship between text and melody in young children's singing. In W. Sims, ed., *Vital connections: Young children, adults and music; Proceedings of the sixth international seminar of the Early Childhood Commission of the International Society for Music Education*. Columbia: International Society for Music Education.

Csikszentmihalyi, M. 1990. *Flow: The psychology of optimal experience*. New York: Harper and Row.

———. 1996. *Creativity*. New York: Harper Collins.

———. 1997. *Finding flow*. New York: Basic Books.

Custodero, L. 1997. *An observational study of flow experience in young children's music learning*. Ph.D. diss., University of Southern California, Los Angeles.

———. 1998. Observing flow in young children's music learning. *General Music Today* 12 (1):1–27.

———. 2000. Engagement and experience: A model for the study of children's musical cognition. In G. L. C. Woods, R. Brochard, F. Seddon, and J. A. Sloboda, eds., *Proceedings of the sixth international conference on music perception and cognition*. Keele, UK: Keele University Department of Psychology.

De Casper, A. J. and Fifer, W. P. 1980. Of human bonding: Newborns prefer their mother's voices. *Science*, 6 June, 1174–1176.

Dissanayake, E. 2000. Antecedents of the temporal arts in early mother-infant interaction. In: N. L. Wallin, B. Merker, and S. Brown, eds., *Origins of music*, 389–410. Bradford, UK: Cambridge.

Elliott, D. J. 1989. Key concepts in multicultural music education. *International Journal of Music Education* 13:11–18.

———. 1990. Music as culture: Toward a multicultural concept of arts education. *Journal of Aesthetic Education* 24 (1):147–166.

———. 1992. Music education and the new South Africa. In J. Van Tonder, ed., *Proceedings of the Fourth National Music Educators' Conference*, 1–15. Cape Town: South African Music Educators' Society.

———. 1995. *Music matters: A new philosophy of music education*. New York: Oxford University Press.

Flohr, J. W., D. Miller, and D. Persellin. 1996. Children's electrophysiological response to music. In S. Woodward, ed., *Universal and particular elements of early childhood education: Proceedings of the seventh international seminar of the Early Childhood Commission of the International Society for Music Education*. Winchester, UK: International Society for Music Education.

Flohr, J. W., S. C. Woodward, and L. Suthers. 1998. Rhythm performance in early childhood. In S. Woodward, ed., *Respecting the child in early music learning: Eighth international seminar of the Early Childhood Commission of the International Society for Music Education*. Cape Town: International Society for Music Education.

Flowers, P. J. 1993. Evaluation in early childhood music. In M. Palmer and W. L. Sims, eds., *Music in preschool: Planning and teaching*. Reston, VA:[3] Music Educators National Conference.

Fung, C. V., and J. Gromko. 2001. Effects of active versus passive listening on the quality of children's invented notations for two Korean pieces. *Psychology of Music* 29 (2): 128–138.

Gromko, J. 1994. Children's invented notations as measures of musical understanding. *Psychology of Music* 22:136–147.

———. 1996. In a child's voice: Interpretive interactions with young composers. *Bulletin of the Council for Research in Music Education* 128:37–58.

Gromko, J., and A. Poorman. 1998a. The effect of music training on preschoolers' spatial-temporal task performance. *Journal of Research in Music Education* 46 (2):173–181.

———. 1998b. Does perceptual-motor performance enhance perception of patterned art music? *Musicæ Scientiæ: Journal of the European Society for the Cognitive Sciences of Music* 2 (2):157–170.

Gruhn, W. 1999. About the difficulties to move knowledge into action, theory into practice. *International Journal of Music Education* 34:57–63.

Hepper, P. G. 1988. Fetal "soap" addiction. *Lancet* 1:1374–1348.

Hetland, L. 2000. Learning to make music enhances spatial reasoning. *Journal of Aesthetic Education* 34 (3–4):179–238.

Leader, L. R., P. Baille, B. Martin, and E. Vermeuken. 1982. The assessment and significance of habituation to a repeated stimulus by the human fetus. *Early Human Development* 7: 211–219.

Littleton, D. 1991. *Influence of play settings on preschool children's music and play behaviors.* Ph.D. diss., University of Texas.

———. 1994. Cross-cultural perspectives on preschool children's spontaneous music behaviors. In W. Sims, ed., *Vital connections: Young children, adults and music; Proceedings of the sixth international seminar of the Early Childhood Commission of the International Society for Music Education.* Columbia: International Society for Music Education.

Loots, A. 1997. *A critical approach to rock music from a cultural, historical, and theoretical perspective.* Ph.D. diss., University of Port Elizabeth.

Manins, S. 1996. An autobiographical case study of steps towards bicultural sensitivity. In S. Woodward, ed., *Universal and particular elements of early childhood music education: Proceedings of the seventh international seminar of the Early Childhood Commission of the International Society for Music Education.* Winchester: International Society for Music Education.

Maslow, A. H. 1970. *Motivation and personality.* New York: Harper and Row.

McLaughlin, H. 1998. Babies and toddlers as musicians. In S. Woodward, ed., *Respecting the child in early childhood learning: Proceedings of the eighth international seminar of the Early Childhood Commission of the International Society for Music Education.* Cape Town: International Society for Music Education.

McMahon, O. 1986. Implications of recent research into aspects of music in early childhood. *International Society for Music Education Yearbook* 13:161–164.

Metz, E. 1989. Movement as a musical response among preschool children. *Journal of Research in Music Education* 37 (1):48–60.

Minami,Y., and H. Nito. 1998. Vocal pitch matching in infants. In S. Woodward, ed., *Respecting the child in early childhood learning: Proceedings of the eighth international seminar of the Early Childhood Commission of the International Society for Music Education.* Cape Town: International Society for Music Education.

Moog, H. 1976. The development of musical experience in children of preschool age. *Psychology of Music* 4:38–45.

Moorhead, G., and D. Pond. 1978. *Music of young children.* Santa Barbara, CA: Pillsbury Foundation for the Advancement of Music Education.

Nettl, B. 1998. Foreword. In P. S. Campbell, *Songs in their heads: Music and its meanings in children's lives.* New York: Oxford University Press.

Omi, A. 1992. Explaining children's spontaneous singing. In W. Sims, ed., *Proceedings of the fifth international seminar of the Early Childhood Commission of the International Society for Music Education.* Tokyo: International Society for Music Education.

Papoušek, H. 1996. Musicality in infancy research: biological and cultural origins of early musicality. In I. Delièege and J. Sloboda, eds., *Musical beginnings: Origins of the development of musical competence,* 37–55. New York: Oxford University Press.

Poch de Grätzer, D. 1999. Can music help to improve parent-child communication? *International Journal of Music Education* 34:47–56.

Scott-Kassner, C. 1992. Research on music in early childhood. In R. Colwell, ed., *Handbook of research on music teaching and learning.* New York: Schirmer Books.

Sims, W. L. 1986. The effect of high versus low teacher affect and passive versus active student activity during music listening on preschool children's attention, piece preference, time spent listening, and piece recognition. *Journal of Research in Music Education* 34:173–191.

———. 1990. Characteristics of young children's music concept discrimination. *Psychomusicology* 9:79–88.

———. 1995. Children's ability to demonstrate music concept discriminations in listening and singing. *Journal of Research in Music Education* 43:204–221.

———. 2001. Music listening experiences for young children. *Florida Music Director* 2 (3): 15–16.

Sloboda, J. A. 1985. *The musical mind*. Oxford: Clarendon Press.

Small, C. 1977. *Music, society, education*. New York: Schirmer Books.

Sumner, W. G. 1960. *Folkways*. 3rd ed. Boston: Ginn.

Suzuki, S. 1969. *Nurtured by love*. New York: Exposition Press.

Tarnowski, S. 1996. Preservice early childhood educators' observations of spontaneous imitative song in preschool children age two to five years. In S. Woodward, ed., *Universal and particular elements of early childhood music education: Proceedings of the seventh international seminar of the Early Childhood Commission of the International Society for Music Education*. Winchester, UK: International Society for Music Education.

Tarnowski, S., and J. Leclerc. 1994. Musical play of preschoolers and teacher-child interaction. *Update: Applications of Research in Music Education* 13 (1):9–16.

Tommis, Y., and D. M. A. Fazey. 1996. The acquisition of pitch element of music literacy skills. In S. Woodward, ed., *Universal and particular elements of early childhood music education: Proceedings of the seventh international seminar of the Early Childhood Commission of the International Society for Music Education*. Winchester, UK: International Society for Music Education.

Trevarthen, C. 1999. Musicality and the intrinsic motive pulse: Evidence from human psychobiology and infant communication. In *Musicæ Scientiæ: Journal of the European Society for the Cognitive Sciences of Music*, special issue (1999–2000):155–215.

van Rysselberghe, M. L. 1992. Multicultural models as teachers of early childhood music. In W. Sims, ed., *Proceedings of the fifth international seminar of the Early Childhood Commission of the International Society for Music Education*. Tokyo: International Society for Music Education.

Verny, T. 1981. *The secret life of the unborn child*. New York: Dell.

Woodward, S. C. 1992a. Intrauterine rhythm and blues? *British Journal of Obstetrics and Gynaecology* 99:787–790.

———. 1992b. *The transmission of music into the human uterus and the response to music of the human fetus and neonate*. Ph.D. diss., University of Cape Town, South Africa.

Zimmer, E. Z., M. Y. Divon, A. Vilensky, Z. Sasna, B. A. Peretz, and E. Paldi. 1982. Maternal exposure to music and fetal activity. *European Journal of Obstetrics, Gynaecology and Reproductive Biology* 13 (4):209–213.

14

What Matters in General Music?

PAMELA BURNARD

Music educators commonly agree that the primary purpose of general music education is to enable young people to progress musically by acquiring skills and understandings through musical experience itself. The praxial philosophy offers direct assistance to general music teachers because Elliott's concepts of music making and listening take us deep into the primarily embodied nature of music and offer us clear guidance for musically educating children.

My own teaching has been very much inspired by Elliott's praxial philosophy because it firmly locates the musical understandings of teachers and learners within our personal autobiographies of learning, so that we find authority in our individual musical experiences. Furthermore, the praxial view of general music education affirms the complexity of children as reflective music makers and validates listening, performing, improvising, composing, arranging, and conducting as interdependent forms of creative doing. This philosophical acknowledgment of the musical wholeness and complexity of children as reflective music makers is to be applauded. What matters in general music, then, is that we affirm children's musical potentials and capabilities, widen their musical access, and strengthen our professional practice.

My intention in this chapter is to make explicit how practical applications of the praxial philosophy can enhance the quality of general music programs.

Teaching General Music: Change and Continuity

Educational change has been commonplace in many countries for decades. Over the past several years, however, teachers have faced accelerated and intensive changes. With progressively greater emphasis on efficiency and accountability, literacy and numeracy now form the critical axis of the curriculum; all other subjects are subjugated. Literacy and numeracy are seen as the means to success. As a consequence, in some settings, music faces extinction from the curriculum, if it has not already disappeared.

Also, some countries have witnessed a shift toward the use of frameworks that facilitate standardization in education. For example, in the United States there are "National Standards for Arts Education"; in Britain, there is the "National Curriculum for England"; in Australia, there is a "Curriculum and Standards Framework." However, and despite great variation within and between countries, common educational values have been identified. For example, "all learners should have the opportunity to grow in musical knowledge, skills and appreciation so as to challenge their minds, stimulate their imaginations, bring joy and satisfaction to their lives and exalt their spirits" (International Society for Music Education 1994, 49).

Although pedagogical practice is influenced by regional variants in philosophical, cultural, and contextual commitments to education, they all emphasize the development of skills, knowledge, and understanding. The common ideal is that every student should reach certain standards in order to "express himself or herself through singing, playing instruments, improvising and composing" (Lehman 2000, 94). These standards (whether national, state, or local) provide the basis for the general music programs in middle (eight to twelve years of age), junior high (twelve to fourteen years) and secondary schools (fourteen to eighteen years).

Elliott describes the most basic conditions for musical continuity:

> Because all music education programs share the same aims [Elliott's aims include self-growth and enjoyment, among others], all music education programs ought to provide the same basic conditions for achieving these aims: (1) genuine musical challenges and (2) the musicianship to meet these challenges through competent, proficient, and artistic music making. What will differ between and among music education programs across grade levels and school regions is not the essential content of the music curriculum (musicianship) but the kinds and levels of musical challenges inherent in the curriculum materials chosen for (and, perhaps, with the co-operation of) one's own students. (1995, 260)

General music programs are usually regarded as primarily egalitarian in nature because they attempt to accommodate and motivate students from a diversity of musical backgrounds. Music teachers attempt to accommodate everyone, including students who have not previously performed in traditional ensembles. "General music" is based on the educational ideal of relevant music instruction for all students regardless of their prior musical experiences.

What, then, is required of the general music student? The music curriculum requires the general music student to primarily engage in performing, composing, improvising, arranging, listening, and appraising music. The general music program runs within the school's curriculum in the form of a class, which is a discrete entity (not part of a band, orchestra, choir, or other performing group). In North America, students who take general music as an elective class are usually those not heavily engaged in performance programs. Sometimes, too, the music classroom facilitates the musical development of so-called less able or disadvantaged students (*not* my terms) with no musical training. However, in the United Kingdom, children who elect to take music in years 9 and 10 are often "serious" music students (that is, a school's "musos") who aspire to continue music studies at a tertiary level.

But how can general music best be taught? How do we provide opportunities for well-disposed and well-motivated engagement in general music classes at the middle and secondary school levels? This is a great challenge to teachers in general and music educators in particular. Elliott offers a way forward when he says:

> All music students (including all general music students) ought to be viewed and taught in the same basic way: as reflective musical practitioners engaged in the kind of cognitive apprenticeship we call music education. Indeed, the fundamental natures of MUSIC and MUSICIANSHIP point to the conclusion that authentic music making (which always involves listening intelligently for the music one is making) ought to be the focus of all music education curricula. (1995, 74)

This view promotes an ethos that is all about engagement and involvement. It resonates with musical understanding "based on artistic musicing and listening through performing and improvising in particular" as well as "composing, arranging and conducting whenever these are possible and relevant" (1995, 260). There is nothing elusive about this approach. Its significance lies in treating all students as reflective musical practitioners "and by teaching all students how to find and solve musical problems in 'conversation' using ongoing musical practices and music educators to situate students' musical thinking and knowing" (266).

To this end, Elliott offers a good picture of how the general music teacher can begin to teach by indicating the goals of engagement and involvement, as well as signposting the trap of judging musicality by performance ability. Every student or teacher, regardless of educational background, preferences, or chosen musical genre, has the ability to make valid choices and valuations. Thus, music is seen as a praxis, and musical understanding is embodied within the acts and actions of musical behaviors.

Does this praxial approach resonate with young people? Byrne and Sheridan (2000) provide affirmation in their report on "an upturn in the numbers of pupils studying music" (46) in Scottish secondary schools when rock music was accepted as "a valid form" of music within the curriculum. Similarly, Hargreaves et al. (2002) found that British students, like their American counterparts, enjoyed music making most when they were presented with challenges attuned to their perceived level of skills.

A report on the effects and effectiveness of secondary school arts education in secondary schools in England and Wales (Harland, Kinder, and Lord 2000) linked musical learning to a heightened sense of enjoyment, excitement, and fulfilment. They also found that perceptions of music students' enjoyment of music were conditional upon the teacher. Thus, disaffected pupils became more apparent in the transition from primary to middle school, and from middle school to junior high or secondary schools. The idea that the "teacher equals subject" often made it very difficult for adolescent-age students to cope with transitional changes to a more demanding system of learning. Similarly, Mills and O'Neill (2002) found that where teachers praised children frequently and taught them music they liked, musical enjoyment was ranked highest.

Although music is the preserve of all, it is not necessarily a subject that every child enjoys at school. Elliott offers a solution when he says "implicit in all this is the broader requirement that all music students be engaged in rich and challenging music making projects in classroom situations that are deliberately organized as close parallels to true musical practices" (1995, 261).

In Britain, a report entitled "All Our Futures" (National Advisory Committee on Creative and Cultural Education 1999) heralds "forms of education that develop young people's capacities for original ideas and action" (or "creative education") and "forms of education that enable young people to engage positively with the growing complexity and diversity of social values and ways of life" (or "cultural education"). This report stresses the importance of "good" teaching that balances "formal instruction of content and skills with giving young people the freedom to inquire, question, experiment, and to express their own thoughts and ideas." The essence of the report, intended to cover a wide span of educational activity, has commonalities with Elliott's praxial philosophy in terms of a shared vision of teachers and learners having the space for personal involvement in their musical learning.

Let us now look at how this may be achieved through the application of praxial principles.

The Praxial View of General Music: Knowledge in Practice

Music is something we do ("do," to Elliott, means both listen for and make music). Doing is characterized by the experiential quality of practical knowledge. It is a social practice that gets embodied in the context of personal life histories and backgrounds. Elliott rightly recognizes that teachers and learners have a sociocultural and an emotional relationship to music. He goes on to articulate this process of musical learning as a form of praxis. His emphasis is on the importance of students' not only engaging in a dialogue between knowledge and musical activity, but also learning how this occurs within the social context of musical experiences. In this praxial view, Elliott focuses on the nature of musical experience in terms of the relationships between a range of "knowings" as manifested in the processes of listening, musicing, and of musical learning. This kind of learning pivots on developing one's listening abilities as one learns to make music—processes that Elliott views as socially, musically, and contextually situated as an integrated complex of knowledge-in-practice. The interrelationships between the types of music-related knowledge are central to this philosophy.

What knowledge is most worth learning by all general music students? Elliott's answer is clear:

> Musicianship is the key to achieving the values, aims and goals of music education. Musicianship, which includes listenership, is a rich form of procedural knowledge that draws upon four other kinds of musical knowing in surrounding and supporting ways. Musicianship is context-sensitive, or situated: that is, the precise nature and content of musicianship differs from musical practice to practice, and musicianship develops through progressive musical problem

solving in teaching-learning environments designed as close likenesses of real music cultures. (1995, 259–260)

The main way to achieve musicianship and listenership is the making of music from one's own experiences. Within this, what we introduce to students must be meaningful to them, to enable them to articulate their responses to music through music making of all kinds. Indeed, it is important to remember that the praxial philosophy encompasses all manner of participation—listening, composing, improvising, arranging, performing, and conducting—as music making situated in the mainstream of one's own experiences.

Young people are embroiled in varied living and musical cultures operating outside school. The praxial philosophy acknowledges the many musics of the world and the musical worlds of young people. The principal focus of general music programs must be on how children and young people relate to music. Thus, "the musical authenticity of the teaching-learning situation is a crucial determinate of what music students learn and how deeply they learn" (Elliott 1995, 72). In this view, Elliott invites us to think about general music programs as planning for embodied "'conversation[s]' with ongoing musical practices" (266) wherein students have the opportunity to interact, encounter, and encode musical experiences in conjunction with adult models. What Elliott seeks is teaching from a pluralistic perspective with strategies extrapolated from many types of musics so that culturally differentiated views of music can be acknowledged along with their intrinsic teaching methods. For if we really are interested in good teaching, then it is critical to apply teaching strategies that are relevant to each type of music. Elliott emphasizes the importance of contextually situated engagements between students and a reasonable range of musical practices (chosen with several criteria in mind: see 211–212).

Clearly, young people are more inclined to relate to music when their own knowledge and experiences are valued. An affirming environment encourages engagement and involvement and offers a greater opportunity for students to become inspired, motivated, active, interested, challenged, and fulfilled through musicing. Of course, teachers must also become inducted into the particular music practices valued by the pupils.

Another determinate of the musical experience is how we attend to and respond to music. In this, the praxial philosophy emphasizes listening as a central tenet. Elliott spends much time in his book (chapters 4, 6, and 8) developing a framework for music listening and the teaching of music listening. As he states (198–201), what is offered is a "multidimensional" concept of musical works—a "map" for guiding teachers and students toward "finding" or constructing the range of meanings that a work may involve.

The praxial view of musical works has many implications for teaching in general music programs. Elliott makes explicit what teachers need to know. The three points of significant relevance for Elliott are that teachers themselves need to know what each musical work involves in terms of its combination of dimensions; that teachers must teach music listening deliberately and systematically in the process of teaching all forms of music making; and that teachers need to develop listeners who are critically reflective about all dimensions of musical works.

What Elliott refers to as "musicing" gives consideration to the cognitive nature of musical experience as forms of knowing or "know-how." This procedural knowledge forms the core of musicianship otherwise described as a form of "working understanding" that resides at the center of all listening and music making. By "musicianship" Elliott means a multidimensional form of knowledge that is "demonstrated in actions not words. It is a form of practical knowledge, or reflective practice" (1995, 53–54). This has particular importance in defining our approach to good teaching in general music programs.

Musical understanding is shaped, informed, and influenced by many kinds of knowing. These are procedural knowledge, formal musical knowledge (concepts, ideas, facts, and descriptions), informal musical knowledge (common sense that comes from accumulated musical experiences), impressionistic musical knowledge (feelings and emotions), and supervisory musical knowledge (self-regularity, reflective and metacognitive in nature, embroiled with imagination). Listening requires the development and fusion of all five forms of knowing; so, too, with music making of each kind. Musical understanding constitutes the integration of all ten.

It seems reasonable to suggest, then, that in this praxial view of general music, programs should emphasize active musical involvement with music of relevance to young people, where authentic musical experiences consist of both student decision making and choice. Again, this has particular importance for how we approach general music. For if the significance of musical experience lies in the embodied nature of "doing music" (as listeners and makers), then the teaching-learning situation must embody the dimensions of knowledge-in-practice that inheres in musical situations and relations in ways that encourage critical reflection. This requires that "students be inducted into and immersed in musical practices through meaningful music making" (Elliott 1995, 101).

Situated Practices: Some Accounts of Action

At the center of the praxial view is the idea that all forms of music making and listening are purposeful, thoughtful, and "situated." That is, a musical situation of making and/or listening to music evinces not only the observable aspects of how music is improvised (for example) and the characteristics of the setting where a particular style of improvisation (e.g., bebop improvisation) takes place; such events are also situated in the sense that they bring into being an artistic-social context that has its own standards, history, and tradition of making and listening to music.

By defining musicing in this deeply contextual way, Elliott validates the actions and intentions of all people present in a musical setting. In this view, it is everyone, together, as a collective, who shapes musical courses of action and response. It is therefore essential that general music students come to understand, feel, and enjoy the contexts of musicing as purposeful action-settings in which their efforts shape (and are shaped by) musical roles, goals, and means (Wertsch 1985). In such settings, says Elliott, "the feedback that arises from one's reflection is used to improve one's expertise and to refine (or redefine) the goals that guide one's making and doing" (1995, 69).

In the next section, below, I introduce three accounts of creative action by praxial learners that further illuminate the nature and potential of Elliott's philosophy. At the heart of this section lies an invitation to readers to reflect on their own teaching contexts.

Children as Reflective Musical Practitioners

To many children, "composing" means making a piece for a particular performing medium (e.g., composing a piece to play on the piano or guitar). Notice how such thinking invokes specific parameters for the "making of a piece I play." This involves a reflective process in which ideas are found, focused, fixed, and finalized circuitously by deciding about sounds children have come to know and understand as music makers (Elliott, 105). This knowledge exists not only, or principally, by deduction or extraction from the music, but directly in the acts of musical attention and decisions themselves.

What constitutes the "praxial learner" is well illustrated in the collaboration between Sidin and Maria. As members of a lunchtime Music Creators Club who met weekly over six months, these twelve-year-olds produced three versions of a "Piece for Piano," which they co-composed over as many weeks. Maria was the more experienced player, and, as Sidin's newly acquired friend and "piano teacher," she assumed a leadership role. This music making illuminates Elliott's notion (1995, 102) of "listenership and its component knowings" as procedural knowledge that feels and sounds in bodily actions learned from inside the musical practice of one player, who transfers it to the other. Figure 14.1 demonstrates a working understanding of musicianship as told by two twelve-year-olds who, for the first time, "made their own piece for piano" collaboratively.

This composition illustrates the norms and conventions familiar to pianists. It features, as Maria describes, "two main ideas" across "four sections," complete with an introduction, coda, key changes, and the use of alternation and repetition; it ends on a perfect cadence. Overall, then, the form is A–A1–(link)–B–A–coda. There are four clearly delineated sections that use transitional links as time points or markers. The links serve to function as time points that direct the players to where they are located in the piece. They assemble sections, as we are told, according to a plan that was decided prior to starting work at the piano. Maria said: "I figure out a couple of ideas first. Then I play them and Sidin makes something up and then we stop and talk. We keep starting and stopping and then going back over and over parts and then playing the whole thing through loads of times" (lunchtime interview). The praxial learner comes to life in this working process, which includes externalizing decisions, feeding back opinions, reinforcing ideas, and making explicit her musical plans. The planning is made explicit by a process Sidin described as "confirming," whereby they play and then purposively stop in order to share feedback with each other on the worth of an idea. As a revisionist strategy, confirming appears to be central to the process of composing and indicative of what a composer and performer understands procedurally, formally, informally, impressionistically, and in supervisory ways (Elliott 1995, 71).

> *Composition for Piano*, by Sidin and Maria. This piece be-
> gins with an introductory harmonic motive that then accom-
> panies a simple motive (G–F#–E–F#). The tempo changes
> before a middle section in which slower rhythmic and per-
> formance tempi lead to a pause announcing the oncoming re-
> turn to the A section *a tempo*. Another tempo change ushers
> in a closing phrase of classical cues based on a tonic triad fol-
> lowed by tonic tones in descending octave leaps. Overall,
> then: A–A1–(link)–B–A–coda.

FIGURE 14.1 Composition for Piano

Fashioning pieces from known melodies and rhythms picked up by ear from popular music or instrumental repertoire is a common experience expressed by many young composers (Burnard 2000a, 2000b; Burnard and Younker 2002). Not surprisingly, children seem to store and draw ideas from known and existing pieces. For example, Lia made and played several of her own compositions for guitar over the six months she was a member of the Creator's Club. Each piece features the use of familiar musical material where we see her thinking "musically in the actions of musicing and listening" (Elliott 1995, 97). One particular "made-up piece" provides multiple insights about and from her experiences. In this piece (see Fig. 14.2) we see evidence of the effects of Lia's prior guitar lessons, her familiarity with popular music, and her notion of composition as a major source of the building blocks from which her identity as a guitarist emerges.

This was a piece anchored in all that Lia knew and found playable (that is, in her "knowledge-how"). Playing it involved her conscious recognition of choices in which her performance techniques and performance repertoire played major parts. Lia's skills and orientations were mirrored back through her composition, which, as a piece performed "without anyone else," displayed her present limits and potential as a guitarist, at this time, integrated with qualities to which she aspired. As Lia said:

> You have to think about what the piece is. Sometimes you might just play any-
> thing but when I play a piece that I made up I worry about what people might
> think and so I try to do it as best as I can. . . .With my own guitar piece, though,
> I made it up by myself. Like this is a made-up piece that I can show everyone
> myself—not with someone else. I started with bits of a song I can play. These
> twiddled bits got me started and then I thought about some different ideas and
> anchored it by playing it over a bit at a time. (Focus Group Middle Phase)[4]

We could argue that in thinking about "what the piece is" she values composing as a way of articulating what she knows and is able to do. Playing "anything" leaves her with less to worry about, whilst "a made-up piece, that I can show everyone myself," means giving prominence to the expectations of the piece by taking "quite a bit of time" to "anchor it." Thus, Lia's composing depended upon a specific kind of situated cognition that she used to call up certain musical conventions as reflected by the expectations of both player and audience. Learning to notice these dimensions of

> *Composition for Guitar*, by Lia. This composition, lasting fifty-five seconds, features three main sections. The first section (A) opens with a phrase that features an ascending three-note motive chained to a descending four-note motive, both of which are repeated before being developed. A link of rising and falling quavers connects to the second section (B), which alludes to a borrowed tune (a Spice Girls song called "Mama") based on a descending stepwise motive over a syncopated rhythm. Here we realize that the opening phrase uses the same pitch in varied configuration and rhythmic patterns. New material is introduced in the third section (C), comprising a variously configured four-note motive to end with notes of longer duration. Overall, then: A–(link)–B–C.

FIGURE 14.2 Composition for Guitar

"artistic knowing" rests, according to Elliott, "upon an independent form of situated thinking and knowing. Hence, each kind of artistic knowing needs to be taught and learned in its own context through active involvement in artistic making" (1995, 249).

So, in what kind of teaching-learning context were these pieces created and performed? These pieces were created during a doctoral research project within the context of weekly music-making sessions attended by eighteen self-selected members of a Music Creators Club involving twelve-year-old children from a multiethnic, comprehensive middle school in West London, England (see Burnard 1999, 2000a, 2000b, 2000c, 2002a, 2002b; Burnard and Younker 2002). As the researcher, I circulated, listened, discussed, and observed a community of learners mutually engaged in composing and improvising. No plan or guided learning objectives were set. There were no "reductionist objectives" (Elliott's term) that specified behaviors and verbal concepts about musical elements, processes, and styles. Instead, learning and coaching proceeded through musical engagements, concerned with musical-contextual issues that embrace the totality of an experiential situation.

This context defines "situated knowing and thinking" in music where praxial learners become aware of the dimensions of musical knowing in the process of constructing various ways of composing. This musical practicum was characterized by a "continuous and active immersion in meeting significant musical challenges" (Elliott 1995, 246) set by the children themselves.

What can we, as teachers, learn from this teaching-learning situation? In this case, the context was a community of learners who negotiated and set their musical parameters. As reflective musical practitioners, children set themselves challenges, as do their teachers, from which they come "to assess their own musical thinking-in-action by learning what counts." These praxial learners were given the opportunity "to reflect on the results of their musicianship and that of their peers" (Elliott 1995, 264).

Consider a further example of children's music making that highlights other characteristics of intentional, contextual (praxial) thinking-in-action. This time the children are engaged in an improvisation. The way these children narrated the "situated" jour-

> *Improvisation on Clarinets and Tuned Percussion.* Ashton begins by playing a rising step-wise pattern on metallophone. He starts in a fast tempo and quickly slows the tempo. Loreen enters, playing a low sustained tone that leaps a sixth to descend by steps. Diane enters quickly and adjusts from playing seconds to unison. Loreen leaps a sixth to hold a long note; Diane leaps down to an octave lower. They pause on these notes. Ashton weaves a descending line, creating a harmonic anchor. Rhythmic activity increases as Loreen plays a series of step-wise notes in her upper pitch register. Diane responds with a counterpoint of independent rhythm in a descending line, going lower. They pause together on their last note. Ashton introduces a new sonority—a roll (oscillating between neighboring tones); Loreen imitates by sounding a trill. A glance is exchanged between Loreen and Ashton. Diane plays a cadential-type melodic pattern around the subdominant (signaling an ending); Loreen takes over by playing a three-note descending *ritardando* to the final tonic, which Diane plays at the octave. This is prepared by a synchronized pause (a breath) before the sustained tonic. Ashton plays a final slow rendition of his opening pattern. The audience applauds; Ashton signals his pleasure and pride.

FIGURE 14.3 Improvisation

ney of improvising was repeatedly referred to in descriptions of what they played, how it was played, when it was played, and with whom. The experiential qualities emerged in the form of a definition of the surroundings or environments set by each other in which each performance was played out. Improvisation possessed a shared and negotiated space, which was more often filled with uncertainty about the events that were to follow. This was a performance space in which the children preferred to involve each other within a framework where each player seemed to develop subtle ways of responding to musical uncertainty. Figure 14.3 provides a description of their trio improvisation as done by Diane and Loreen (clarinets) and Ashton (metallophone). There is no predetermined decision regarding who is to start or finish. The relationship between players reflects a musical trust. Ashton describes it this way:

> I didn't go into my own world. I thought it was unfair on the others. You have to be there together. I took a bit of a chance, but it paid off, as there were no serious collisions. . . . You have to listen to what they are playing and listen harder to what you're playing so it goes together. What I tried to do was to keep on with what I was playing and . . . keep on thinking about what else I can do against them, and then I'll change it. Then by this stage my own ideas come into it. Sometimes I added some of my ideas and then they'd take bits of my ideas to play. (Focus Group Middle Phase)

Significantly, the music becomes a meeting place defined by the shared space in which musicianship and musical creativity are developed. The character is of a musical event where "ideas" cannot be "take[n] back"; a pathway is mutually established for the continuation of a shared, collective encounter. As Chloe noted, "It's not like it's your own piece." Within the joint action of improvisation, the players focus their attention on the immediate musical challenges met during the performance. This is followed by reflection on the musical understandings gained. Thus, the actual musicing-of-understanding is perhaps the most fundamental ingredient of general music education. This example of understanding-as-doing music (i.e., listening and making) underscores the praxial philosophy.

Teachers as Reflective Practitioners

At the heart of the dynamic of praxial philosophy are the personal constructs of the teacher, a complex amalgam of past knowledge, experiences of learning, a personal view of what constitutes "good" teaching, and a belief in the aims and values of music education. "To teach music effectively, a teacher must possess, embody, and exemplify musicianship. This is how children develop musicianship themselves—not through telling, but through their actions, transactions, and interactions with musically proficient and expert teachers" (Elliott 1995, 262). Elliott insists that school music should be taught by teachers who have competent or proficient levels of musicianship themselves.

Deeply embedded in Elliott's situated approach to music education is the notion of participation in communities of practice where musical understanding resides not just in the teacher, but in the context as a whole: in the community of practice in which the teacher participates (as "first among equals"). In other words, children are also viewed as musical; they are treated as musical; they are seen as being in the process of developing musical understanding as apprentices set within a reflective musical community and centrally involved in its activities. It crucially involves learning through participation—of absorbing and being absorbed in the culture of musical practice. At the center of this community of practice is the musically competent teacher.

Consider, for instance, the community of practice underlying the group of children introduced earlier. As the researcher, I was not permitted participation as a way of learning in the culture of practice within this community of children. However, just as the serendipitous surprises in research are a reflection of life itself, in the final week of the Soundings Project a performance was held in the school hall. This was a "final concert" bringing together the head teacher, the class, music teachers, parents, family members, and friends of the Soundings members. The idea was to capture aspects of the Creators Club with old and new compositions presented along with a range of improvisations (with varied instruments), students, and settings chosen by the children. (To this point, the researcher had not performed for or with the children.)

It was close to the end of the concert when an invitation made by the children to "make a piece on the spot for us" came to me. This came as a complete surprise. Naturally, I was struck with panic and pleasure—panic at the pressure of performing without warning, and pleasure at being asked to perform. It was both politically correct and right to accept the invitation, and I would naturally be judged. At that moment I was struck by the fact that participation in any improvisatory effort depends upon a willingness to take risks. What I felt was not painless. The key question was: "What to do?" I was not sure which instrument to play; I had given no thought to the possibility of what to improvise at this concert. I wondered what they would like me to play; I asked if they would like to make any choices on my behalf. I asked: "Which instrument? What setting?" At this stage, the cameraman (a musician, too) was also called to play a duo with me.

Their response was overwhelmingly unanimous—selecting me to play the piano in a duo setting—so they could observe who would play what in the ensuing musical interaction. Our performance reflected a lot of energy and moved through various polyphonic textures, pitch clusters, abrupt shifts of rhythmic dissonance, varied metric groupings, and other tensional qualities. There were sufficient regularities (and commonalities) in events and patterns to unify the piece. Nevertheless, I recall consciously thinking that we needed to make the piece sound a bit more agreeable. I felt an expectation to continue until we had resolved some of the musical tension and reached a point of resolution. All sounds were not anticipated, nor all movements controlled or directed. It was very apparent that musical change was the result of role shifting and monitoring. The options that were allowed, or downplayed and excluded, were reflections of our immediate musical interactions. In effect, our performance typified the nature of a duo improvisation as a musical narrative lived for the moment.

As musicians, teachers, artists, and mentors, we provide models and feedback to our students in different forms. Knowing when and how to do this is the challenge. As Elliott puts it, "knowing how to provide appropriate feedback to students rests on knowing how to model and how to explain why and how" (1995, 134). It is knowing which form of explanation is appropriate that rests heavily on the shoulders of teachers. As Elliott explains:

> Music educators are diagnosticians of musical thinking. We consider what our students are giving attention to, what they fail to notice and understand, what they find difficult to solve, what they feel right or wrong about musically, and so on. On the basis of these analyses, we target students' attention and guide their thinking-in-action by using different languages of instruction including modeling, demonstrating, explaining in words, gestures, diagrams and metaphors. (1995, 75)

Music Classrooms That Matter

Elliott establishes a theoretical framework that forms the basis of valuing musical action, thereby providing insights into the nature of music, musical experience, and musical development. He recognizes the multidimensional nature of music and the importance of what learners already know, think, and do. He highlights the significance of the teacher-learner relationship's being based on practical experience and the need for genuine musical engagements to aid the development and growth of musical knowledge. The praxial focus is on the promotion of genuine experiences of and for children as listeners, performers, composers, improvisers, arrangers, and conductors. The application of highly organized or prescribed lesson plans is not advocated. The experience of developing musical understanding using critical reflective practice requires learners to discuss what is intrinsic to their own musical experiences, to identify themselves not only as music makers but as music listeners and creators, and to reflect on what it is to be a musician.

At the heart of praxialism is a conception of teaching that takes its point of departure from within the conscious contents of musical experience. It invites us to look for musical understanding inside music making and our reflections upon it. It challenges us to exert our musical agency and creativity by cultivating our students as reflective musical practitioners. And it urges us to explore our own ways of thinking as reflective musical practitioners whilst sustaining both our "educatorship" and our mission as teachers.

In presenting exemplars of musical engagement, I have attempted to provide insights into the "replication of results" that is appropriate to the field of reflective practitioners and to demonstrate how the praxial philosophy can provide "the keys to understanding the uniqueness and power of musical experiences and music education" (Elliott 1995, 128).

References

Burnard, P. 1999. Bodily intention in children's improvisation and composition. *Psychology of Music* 27 (2):159–174.

———. 2000a. Examining experiential differences between improvisation and composition in children's music making. *British Journal of Music Education* 17 (3):227–245.

———. 2000b. How children ascribe meaning to improvisation and composition: Rethinking pedagogy in music education. *Music Education Research* 2 (1):7–23.

———. 2000c. Making a piece you don't play and forget: Children composing and the role of context. *Australian Journal of Music Education* 1:30–39.

———. 2002a. Investigating children's meaning making and the emergence of musical interaction in group improvisation. *British Journal of Music Education* 19 (2):157–172.

———. 2002b. Teaching and assessing children's improvisation. In D. Harris and A. Paterson, eds., *How are you doing: Learning and assessment in music*. UK: National Association of Music Educators.

Burnard, P., and B. A. Younker. 2002. Mapping pathways: Fostering creativity in composition. *Music Education Research* 4 (2):245–261.

Byrne, C., and M. Sheridan. 2000. The long and winding road: The story of rock music in Scottish schools. *International Society for Music Education* 36:46–57.

Department for Education and Employment 2000. *The national curriculum for England*. London: DfEE.

Elliott, D. J. 1995. *Music matters: A new philosophy of music education*. New York: Oxford University Press.

Hargreaves, D. J., A. M. Lamont, N. Marshall, and M. Tarrant. 2002. Young people's music in and out of school: A study of pupils and teachers in primary and secondary schools. Interim report to National Music Education Forum, QCA, London, June.

Harland, J., K. Kinder, and P. Lord. 2000. *Arts education in secondary schools: Effects and effectiveness*. Slough, UK: National Foundation for Educational Research.

International Society for Music Education 1994. Declaration of beliefs for worldwide promotion of music education. *International Journal of Music Education* 24:1–96.

Lehman, P. 2000. How can the skills and knowledge called for in the national standards best be taught? In C. Madsen, ed., *Vision 2020*. Reston, VA: Music Educators National Conference.

Mills, J., and S. O'Neill. 2002. Different points of view? Evaluating the school music provision for children aged ten to eleven years. In G. McPherson, ed., *Proceedings of the Seventh International Conference on Music Perception and Cognition*. Sydney, Australia: ISME.

Music Educators National Conference. 1994. *National standards for arts education*. Reston, VA: Music Educators National Conference.

National Advisory Committee on Creative and Cultural Education. 1999. *All our futures: Creativity, culture and education*. London: DfEE.

Wertsch, J. V., ed. 1985. *Culture, communication, and cognition: Vygotskian perspectives*. Cambridge: Cambridge University Press.

15

Elementary Music Education

Building Cultures and Practices

LORI-ANNE DOLLOFF

Music is a natural part of children's lives. They often make up songs to accompany their play, move rhythmically between tasks, and "play" with music. Campbell (1998) says of children:

> Music is on their minds and in their bodies. It is evident in their conscious musicking alone and together, and in the various musical expressions they produce. . . . Music serves children in many ways. They group together to socialize through music, but they also take music into themselves at their most private of times. They receive it from many sources, and they learn to sing it, play it, and dance to it. (168)

Elliott's praxial philosophy of music education holds that music education must embody the essence of music as a worldwide array of social-artistic practices, as something that people everywhere "do" musically (as listeners and makers). This is especially the case in the education of children. Young children do not separate thinking, listening, doing, playing, and learning. Based on her observation of preschool children, Pramling (1996) found that they conceive learning as "learning to do something" (567). Many approaches to childhood education stress the active participation of children in music making prior to learning theoretical concepts about music (Elliott's "formal knowledge"). In this chapter I consider the varied and dynamic world of elementary music education in relation to selected principles in Elliott's *Music Matters*.

At the outset, I wish to emphasize that I do not conceive of "elementary music education" as something different from music education at or for any other age of life. The principles I apply in my teaching of young children are the same as those I apply to my work with undergraduate music education majors and other adult community groups. The differences arise from (as Elliott would say) the "levels of musical challenge" that I select for young children and the vocabulary I use with them. In my view, other key components of elementary music education (e.g., active involvement, movement, drama, poetry, and "play") apply to music teaching and learning for all ages.

Praxialism and Traditional Approaches

Elliott's praxialism is compatible with many traditional approaches to elementary music education. For example, the Orff approach seeks to involve the whole child—mind, body, and spirit. Orff (1962) stressed the importance of children learning music as a humanizing and self-realizing force (3). "Elementary music, word and movement, play, everything that awakens and develops the powers of the spirit, this is the 'humus' of the spirit, the humus without which we face the danger of spiritual erosion" (Orff 1962, cited in Dolloff 1993, 9).

Active music making in a musical community is a primary feature of the Orff approach. Orff emphasized the importance of involving the whole body in the experience of music. Children sing, play, move, arrange, improvise, and compose within the context of a musical ensemble. The original five volumes of *Das Schulwerk* were meant to provide models of repertoire and examples of children and teachers interacting with songs, poems, and dances. Orff intended that teachers should explore music with their students in a creative partnership, working together to create musical experiences. This description of the teaching-learning partnership matches Elliott's portrayal of music learning as musical apprenticeship.

The Orff instrumentarium—xylophones, metallophones, glockenspiels, and a host of rhythmic instruments—can be a rich way of allowing children to create music by performing instrumental music, accompanying singing and arranging, composing, and improvising. The Orff ensemble was modeled on Balinese gamelan ensembles. While not a traditional musical ensemble, the timbres of Orff instruments can be magical for students of all ages. I have witnessed expressive Orff ensemble performances in many styles of music. Of course, the use of these instruments is not without its dangers. One problem with adapting the repertoires of various musical cultures for an Orff ensemble is the forced homogeneity of timbre and style that is created. This is also a concern to Elliott, who maintains that we should respect the integrity of the traditions and standards of musical practices. I agree. Not every style of music will be appropriately transferred to xylophones, for example.

So, in the process of developing arrangements for the Orff instrumentarium, children must be taught the authentic features of the musical cultures in which they are working by listening to live and recorded performances, for example, as Elliott also insists (1995, e.g., 104, 207, 274, 285). By engaging in listening and critical decision making, teachers and students may decide to adapt a piece for Orff instruments or decide that a piece will be more expressively arranged in other ways. Allowing children to examine these possibilities is a powerful way of involving them in critical reflections on the values of a musical practice and also weaves verbal musical knowledge into lessons.

Consider, next, that the Orff approach is rooted in a specific musical practice: German folk music. Many features of the Orff repertoire reflect this tradition. In particular, the use of rhythmic body-percussion is a basic way Orff incorporates movement. This grew out of the German traditional dance style of *Schallplatten*, in which dancers perform rhythmic patterns on their bodies by slapping their heels, thighs, and chests in sometimes elaborate and technically challenging movement patterns. Orff wanted teachers to explore the possibilities of their own musical cultures for musical experiences to pursue with children. To this end, music educators worldwide have made adaptations (not translations) of the five original Orff books based on the folk traditions of their own local musical cultures. Other specific musical practices—such as Celtic mouth music or Zulu singing, dancing, and drumming—should be approached from the traditions of movement and pedagogy inherent in those practices.

The Kodály approach to music education also celebrates folk music to the highest degree. Zoltán Kodály and Béla Bartók undertook extensive travels to collect and preserve the folk music of various musical cultures in Hungary. Kodály held that developing the musicianship of children was the central responsibility of music education. He equated musicianship with being musically literate, which he defined as "being able to look at a musical score and 'think' sound, to read and write music as easily as words" (Choksy 1988, 11). Although Kodály's definition of musical literacy is a multidimensional one, it tends to restrict the notion of informed musicianship to Western European traditions. However, while I acknowledge that the development of musical literacy is an important component of learning some musical traditions (in the holistic, cultural sense that Elliott means), I urge that we keep in mind the countless other musical practices that pivot on nonnotational, aural literacies (e.g., Donegal[5] fiddle music or Ewe drumming).

In many ways, Elliott's praxialism is also compatible with the Kodály approach. First, both views want children actively involved in a combination of music making, singing, creating rhythmic and vocal accompaniments to songs, and active listening. Second, the Kodály approach offers a rich array of tools and concepts for the development of musical literacy. Third, Kodály specialists have been at the forefront of the movement to include world folk musics in the curriculum. Fourth, Kodály teaching techniques provide excellent ways of approaching what Elliott calls "musical problem solving" and "problem reduction" in music education. Fifth, children who study music in a Kodály-based program tend to develop lifelong skills and excellent musical ears. Sixth, the commitment of Orff and Kodály specialists to involving children in making music—singing, playing, dancing, composing, and improvising—fits completely with the principles that Elliott proposes.

On the other hand, there is a difference of focus between the traditional approaches of Orff and Kodály and the new praxial philosophy. For example, practitioners need to examine their choices of repertoire and the organization of their curricula in light of Elliott's praxial arguments for musical pluralism. Also, the organization of curricula based on a progression of verbal concepts (in the case of Kodály), or historical musical forms (in the case of Orff), means that repertoire is chosen for being the "best example" of a particular concept or form.

In contrast to these organizing strategies, Elliott holds that music curricula should be based on careful choices of musical works (in a reasonable variety of styles) that have the best potential for developing a range of musical understandings and skills and, therefore, maximizing children's musical enjoyment. This is essentially what good music teachers have always done: they make excellent and authentic musical works (not verbal concepts) the focus of their curricula so that children will experience the power and beauty of music.

Educating Musicianship

Traditional approaches to music education begin with the child's body; specifically, the voice is considered a primary vehicle for musical experience. Singing in the elementary music classroom is one of the most easily implemented musical components of the curriculum and, often, the most misunderstood. In our efforts to make all children feel comfortable in the singing classroom, we are sometimes guilty of accepting whatever they offer and giving no guidance or constructive feedback for their musical-vocal improvement. This is especially the case in elementary singing contexts. We are eager to encourage children to sing; we strive to "bring out" their voices. However, some teachers fear that they will dampen children's enthusiasm for music if they teach them how to use their voices healthfully and beautifully. Other teachers feel that, by teaching children techniques of vocal production in the contexts of performing, composing, listening, and so forth, we will make singing more technical and less spontaneous.

Bad music teaching can have these results, of course. However, when music is taught musically in context, as Elliott proposes, children learn to use their voices comfortably, with the result that they become musically empowered to sing with confidence and to tackle the challenges of a broader and deeper range of pieces and styles.

How can we structure singing-based classrooms to be congruent with the principles of *Music Matters*? Elliott suggests structuring classes as "reflective musical practicums." This means using excellent music from several styles as the foundation of children's action (making and listening) and study. In a practicum, students and their teacher work together to explore the many possibilities of carefully selected works of choral music. By "possibilities" I mean the interpretive possibilities of a given piece, or the several dimensions of meaning that a piece can present for deep listening (Elliott provides a map of what to listen for in music: Elliott 1995, 199), or the possibilities of listening to recordings of similar pieces in the same style-practice, or composing pieces in the same style as the piece of music chosen for choral singing.

So, instead of merely singing through a number of songs, or merely identifying the structural elements of songs, the singing experience as a reflective practicum is embedded in the musical world that swirls around each piece selected for singing-listening and other possibilities.

Yes, students also learn how to use their voices to produce tone well, how to practice the music reading and writing skills that arise from the context of the repertoire being studied, and how to perform expressively and with stylistic integrity (see Dolloff 1998).

In these ways, the praxial philosophy offers a concept of music education that goes far beyond teaching disembodied skills and concepts that have little transfer to children's musical lives, present or future. Drawing on the research literature on situated cognition, Elliott reminds us that teaching skills, such as breath management, vocal technique, and counting, are instances of mere problem reduction: that is, skills that need to develop and become automatized gradually and parenthetically in the processes of making and listening to music enjoyably. In other words, the praxial curriculum remains centered on musical problem solving (not mere technical-problem reduction) in relation to real musical practices and and excellent pieces of music conceived as multidimensional challenges.

In the praxial view, a major outcome of children's learning is the development of their musicianship (which, Elliott insists, always includes "listenership") as demonstrated in their singing and listening, and in their reflections about their musical experience of singing. Elliott (1993) describes the way musicianship is developed through music performing or any other kind of music making:

> Moving "inside" and becoming part of musical practices by learning to make music well is the only way that all the component knowings of musicianship develop and cohere. Learning to interpret and perform music is a matter of progressive musical problem finding and problem solving. It is through active music making, in relation to standards and traditions of creative musical practice, that early, middle, and secondary school students develop musicianship. (14)

Singing in the classroom is often underestimated for the richness of possibilities it holds. That is, when singing is the medium of music education there are numerous ways of expanding the singing-listening experience, depending on the musical style practice chosen (e.g., an Irish song, a Zulu song, a Bach chorale, or a jazz selection). As Rogoff, Matusov, and White (1996) propose, members of communities have varying roles to play in the activity of each community. These roles rotate as members engage in a variety of projects. This holds true for the singing classroom, too. Even in the most traditional Western European musical practices (e.g., Renaissance, baroque, classical, romantic) there are a variety of roles students can and should experience. Think of the traditional performance roles in choral music—conductor, arranger, singer, singer-as-listener, audience member. In Elliott's "community-practicum" model of music education (1995, 269–288), students-as-participants rotate these roles as they solve the musical problems inherent in their repertoire. This is what Elliott intends when he discusses apprenticeship and the need to immerse students in musical style-communities or "musical practices."

Moreover, students who usually sing in response to the gestures of their conductor should also have opportunities to experience the responsibilities, perspectives, and feelings that go with acting as their own conductors. For example, students should be encouraged to reflect on and monitor their own vocal responses and constructs and to learn to listen to their peers as they conduct small parts of pieces that their chorus is learning. The latter may involve students in keeping the musical pulse, using hand signs, mapping the contour of phrases in the air, or using conducting gestures as they sing or move to the music. Students should also take on the role of musical coach to their peers as they listen to each other sing, and as they reflect on how they can collectively meet the challenges of the pieces they are learning. Through the use of video and audiotapes, students can also be their own audiences, listening to their rehearsals and performances with an artistic ear to what they would like to improve.

Arts Propel, a curriculum and assessment project developed by scholars at Harvard, provides excellent ideas for students' self-assessment, which Elliott (1995) draws upon, too (282–285). Elliott insists that teachers should also develop students' listening skills by means of "ensemble critiques" and "listening logs" in addition to continuously targeting students' attention to various dimensions of the musical works they are learning to perform, improvise, compose, and conduct.

Students are not the only participants who should be flexible. Teachers must be prepared to switch roles from conductor to performer, demonstrating their musicianship by singing ideas for the students. In this way, they make their musical decision-making processes accessible and available to their students through their active performances in the classroom, and they target students' attention to key details of the music the students are learning to produce, interpret, perform, and listen-for.

Yes, sharing responsibility with one's students can be an unsettling experience at first. However, the key to designing the music classroom as a reflective practicum is to allow students' skills and understandings to emerge through authentic interactions with excellent pieces of music. This can be a powerful teaching tool, because students learn to listen with discriminating ears when they can reflect critically on their own and their teacher's interpretations and performances, identifying positive elements and offering suggestions for improvement. Regular opportunities to do so will give students many openings to verbalize what they hear, or do not hear, and what they are learning about the kinesthetic and vocal principles they have been learning in practice (Elliott 1995, 92).

Composing, Arranging, and Improvising

About these forms of musicing, Elliott says: "Composing and arranging are *major* aspects of the praxial curriculum. Composing and arranging can and should be learned in close connection with listening, performing, improvising, and conducting" (1997, 5).

Composing, arranging, and improvising are aspects of a multidimensional elementary music classroom that teachers often fear. Similarly, although the Orff and Kodály approaches make composing, arranging, and improvising key elements of their curricula, Orff and Kodály teachers often lack the knowledge and experience needed to compose and improvise themselves, let alone teach others to compose and improvise. Thus, they are not able to take their students beyond the novice stages of these ways of making music. Elliott lists some specific ways in which composing, arranging, and improvising should be part of music education. (In chapter 14 of this book, Pam Burnard provides excellent narratives about the composing experiences of students she has observed.)

Very specifically, now, let us ask: Can children be taught to improvise? Many teachers believe that improvising is a natural ability. However, if we think of jazz improvisers, we need to consider how they are able to create melodies on the spot. In fact, as Elliott explains, jazz musicians intentionally build a bank of riffs or characteristic bits, as Howard Gardner calls them. In other words, jazz improvising is a matter of building up and then accessing these patterns to play with and combine in new ways during actual performances. (Jeff Martin concurs with this view; see chapter 9 in this book.)

We can and should teach children to do this kind of building, playing with, and combining toward individual expressions and variations through improvising. Elliott details ways of developing such musical creativity (see, for example, Elliott 1995, 224–227, 234). Unfortunately, by the time classical musicians reach university, most are terrified of improvising. In my elementary music education classes at the University of Toronto I deliberately help students regress to their earliest stages of joy in *playing* with sounds, improvising by playing with riffs, and so on. Many have never been told that "it's okay to play with sounds," to explore possibilities. (This situation highlights a major failure in the elementary music education programs of these future music educators.)

To paraphrase Donna Brink Fox, novice music educators don't need to reclaim childhood music education experiences; they need to create them. This is especially the case with composing and improvising. Many music teachers do not have a repertoire of composing and improvising experiences and ideas they can draw from with confidence. The result in the classroom can be minimally satisfying for students and teachers alike.

Improvising and composing can and should be forms of music making that students and teachers learn how to do. Student teachers should learn how to organize composing and improvising projects as natural corollaries to musical performing and listening, in various styles, in order to provide their future students with a palette of materials and strategies for their future use and enjoyment. Central to this is the understanding that composing and improvising are contextual in nature. That is, as Elliott (1995) emphasizes, composing and improvising always occur in relation to some specific musical style-practice context (169–170). It is not simply a matter of "improvising" and judging such creativity in purely subjective terms; it is always a matter of improvising in relation to a musical practice-style context. Even an aleatoric style of improvising has a particular history attached, specific recorded examples for listening and specific ways of doing the improvising, and so on. This praxial view of creativity (endorsed by Howard Gardner and Mihaly Csikszentmihalyi, among others) makes the teaching and learning of composing and improvising much easier. Why? Because the praxial-contextual idea of creativity acknowledges and utilizes the "operating principles" of each specific musical style of improvising and composing (e.g., blues improvising using the blues scale with the help of blues recordings), which, in turn, gives teachers and students practical guidelines, models, demonstrations, and boundaries (but not fixed rules and regulations) for their efforts.

Traditional Approaches Revisited

The Orff approach to music education is predicated on the development of children's compositional and improvisational skills. Improvisation precedes composition and develops out of singing and playing experiences. The initial use of ostinato and limited pitch ranges provide "scaffolding" in early experiences with improvisation. Students complete phrases in call-response forms (which occur in many music cultures). Next, students create longer phrases; eventually, they improvise larger forms. As children remember, reproduce, and edit their improvisations, they enter the realm of composing. The use of the pentatonic scale is an important early stage of singing, improvising, and composing in the Orff approach.

Unfortunately, some Orff programs never progress past the use of pentatony. The richness of tonality available in a variety of modes, and the musical forms that are possible beyond the rondo, are rarely tapped. It is here that it is useful to reiterate Elliott's maxim that musicians don't "just improvise"; instead, musicians improvise within specific musical-practice (style) contexts (e.g., North German baroque organ music, Cape Breton fiddle music, Chicago blues, Kansas City swing) governed by traditions and standards that are embodied in the recordings, live performances, histories, and theoretical concepts preserved in the writings and oral histories of music makers (performers, composers, et al.) who make music of a particular kind.

Arranging song material is also an important component of the Orff approach. Elliott mourns the fact that arranging is not given a more prominent place in music education. Arranging is a potent form of music learning because in the process of musical arranging, children are compelled to reflect on the full range of a work's musical dimensions in choosing how to express their conception of a piece through their arrangement.

The Kodály approach to composition and improvisation grows out of music making and listening experiences. Here, too, composition follows improvisation. Characteristic compositional activities can take the form of changing the mode of known songs, using a sequence to extend melodies, augmenting or diminishing rhythms, or other techniques for writing variations. For example, after such experiences with (say) "Frère Jacques," students could listen to Mahler's Symphony no. 2 in order to focus on the choices that Mahler made. It is in these circular patterns of performing, composing, and listening that the Kodály approach comes closest to the praxial curriculum proposed by Elliott.

Technology

Technology is changing the way that we interact with music. It offers huge opportunities to enhance the teaching of composition. Children can use computers to listen immediately to the results of their compositions. They can work out a musical idea in steps, play it in stages, and hear it back with a richness of texture, dynamics, or tempo variations. It becomes much easier to realize orchestrations and to share compositions electronically.

As I have mentioned several times, one of the most significant tenets of *Music Matters* is the importance of musicing with an awareness of the traditions and standards of each style-practice. As we rush to keep up with the ever-changing world of music technology, we are also involved in establishing new traditions and exploring new standards of music making and listening. Children often have a capacity and comfort with technology that surpasses ours. It behooves us to critically explore the ways technology can enhance our teaching and our experiences of music, and the ways in which it may change our conceptions of making and listening to music.

Conducting

I remember, as a five-year-old, standing in the sunshine in my living room, listening to a recording in which a mellifluous voice talked me through the process of conducting an orchestral piece. I have searched unsuccessfully for that recording since I began teaching conducting. In tones that motivated me to imagine the orchestra sitting before me, my guide directed my attention to the violins, the brass, and the woodwinds while the orchestra played a symphonic work. I was encouraged to cue the strings and perform all sorts of musical directions, many of which were over my head. What has remained with me all these years later is the manner of instruction. The instructor guided me through the process of finding specific problems in conducting: for example, learning to look in the direction of the instrumental section as it entered, showing dynamic changes through the size of my gesture, and guiding the tempo. In a very real way, I felt as if I were creating music along with the orchestra while learning how to do it.

All of this echoes Elliott's proposals for teaching listening and conducting together. Often, we teach conducting only after students achieve a high level of musicianship in another area. This presupposes a Western European view of the conductor as the musical expert or "maestro." In contrast, Elliott lists conducting as one of the basic ways of developing all children's musicianship. I agree and propose that teaching young children to conduct (in the broadest sense of this word) is one way of establishing a kinesthetic relationship with music and a valuable way for children to participate in music making.

Pedagogues who follow the Dalcroze approach to music education have been doing this for years. Full-body movements performed in time with a qualified and—most important—musically sensitive teacher's improvised piano accompaniments provide an important step in establishing children's awareness of meter, according to Dalcroze. Large movements, for example, demonstrate a child's awareness of accent and unaccented beats (i.e., meter). What is missing here, however, is the richness of the experience of gesture and the experience of specific musical works.

By way of example, let me offer a vignette. Involving students in conducting can be a technique to use for problem reduction. That is, I often ask students in performance groups to conduct along with me in order to reinforce their understanding of how long to sing a sustained note, where to place a cut-off, and how to feel a tempo change. Group conducting is also a potent way of allowing students who are less comfortable with their bodies (particularly as they reach the upper ends of elementary school) to express music kinesthetically. And conducting allows students to get "inside" a musical style-practice, develop their "supervisory listening knowledge" (Elliott 1995, 66–68) of a work of music, promote their listening-for, and encourage children to make decisions about musical interpretation based on stepping back for the big picture of their own and their group's efforts to perform musically.

Conducting is also a way for children to express their musicianship, a way that they can demonstrate their musical understandings through the qualities and choices of their gestures. Even very young children enjoy this experience.

A word of caution is in order. Just as there are different standards and traditions for performing vocally or instrumentally in various musical practices, children should learn that the role of a conductor, and a conductor's physical instantiation of musical ideas, will differ in different musical traditions. Hence, it is not appropriate to teach children to conduct traditional Ewe music from Ghana in a Western European style, although it would be essential to involve children in moving to this music as Ewe dancers-listeners do.

Movement

In the Western European tradition, musicians tend to view movement as extraneous, except where moving is absolutely necessary for the manipulation of instruments. In childhood, however, movement is a natural aspect of music. The body lifts, sways, bounces, or taps with the music. Somewhere along the way we tend to eliminate this natural connection from music making. This is wrong. Elementary music education must capitalize on the natural inclination of children to move to music. The Dalcroze approach is grounded in the belief that "the acuteness of our musical feelings will depend on the acuteness of our bodily sensations" (Jaques-Dalcroze, cited in Finlay 1971, 3).

Movement is often neglected in music classrooms because teachers forget many natural connections between music and movement. In many musical traditions, movement is the motivation for music making. For example, in mouth music—a tradition in many world music cultures—vocables and text are used to create instrumental textures. In other traditions, such as Irish lilting, Scottish *puirt a beuil*, and Acadian *reel a bouche*, dance steps set the tempo and style of the music. Movement underpins tempo, style, and rhythm, whether people are singing a strathspey, a jig, a hornpipe, or a reel. While studying mouth music in Cape Breton (Nova Scotia, Canada), my teacher would always stand up and dance a few steps to set the tempo before we began. Why? Ask yourself this: is it possible to sing mouth music well without knowing that it is a kind of dance music and without knowing how to dance (to some degree) the steps and style of this dance music? No. Without these kinds of knowing, teachers and children will miss the heartbeat of this musical style, practice, and tradition.

The power of movement and music was brought home to me very poignantly during the opening ceremonies of the 1998 Olympics. The conductor Seiji Ozawa conducted a performance of the final movement of Beethoven's Ninth Symphony with choirs singing in sites around the globe. During the performance, the television cameras alternated between Ozawa and the orchestra in Japan and the various choirs worldwide. It was a glorious technological achievement to have all these singers coordinated from all points of the globe—the Brandenburg Gate, the steps of the Sydney Opera House, the United Nations building in New York City, and the ocean shore in South Africa. When the camera panned to the South African choir, they were moving while singing in a style reminiscent of traditional African dance. To me, this was completely natural, an expression of their musical relationship with Beethoven. It made me hear Beethoven in a way that I have never heard it before. Now, I am not suggesting that we choreograph all Western choral performances. I am only repeating my view that movement is a basic component in the musical education of children. We should enable them to expand their musical experiences through the use of movement, reinforce their use of movement to focus on musical features, and make them aware of movement as a natural partner in many musical traditions and as a natural expression of their musicianship.

Listening

Elliott insists that listening should be taught continuously and systematically while students learn to make music in several ways: "artistic music listening can and must be developed in relation to the musical works students are learning" (1995, 179). He proposes a reciprocal relationship between music making and music listening, and he views informed music listening as a manifestation of musicianship.

Where do we start to extend the palette of children's listening experiences and to build their capacity to "do" music listening deeply and critically? Elliott proposes that children be taught to listen by learning to listen to several dimensions of their own performances, to other performances of the same work (via recordings), and to recorded examples of pieces from practices that are the same as or related to those they are working in.

For many years, excellent music educators have been doing just these things in order to give students access to larger works that they are not able to perform themselves. For example, many textbooks suggest that when children sing the Shaker melody "Simple Gifts," this should be followed by a guided listening experience with the Copland composition "Variations on a Shaker Melody." In *The Kodály Method,* Lois Choksy includes a valuable appendix of such "listening themes."

Elliott makes a similar proposal, but he insists that singing should be taught well so that children learn to interpret and learn to listen-for all six dimensions of a work, which he explains and diagrams in the listening guide he summarizes after several chapters of development in *Music Matters* (1995, 199). However, the characteristic that distinguishes the praxial approach to music listening is Elliott's postmodern emphasis on teaching children to attend to much more than the formal design components of works and to apply and sharpen their music listening skills (in all dimensions—structural, interpretive, emotive, ideological, and so forth) in their music-making experiences. Again, Elliott reminds us that musical works are contextual. Whether we perform, compose, or listen to music, we are doing so within a set of cultural expectations. "If music listening and musical works are culturally informed and informative, what is the most appropriate way to develop students' understandings of them? My answer is: by teaching students to meet significant musical challenges in teaching learning situations that are close approximations of real music cultures" (206).

Listening charts of musical elements are central in the aesthetic approach to music education. One of the important tools for making listening accessible to students is the listening chart. But the major weakness of the aesthetic-education concept of a listening chart (e.g., Reimer 1984) is its one-dimensional, modernist notion of musical works, which Elliott challenges and replaces with his multidimensional model. The challenge for today's teachers is to redesign listening charts. We must capture the complete nature and richness of musical works (see Elliott 1995, 199), which means opening students' minds and ears to the several dimensions of musical meaning that musical works embody and present in a variety of combinations: structural, interpretive, traditional, expressional, ideological, and representative dimensions of meaning. And, says Elliott, we must strive to do so in ways that are age appropriate and enjoyable.

At this point, I need to say a word about musical notation. In practical terms, I believe it is important for children to see notation (graphic or traditional staff forms) embedded in the other aspects of a listening chart. Some of the most powerful examples I have seen include:

- the notated version of the a melodic theme;
- images of the performing ensemble or instruments used;
- graphic representations of musical movement, such as dynamic or rhythmic changes, textural or timbral complexity; and
- other representations of important features of the music, such as emotive or representational meanings.

To summarize: listening charts can target students' attention to single or multiple events, layers, and combinations of meanings. Hand in hand with listening to music by means of listening guides is the idea of teaching and permitting students to do "listening homework" or "listening projects" by having them design their own listening charts. Even for the youngest children, the making of personal listening charts for class sharing and demonstration can be a dynamic way of understanding what children hear or fail to hear in specific pieces. The process of teaching our students how to create listening charts is another example of Elliott's reflective practicum in which the teacher demonstrates explicitly how he or she makes sense of his or her listening experiences.

Integration

In the current educational climate, it is not unusual to hear phrases such as "music across the curriculum." This often means using music as a tool for teaching such things as math, grammatical rules, historical facts, and so on. Music can be a powerful means of assisting memory and learning. (I still remember all the words to "Schoolhouse Rock" and "Conjunction Junction," a 1970s-era series of educational shorts on television.) This approach does not represent true integration, however. It is merely another approach to teaching math or language skills by means of music. Many students find it a helpful learning tool, but it is not music education.

Elliott argues against forcing integration by means of unmusical "common elements" approaches and the like. He argues that there are many opportunities in teaching musical practices for authentic, integrative experiences without creating artificial ones. In cooperation with specialists in other artistic areas, we need to strive to create realistic situations of integrative practice. As Elliott (1995) says:

> the relationships between music making and dance, poetry, and drama are an important part of what specific practices and works present for our understanding and enjoyment. These relationships are part of the cultural-ideological dimension of listening and listenables. Accordingly, to learn how to make and listen for musical works that involve other artistic practices requires reference to the whole web of beliefs, concepts, traditions and standards that explain how certain musicers and listeners understand the contribution that other performing and nonperforming arts make to their music cultures. (248)

Many activities that teachers have traditionally thought of as integration are, for Elliott, a basic and natural part of learning particular styles and works because other arts are part of the sociohistorical tradition of such styles and works. It is important to engage students in exploring the cultural context of a piece. The social ethos of its performance setting; the ritualistic meaning or role of a piece; and the political underpinnings, dance, drama, or costumes that are part of its meaning—none of these are considered extramusical in Elliott's view; rather, all of these dimensions, and many more, are part of the musical nature, values, and meanings of that piece of music.

For example, the musical culture of Cape Breton in Nova Scotia, Canada, owes its development to the cultures of its early settlers, to their geographical isolation from much of Canada, and to their continuing usage of the Gaelic language. Although it would be possible for young children to enjoy and perform a piece of Cape Breton folk music as a "song," doing so would forfeit much of the musical significance of that piece and its musical practice. I have taught simple milling songs as part of an elementary music curriculum to children aged eight to twelve. In the process of performing and learning how to sing these songs stylistically, I have pointed out, for example, that the strong beat comes from the original setting for which milling songs were composed or improvised. That is, before the mechanization of cloth production, a whole community would gather to help an individual "mill" or preshrink a yardage of handwoven cloth. They would soak the cloth and then sit around a table in a circle, twisting the cloth, beating it on the table, and passing it around the circle between beats. To make the work pass more quickly, the circle would sing milling songs—a tradition that arrived with settlers from Scotland, where they were originally called "waulking" songs. The "milling frolic" became a center for the preservation and creation of song. Milling songs take a call-and-response form, which makes them ideal for improvisation and composition. When I teach children these milling songs, I use lengths of fabric, sewn into a circle, to approximate the cloth; thus, we sing the songs in a way that closely resembles how they are still performed in rural communities of Cape Breton to this day. Children also listen to recordings made by traditional singers of the milling songs that they are singing. A logical educational extension to the singing of these songs is the improvisation of verses to traditional songs, or the composition of new songs. Students may also want to explore weaving in art class, or investigate the patterns and meanings of tartans or the clearing of the Highlands that forced Scottish migration to Nova Scotia. To me, this is integration at its best: exploring the richness of a musical practice as it informs and is informed by its cultural context. This is what Elliott's praxial philosophy intends and recommends.

Myths about the Education of Children

Some educators feel offended by the use of the word "excellence" in connection with the musical education of children. They view "excellence" as elitist. On the contrary, I believe that to strive to do something well is to set standards—to affirm that something is worth doing well. After all, we wouldn't tell a child who presented us with $2 + 2 = 5$ that he or she is "close enough." In music, the answers are not written in a list of tables. This doesn't mean, however, that we should decline to help all children learn how far they can develop their musicianship. This is not possible if we only accept first answers, first attempts, or spontaneous reactions. At the same time, of course, we must not allow the gradual and systematic development of excellence to take precedence over our children's emotional well-being.

Another myth surrounds relevancy. One movement in general education seeks to make all curricula more relevant to children. However, what teachers sometimes consider relevant for children is not what children themselves consider relevant. Relevancy, for children, often equates with familiarity. The developmental psychologist Margaret Donaldson cautions that to insist that all education be directly relevant to children is a trap. Donaldson (1996) points out that while the intuition underlying the relevancy issue might seem sound, insistence on teaching only those things that are immediately relevant can be limiting. She holds that doing so "can lead to neglect of the fact that education is about *changing lives*. It is about opening up new directions in which the life may move and thus enlarging the range of relevance. It is about proposing new purposes, new desires" (340; italics in original).

Elliott affirms this view of relevance by insisting that the music curriculum be constructed around a reasonable diversity of musical styles. Some will be familiar to children; others will be new and will offer children opportunities to make previously unknown musics accessible, understandable and, hopefully, a satisfying part of their future musical lives in the sense of what Elliott discusses as "tones for us" (877–889). So, we must not confuse instant appeal and relevance.

Conclusion

The praxial curriculum is multidimensional. Elliott insists that lifelong learning in music and a lifelong involvement with music will result only from enabling children to

> live-into different music cultures through artistic action, induction and immersion. Becoming actively engaged in the contexts of different music cultures—engaging musical works in their contextual nature as artistic-social-cultural achievement from multiple perspectives—enables students to build understandings and informed evaluations of individual pieces. But there is more: deep engagements of these kinds tend to motivate students to support and seek

the multiple values of musical engagements as a *life-theme*—as a central part
of their lives. (1997, 14; italics in original)

One of the key features of the praxial philosophy applied to the elementary music
classroom is the emergent nature of the teaching and learning experience. As teachers and students address the full musical potential of a piece of music, they will be
presented with many options for the organic inclusion of a multifaceted experience.
Moving between forms of music making, singing, dancing, conducting, composing,
arranging, improvising, and listening allows students to engage a musical work from
a variety of perspectives. Accordingly, many opportunities for teaching "about"
music (for developing "formal musical knowledge" that official state curricula require) will arise naturally and fluidly if we respect the multiplicity of meanings in the
musics we are studying and if we keep our pedagogical senses tuned to deepening
students' understandings actively and contextually.

Permit me to conclude with a poem by David McCord (cited in Booth 1982) that
speaks to the unity of body, spirit, and music that is the natural state of the child before we teach him or her to compartmentalize.

Blessed Lord, what it is to be young:
To be of, to be for, to be among—
Be enchanted, enthralled,
Be the caller, the called,
The singer, the song and the sung.

This is the aim of praxial music education for children. The values of music do
not inhere in making distinctions between mind and body, between verbal and nonverbal, or between performance and perception, but in recognizing the multiple layers or meaning and interpretation that exist for musical participants (doers *and*
listeners). Separating musical doings does not recognize the interconnectedness of
performing, listening, composing, improvising, and conducting (and other ways of
making music) that Elliott's philosophy embraces and wants for children.

Likewise, in a child's musical experience, there is no distinction between the musician, the music, and the making of music. During the moments that a child is
musicing, he or she *is* "the singer, the song, and the sung." Thinking in these ways
about music education will help us to respect the nature and values of music and the
way children learn music most enjoyably. Our elementary music classrooms can be
places in which we nurture the fullness of musical experience. By allowing children
to immerse themselves in pieces of music in ways that cherish the child and the
music, we are enabling our students to embrace music as one of their most important
life-themes.

References

Booth, D. 1982. *Poems please!* Toronto: Prentice Hall.

Campbell, P. S. 1998. *Songs in their heads: Music and its meaning in children's lives.* New
York: Oxford University Press.

Choksy, L. 1988. *The Kodály method.* 2nd ed. Englewood Cliffs, NJ: Prentice Hall.

Dolloff, L. 1993. *Das Schulwerk: A foundation for the cognitive, musical and artistic development of children.* Toronto: Canadian Music Education Research Centre.

———. 1998. The singing classroom: A community of musicians. In B. Roberts, ed., *Sharing the voices: The phenomenon of singing; Proceedings of the international symposium,* 89–96. St. John's: Memorial University of Newfoundland.

Donaldson, M. 1996. Humanly possible: Education and the scope of mind. In D. Olson and N. Torrance, eds., *The handbook of education and human development,* 324–344. Cambridge, MA: Blackwell.

Elliott, D. J. 1993. When I sing: The nature and value of choral music education. *Choral Journal* 33 (8):11–17.

———. 1995. *Music matters: A new philosophy of music education.* New York: Oxford University Press.

———. 1997. Continuing matters: Myths, realities, rejoinders. *Bulletin of the Council for Research in Music Education* 132:1–37.

Finlay, E. 1971. *Rhythm and movement: Applications of Dalcroze eurhythmics.* Evanston, IL: Summy-Birchard.

Orff, C. 1962/1977. Demonstration with recordings. Lecture at the University of Toronto. Reprinted in I. McNeill-Carley, ed., *Orff re-echoes,* 53–59. American Orff-Schulwerk Association.

Pramling, I. 1996. Understanding and empowering the child as a learner. In D. Olson and N. Torrance, eds., *The handbook of education and human development,* 565–592. Cambridge, MA: Blackwell.

Reimer, B. 1984. *Developing the experience of music.* Englewood Cliffs, NJ: Prentice-Hall.

Rogoff, G., E. Matusov, and C. White. 1996. Models of teaching and learning: Participation in a community of learners. In D. Olson and N. Torrance, eds., *The handbook of education and human development,* 388–414. Cambridge, MA: Blackwell.

16

Why Don't I Feel Included in These Musics, or Matters

PATRICIA O'TOOLE

As I read *Music Matters*, I become aware of the differences between the worlds in which Elliott and I speak about and make music. Our differences are based on our identities as musicians. The problem I have is that my identity has radically shifted since my formal education in music to the extent that I feel as if I barely fit into the category of "music educator." As a feminist (a precarious title at best) I am no longer accepting of the ways girls are positioned and neglected in musicing, or the ways boys are damaged by too much privileging, and I want these concerns and problematic identities on the table—and in Elliott's book. Additionally, I have worked with city kids in a youth choir who have challenged my notions of race and class issues while teaching me that music education methods are not universal; they legitimize the experiences of white suburban children. Identity issues of city children are not part of our professional conversations or teacher training.

So, how do I write myself, the experiences I have had, and the students I work with into *Music Matters*, or at least clarify our presence? I will pry open Elliott's definition of musicing with help from Chris Small, who agrees (1990) that music is a verb but finds musical meaning by "centering on relationships in music—relationships between person and person, between person and society, between humanity and the natural world, etc. (5)." I will also argue that a primary reason for music making is identity affirmation, and that though Elliott has hinted at this in his text, mostly he is concerned with technical and performative aspects of musicing, which offer musicers limited identities. Because context is the playground for identity formation, I will visit Elliott's discussion of context and offer some extensions. I will then give several examples from my own teaching of contexts that suggest diversified issues for Elliott's theorizing.

As an aside, I approach all of this from my feminist politics, which celebrates and recognizes difference. In this chapter, I do not plan to spin out or explain differences in feminisms, but merely offer grounding with this quote from bell hooks (1989) that feminisms are "a commitment to eradicating the ideology of domination that permeates Western culture on various levels—sex, race, class, to name a few" (6). It is from this standpoint that I engage Elliott's book.

And, because Elliott's text focuses on praxis—a theorized practice—I find it imperative to challenge the theoretical with the practical, in hopes of closing the usual gap between practitioners and theorists. I realize that in sharing anecdotes I risk being dismissed as merely anecdotal, as finding the anomalous example to unhinge a theory. However, I find my "anomalous" experiences accumulating and, therefore, moving toward common occurrences that merit attention. In fact, scholars in other parts of the academy such as education, anthropology, women's studies, cultural studies, and sociology have heavily theorized these experiences. It seems that only music education hesitates to recognize them as crucial sites of inquiry and theorizing. As a result, I hope readers can approach these anecdotes as representations of serious issues taken from earnest practice.

Musicing and Musicking

When I taught at the State University of New York–Buffalo I took my music education students to observe Charlie Keil's MUSE (Musicians United for Superior Education) program, where traditional drummers and dancers teach their country's music in elementary city schools that otherwise have cut formal music education. Most of the MUSE teachers do not have Western music or education training, so they teach as they were taught in their home countries as children. University students were usually overwhelmed when they observed this program. First, they were confronted with media-created fears about dangerous city schools and neighborhoods, as they braced themselves for a random drive-by shooting (which, they were certain, happens every day). Then, they observed a music lesson that looks nothing like any music lesson they have ever experienced. Within the MUSE classroom the drumming instructor frequently teaches drumming at the same time the dance instructor teaches dancing. There is no tidy categorization of skills; both drumming and dancing are learned, taught, resisted, and negotiated—all at the same time. As a result of the drumming and activity level, the classroom atmosphere is generally noisy, chaotic, and full of seemingly off-task behavior. However, when the student drummers and dancers synchronize at the end of the class period to perform their newly learned skills, the university students were usually surprised and impressed by the proficiency the young drummers and dancers were "suddenly" able to display.

Unfortunately, my university students typically would not categorize this experience as music education; they thought it was more akin to a physical education class than a music class. The reasons for this dismissal are not difficult to imagine. Most of the university students have never heard music like this before; they do not learn music like this, in places like this, or in this manner; and they cannot perform music like this. Hence, everything they know about music education and musical training is missing from the MUSE context. Because this music education experience wipes out their identities as musicians, they in turn wipe out the MUSE experience.

How do we make sense of MUSE within conventional music education? Elliott begins with the notion that music is a diverse human practice, with emphasis on practice; music is something you do. Small (1990) takes the same notion—that music is a verb instead of a noun—but extends the definition to include the social grounding of music:

> To music is to take part in a musical performance, not just as performer but also as listener, or as provider of material for performance—what we call composing—or in any other way, dancing, for example, should anyone be dancing, or even perhaps taking the tickets at the door or shifting the piano around. Musicking is thus not the same as either "making music" or "performing," since both those words apply only to what the performers are doing. (5)

Musicking, then, is something that people do together. Small uses one verb to describe all possible interactions with music because he does not wish to distinguish between performers and all other participants in a music event. He argues that it is these distinctions that lead to hegemonic valuing of musics and those involved. Small suggests that there is significance in what music is being performed, but the musical genre does not determine the meaning of the event as a whole. Ultimately, musicking takes place in a physical and cultural context, and therefore it is the diversity of musickers within a specific context who make meaning and give structure to their experiences. As a result, through the act of musicking, Small suggests, we affirm, explore, and celebrate our identity; musickers are saying, for right now, "this is who we are" (1990, 5). In the case of MUSE, the music students were creating and affirming identities, and all participants, from the university observers to those "goofing off," were significant to the musicking.

Elliott focuses on some of the same concerns as Small, as exemplified in the following quote:

> To develop full musical understanding and appreciation, we need to re-mind ourselves and others that MUSIC is a diverse artistic-social-cultural practice. As Wolterstorff insists, "we shall have to renounce our myopic focus on works of art and look at the social practices of art. . . . We shall have to look at the interplay between works, practices, and participants in the practices." At the same time (and not surprisingly), one of the most important benefits of a more comprehensive concept of music is a more complete understanding of the nature and significance of musical works. (1995, 198)

Although Elliott is arguing for experiencing a "fuller measure of the human values that musicing and listening involve" (1995, 201), he limits musicing to performers, has a separate category for listeners, and does not include any other kind of participant nor the identity issues Small addresses. Further, his inclusion of the term "artistic" suggests a conventional bottom line that supports a hierarchical stacking of musics and skills.

I fear Elliott's language in *Music Matters* encourages dismissal of nontraditional ways of musicing, as in the case of MUSE. The institution of music education offers narrow musical identities to its musicers and closes down alternatives that challenge normative practices, as illustrated above. A difficulty I encounter in preservice education is convincing students that musicing is primarily an act of creating, exploring, and affirming identities. As teachers, then, we need to recognize, support, and offer a variety of identity positions to accommodate and encourage differences between students. It is perfectly reasonable for children to explore their and others' ethnic identities through music, even if this process looks different from conventional music education, as in the MUSE example. Otherwise, by seeing all students as the same, we see them as ourselves, which in the case of most music teachers means white and middle class. It is ludicrous to think that all white, middle-class people have had the same experience, let alone people of Asian, African, Hispanic, or Jewish descent. It is equally ludicrous to believe that one form of musicing can incorporate all of these identity positions. However, in music education, our conventional methods suggest that we believe this to be true.

Identity is the process of becoming that is as much about who one imagines oneself to be or not to be. Fundamentally, all identities are unstable because they are always in process and music is one of the sites of identity that is engaged in the process of identification. Virginia Caputo (1996) argues:

> It is this point that has much to do with how music can play a profound role in understanding students' interests, hopes, and aspirations, and especially in how they wish to identify themselves, their differences and commonalties. Music can enable one to suspend expected ways of behaving and play with other imagined identities. Students can engage with music to understand similarities and differences as they are lived and not by appealing to biological explanations and other quantifiable "truths." Rather, through discourses such as popular culture, for example, students can speak and make sense of their social relations, making the process of identification an open-ended and shifting one. (6)

Elliott continually uses musical examples from a variety of cultures and ethnicities in an attempt to include a variety of new identities in music education. However, he never includes in his examples or discussion such subject positions as race, class, gender, sexuality, patriarchy, consumerism, age, and ability. Chris Small would argue that musical meaning does not reside in answering the question, "What does this music mean?," which is the question he claims is the preoccupation of the majority of Western musical criticism, theory, and music education. Rather, Small claims that musical meaning lies in negotiating identities within a culturally and historically defined context (1990, 7). In the MUSE classroom, then, musical meaning is found in a number of relationships between traditional African drummers and dancers and city children who bring diverse cultural and ethnic backgrounds to this setting; between the experiences the artists had learning music in their countries and the teaching of it to city children within the confines and definitions of an American classroom; and between how the children imagine their musical selves and the Afrocentric musical experiences they were encountering, to name a few.

Context

As stated previously, musicing is primarily an act of creating, exploring, and affirming identities, and context is the playground for this formation. In this section I review how Elliott describes context in *Music Matters* and scrutinize what sorts of identities and relationships these contexts encourage.

Elliott defines context as "the total of ideas, associations, and circumstances that surround, frame, and influence something and our understanding of that something." Context, then, is delineated as having four dimensions: what is done (the composition), what it leads to (historical development of performance practices), where it comes from (the outgrowth of historical performance practices), and the immediate context of its use and production (1995, 40). Elliott further states that, because these four dimensions exist in a dynamic relationship, the intersections create a context that is social, so that "we can expect these relationships to generate beliefs and controversies about who counts as a good musicer, about what counts as good music making, and so on" (41).

While there are various examples of context given throughout the book, I read "context" in *Music Matters* to mean the conventional aspects of music and performance analysis, such as composer, historical connections, performance practice, functions of the elements of music, and sociological aspects (mostly when discussing non-Western musics).

Further, the examples in *Music Matters* lead me to believe that context is something you step into as you learn or perform music, and therefore, it exists outside of those who are going to make the music. Context is preexisting, and, moreover, the context for Western music education historically is predetermined by white, Western men; therefore, we can assume appropriate limitations on the boundaries of musical preferences.

In addition, the autonomy of context in *Music Matters* is supported by Elliott's scientific approach of breaking it down into numbered dimensions (context begins with four dimensions, each of which then breaks down into another four, etc.). The science hypothesis asserts that knowledge exists in the world to be discovered; all one needs to do is develop or find the right tool to discover that knowledge. The present academic critique of science argues that the tools used in an experiment determine the type of knowledge discovered. For example, if one uses a hammer to put a metal piece into wood, one discovers that it goes quickly and smoothly with the right amount of force. However, if one uses a screwdriver, one discovers the need to twist and turn the metal piece. Hence, each of these tools leads to different understandings of the physical world. Moreover, each of these tools *produces* different knowledges about the metal and wood. *Music Matters* is missing discussions of how the tools (i.e., music history, music theory, music psychology) used to understand music or to determine what music matters have produced specific knowledges about music. These produced knowledges have become part of our professional "common sense" and, therefore, are difficult both to detect and to change.

For example, it has become common sense within the Western classical vocal tradition that men are encouraged to develop the upper part of their ranges (i.e., falsettos and alto ranges), while women are discouraged from developing their lower ranges and are limited to soprano and alto voice parts. This common sense is supported by the scientific notion that women who develop their lower ranges will harm the upper register and longevity of their voices. However, women have tenor and bass ranges, as we see readily in community and church choirs. Furthermore, what does it matter if a woman cannot sing high Cs all of her life? There are many ways for women with a low range to participate in music, as exemplified by jazz, Broadway, Sweet Adeline, and pop singers (e.g., Kim Carnes had an amazing career with a severely damaged voice).

What is not spoken in this discourse is that female vocal ranges are determined also according to cultural definitions of femininity; in the *bel canto* choral culture, women belting out resonant bass tones are not considered feminine. In this example, the tools used to determine vocal ranges, scientific vocal health, and cultural notions of femininity have created rigid institutionalized approaches to voice training that severely limit women's music making.

Take, for example, the twelve-year-old female tenor Ruby Helder (1896–1940, England). Helder, a child prodigy, was described by a famous English baritone, Charles Santley, as possessing "a natural, pure tenor voice of great beauty and power. She also possesses what few can boast—a thoroughly artistic temperament . . . in my opinion she has no rivals among the artists of the day" (Haynes 1993, 126). By the age of twelve she was making recordings, had been endorsed by Caruso, and was being offered roles at the Metropolitan Opera. However, by 1925 she received such reviews as:

> *Gramophone*: Miss Helder, if she will forgive my saying so, has a freak voice; a tenor, yet not tenor. I feel the same about it as I do the male alto, so I will not attempt to review this record.

> *The Times*: The voice has something in its quality akin to that of a true tenor; otherwise it might be described as a contralto. . . . It is quite lacking in the characteristic power and expression of the tenor's top register. (Haynes 1993, liner notes)

These two music critics live up to critics' notorious reputation for inhumanity; but in addition, they both show an inability and an unwillingness to deal with Helder's extraordinary voice. As a result, they dismiss her as deviant, with a harsh critique of a voice she does not have (that of a mature male tenor).

According to the biographer who wrote the CD liner notes, no recordings or performances of Helder can be found that postdate these unfavorable reviews. The remaining fifteen years of her life are untraceable in public records, so the end of her life and career is a mystery.

Ruby Helder is not mentioned in any of the history books that constitute common music history lore. Men who sing in female ranges were not seen as undesirable deviants from normative male singing, and they have a legacy and history. There have been no other female professional singers who have packaged themselves as tenors; Ruby Helder, an exemplary musician, did not inspire a generation of female tenor soloists. There is even disdain for and suspicions about choirs who use female tenors. Since there is no place in the rigid institution of Western music for women with male registers, the profession has all but erased Ruby Helder. I found her CD in a bin at Half Price Books for $3.95.

Expanding Contexts

The following are examples from my praxis that include identity positions not typically recognized in music education and that require an institutional critique in order to take seriously how these contexts affect musicing. Once again, I want to remind the reader that these contexts and identity issues are not mere aberrations, they have been recognized and researched, and they have entire bodies of literature written on them in other academic disciplines.

Gender as Context

In the past, I advised a male and and a female a cappella group (the women's group began a year and a half after the men's). It is an unusual arrangement for a men's a cappella group to have a feminist as director; it truly changes the context in which music is made. For the first two years, the men's ensemble was extremely aware of how their songs positioned women and why it might be bad to delight in such lyrics as "Brandy, what a good wife you'd be," or "Come on, come on, come on, come on now touch me babe." The ensemble rehearsed twice a week; once with me coaching and once coaching themselves. When I rehearsed them, I made fun of overt macho approaches to performing and joked about a "kinder, gentler" approach to singing that did not always have as its goal the conquest of women. However, and although I do not know for certain, I imagine that they gleefully practiced their macho identities during the rehearsals when I was absent; as they admitted quite freely, it was the hope of increasing their chances with women that attracted and (for some) sustained their interest in the group. This tension made rehearsals with and the advising of this group interesting and lively.

During the women's first year, the men offered them a chance to perform on the big Valentine's Day concert as a way of introducing themselves to the community. The women sang three songs, and, by conventional musical standards, they were mediocre—as the men had been, one year earlier, when they were first introducing themselves. The difference was that, at the end of their first concert, the men were embraced with standing ovations and an immediate formation of an informal fan club. On the contrary, the women received warm applause akin to a paternal pat on the back. Moreover, after their performance, conversations focused solely on how sleazy the women looked on stage in their short skirts and, for some, tight shirts.

It is not a new story that men and women engaging in the same act are judged by different standards. Men are more frequently judged on their merits or potential; women tend to be judged on how successfully they present their femininity, that is, their clothing, hair, make-up, and body shape. It is not even a new story that a group of pudgy, good-hearted guys who find the courage to perform are embraced as sex symbols; the success of the movie *The Full Monty* is tribute to this twisted phenomenon. The story that music education seems reluctant to tell is how being female changes the context of musicing. Lucy Green (1997) argues that musical meaning is determined in part by "delineated meanings" she defines as "a plethora of contextualising, symbolic factors (7)." She writes:

[There is] something definitive about the femininity of the woman musician, I will argue, [that] itself forms a part of her music's delineated meanings. . . . But the gendered delineation of music does in fact not stop at delineation: it continues from its delineated position to become a part of the discourse on music, and from that position to affect listeners' responses to and perceptions of inherent meaning, and thus our very musical experiences themselves. (16)

A woman musician and her musicing, then, is already differentiated from male musicians and his musicing. There is an anticipation of femininity in the performance that includes physical presentation as well as musical. Although male performers are met with similar expectations, they are afforded a wider range of possibilities. They can be sensitive, aggressive, passionate, and pudgy. But women who are too aggressive, overly sexualized, or physically unattractive will meet with resistance and possible dismissal. Including gender in context discussions forces us to recognize that musicing is always and already gendered. By not including gender, we fool ourselves into believing that boys and girls have the same experiences in music when, clearly, they do not. More importantly, not including gender in music matters continues to support existing identity positions that tell boys they are special and girls they are ordinary, as in the case of the student a cappella ensembles.

Sexuality as Context

In the following example, students learning a folksong shift the context from gender to the less comfortable context of sexuality. I was conducting a fifth- and sixth-grade all-county chorus singing "Kookabura," arranged by Mary Goetze. We had been singing for four hours. The students needed a break, so I asked them to sit back, relax, and tell me why they thought Kookabura was a guy ("Merry, merry king of the bush is he"). Feeling confident in my ability to engage ten- and eleven-year-olds in a gender discussion and hopeful that if this discussion went well these students might go on to question problematic images on television and in other media sources, I waded through the silence with great anticipation. I could see that the teachers observing in the back of the classroom were impressed by this question, and they, too, were carefully pondering the gender issue at hand. Suddenly, with great enthusiasm, a lad sitting in the middle row raised his hand and blurted out, "It's because he's gay ('Laugh, Kookabura, laugh, Kookabura / Gay your life must be')!" As I felt my tonsils tightening, I noticed that most students were shaking their heads in agreement, while the teachers used their hands, music, and bits of clothing to cover up snickers, gasps, and giggles. Although I felt confident leading a discussion about gender issues as a guest conductor, I did not feel secure leading fifth and sixth graders in a gay pride discussion, so I responded, "Two, three, four. 'Kookabura sits in the old gum tree. . . .'"

Just as gender shapes our delineation of music performance, so does sexuality, an almost forbidden context within the puritanical system of public schools. A colleague of mine was a clinician on the gay men's chorus circuit for a number of years and described the embarrassment she felt as she innocently barked out her first direction, "Okay men, stand up straight!" Contexts slip and slide as conventional musics are remade within less conventional settings. A gay men's chorus singing "My Love Is Like a Red, Red Rose," or a lesbian chorus singing "Full Fathom Five My Father Lies," will be a different musicing experience than the one heterosexual choirs have. Although queer theory has been accepted in many parts of the academy, our profession is not yet comfortable with discussions of sexuality and musicing and actively silences identity positions based on sexuality. The silencing has been so effective that gay and lesbian choruses have had to create their own music publisher (Yelton Rhodes Press) because mainstream publishers will not carry this music, supposedly for ethical and economic reasons. With these sorts of institutional policies, gay teens who find their way into choirs are confronted with stifling politics and little support for their emerging and complex identities.

Race as Context

For two years I conducted an inner-city children's choir. One spring I decided to feature gospel music because a number of the students sing in gospel choirs, and I wanted to validate their musical background and introduce this music to the other choristers. As a result, I invited a gospel artist, Ken, from Wisconsin to come for a weekend, polish our music, and perform with us on the concert. To back him up, we hired a local R&B band. We sang four songs; two of these were Kirk Franklin tunes (Franklin is extremely popular among kids who listen to gospel music). When I first played the Kirk Franklin tunes for the ensembles, all of the students were excited, but it was clear that there was a subtle shift in emphasis on who was important in our music making. Most of the students who were experienced gospel singers did not come from schools with music programs. Consequently, where they may have felt like slow learners of conventional choral skills, they now moved into more comfortable positions as hosts in their familiar musical world. In addition, they offered a new way of being with music as they related to each other with choreographed gestures, responded to musical codes that those of us who were less experienced did not recognize and, quite frankly, intimidated us. This shift in whose identities were being supported that I hoped would happen so that we would all experience new roles in our choral setting had in fact occurred.

The day that our guest artist, the R&B band, and the choirs were to bring everything together was a disaster. Ken's plane was delayed, so he missed all but an hour and a half of our rehearsal; the band's van broke down, so they were two hours late; moreover, they had not learned the music (which was in the form of tapes from CDs, not notated music). The band came expecting that their musical parts would be worked out as the choir rehearsed, as is traditional with church gospel choirs (and similar to the MUSE program). I found it too chaotic to coordinate a rehearsal of both the band and the choir, so I left the band to rehearse on their own while I rehearsed the choir in a separate room.

As I left, a band member, trying to be reassuring, said to me, "I'm sure this will work better once the gospel artist comes." While I smiled and nodded my head in agreement, his comment irritated me. I knew this music inside and out. I could sing every instrumental riff, every drum fill, and all the vocals. I was prepared. However,

when the artist came, the band relaxed and felt confident about his knowledge of the
music. As a result, things did come together quickly. As much as I did not want to believe it, an Irish American, white, middle-class, female professor does not necessarily instill confidence in African American city musicians, no matter how well prepared she is. What I did not pick up were the subtle codes of interaction that makes
gospel music "feel" right. No matter how much studying I did, I was an outsider to
these musicians.

At our dress rehearsal the next night, we only had thirty minutes to practice all
the gospel music. For whatever reason, when the choir sang with the band, they forgot all their harmony parts and ended up shouting instead of singing. I stopped Ken's
rehearsal and asked him to at least improve their tone production, figuring we had
time to fix only one musical element. He told me that he did not think it was too bad
for gospel music and that, in his church, people leave services with husky voices
every week. While I recognized that gospel vocal production would not sound like
bel canto, I told him I hoped we could find a middle ground. Ken, a classically trained
tenor and a public school teacher, agreed to try.

With only fifteen minutes of rehearsal left, I took a deep breath, decided to leave
this in Ken's capable hands, and stepped away from the podium. As I did so, the entire musical event changed. I could now see children's faces, eyes, and bodies. They
were engaged; they were sparkling; they were grooving. Although I still heard children screaming, it was transformed from vocal abuse to screaming new identities.
Several white boys discovered that night that they could dance. Several stiff, inhib-
ited girls discovered they could be physically present in music—that they could be
cool. Several African American children discovered that important parts of their identities could count in organized music, and in a setting of diversely musical children.
As they found new relationships with themselves, their peers, and the music, these
students learned new things from the music. All these students found a space where
they felt comfortable together crossing, blending, and mixing identities and cultures.
I felt my eyes well with tears as I watched all of these new beginnings. Even though
what I was hearing went against everything I have been institutionally trained to
value, this was one of the most amazing events of my musical life.

Summary

I started with the notion that in our society there is a conspiracy, produced by values
of the dominant class, to silence and erase a multitude of diverse experiences, and that
this is bad. I also started with the notion that schooling is supposed to be a primary
mechanism through which we understand how to be in the world, and how we learn
to make and change the world, and that music is one place where people can actively
engage in this process. This is contrary to most music educators' approach to teaching music: they hide behind a claim of neutrality (a graduate student recently wrote
to me that "we are not activists in the classroom, we are music educators and the only
thing we teach is music!"). So, in my praxis I continuously engage students in institutional critiques to create awareness of and spaces for multiple identities. I use the

following questions, which have arisen from musics and matters I have encountered in my praxis, to help us think outside the boundaries of our rigid educations:

- What sense is being made out of this musical moment by the individual, those involved, competing discourses, etc.?
- Who created the standards by which this music is performed?
- How have these standards become hegemonic across music? In other words, how do these standards create desires for certain types of musicing and not others?
- How can performers see their position within existing structures, histories, and discourses and be able to respond from somewhere else?
- What is the political act of performing music?
- How does all this differ across lines of class, race, gender, sexuality, patriarchy, capitalism, and consumerism?

The problem I encounter is that the music education profession generally dismisses issues that significantly affect musicing as "nonmusical" concerns. However, to make the point one final time, these issues are considered serious, even dire in the rest of academy. My challenge to Elliott is, how can we have a theorized practice of performativity that makes apparent (and does not just imply) institutional critiques and multiple identities including gender, class, race, sexuality, patriarchy, and so forth? How can the musics and practices created from these positions and concerns come to matter? When will music education theorizing catch up with and recognize the last twenty years of theorizing in other disciplines?

Note

An earlier version of this chapter by Patricia O'Toole was published as "Why Don't I Feel Included in These Musics or Matters," *Bulletin of the Council for Research in Music Education* 144:28–39.

References

Caputo, V. 1996. *Music, culture and the politics of identity; Combining anthropological and musical insights for music education*. Paper presented at the national meeting of the Music Educators National Conference, Kansas City, KS.

Elliott, D. J. 1995. *Music matters: A new philosophy of music education*. New York: Oxford University Press.

Green, L. 1997. *Music, gender, education*. Cambridge: Cambridge University Press.

Haynes, C. 1993. *Ruby Helder: "The girl tenor."* Sparrows Green, England: Pavilion Records.

hooks, b. 1989. *Talking back*. Boston: South End Press.

Small, C. 1990. *Whose music do we teach anyway?* Paper presented at the national meeting of the Music Educators National Conference, Washington, DC.

17

Community Music and Praxialism

Narratives and Reflections

KARI K. VEBLEN

Music education is not merely desirable but essential to the full development of every student because the primary values of MUSIC and music education overlap the essential life values that most individuals and societies
pursue for the good of each and all: personal growth, differentiation, complexity, enjoyment, self-esteem, and happiness. The welfare of a society
depends on the ability of its citizens to pursue and achieve these values
regularly. The quality of individual and community life depends on providing people with the knowings and the opportunities they require to make
a life as well as a living.

—David J. Elliott, *Music Matters* (1995)

David Elliott's praxial philosophy targets formal music education more than nonformal music instruction, or what many people now call "community music" (or CM,
for short). Still, the spirit of his philosophy and many of his basic principles have been
welcomed warmly by CM practitioners around the world. In turn, the CM projects
Elliott has witnessed and investigated in many countries have caused him to expand
his thinking about the nature and values of music education. Indeed, Elliott has become a strong advocate for CM. His recent writings and conference papers evidence
this cross-fertilization of ideas and ideals, which is rich and still in midflight.

A key concept behind CM is that most of the world's music education occurs outside the classroom. Said another way: much music teaching and learning is facilitated
by excellent musicians who may or may not call themselves "teachers" and who do

not hold official teaching certification. As Finnegan notes (1989), these are not covert activities but, rather, unrecognized activities. The diversity and complexity of music making and music teaching in every human society suggests that these robust activities are significant and deserve more serious consideration by all music educators.

In this chapter I examine "hidden" or nonformal musics, processes, and frames of reference (which I sum with the term "community music"). To probe what may be valid for a variety of musical contexts, I will examine contemporary concepts and articulations of CM and compare them with details of Elliott's praxial philosophy.

In writing this chapter, I cannot pretend to offer a detached critique of *Music Matters* because David Elliott and I collaborate on many projects. Furthermore, my long involvement in CM has made David more aware of the complexities of CM during the past seven years. Accordingly, in nature and purpose, this chapter fuses narrative inquiry, ethnography, and conceptual analysis.

Community Music Scenarios

Consider these three scenarios:

In Tlalpan, near Mexico City, Mexico
It is early evening on Thursday and the purple jacaranda trees in the courtyard of St. Augustine Church are lovely against the darkening sky. We stand in front of the church eating mango and chili fruit ices and listening to a guitar and voices rehearsing. Or is this an evening service? A strong baritone leads perhaps a dozen choir members . . . mixed voices in sweet tempered thirds. These must be hymns, but they are definitely Mexican . . . graceful melodies infused with lively rhythms.

Our treats finished, we enter through the portico to a grand but austere main apse. This church is one of the oldest in North America, built sometime in the early 1600s by the early Spanish conquistadors. In addition to the choir practice held in one of the chapels, other groups are using the space. A man talks quietly with a small group near the altar. Older people and young couples stroll. Families arrive for prayers.

A side chapel to the left seems to be much older than the main part of the church. Candles flicker against a pantheon of saints cup boarded in a baroque, gold-encrusted wall. Ribbons with writing on them and flowers are arranged before St. Charbel, a favorite saint in Tlalpan, who works miracles with lost causes. My friend whispers that these centuries-old statues are carried annually in religious processions. The soft cadences of the choir, the sibilance of praying, and the peaceful ease of this beautiful place hold us for some time.

In Toronto, Ontario, Canada
This event is perplexing—it feels immediate and intimate, like a family reunion. It also feels impersonal and massive. It's hard to tell exactly how many people—but there are many—are jammed into this concrete structure on this

Sunday afternoon in July. We watch amazing patterns of people ebb and swell in time to music; hundreds of dancers in colorful hand-loomed costumes move in perfect design and grace to Lithuanian music.

The precision and coordination of this spectacle are awe inspiring, particularly when one realizes that the forty-one dance troupes performing here met for the first time this weekend. With the exception of a small professional group from the motherland, the dancers are all amateurs. Whole families dance, beginning at a very young age. There are specific dances for each age group and massed dances for all ages.

This occasion—the eleventh international Lithuanian folk dance festival, or Sokiu Svente—brings all parts of the Lithuanian diaspora together. Each team is one small part of a large, intense kaleidoscope of color, music, and motion that fills the entire coliseum. An international central committee selects the dances and music for each international meeting and then choreographs the pageant, held every four years. Instruction in music, arts, and language often accompanies the dance instruction. Because teams from Brazil and Argentina were sandwiched between groups from Detroit, Boston, and Lithuania, the dance instruction (and much of the casual talk I hear during rehearsals and performances) is spoken in Lithuanian.

This event offers a stunning example of a displaced cultural community gone global. There are paradoxes here in the contrast between the rural dances (dances of harvest, milling, plowing, sowing, and horse husbandry) and the extremely well educated and urbane people who gather to dance at and celebrate this event. Likewise, the music (either performed live by a folk ensemble, or piped in for the dancers) sounds sweetly old-fashioned, even fragile, and generations removed from the lives of modern Lithuanian immigrants. However, the precision, grace, gestures, and symbols of this musicing and dancing epitomize Lithuanian ethnicity and identity for its participants.

In Maia, Portugal

It's almost nine in the evening and there's a distinct buzz in the air. This isn't the regular Friday night jam, but a bonus night complete with international guests. For the musically inclined youth of Maia, a small and beautiful old town not far from Porto, it is a welcome diversion. Six young people congregate with guitars and instruments, with handshakes and bilingual jokes all around.

Alexandrina Pinto, the originator and director of her own Maiorff Music School, leads us past classrooms and vivid student drawings down to a basement club. Suddenly, we are in a place that feels like a dimly lit cabaret. A small stage with a state-of-the-art audio system dominates one corner. Small tables with jugs and candles surround it. A piano, a side bar, and posters for rock bands complete the space. Young people arrive in twos and threes. Alexandrina brings over a large creamy cheese with a knife in the middle, freshly baked bread, and port wine. We chat as the musicians begin to tune, adjust their reverb, and noodle around with leads and rhythmic fragments.

Gradually the night stretches out into high-octane performances as the school's premiere guitar, keyboard, and percussion teachers, all teenagers, run through their paces for us. All the chairs fill up, then the floor, and then the stairs. This basement cabaret is quickly lined with students and local fans. One young boy who looks no more than eleven watches the fingers of one of the guitarists like a hawk. Another flushes with embarrassment and delight when he is invited to join the musicians in playing the riffs he has recently mastered. Others sip pop (or wine, if old enough) and make asides to their friends, unheard above the pounding beat and fiery melodic runs.

This CM school, which opened a scant decade ago, offers early childhood music classes through adult classes. Instruction is offered on a dozen instruments and voice. Likewise, there are ensembles and choirs for students to join. Enthusiastically welcomed by the people of this small town, the Maiorff Music School is the focus and motivator of numerous CM events, festivals, productions, and activities.

These international scenarios are a just few of the many possible settings that qualify for inclusion in the category of community music. Other scenarios might feature brass bands, seniors' choirs, orchestras, toddler playgroups, garage bands, private piano lessons, jazz ensembles, or community schools. The Lithuanian scene described earlier offers one example of technology, music, and globalization. Other possibilities might include the use of music technology with gifted or challenged populations.

CM takes many different forms. The term may be used to indicate music "programs that, unconstrained by any educational bureaucracy, have found solutions that fit the needs of particular communities," as Letts (2000) defined it in the *International Journal of Music Education*. In some places, "community music" connotes webs, networks, or pathways through which music making happens. The term can also distinguish between informal and formal musical settings and music-teaching processes. In some countries, CM signifies therapeutic, social, or educational contexts in which a facilitator works with various kinds of "clients." Here are several basic characteristics of community music activities (Veblen and Olssen 2002):

- Emphasis on a variety and diversity of musics that reflect and enrich the cultural life of the community and of the participants
- Active participation in music making of all kinds (performing, improvising, and creating)
- Development of active musical knowing (including verbal musical knowledge where appropriate)
- Multiple learner/teacher relationships and processes
- Commitment to lifelong musical learning and access for all members of the community
- Awareness of the need to include disenfranchised and disadvantaged individuals or groups
- Recognition that participants' social and personal growth are as important as their musical growth
- Belief in the value and use of music to foster inter-cultural acceptance and understanding

- Respect for the cultural property of a given community and acknowledgment of both individual and group ownership of musics
- Ongoing commitment to accountability through regular and diverse assessment and evaluation procedures
- Fostering of personal delight and confidence in individual creativity
- Flexible teaching, learning and facilitation modes (oral, notational, holistic, experiential, analytic)
- Excellence/quality in both the processes and products of music making relative to individual goals of participants
- Honoring of origins and intents of specific musical practices

As official networks promote and deliver services in Australia, Europe, and North America, various organizations and individuals are attempting to define CM, locally and internationally. The focus changes from individuals and programs through larger structures and overlapping systems to the wider world of participatory music making. All levels of this narrative illustrate the complex and sometimes contradictory ways in which people use music to make meaning for themselves and their lives.

Of course, there is nothing really new about CM. Music educators interact regularly with many populations and in many circumstances. Participatory music making is certainly not novel, either. What *is* new and notable is educators' growing awareness and professional recognition of the connections between CMians, music making, and education. International trends and research support the thesis that what is happening in CM constitutes a paradigm shift in music education. This is not surprising, as CM parallels and encompasses other postmodern developments such as multicultural music education, the use of technology, and the praxial philosophy of music education.

Community Music and Praxial Philosophy

It seems appropriate at this juncture to sketch a chronology of Elliott's association with CM. In 1996 he was a guest at a seminar held by the International Society for Music Education's Community Music Activity (CMA) Commission.[1] The dialogues and experiences at that seminar inspired him to find correspondences between his philosophy and the CM contexts described by seminar participants. Elliott was then invited to join the ISME CMA commission (composed of six members). He and I drafted a final statement for the Liverpool seminar based on the dialogues we heard. The CMA commission then presented our statement to the ISME board. Our statement served as a starting point for subsequent CMA debates. It has been modified, augmented, altered; at present, it serves as the ISME CMA Mission Statement.[2]

That year, 1996–1997, proved to be even more influential. At the invitation of Michael O' Súilleabhain, director of the Irish World Music Centre, Elliott and I assisted in developing an original and foundational curriculum for a new College of Performing Arts at the University of Limerick. This college offers unique programs in graduate music studies that combine theory and practice in ways that Elliott proposes in *Music Matters*.[3] For instance, a student may elect to do a master's degree in liturgical chant. To do so, however, the student must apprentice to the daily musical lives of monks at nearby Glenstal Abbey in order to supplement scholarly studies. Another course we helped to design is a master's degree in CM.[4] In doing so, we met and worked extensively with CMians in the United Kingdom and Ireland.

The years 1997 through 2000 were filled with travel and research into CM programs in Japan, New Zealand, Portugal, and other countries. The 1998 ISME CMA seminar met in Durban, South Africa; Elliott and I hosted the 2000 meeting in Toronto; our 2002 meeting was held in Rotterdam. All of these events fueled Elliott's thinking. During his tenure as a CMA commission member, Elliott has taken an active role in posing questions, leading discussions and initiating actions on behalf of CM. In his new role as director of music education at New York University, he intends to institute a master's program in CM.

Musical Practices

Throughout *Music Matters* (1995) Elliott offers a variety of scenarios to illustrate his concepts of music teaching and learning. His examples include a sweep of classroom settings (from general elementary music classes to band and choral rehearsals) as well as nods to a Bulgarian bagpipe student, Dgomba drummers, jazz players in a session, and others. How do Elliott's illustrations and the inferences he draws correspond to the diverse and myriad realities of music transmission found in CM?

One of the most significant themes of the praxial philosophy is Elliott's concept of "musical practices." Elliott argues that there is not one universal idea of music; instead, there are many thousands of individual musics, all of which are socially constructed and specific to a culture or community. All of these individual musics—and the musical products of these communities—make sense to their culturally and artistically affiliated listeners, but not to all listeners everywhere in the world.

Because a musical practice (such as zydeco or Appalachian ballad singing) is a social practice, it can be most easily visualized as a sphere containing listeners and makers, as Elliott pictures in *Music Matters* (1995, 44, figure 2.5). The integrated pairing of makers and listeners, showing them all as active participants in the events of music making and listening, contradicts received notions of the "active" performer and "passive" receiver. It acknowledges the reality and necessity of each music's being rooted in community, or in situ, where a music's community may be local, regional, or global (e.g., the Dixieland jazz community of makers and listeners, professionals and amateurs, distributed internationally).

Elliott's interactive concept of music making and listening is illustrated in an ancient Taoist story. Once, the story goes, there was a virtuosic lute player who played wonderful music for a beloved friend. One day, the listener died. In grief, the lute player cut the strings of his instrument because, to him, the music was not only meant to be played, it was meant to be heard and understood by the heart of his dear friend.

Similarly, the equal and mutual relationship of music maker and listener is found in modern times. For instance, a modern Irish *sean-nós* singer ("old-style" singing in the Irish language) may clasp the hand of an empathetic listener, as Ciaran Carson (1996) describes:

> In the "hand-winding" system of the Irish *sean-nós*, a sympathetic listener grasps the singer's hand; or, indeed, the singer may initiate first contact, and reach out for a listener. The singer then might close his eyes, if they are open (sometimes, he might grope for someone, like a blind man) and appear to go into a trance; or his eyes, if open, might focus on some remote corner of the room, as if his gaze could penetrate the fabric, and take him to some far-off, antique happening among the stars. The two clasped hands remind one another of each other, following each other; loops and spirals accompany the melody, singer and listener are rooted static to the spot, and yet the winding unwinds like a line of music with its ups and downs, its glens and plateaus and its little melismatic avalanches. One hand prompts the other as they internalize the story of the song, or the yarn behind the song—*údár an amhráin*—deferred to in a few obeisant vocal fragments, spun out in a run or ornament, a cheironomic flourish. (27–28)

The bonds between performer and listener signify shared community and a commitment to particular musical values and understandings.

Another significant aspect of musical practices in the praxial philosophy is the concept that each musical practice is a unique system. Elliott visualizes the breadth and variety of musics around the world as floating "bowties" (45, figure 2.6) signifying a world of more or less related individual communities, all of which involve musicers, musicing, listening, listeners, and so on (as Elliott pictures: 42–43, figures 2.3 and 2.4).

Elliott's concept of each kind of music's being a community of practice is in perfect accord with CM tenets. In theory, CM encompasses all musical genres. There is strong resistance to any hierarchical system that favors one music above all others (e.g., the notion that Western classical music is superior to all other musics). Some CM organizations derive their impetus from underrepresented local musics. Some CM programs consider it their mission to offer a wide selection of musical experiences. Examples include Ukusa in Durban, South Africa;[5] pilot programs with Aboriginal groups in the Northern Territory of Australia;[6] the range of music classes at the University Settlement House, Toronto, Canada;[7] and many more.

Musical Context

In addition to an emphasis on music as a global tapestry of musical practices and the assertion that all practices pivot on "musicianship" of some kind, the praxial philosophy emphasizes the importance of context:

> because the dominant forms of knowing that constitute musicianship are essentially nonverbal and situational, the development of musicianship is intimately related to the authenticity of the musical situation in which it is taught, learned, and used: that is, musical action and musical context work together to co-produce musical understanding. (Elliott 1995, 161)

In other words, the context of a given practice (or style, or genre) will determine expectations for improvisation, creativity, performance, and listening. Although musicianship is learned through interactions with individual teachers, according to Elliott's approach a student also learns through encounters with an entire social-musical community:

> with the community of practitioners who have established, maintained and advanced the musical domain a novice wishes to learn. When the musicianship of a practice is complex, a variety of people become involved in the teaching-learning enterprise, both directly and indirectly. Even a person who is largely self-taught inevitably makes use of past and present practitioners directly (through personal advice) and indirectly (through books, concerts, recordings, and videotapes). (161)

His emphasis on context is grounded in his own early music-making experiences. He comes from a musical family and grew up with music in the home:

> Church activities were a big part of my parents' lives as they were growing up. Their life-long circle of friends grew up as friends in the church, and music (singing songs around the piano) was a major part of their social lives. . . . I began playing piano at 4 because I wanted to do what my dad was able to do: play the piano for the weekly Saturday-night "sing-song" parties when all the adults came to the house and gathered around the piano . . . there was no stopping to correct mistakes—I really learned to "fake" and get the musical "Gestalt" in that situation. (Elliott 2001, personal interview)

As a teenager, Elliott became involved in the world of jazz—from settings such as smoky clubs, dance halls and concert settings to jazz personalities, mythologies, repertoires, and recordings. He performed piano and trombone in a variety of jazz groups, arranged and composed and gigged as a local musician—all while studying classical music formally at the university and conservatory. These two aspects of his life seemed "utterly natural and as regular as day and night to me. Well, they *were* day and night to me. Didn't sleep much for a few decades in there" (Elliott 2001, personal interview).

Context is clearly a point of correspondence between Elliott's life in music, praxialism, and CM; indeed, a key determining aspect of CM is the *type* of music-making setting, not to mention the diversity of music-making settings. For instance:

- the New Horizons Seniors' Orchestra performs their annual spring concert in the university hall;
- dancers and drummers participate together at an intertribal powwow;
- toddlers in an early childhood program learn "bouncing songs" and finger play sitting in a circle on a rug with their mothers and fathers;
- the Sweet Adelines work on their four-part harmonies in large groups, then separately in quartets in the high school choir room on Tuesday nights;
- bell ringers ring changes on Easter Sunday.

More to the point, the bell ringers may study their parts individually, read about bell ringing theory and technique, listen to other groups, and so forth. But all such activities complement the "real" bell ringing, which happens as a group, on site, and to a common purpose. Thus, context defines CM. The context—the circumstances and setting—constitutes and embodies the learning, listening, and performing expectations, all of which square with the praxial perspective.[8]

The Teacher-Musician

The music educator evoked in *Music Matters* embodies both musicianship and what Elliott terms "educatorship" (1995, 252). These qualities are interdependent. Both are necessary. Musicianship is displayed through words and actions and through the procedures of making music (in all its forms). Likewise, educatorship also draws upon procedural knowledge, which, "in turn, draws upon other kinds of educational knowledge, including formal, informal, impressionistic, and supervisory educational knowledge" (262).

In the same vein, CM practitioners embody the standards and traditions of the musics they teach (e. g., tradition bearers, amateur and professional rock musicians). It could be argued that many CM workers teach without formal educational knowledge (i.e., educational psychology, curriculum theory, child development theory, or philosophy). However, much about teaching can be learned informally, "on the job," especially when students tell their instructors what they need—which is what happens in many CM situations. At this time, there is a growing awareness that these CM workers need more preparation; accordingly, several university programs for CM workers have begun in the past decade, most prominently in the United Kingdom.

Elliott's own musical education was heavily embedded in CM contexts, as well as in school music programs. His music teachers ranged from family members (such as his grandfather, uncle, and, especially, father) to a private piano teacher, a private trombone teacher, and two band directors he recalls fondly from his junior high and high school days, as well as composition teachers, ensemble directors, and university colleagues. His great-grandfather, John Elliott, played the button-box accordion in Ireland and exhorted his Protestant congregations in western Ireland in the late 1800s.[9] Elliott's grandfather, John's son Harry, was also a musician:

> My grandfather (Harry) was the youngest of 13 kids. He learned to play the "box" (the Irish button accordion) as a child on my great-grandfather's farm (located near a village between Galway and Limerick). Harry Elliott was well known in the area for playing at Irish dances as a teenager. Harry immigrated to Canada . . . Harry continued to play the box all the time as a young man in Toronto. As a laborer working at all sorts of backbreaking jobs, Harry was still able to buy my dad and his brother a piano, but not lessons (no money for lessons). (Elliott 2001, personal interview)

Although there was no money for his father's music lessons (this would have been during the Great Depression), music was in the air. The Elliott boys were quick studies and were sought out to play for parties in their neighborhood:

> My father and uncle learned to play the piano by ear—they played popular WWII songs they "lifted" from the radio, Irish songs, Tin Pan Alley songs, big

band tunes, jazz of many kinds. My father had a great musical ear and was able to "grab" most things he heard very fast (as my grandfather was able to do, too). He didn't have perfect pitch, but he had amazing relative pitch and an unfailing sense of rhythm. (Elliott 2001, personal interview)

David's father, Jim Elliott (1919–2001), began playing piano before he attended public school; he played in public until the last two weeks before his death.

His main, life-long passion was music. After the war (WWII), my dad worked as a salesman (in the steel industry) until his retirement at 65; but music (specifically, playing the piano) was something he did daily, all his life, without fail, for his own intrinsic enjoyment and as preparation to play for others (anywhere, anytime). Wherever he went, he sought out a piano to play. It got to be embarrassing for me as a teenager (especially) when we would go to a restaurant or a wedding (or whatever) and my father would end up (inevitably!) playing (much to everyone's delight). In other words, my father was the epitome of the "amateur" musician—totally in love with music, fascinated with how it "worked" and why it was so powerful. He was always learning to sing and play new material; and he "composed" hundreds of songs (in his head) during his lifetime (and then paid people, including me—when I was old enough) to notate his songs on paper. (Elliott 2001, personal interview)

In addition to such informal music making in the home, David Elliott took lessons with a teacher in the neighborhood. He describes these early experiences in the North York Music School:

My father got me "jazz and pop" piano lessons (ages 5–11) with a wonderfully kind and down-to-earth, gigging dance-band piano player named Valli Cinnanni (his day job was sales, too). My lessons were taken at a local, independent music school (in a big, drafty old farm house divided into tiny studios) a few miles from my house . . . the jazz approach taught me a great deal about harmony, "comping," playing by ear and "faking" very early on. (Elliott 2001, personal interview)

His elementary school music teacher did not inspire young Elliott. However, his junior high band director did:

My first day of junior high . . . was a HUGE turning point in my life. I met Mr. (Glen) Wood for the first time in our first band class. . . . Glen was a wonderful trumpet player. . . . He was very engaging, kind, happy, humorous, and he constantly sang and played for us. I had enormous respect for his ability to model and demonstrate with his trumpet, as did all the kids. (Elliott 2001, personal interview)

One day, when Mr. Wood was late for class, David began conducting the band class, to his teacher's approval:

After he came into the classroom and saw me conducting, Mr. Wood asked me if I'd like to conduct the class band and the school band regularly. He taught me how to read scores, conduct patterns, and how to "teach-and-interact" with my peers. He did all these things in a very informal, coaching-mentoring type style. He put a lot of trust in me and let me "risk" making mistakes. Also, though, my peers were very supportive. They didn't make a big deal of me being a kind of "first-among-equals," which is how I always saw my nascent teaching-conducting role. (Elliott 2001, personal interview)

Elliott reflects that Glen Wood's academic values (he was also a fine English and math teacher) affirmed to David that musicianship and scholarship could and should go together:

> For me, Glen embodied the perfect integration of music making, critical think-ing, excellent academic standards, and an enthusiasm for reading about, writ-ing on, and discussing ideas related to music and many other topics—all of which I love and treasure to this day. (Elliott 2001, personal interview)

Elliott's high school band director, Bob Cringan, was also a powerful model:

> Bob was a superb musician. He was a fantastic clarinet/sax player and a bril-liant professional arranger. He was a working musician during all the years he taught (about 35 years of high school teaching). During WWII he played in and arranged music for the Canadian Army's equivalent of the Glen Miller Or-chestra . . . (in Elliott's high school), he was a LEGEND in Toronto. (Elliott 2001, personal interview)

Other influential people in Elliott's musical development included members of the professional jazz bands he played in, arranged and composed for, and directed; musicians in the Toronto jazz scene; colleagues from the University of Toronto; and his private music composition teacher in the 1970s, Gordon Delamont, a highly cele-brated and revered Canadian jazz composer, author, theorist, and pedagogue. Clearly, Elliott's experiences persuaded him that there are multiple models for excellent music educators and that they operate in a variety of settings.

The Student

In CM settings, the students may be of all ages, early childhood through elderly, and of a variety of dispositions. Some programs are aimed at a specific clientele who are disadvantaged (perhaps in a prison, hospital, or other institution). Others are offered to multiple groups. Indeed, many programs strive to offer services for all populations. Martin Dempsey (1999) notes:

> Established as a charitable organization as long ago as 1956, the Liverpool Music Centre is one of the oldest community based music organizations in the country [United Kingdom]. The initial aims were to create accessible opportu-nities for music tuition, rehearsal and performance, regardless of age, race, gender, and level of skill or financial provision. (45)

Other CM centers with similar aims have been developed in other parts of the United Kingdom, Ireland, Scandinavia, North America, Australia, and New Zealand.

Each learner and each group bring individual expectations and abilities to a situation. CM settings allow the possibility for a group of students to be different ages; this situation is usually not encountered in school settings, where students are banded by age. Likewise, CM settings may provide for large and small groups as well as individual instruction.

The role of the student is determined to a great extent by how much choice he or she has in initiating a musical experience. For some—the very young, or those in institutions—there is little choice. Consequently there is not as great an obligation to participate. But many students elect to play the saxophone or sing in the choir, thus accepting responsibility for their part. A number of recent studies touch upon the role of the learner in community choirs (Green 1998; Holmquist 1995; Schaffer 1992; Spell 1989; Tipps 1992; Vincent 1997) and bands or orchestras (Bowen 1995; Hosler 1992; Park 1995; Spencer 1996; Thaller 1999).[10]

Music Matters focuses more on the role of the teacher than the role of the student, which is natural since the book addresses itself to music educators. Students are portrayed in sympathetic terms. However, much is assumed about who the student is and what the student should do. Although Elliott's text is a primarily theoretical one, future realizations of the praxial philosophy might attend to the learner's role(s) in the teaching-learning dynamic, perhaps contrasting music students in several settings.

Teaching and Learning

Teaching and learning musicianship include teaching and learning different kinds of musical obligations and ethics as they apply in different musical communities.

—David J. Elliott, *Music Matters*

Learning to enjoy music as an informed listener and music maker should be the primary aim of any music education program, according to *Music Matters*. The praxial philosophy of music education takes its name from and refers to the procedural essence (the action-centered nature) of musicianship. (By "action" Elliott means listening and all forms of music making.)

From the premise that actions are nonverbal forms of thinking and knowing, in and of themselves, it follows that performing is not simply producing. Music making isn't merely chording a guitar or fingering a flute. Music performing embodies different sorts, levels, and layers of understanding, including formal, informal, impressionistic, and supervisory knowledge. Formal music knowledge—notational skills, verbal terms, and facts about theory, history, and so forth—are most often encountered in classrooms. Informal knowledge refers to that which is passed on in musical context, often unstated, but known. Impressionistic knowledge denotes the intuitive, thinking and/or feeling moments where the musician chooses one course over another because it "feels right" musically. Like informal knowledge, impressionistic knowledge is situated within a context. Decision making and interpretation are learned in realistic settings, not in abstract ones.

A performer's musicianship, according to praxial thinking, is learned within chosen musical genres, and, thus, certain skills are developed. Performers in musics such as jazz or Indian classical traditions expect to create original variations and improvisations that will fit the genre. Other performers, such as bluegrass or rock musicians, may strive to duplicate their recorded hits for eager fans. In other words, the musical practice mandates certain expectations of training and listening.

The teaching and learning processes found in CM settings are many and varied. However, there are many correspondences between these processes and the praxial approach. First, most CM situations are "apprenticeships " in the praxial sense of the word. Second, in CM, the development of active musical knowing (including verbal musical knowledge, where appropriate) is stressed. People in CM programs come together to learn and to make music. Furthermore multiple relationships and processes may be encountered. Connections between teacher and learner may take the form of apprenticeship, partnership, or collaboration. Interactions may take place within group settings, but there is often room for unique expression and individual instruction. Sometimes the setting allows for participants to teach each other.

The facilitation and teaching methods used may be flexible, using diverse modes such as oral, notational, holistic, experiential, and analytic. Another important aspect of teaching in CM programs is that the processes of music making may be conceived as more important than a final performance or product.

Curriculum

> This praxial philosophy recommends that all music education curricula . . . be organized and carried out comprehensively—in terms of musical practices and artistic musical actions—not narrowly in terms of verbal concepts about autonomous works. For it is always the musical community or practice that determines the nature and appropriate use of musical understanding.

> —David J. Elliott, *Music Matters*

Elliott's concern for developing music curricula in relation to the contexts of musical practices is reflected in the organization and operation of many community music programs. Indeed, most CM programs do not plan their programs in relation to verbal concepts about works; instead, they organize their students' efforts around making the musics that the students want to learn and the musics their CM teachers are expert in making and listening to. For example, many CM programs offer students opportunities to learn various styles of rock music. Here, participants play electric guitars, synthesizers, and drum kits; they compose and record with the latest technologies; accordingly, they emulate (and, often, learn to think critically about) the value systems and repertoires of contemporary rock musicians. Other programs— such as pipe bands, madrigal groups, and Suzuki violin classes—pivot around the doings and values of other musical-social traditions.

Why is this kind of learning important in music education? In praxial terms, and at their best, these CM forms of Elliott's curriculum-as-practicum contextualize and situate students' development. Everything is linked to real-life music making. Thus, for many students, the musics they are learning have meanings, histories, and values far beyond learning an isolated song or concept.

Elliott's practicum idea is something he views as a "knowledge-building community that actualizes concepts authentically so that students not only learn comprehensively, they learn how to learn" (1995, 270). The emphasis is on providing a safe and interactive sphere of learning where, in the course of music making, students identify, question, probe, explore, and make musically artistic choices. This group activity allows all participants to witness how their individual and collective musical thinking develops, improves, and pays off in their musical compositions, performances, and so forth.

Elliott draws from Howard Gardner's views on curriculum-as-practicum. Gardner believes that the contemporary practicum-apprenticeship model is effective instruction because it is

> heavily punctuated with sensorimotor experiences and with the contextualized use of first-order forms of symbolization, such as natural language and simple drawings or gestures. To the extent that they feature more formal notations or concepts, these are introduced to the learner directly in the context in which they are wanted, and the learner sees for himself the ways in which they may be applied. (Gardner 1991, 124, cited in Elliott 1995, 270)

Let me step back now for a broader, macro-level view of curriculum. When music teachers consider music's values (i.e., in terms of the aims and purposes of music in education), they often do so in relation to the school's curriculum as a whole. Parents and colleagues continuously ask teachers, "Where does music fit?" Under pressure to answer and to advocate for protecting the place of their school music programs, music teachers know all too well how music is often treated or eliminated as a "frill subject."

How do we explain the persistent notion in Western societies that the arts are superfluous? One theory of curriculum (as articulated by Michael Apple and others) suggests that "top-down forces" oblige teachers (who may personally endorse the values of music and the other arts) to accept and impart curricula designed and produced by others who may not value the arts and who are not directly involved in the daily teaching-learning enterprise. In this way, societal forces outside the control of teachers (e.g., federal, regional, or local governments, or professional organizations) enforce a prescriptive agenda. Accordingly, teachers are obliged to cover a dictated curriculum as best they can with the time and resources they are allotted (and, implicitly, according to how they were prepared during their university teacher training).

In *Music Matters*, Elliott echoes Apple's criticisms of this top-down, prescriptive approach to curriculum making and taking. In addition, however, he pinpoints several other ways Western societies contradict, negate, and dumb-down the aims of education they state and publish for their citizens. Elliott suggests that a central enemy of our society's educational ideals is our system of schooling. Specifically, Elliott addresses two unspoken expectations that most Western governments and parents have for their schools: the allocative and the custodial. The allocative function of schools pertains to how societies use schools to filter and certify students for jobs and careers. Elliott describes the custodial function this way:

> The school system is expected to "hold" students until such time as they can be absorbed by employment or supported in their unemployment.... In areas where this custodial function has broken down (e.g. parts of Latin America, Britain and the U.S.) social stability is threatened.... We must recognize therefore, that in essence, the school is not what society says it ought to be, but what society obliges it to be: a benign asylum for vocational sifting, sorting and certification. (1995, 141)

This discrepancy between what Western societies say they want their schools to do educationally and what they expect schools to do in everyday life serves to marginalize music education in most Western curricula. In other words, whereas Western societies invariably want education to provide a "balanced curriculum for the whole child" (a credo that assures the place of music in the curriculum), most schools, Elliott notes, focus on sifting children for jobs or keeping them safe and controlled in classrooms (1986). From this perspective, Elliott suggests that we may want to rethink the traditional setting of music education, a theme he advanced ten years before the publication of *Music Matters* in the *British Journal of Music Education*:

> In most North American minds, music education is synonymous with public school music instruction. Perhaps it is time for some of us to change keys. Perhaps it is time to consider transposing what we know and do well out of the school and into the community.... We often forget that our strongest agent is the making and experience of music itself; not words about music. We ought to make such experiences more available for our society. Indeed, we are presently neglecting a large pool of adult learners, not to mention the available preschoolers. An investment in either or both ends ... would pay dividends to community, business, and industry-based programs.... We need people who are willing to rethink our traditional (and limited) concept of music education. (Elliott 1986, 146)

Elliott's article continues in this vein. In one section of his discussion he makes direct reference to CM programs and offers innovative ideas for CM projects.

I was elated to discover Elliott's early writing on community music, not only because of my long-standing involvement in and advocacy for the recognition of community music programs, but also because his article explains much about the genesis of his praxial philosophy and his belief in CM. Although his initial views on both topics were in their embryonic stages in 1985, he voiced strong support for (and suggested creative connections between) school music education programs and CM work at that earlier time. In many ways, he predicted what we now see happening in many CM programs around the world.

My delight in finding these scholarly links does not mean I subscribe to Elliott's views that teachers often tend to receive and implement a manufactured curriculum, or his suggestion (strong, at times) that CM programs are the answer to many problems faced by school music programs. For example, although the allocative and custodial imperatives of many school systems—and the cookie-cutter nature of mandated curricula—can and do cripple the efforts of many music teachers, there is another reality. There are in fact many teachers today who reflect critically, reason independently, and, often, take collective action. After all, teachers *are* a school, to a very large extent. Teachers work within, without, for, and against the systems that may isolate and alienate them and/or nurture and optimize their efforts. Likewise, while noting that community music programs may intersect and enrich formal school programs, it would be a serious disservice to schools (and to all children) to give up on school music in favor of CM programs. What he is suggesting (but too indirectly) is that, instead of looking to CM to "save school music" (as some CM practitioners argue), we might do well to broaden our views of what "music education" is, what it can be, what CM programs around the world have been doing for decades to educate people of all ages in and through music. More pointedly, we should ask, "How can and how do formal and informal music education systems reach every citizen?"

Values and Goals of Music Programs

Why is music education (in the broadest sense) important? The praxial view suggests several answers. Elliott emphasizes that music is significant in human life, and in school life, for many reasons and on many levels: affective, cognitive, psychological, social, artistic, expressive, cultural, and more.

In particular, Elliott (following Csikszentmihalyi 1990) suggests that self-growth and enjoyment (or "flow") are among the "primary values" of both musicing and listening (1995, 120–123, 129). Elliott echoes Csikszentmihalyi in suggesting that musical flow experience occurs when the challenge of a musical activity (where "challenge" means any form of making or listening to music on a wide continuum between high or low) is well matched to an individual's abilities.

In addition, however (and this is something overlooked by most commentators), Elliott extends the concept of musical flow (challenge matched to ability) to music teaching and curriculum planning (Elliott 1995, 309–310). He posits that the intense concentration needed to perform effectively as an educator—in the moment, on one's feet—and (then) the exhilaration that arises from and in the processes of meeting specific teaching challenges are key attributes of what teachers otherwise describe as the most satisfying, meaningful, or fulfilling parts of their work.

Elliott's explanations of musical and educational significance fit many CM situations, too. Many if not most structured networks of CM providers and services describe their aims and experiences in terms that closely resemble Elliott's themes of enhancing self-growth, self-knowledge, enjoyment, and self-esteem. Numerous CM teachers I have interviewed also describe their CM teaching experiences in words that echo descriptions of flow. In short, CM practitioners tend to agree that the several values of their work are in consonance with Elliott's praxial thinking on this topic.[11]

Still, for me, the praxial view of musical values falls short in explaining some key benefits of CM programs. For example, the special social qualities of informal CM settings, the varieties of human interactions that take place in CM settings, how participants feel about the social and political aspects of their musical efforts—these call for additions to Elliott's discussions of values. From my observations and studies, I find that CM situations often evince a sense of the collective, of group dynamics, and collective flow. In fact, I would make the case that music making in CM situations often serves as a metaphor for people doing things "in sync," "in harmony," or "together." This metaphor can be traced through other cultures. For example, *samspel* is a Norwegian word for "working together" in music and in other areas of human activity. Similarly, the African term *ubuntu* connotes people acting in accord, musically and otherwise. Marie McCarthy (1999) writes:

> *Ubuntu* is an age-old African concept of community, which roughly means "humaneness," caring, sharing, being in harmony with all of creation. The interdependence of all people is at the heart of Ubuntu, which literally means "I am because we are." Ubuntu may be considered a social-organizational metaphor with its emphasis on how people live together in harmony, how individuals develop their potential in the context of community . . . and how community and individuality are interdependent forces in the advancement of humankind. . . . Ubuntu as a metaphor synthesizes the social and the spiritual and in that sense may be transferred easily to the province of music-making and the development of musical practices. (47)

How do things get done in a large group of people — say, in a collective or a group bound together by a national or religious identity? Sometimes there are strict protocols, lists, and ordered structures. But often, it seems, one action sparks another, people join in, and energy wells up to satisfy an outcome. This dynamic, which is familiar to members of coffeehouse collectives and other volunteer groups, deserves more study as a phenomenon of *community* music.

A more dramatic manifestation of group energy arises in response to political or social situations. In some instances, a CM group emerges suddenly, like molten lava from seams in the culture. One case in point is the Estonian "singing revolution." Estonians customarily congregate every five years for song festivals at which church, youth, and traditional musics are sung. Pierson (1998) documents how one such gathering in 1988 became the focal point for a peaceful protest by Estonians against Soviet repression. (By 1991 Estonians had gained their independence.) Other examples include Flam's (1988) study of Holocaust songs from a Polish ghetto and Koehler's (2000) analysis of the sociopolitical implications of the German Workers' Choral Association (comprised of nearly 500,000 Germans) during the Nazis' rise to power.

When we examine the energy and development of CM organizations, we often see musical-social collectives developing in nonlinear, creative ways. There is a sense of organic unfolding. CM programs often formulate or realize their aims, goals, strategies, clients, financial resources, and so forth in day-to-day emergent patterns (as opposed to formal preplanning).

There is an element of chaos theory in all this. Originally put forth as a scientific hypothesis, chaos theory proposes that the universe is a vast "mind" or system, rather than a tidy Newtonian machine based on laws and interactions.[12] Today, chaos theory is frequently used as a cultural metaphor. In any event, a chaos-theory mindset is a useful tool to keep at hand when attempting to understand the birth and genesis of some CM programs.

For example, and in reply to Elliott's neat flow model of musical enjoyment and self-growth, I suggest that in many CM settings the values and aims of music seem to go beyond individualistic flow, self-esteem, and self-knowledge. Instead, or in addition, collective musical impulses, memories, and energies go beyond what one person may feel, conceptualize, or do. There is a complex interplay between and among individuals and the whole of the CM collective.

Thus, while the praxial view offers a persuasive and useful explanation of many musical values, it doesn't do justice to the social-affective dynamics of many CM situations I know, nor does it fully explain why groups of people are driven to make and listen to music *together*.

Conclusions

Elliott's rethinking of what music is and how musics should be taught has sparked controversy since his book appeared in 1995. Debates over issues raised in *Music Matters* have engaged musicians and educators worldwide. In addition, however, one of the most interesting outcomes of this book is the fact that community music practitioners have become actively involved in the dialogues surrounding Elliott's topics and proposals.

This input and involvement of the CM constituency is new. Although CM musicians and teachers constitute a very large group within our global family of music teachers, their voices have seldom been heard by school music teachers, and their interests have not be engaged by traditional theorizing in music education. In contrast, Elliott's praxial approach is well received by CM workers and music therapists who believe in active music making (e.g., music therapists using the Nordoff Robbins approach).[13] And although Elliott's philosophy was not primarily intended for community music workers and music therapists, many ideas in *Music Matters* address deep concerns and echo common practices in these constituencies: for example, Elliott's concerns for teaching music holistically, in terms of musical practices; his concept of the curriculum-as-practicum; his emphasis on empowering all people to perform, compose, listen, improvise, and join in music making at the level they desire; his emphasis on situated cognition and nonverbal forms of knowing; and his allowance for flexibility in selecting teaching modes.

Altogether, then, Elliott's praxial philosophy is a substantial contribution to the efforts and aspirations of community music practitioners. In this context, Elliott's recent contribution to CM is no surprise. In November 2003 he founded the *International Journal of Community Music*, an online e-journal for the publication and dissemination of many forms of research, reports from the field, conference proceedings, and multimedia presentations for the benefit of community music and its practitioners.

Notes

1. The International Society for Music Education was formed at a conference convened by UNESCO in 1953 "to stimulate music education as an integral part of general education. . . . In

the years that followed its formation, ISME gradually evolved to what it is today: a worldwide service platform for music educators who want their profession to be taken seriously by educators in other disciplines, by politicians and policy makers, by international organizations that promote culture, education, conservation, and durable development of cultural heritage" (retrieved 1 June 2003, from the Web site of the International Society for Music Education: www.isme.org/).

The International Society for Music Education has established seven commissions to investigate, report on, and develop particular areas of importance. The ISME commissions are Music in Schools and Teacher Education; Research; Education of the Professional Musician; Music in Educational, Cultural and Mass Media Policies; Music in Special Education, Music Therapy, and Music Medicine; Early Music Education; and CM Activity.

2. This statement, and other information about the ISME CM Activity Commission, is found at http://www.isme.org.

3. For further information on all programs at the University of Limerick, consult www.ul.ie/~iwmc/flash.htm.

4. Our colleagues included Phil Mullen, Georgette Mulheir, and Keavy O'Shea. Our purpose was to investigate the state of community music programs in Ireland through a series of seminars held at Limerick, Dublin, Galway, and Belfast.

5. Elizabeth Oehrle started Ukusa in Durban, South Africa, in 1988. This weekend music program, whose name means "sunrise" in Zulu, offers music instruction and organizes choirs, jazz bands, and other musical groups.

6. See Harrison (1996).

7. The mission of the Toronto Settlement Music and Arts School is to make the arts accessible to all and to provide a welcoming family atmosphere. Lessons are offered on seventeen instruments and voice in a wide range of styles taught by more than thirty teachers. See Veblen and Elliott (2001).

8. I prefer the American Heritage dictionary definition (1992) of "context": "The part of a text or statement that surrounds a particular word or passage and determines its meaning."

9. Elliott adds: "My great-grandfather, John (who lived during the late 1800s) was a preacher/farmer sent from Scotland by the Protestants to 'save' people in the Republic of Ireland in regions (like Southwestern Ireland near Shannon and Limerick) where the Catholics were still not organized at that time. By all accounts, he was a passionate orator, a fine musician, and an avid reader. . . . Great-grandfather John used music in his services to attract converts!" (Elliott 2001, personal interview) In fact, some ethnomusicologists in Ireland tell me that John Elliott was very likely a prominent historical figure in terms of introducing the accordion—in its button-box form—to Ireland around 1900.

10. These profiles trace factors such as demographics, educational levels, musical experiences, and motivation for participation by participants.

11. Other CM practitioners have expressed concerns that *Music Matters* emphasizes musical outcomes to the exclusion of other important values. In many programs, particularly those with therapeutic and social purposes, the participant's interactive and personal growth is of equal (or, perhaps, greater) importance as self-growth.

12. Briggs and Peat (2000) write: "Chaos turns out to be far subtler than the commonsense idea that it is the messiness of mere chance—the shuffling of a deck of cards, the ball bouncing around in a roulette wheel, or the loose stone clattering down a rocky mountain side. The scientific term 'chaos' refers to an underlying interconnectedness that exists in apparently ran-

dom events. Chaos science focuses on hidden patterns, nuance, the 'sensitivity' of things, and the 'rules' for how the unpredictable leads to the new. It is an attempt to understand the movements that generate thunderstorms ... gnarled coastlines, and complex patterns of all sorts, from river deltas to the nerves and blood vessels in our bodies" (1–2).

13. Interestingly, *Music Matters* is used as a basic text in graduate courses at the Nordoff Robbins music therapy program at New York University.

References

Apple, M. 1990. *Ideology and curriculum*. New York: Routledge.

Bowen, C. K. 1995. *Adult community bands in the Southeastern United States: An investigation of current activity and background profiles of the participants*. Ph.D. diss, Florida State University.

Briggs, J., and F. D. Peat. 2000. *Seven life lessons of chaos: Timeless wisdom from the science of change*. New York: HarperCollins.

Carson, C. 1996. *Last night's fun: A book about Irish traditional music*. London: Jonathan Cape.

Csikszentmihalyi, M. 1990. *Flow: The psychology of optimal experience*. New York: Harper and Row.

Dempsey, M. 1999. Communities, music, and technology, Liverpool '99. In L. Higgins, ed., *CM and new technology: Conference report and reflections*, 43–47. Liverpool: Liverpool Institute for Performing Arts.

Elliott, D. J. 1986. Finding a place for music in the curriculum. *British Journal of Music Education* 3 (2): 135–151.

———. 1995. *Music matters: A new philosophy of music education*. New York: Oxford University Press.

Finnegan, R. 1989. *The hidden musicians: Music-making in an English town*. Cambridge: Cambridge University Press.

Flam, G. 1988. *Singing for survival: Songs of the Lodz ghetto, 1940–1945*. Ph.D. diss., University of California, Los Angeles.

Gardner, H. 1991. *The unschooled mind*. New York: Basic Books.

Green, V. B. 1998. *Enhanced musical literacy through participation in the adult amateur / volunteer chorus: A descriptive study*. Ph.D. diss. Columbia University Teachers College.

Harrison, G. 1996. Community music in Australia. In M. Leglar, ed., *The role of community music in a changing world: Proceedings of the 1994 seminar of the Commission on Community Music Activity*, 39–45. Athens: University of Georgia Press.

Holmquist, S. P. 1995. *A study of community choir members' school experiences*. Ph.D. diss., University of Oregon.

Hosler, N. 1992. *The brass band movement in North America: A survey of brass bands in the United States and Canada*. Ph.D. diss., Ohio State University.

Koehler, W. S. 2000. *"The politics of songs": The German Workers' Choral Association as a cultural and sociopolitical entity in comparative perspective, 1918–1933*. Ph.D. diss., Brandeis University.

Letts, R. 2000. Editorial. *International Journal of Music Education* 35:1.

McCarthy, M. 1999. Ubuntu: A metaphor for the origins, role, and development of the International Society for Music Education. *International Journal of Music Education* 33:47–56.

Oehrle, E. 1996. Structures for transformation through music in South Africa. In M. Leglar, ed., *The·role of community music in a changing world: Proceedings of the 1994 seminar of the Commission on Community Music Activity*, 29–38. Athens: University of Georgia Press.

Park, J. H. 1995. *On the margin between 'high' culture and 'ordinary' everyday life: Social organization of the amateur orchestra and its musicians.* Ph.D. diss., Syracuse University.

Pierson, S. J. 1998. *We sang ourselves free: Developmental uses of music among Estonian Christians from repression to independence.* Ph.D. diss., Trinity Evangelical Divinity School.

Schaffer, R. E. 1992. *History of the Phoenix Boys Choir: From 1947 through 1989.* Ph.D. diss., Arizona State University.

Spell, G. M. 1989. *Motivational factors and selected socio-demographic characteristics of Georgia community chorus participants as measured by the education participation scale, the community chorus participation scale, and the personal inventory form.* Ph.D. diss., University of Georgia.

Spencer, W. D. 1996. *An attitude assessment of amateur musicians in adult community bands.* Ph.D. diss., University of North Texas.

Thaller, G. P. 1999. *The community contributions, recruitment, and retention practices of select adult community bands in eastern Massachusetts.* Ph.D. diss., University of Cincinnati.

Tipps, J. W. 1992. *Profile characteristics and musical backgrounds of community chorus participants in the Southeastern United States.* Ph.D. diss., Florida State University.

Veblen, K. K., and D. J. Elliott. 2001. Community music: Foundations and practices. In K. K. Veblen and S. Johnson, eds., *Lived music, shared music making: Community music in the new millennium.* Toronto: Centre for Research in Music Education.

Veblen, K. K., and B. Olssen. 2002. Community music: Towards an international perspective. In Richard Colwell and Carol Richardson, eds., *The new handbook of research on music teaching and learning.* New York: Oxford University Press.

Vincent, P. M. 1997. *A study of community choruses in Kentucky and implications for music education.* Ph.D. diss., University of Kentucky.

Interviews

David J. Elliott	July 18–19, 2001	Toronto, Canada
Deborah Kmetz	July 12, 2000	Toronto, Canada
Alexandrina Pinto	April 9, 2000	Maia, Portugal
Brenda Romero	April 27, 2001	Mexico City
Annette Sanger	June 19, 2000	Toronto, Canada

Name Index

Subject Index

28314534R00206

Made in the USA
Lexington, KY
18 December 2013